# THE UNIVERSE UNRAVELING

A volume in the series

**The United States in the World**

Edited by Mark Philip Bradley, David C. Engerman, and Paul A. Kramer

*A list of titles in this series is available at www.cornellpress.cornell.edu.*

# THE UNIVERSE UNRAVELING

## American Foreign Policy
## in Cold War Laos

**Seth Jacobs**

Cornell University Press
Ithaca and London

Publication of this book was made possible, in part, by a grant from Boston College.

First published 2012 by Cornell University Press

**Library of Congress Cataloging-in-Publication Data**

Jacobs, Seth, 1964–
  The universe unraveling : American foreign policy in Cold War Laos / Seth Jacobs.
    p. cm. — (The United States in the world)
    Includes bibliographical references and index.
    ISBN 978-0-8014-4547-7 (cloth)
  1. United States—Foreign relations—Laos.   2. Laos—Foreign relations—United States.   3. United States—Foreign relations—1953–1961.   4. United States—Foreign relations—1961–1963.   I. Title.   II. Series: United States in the world.
  E183.8.L3J33   2012
  327.730594090'04—dc23
                        2011045122

Cloth printing   10 9 8 7 6 5 4 3 2 1

For my father and mother

If you want to get a sense of the universe unraveling, come to Laos.

Norman Cousins, *Saturday Review*, 1961

# Contents

Acknowledgments — ix

Introduction — 1

1. "A Long Country Inhabited by Lotus Eaters": Washington Encounters Laos — 21

2. "A Soft Buffer": Laos in the Eisenhower Administration's Grand Strategy — 50

3. "Help the Seemingly Unhelpable": "Little America" and the U.S. Aid Program in Laos — 82

4. "Foreigners Who Want to Enslave the Country": American Neocolonialism, Lao Defiance — 129

5. "Doctor Tom" and "Mister Pop": American Icons in Laos — 171

6. "Retarded Children": Laos in the American Popular Imagination — 209

7. "No Place to Fight a War": Washington Backs Away from Laos — 235

Epilogue — 271

Notes                                                      275
Index                                                      303

# Acknowledgments

There is always a tension in this part of a book's front matter between the need to be brief and the desire to thank everyone. I choose to err on the side of brevity. Apologies to those friends and mentors unacknowledged by name. You know who you are.

My colleagues at Boston College were supportive and empathetic throughout the five years it took to complete this project. Lynn Lyerly in particular furnished extensive feedback and lent her talents to the thankless task of editing my adjective-laden, oft-digressive prose. Courteous professionals staffed all the archives I visited, with Stephen Plotkin and John Waide deserving special mention. Michael McGandy, Ange Romeo-Hall, and Sarah Grossman of Cornell University Press were essential in getting the manuscript into publishable form. Mark Bradley and Andrew Rotter helped me expand and clarify my argument and saved me from numerous errors.

I am indebted to Howard Buell, who allowed me to peruse his father's correspondence and who, along with his wife, Bonnie, hosted me during my stay in Hamilton, Indiana. Jeff Buell was a priceless source of information and anecdote. Charles Stevenson, who wrote his dissertation on U.S.-Lao relations over forty years ago and interviewed dozens of policymakers for that work, kindly supplied me with transcripts and other relevant materials.

As for Joel Halpern—this book would not have been possible without him. Making his acquaintance was the luckiest break of my career. He knows more about Laos than anyone else on earth, and his letters and field notes from the late 1950s were my "eyes on the ground" for several key events addressed herein. Thank you, Joel.

As always, my deepest thanks are reserved for my family. My wife, Devora, and daughters Miranda and Sophie provided encouragement, loving companionship, and—especially in Sophie's case—comic relief when I needed it most. I am dedicating this book to my parents, Max and Helen Jacobs, whose unshakable belief in me and many sacrifices on my behalf I have only just begun to appreciate. My debt to them goes beyond words and can never be repaid.

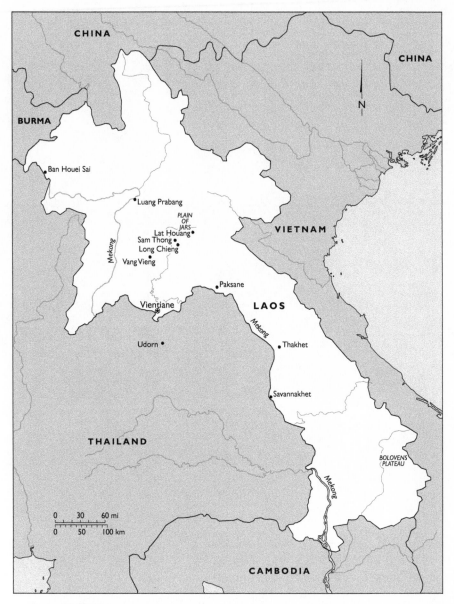

Laos, 1954–1962

# THE UNIVERSE UNRAVELING

# Introduction

John F. Kennedy inherited a powder keg. The presidential transition from Dwight Eisenhower to Kennedy occurred during one of the tensest periods in the history of American foreign policy. Crises simmered and blazed all over the globe: Fidel Castro had established a communist beachhead ninety miles from Florida, rebels in the Dominican Republic seemed poised to turn that nation into another Cuba, Washington and Moscow clashed over a UN-sponsored peacekeeping mission to the Congo, and Soviet leader Nikita Khrushchev was threatening to force the Western allies out of Berlin. Most distressing was the situation in South Vietnam, where America's ally Ngo Dinh Diem had just survived a coup attempt that exposed the precariousness of the Saigon government despite six years of unstinting U.S. aid.

Yet Eisenhower and Kennedy did not talk much about Cuba, the Dominican Republic, the Congo, Berlin, or Vietnam when the outgoing American president briefed his successor on January 19, 1961, the eve of Kennedy's inauguration. Instead, the two men, accompanied by their principal national security advisers, discussed Laos. A three-sided civil war in that country between the U.S.-backed Royal Lao Government (RLG), the communist Pathet Lao, and a neutralist front appeared about to conclude with the reds on top—an outcome that, Eisenhower warned, would mean more than the communization of one country. "[T]he loss of Laos would be the loss of the 'cork in the bottle,'" Eisenhower declared, "and the beginning of the loss of most of the Far East."

Kennedy had great respect for Eisenhower's judgment, especially in military matters, and did not challenge the older man's contention that it was imperative to "defend Laos." Rather, the president-elect observed that the People's Republic of China and the Soviet Union had an advantage in this "military situation" because of their "proximity" to Laos, a point Eisenhower conceded. The president did not think, however, that Beijing wanted to "provoke a major war," and Secretary of State Christian Herter questioned the extent to which "the Soviets would wish to get publicly involved."

Herter was more concerned about another obstacle America faced in Laos. The "factor disturbing us most," he said, was "the unwillingness of the armed forces of the recognized government to fight." Royal Lao troop "morale" was "not good," Herter noted, and this made waging proxy war in Laos "difficult for us" because the forces opposing communism were "so undependable." Eisenhower then raised a point that, in retrospect, deserved more consideration than it received. He said he did "not understand why the communist soldiers in such countries always seem to have better morale than the soldiers representing the democratic forces." Perhaps, the president ventured, there was "something about the communist philosophy" that gave its adherents "a certain inspiration." Kennedy remarked that he was aware of the "weakness of the troops of the government of Laos."[1]

Just what Eisenhower counseled Kennedy to do about Laos is unclear. Clark Clifford, a Kennedy aide who took notes during the briefing, recorded the president advising that the Southeast Asia Treaty Organization (SEATO) "take charge of the controversy." Unfortunately, two of SEATO's members, Britain and France, were opposed to intervening in Laos, and Eisenhower found their proposals for a coalition government with Pathet Lao participation naïve. "[E]xperience shows that any time you permit communists to have a part in the government," Eisenhower declared, "they end up in control." Since a political settlement in Laos acceptable to Washington seemed unlikely, the incoming Kennedy administration would have to weigh military options. According to Clifford's memorandum, Eisenhower "stated that he considered Laos of such importance that if . . . we could not persuade others to act with us, then he would be willing, '*as a last desperate hope, to intervene unilaterally.*'" Yet Secretary of Defense-designate Robert McNamara, who also attended the transition talks, submitted a memo to Kennedy five days later in which he claimed, "President Eisenhower advised *against* unilateral action by the United States with respect to Laos." Kennedy's own aide-mémoire, dictated hours after he spoke to Eisenhower, did not recount the president's advice but concluded that "the Eisenhower administration would support intervention—they felt it was preferable to a communist success in Laos."[2]

Discrepancies in these first-person accounts notwithstanding, what is beyond dispute is that Eisenhower and Kennedy spent the lion's share of their conference focused on Laos, that both men considered conditions there the most important business facing the new administration, and that other cold-war hornets' nests like Vietnam barely registered as immediate concerns. Kennedy later remarked to Deputy National Security Adviser Walt Rostow, "Eisenhower never mentioned the word Vietnam to me." That was untrue—Eisenhower had referred to Vietnam in passing—but Laos topped his agenda. McNamara recalled, "We were left...with the ominous prediction that if Laos were lost, all of Southeast Asia would fall.... The meeting made a deep impression on Kennedy and us all. It heavily influenced our subsequent approach to Southeast Asia."[3]

Historians would do well to bear McNamara's words in mind when assessing the early advisory stages of the Vietnam War. While the decade from Dien Bien Phu to Diem's assassination has been the subject of numerous monographs, scholars have been inclined to treat U.S. policy toward Southeast Asia during this time as though it involved only Vietnam, not all of the former French Indochina. American-Lao relations in particular tend to be marginalized. This is understandable, given that neither Eisenhower nor Kennedy made a direct military commitment to Laos, and few American soldiers died in Laos on Eisenhower's or Kennedy's watch, or even when Lyndon Johnson escalated U.S. involvement in Southeast Asia to levels beyond anything his predecessors had contemplated.[4]

Still, U.S. policy toward Laos under Eisenhower and Kennedy did much to shape America's approach to Southeast Asia during the cold war. Laos was the testing ground for counterinsurgency and nation-building programs that came of age in Vietnam, and many of the features that distinguished those later programs—support of unpopular but pro-Western despots, slugging matches between U.S. civilian and military bureaucracies, and ignorance of the needs and problems of the native populations—first surfaced in Laos. The Eisenhower administration set the precedent for "free" elections in South Vietnam by encouraging its Lao viceroys to stuff ballot boxes, intimidate voters, and otherwise rig the electoral process.

Eisenhower also launched Air America, the Central Intelligence Agency's proprietary airline, on its twenty-year involvement in Southeast Asia when he ordered its planes to drop military supplies to anticommunist forces operating in Laos. And Kennedy sent the first official U.S. combat troops to Southeast Asia in response to Pathet Lao aggression, ordering marines to take up positions across the Lao border in Thailand.

Incongruous as it seems from a post–cold war perspective, Laos occupied more of Eisenhower's and Kennedy's time than did Vietnam. The "Kingdom of a Million Elephants" was considered a vital piece of real estate in the contest between communism and anticommunism, a "domino" whose preservation was essential to America's national security. During Eisenhower's second term, Laos became the only foreign country in the world where the United States paid 100 percent of the military budget. Eisenhower approved the most audacious enterprise in CIA history when he permitted that agency to equip an army of Lao tribespeople to fight against communist guerrillas. Confrontation over Laos brought the United States and the Soviet Union to the brink of nuclear war in 1961–62, as Kennedy's Joint Chiefs of Staff urged the president to use atomic weapons to counter communist advances on the Lao capital of Vientiane. For American statesmen in the early 1960s, Laos was no sideshow, its present erasure from collective memory notwithstanding. A reexamination of the Lao crisis can help rescue this episode from obscurity and deepen our understanding both of why Washington perceived such an immense stake in Laos and why policymakers chose to fight in Vietnam instead.

That latter question is of particular significance. The most compelling reason for scrutiny of Washington's Laos policy in the Eisenhower/Kennedy period is that the capstone to that policy bound America more tightly to its client state of South Vietnam and, by extension, to its longest war. Laos was critically important in transforming America's role in the Vietnamese civil conflict from adviser to combatant. When Kennedy repudiated Eisenhower's support for the Lao right wing and accepted a neutralist government in Laos, this political solution to a Southeast Asian crisis made a military solution in Vietnam harder to avoid. In other words, Kennedy's dovishness in Laos paradoxically dictated hawkishness in Vietnam. Some months after taking office, Kennedy decided that while it was necessary to confront the communists in Southeast Asia, Laos was a singularly unpropitious site to make a stand. Vietnam, the president calculated, would be a better battleground. Thus Kennedy threw his weight behind the neutralist Prince Souvanna Phouma and agreed to American participation in an international conference organized to guarantee Laos's nonalignment. But Kennedy assured South Vietnam's President Diem that these moves in no way lessened U.S. determination to take up arms in Vietnam should the communists seek to extend their sphere below the 17th parallel. "[T]he strategy best calculated to preserve Vietnamese independence and enable your brave people to build a better future," Kennedy wrote Diem in mid-1962, "is clearly very different from the strategy required for Laos."[5]

Why was it different? Scholars who have examined U.S. policy toward Laos in this period argue, in effect, that geography was destiny, that Laos—a landlocked nation made up of deep valleys, triple-canopy jungle, and some of the highest mountains in Southeast Asia—presented American policymakers with what one historian calls "a logistical nightmare" that overwhelmingly favored the communists. Not only were China and North Vietnam closer to Laos than was the United States, which made it easier for them to send troops across the Lao border, but the communist doctrine of "people's war" was suited to countryside both rugged and lacking in railroads, airstrips, or all-weather roads. By contrast, America's mechanized forces would be nearly impossible to supply, defend, or transport in such terrain. Better to confront the communists in Vietnam, with its long coastline, deep-draft harbors, modern airports, and paved road system.[6]

These considerations played a role in Kennedy's choice to content himself with a "draw" in Laos, but they were not the decisive factors. Indeed, Laos possessed some topographical and positional advantages over South Vietnam that made a determination based solely on logistics unlikely. First, much of the fighting between the Royal Lao Army (RLA), the neutralists under rebel captain Kong Le, and the Pathet Lao in the early 1960s took place in the Plain of Jars, a five-hundred-square-mile plateau of rolling grasslands that an observer aptly described as "a sort of giant-sized golf course" where enemy guerrillas did not have the kind of natural cover they could avail themselves of in South Vietnam. Furthermore, there was a pro-U.S. country on Laos's western flank. Laos and Thailand share a border of 1,090 miles, and conservative Thai premier Sarit Thanarat was willing to allow U.S. forces to use his nation as a base from which to attack the Pathet Lao. It was in Sarit's interest to maintain Laos as an anticommunist buffer between his country and North Vietnam. Also, Phoumi Nosavan, America's Lao strongman, was Sarit's cousin; the two men often coordinated their political and military strategies. Washington thus had an ally, contiguous to Laos, where American troops could be stationed and to which those troops could retreat. South Vietnam offered no such conveniences.[7]

More significant than strategic assessments of the Lao landscape were cultural perceptions of the Lao people. U.S. policy toward Laos in the 1950s and early 1960s cannot be understood apart from the traits that Americans ascribed to inhabitants of that country, the manner in which American statesmen and the American media constructed a putative Lao national character that differed from South Vietnam's and that made Lao chances of withstanding communist pressure appear negligible. As several works of diplomatic history taking the so-called cultural turn have shown, it is not sufficient to accuse Americans of generalized "bias" in their cold-war dealings with countries like Vietnam, Indonesia, and China. Policymakers and press lords may have mouthed the domino theory's rhetoric of interchangeability, but they never believed that one Asian nation was much the same as any other. Rather, conceptualization of Asia in the American popular imagination was complex, positing a hierarchy of "good" and "bad" Asians, as Kennedy demonstrated in the above-cited letter to Diem when he contrasted Lao "ineffectiveness" with "the fierce desire of your people to maintain their independence and their willingness to engage in arduous struggle for it." Americans at midcentury considered some Asians "tough" and therefore dependable anticommunist allies and consigned others to the ranks of those who, in the words of a State Department working paper, "will not fight for themselves," much less the free world. No Asians rated lower in American eyes than the Lao.[8]

The record of policymaking deliberations under Eisenhower bristles with complaints about how difficult it was to get Lao soldiers and politicians to behave like cold warriors, or even to recognize that there was a war on. To American strategists, the Lao lacked every virtue desirable in an ally—courage, brawn, intelligence, maturity, acumen, morality, vigor— while possessing in abundance every shortcoming likely to render someone susceptible to red coercion: cowardice, feebleness, ignorance, childishness, injudiciousness, depravity, indolence. It is doubtful whether any people, even Amerindians in the Jacksonian era, have been held in greater contempt by U.S. government officials than the Lao, or that American policymakers ever resented an alliance more keenly than Eisenhower and his lieutenants resented their partnership with Laos in the crusade to keep Southeast Asia out of the communist orbit.

Kennedy found the partnership so vexatious that he ended it, disavowing Eisenhower's hard line and opting for Lao neutralism. In July 1962, the American secretary of state joined representatives of thirteen other nations at Geneva to sign a treaty that left Souvanna in charge of a coalition government, ordered all foreign troops to evacuate Laos, and stipulated that Lao territory would no longer be used as an avenue for the infiltration of neighboring countries. This was not an ideal outcome from Washington's perspective, even assuming the provisions were carried out in good faith, but it was better than large-scale American intervention or Pathet Lao victory. Kennedy has received high marks from historians for obtaining a negotiated settlement in Laos. Kenneth Hill cites the president's handling of the crisis as evidence of his desire "to initiate an era that would be devoid of old clichés and cold war slogans."[9]

Such praise hits wide of the mark. Kennedy was at least Eisenhower's equal in terms of anticommunist pugnacity. He chose to neutralize Laos not because he questioned the view that the United States needed a stronghold on the Asian mainland—in fact, he increased America's presence in South Vietnam while the 1961–62 Geneva Conference on Laos was unfolding—but because he considered the Lao miserable allies. Like Eisenhower, he was disgusted by reports of RLA incompetence. The intelligence briefings that landed on his desk every morning told him that royal troops regularly retreated in the face of a handful of Pathet Lao guerrillas. Sometimes they broke ranks to go swimming or pick flowers. RLA commander Phoumi Nosavan was, in Kennedy's words, a "total shit," and Lao civilian leaders were just as bad: lazy, stupid deadbeats, they soaked up millions of dollars in American aid without offering even verbal resistance to the communist bloc. Theodore Sorensen, Kennedy's chief speechwriter, put the matter plainly: "Do we want an indefinite occupation of an unenthusiastic, dark-skinned population... unwilling to fight for their own freedom?" Kennedy decided that he did not. According to Sorensen, the president justified the new course in Laos in his second State of the Union address, when he proclaimed that "no free peoples can be kept free without will and energy of their own." "He spoke of the world in general," Sorensen recalled, "but he was thinking of Laos in particular."[10]

In this book I trace the evolution of American policy toward Laos under Eisenhower and Kennedy, interpreting that policy as a product of cultural prejudices rather than logistical considerations or other ostensibly more salient imperatives. Nomenclature in a work like this is always problematic, as one strives for precision as well as parsimony, and my efforts to navigate between the Scylla of hairsplitting and the Charybdis of reductionism have convinced me that there is no single term for midcentury Americans' *optique* nuanced and elastic enough to serve the many functions to which it must be put. *Orientalism* and *paternalism* have their merits as explanatory rubrics, but neither encompasses all the feelings, attitudes, and values that drove U.S. policy. *Bigotry,* by contrast, is so vague as to be unwieldy. *Ethnocentrism* could conceivably work, since U.S. policymakers were incapable of understanding anything outside their own purview and presumed that the Lao wanted the same things they did; nonetheless, that expression has always rung tinny to my inner ear—it is too clinical to convey the malignancy of American anti-Lao sentiment, and it sounds, fairly or unfairly, like a word academics employ to avoid saying what they mean.

More useful for my purposes is Mark Bradley's culturally inflected approach to U.S.-Vietnamese relations in the first half of the twentieth century. Rather than relying on one structural category, Bradley writes of the "ensemble of assumptions" Americans brought to Vietnam, the deep-seated beliefs about Vietnamese mental, physical, and moral development that led U.S. statesmen to dismiss Ho Chi Minh's demands for independence and at the same time congratulate themselves for being more enlightened than French colonialists. Some of these beliefs had a racist cast; others grew out of allegedly more progressive views about the influence of environment on aptitude; others reflected faith in the universal applicability of U.S. institutions; still others expressed, in muted form, the missionary impulse to save heathen souls. Together, they made up the prism through which Americans "apprehended the Vietnamese" while crafting policies appropriate— or so they thought—to the situation. As Bradley illustrates, this perceptual framework left Washington unable to appreciate the vitality of Vietnamese national pride and provided justification for what amounted to neo-colonialism. Although American diplomats and military officials deplored France's brutal administration of its Indochinese possessions, none believed the Vietnamese capable of self-government. All were certain that Vietnam would need a period of Western tutelage before it could join the community of nations. Thus blinkered, U.S. policymakers missed their opportunity to establish a working relationship with Ho and condemned their country to an unwinnable war.[11]

The ensemble of assumptions Americans brought to Laos differed in degree and kind from the mental baggage they carried in Vietnam. Policymakers' preconceived notions of the Lao were more dehumanizing, verging more often on social Darwinism. Saving graces that U.S. statesmen were willing to grant the Vietnamese—trainability, desire to move with the times, and, most important, aggressiveness—were absent from the "Lao" portrayed in diplomatic correspondence, position papers, departmental and interdepartmental committee reports, and the minutes of high-level meetings. U.S.

ambassador to Laos J. Graham Parsons, roving ambassador W. Averell Harriman, Undersecretary of State Chester Bowles, Secretary of State Dean Rusk, and other key actors in the Eisenhower and Kennedy administrations vied to come up with the most withering epithets to characterize Washington's ally. They sneered at politicians like Souvanna, derided the RLA's battlefield performance, traded horror stories of U.S. initiatives undone by Lao doltishness, and as a rule spoke and wrote about the Lao in terms that made their stereotypes of the Vietnamese seem flattering by comparison.

America's prestige press, those newspapers and magazines with the widest circulations and most lustrous reputations, echoed such hauteur. Long before Kennedy removed Laos from the roster of disputes between Washington and Moscow, American journalists had identified the Kingdom of a Million Elephants as a losing proposition, and their disdain grew more entrenched as the Pathet Lao went from strength to strength. "The Laotian people have a very passive nature and do not care one way or another about communism or other big questions," observed the *Wall Street Journal* toward the end of the Eisenhower years. "Most don't seem to care much which side—government or reds—wins as long as they are left out of the squabble." *Newsweek* agreed, noting, "No one is less interested in the struggle for his country than the gentle Lao. Bloodshed and violence are alien to his nature. Red threats from the north mean nothing to him." The vision of Laos that arrived at American doorsteps and newsstands from the mid-1950s through the early 1960s was consistently opprobrious, and often presented in contrast to that of Vietnam, whose inhabitants, the *New York Times* declared, were of "different ethnic stock" than the Lao and had "no compunctions against killing." Although *Times* reporter Max Frankel did not answer the question he posed after the signing of the 1962 Geneva Accords on Laos— "Why is a Vietnamese right-wing strongman worth additional American lives, money, and prestige while a Laotian one is not?"—the bulk of received opinion in mainstream U.S. journalism made the answer obvious: because Americans could count on the Vietnamese to fight.[12]

None of the assumptions shaping American policy toward Laos functioned more powerfully than the religious. Laura Belmonte correctly calls religion an "understudied element of U.S. diplomacy in the early cold war years," and while a handful of recent books and articles have addressed religion's influence on midcentury American policymaking, their main contribution has been to show how diplomats like Secretary of State John Foster Dulles conceived of the cold war as a holy war. For Dulles and his contemporaries, writes William Inboden, the "basic outline of America's diplomatic theology" was clear: communists sought to stamp out the worship of God, and the United States had a sacred duty to confront such "militant irreligion." Yet it was not simply a matter of faith versus atheism. There were stalwart religions and inconstant ones. As Andrew Rotter, one of the few historians to take up this issue, observes, policymakers and public intellectuals differentiated between the "forthright, vigorous, [and] combative" Muslims of Pakistan and India's Hindus, whom they considered debauched and pusillanimous. Starker still was the distinction drawn between Catholicism, an obtrusively anticommunist religion, and Buddhism, the dominant faith of Southeast Asia. A study of U.S.-Vietnamese relations under Eisenhower demonstrates that Buddhism was "invariably identified with passivity, unindustriousness, and moral relativism, hardly desirable qualities in an ally when one is waging a crusade." The Catholic Diem, however, seemed committed by his faith to advance America's cause in the cold war, and that is why the Eisenhower administration stood behind him rather than a Buddhist South Vietnamese with greater administrative experience and popular support.[13]

Laos had no Diem. No RLG leader possessed the religious credentials to convince Washington that he would never betray the free world. Even Souvanna, whose "Western" mien attracted much attention from American politicians and journalists, was a Buddhist, and hence unreliable. Indeed, according to the Operations Coordinating Board, an agency set up by Eisenhower to coordinate departmental execution of national security policies, Lao Buddhism was worse than garden-variety Buddhism. "Like everything else in Laos," the board reported, "the Buddhist Church is less energetic, less well-organized, less well-developed, and less unified than similar institutions in neighboring countries. The enervating Lao climate and the amiability and indolence of the Lao people have resulted in relaxed intellectual and moral standards." If the South Vietnamese needed a Christian soldier like Diem to rally them against red tyranny, the Lao required Richard the Lionheart, and no one matching that profile dwelt in what veteran Southeast Asia correspondent Stanley Karnow called "an improbable little landlocked country" where "the passionless sage is still in popular esteem superior to warriors."[14]

Gender perceptions likewise played a role in the formation and execution of U.S. policy toward Laos, especially after Kennedy became president. By *gender* I do not mean biological difference; I accept the definition set forth nearly twenty years ago in an oft-reprinted article on U.S.-South Asian relations: "[G]ender... is the assignment of certain characteristics based upon prevailing ideas of masculinity and femininity to a people and a nation by another people and nation." Many historians, among them Kristin Hoganson and Mary Ann Heiss, have demonstrated how American policy-makers and the American media habitually accorded stock feminine traits to the citizens of poorer, predominantly nonwhite countries; thus nations as dissimilar as the Philippines and Iran were encoded as emotional, irresponsible, and unbusinesslike. Such gendered imagery, along with legitimating foreign policies of domination, led Americans to expect a kind of head-in-the-clouds caprice, a reluctance to face up to problems "like real men," from representatives of those countries, and the Lao—judging by records in the National Archives, the Library of Congress, the Eisenhower and Kennedy presidential libraries, and collections of relevant papers—obliged. U.S. officials repeatedly commented on Souvanna's quixotism, Kong Le's impulsiveness, Phoumi's petulance, and the general inability of any Lao to deal realistically, rationally, and logically with the threat facing the kingdom. While jungle-tough communists massed on Laos's borders and infiltrated its government and army, America's Lao allies were forever throwing parties, reshuffling cabinet positions, sulking because Washington would not give them enough aid, or, worst of all, indulging in the type of wishful thinking that had allowed Czechoslovakia, Hungary, and other nations to slip behind the iron curtain. No matter how often Americans warned them otherwise, RLG leaders clung to the view that coalitions with communists were workable. They felt, as U.S. minister to Laos Charles Yost complained in a typical cable, that if they made "concessions" to the Pathet Lao, "sweetness and light will be restored." Washington considered this a pipe dream. The dean of American journalists, Walter Lippmann, concurred. "In any political marriage," he wrote, "the communists are always the male." People too frivolous to heed the lessons of history were unfit to defend vital interests in Southeast Asia.[15]

The RLA's blasé approach to combat fortified this judgment and the policies that flowed from it. Robert Dean has shown how the Kennedy White House thrummed with a "boundary-defining" masculinity that demanded self-sacrifice, vigor, and physical and moral courage; it is not surprising that this most manly of presidents and his two-fisted advisers should have considered RLA diffidence proof that Laos did not deserve to remain part of the free world. Shortly after taking office, Kennedy forecast that "the complacent, the self-indulgent, the soft societies are about to be swept away with the debris of history." From what Kennedy could gather, Laos epitomized such societies, a view Eisenhower encouraged when he informed his successor that RLA soldiers were "a bunch of homosexuals." Kennedy expanded that slur in the retelling. "Laos," he remarked to special assistant Arthur Schlesinger Jr., "is a nation of homosexuals." In New Frontier–speak, there was no greater insult, and no stronger argument for policy change.[16]

Americans also infantilized the Lao, figuring them as dependents and Washington as their guardian. Naoko Shibusawa's study of postwar U.S.-Japanese relations, the first to deploy *maturity* as a category of analysis, is instructive here, as many of the traits her actors ascribed to the defeated Japanese appeared in American representations of the Lao, albeit in more corrosive form. "[A]dult over child" was a "universally recognized hierarchical relationship" in Truman- and Eisenhower-era America, Shibusawa writes, and this "helped to rationalize" the U.S. occupation of Japan and facilitate the shift in Japan's popular image from enemy to ally. U.S. policymakers assured themselves that Washington was not aping nineteenth-century imperial powers by seizing control of Japanese governmental activities; America, they said, would relinquish sovereignty once the Japanese grew up and were ready to "take on the responsibilities and privileges of an advanced society." Moreover, the Japanese, who had been depicted in U.S. wartime propaganda as demons driven by bloodlust, received gentler treatment from American journalists, scholars, and Hollywood filmmakers in the late 1940s and 1950s. Now they appeared as wayward youths, left to their own devices for too long, needing the stern hand, but also the forgiving heart, of a father figure to guide them to figurative adulthood.[17]

The trope of maturity turned up often in American discourse on Laos. Tom Dooley, beloved "jungle doctor of Asia" and the most influential American interpreter of Laos at midcentury, frequently referred to his host nation as the "Kingdom of Kids" and touted Walt Disney movies as the perfect medium for capturing Lao hearts. News stories devoted to Edgar "Pop" Buell, the Indiana farmer who won fame for his efforts to aid refugees from the Lao civil war, likewise emptied Laos of its adult population as they portrayed Buell as a paternal presence coaching pre-civilized wards on the rudiments of self-help. Similar condescension bled through the mountains of memoranda and other documents flowing over desks in the State Department and White House and ran like a central artery through the reminiscences of U.S. officials responsible for devising policy toward Southeast Asia. Especially revealing were the names Americans posted to Laos gave to the country of their assignment: "Never-Never Land," "The Land of Oz," and other titles drawn from fairy tales. When Souvanna, attempting to ingratiate himself with Dulles, told the secretary that he considered Laos "a child...in relation to the United States," he reinforced American assumptions about Lao immaturity.[18]

Yet Americans saw a different breed of children in Laos from what they had encountered in Japan—or Vietnam. As early as the 1890s, Joseph Henning notes, Japan confounded the West by industrializing and developing a first-rate navy. U.S. diplomats, military men, and journalists struggled to reconcile stereotypes of backward "Mongolians" with the Meiji Restoration. They eventually concluded, as they would during the two decades after Hiroshima, that the Japanese, while inferior to Euro-Americans, were exceptional among Asians in their knack for mimicry and hunger for the fruits of civilization. In other words, the Japanese were gifted children, at the top of the class. Although the Vietnamese ranked a notch below, they were still, according to U.S. ambassador to Burma William Sebald, "super-Orientals," ambitious and ripe for instruction. The Lao, by contrast, were Asia's underachievers, both for reasons of temperament and, some Americans suspected, because nature had not endowed them with much cerebral capacity. U.S. missionary and right-wing talking head Matt Menger went so far as to call them "retarded children." By employing such rhetoric, he and many of his countrymen crossed the line from derision to outright racism.[19]

I use that term with caution, aware that *racism* is the most loaded word out there, guaranteed to set eyes rolling and prompt charges of presentism from more traditional scholars. Let me be clear: the type of racism exhibited by Americans in Laos during the 1950s and 1960s was historically specific. It ought not to be confused with justifications for chattel slavery in the antebellum South. Midcentury Americans would never have asserted that the Lao were a separate biological group possessing genetically distinct talents. Nor would they have blamed Laos's myriad troubles on innate inferiority. Quite the reverse: many Americans saw the free world's challenge in Laos as one of accelerating progress, of helping the Lao fulfill their economic and political potential. In conformity with the principles of then-regnant modernization theory, Washington sought to catalyze a Lao "takeoff" toward capitalism, industrialization, and representative government before Marxist revolutionaries could exploit local grievances and communize the recently emancipated colony. America's whole cold-war campaign in Southeast Asia rested in large part on the premise that indigenous peoples were capable of ascending the rungs of a developmental ladder, even if some of them, namely the Lao, needed to start at the bottom.[20]

Fashionable theories aside, though, many American politicians, journalists, and opinion leaders wrote and spoke about the Lao with such poisonous antipathy that no expression save *racism* will suffice. Men like Parsons and Harriman openly despaired of ever getting the RLG or the RLA to behave like citizens of the free world. They viewed their allies as uneducable, sleep-drunk, affectless, content with the most limited horizons. If they never distinctly called the Lao a lesser breed of human beings, they conducted themselves with sufficient arrogance to earn the label "racist" and the reproachful connotations it entails.[21]

Not every American sank to their level. Indeed, Parsons's two successors at the Vientiane Embassy, Horace Smith and Winthrop Brown, held markedly more forbearant views than their colleague. Younger, lower-echelon Americans in Laos, like the anthropologist Joel Halpern—who might qualify as this book's hero—also approached their task from a perspective that, by the standards of the day, was quite broad-minded. Yet even the most charitable Americans looked down on the Lao. For example, Halpern, when asked in 1959 if communist leadership could instill "rigid discipline" and "a strong sense of national dedication" in Lao villagers, quipped that he doubted whether the communists had "enough No-Doz to stay awake."[22]

This was mild teasing compared to the bile spewed by Halpern's superiors in Vientiane and Washington; still, it betrayed a strain of contumely to which no midcentury American was immune, a strain that centered on one Indochinese country, not the entire region. Christian Chapman, the State Department officer in charge of Lao affairs during Eisenhower's second term, spoke for many of his associates when he contrasted the Vietnamese, "a dynamic, energetic, determined people," with the "relaxed," "noncompetitive" Lao. "The Lao are...not very vigorous," Chapman noted, "and they don't work too hard.... They're very humble and say, 'Oh, we're just three million people in the middle of Southeast Asia, and there's just so much we can do.'" While putting these words in Lao mouths hardly made Chapman a pith-helmeted imperialist, he would not have attributed comparable views to the inhabitants of another country, least of all his own, and the ease with which he invoked a monolithic Laos, shrugging its collective shoulders and hanging its communal head, was telling, especially if we position his relatively tame comments over against a random sample of descriptors favored by other policymakers and the American press when discussing the Lao: "docile," "apathetic," "gutless," "spineless," "useless," "feeble," "dreamy," "unprepared philosophically to defend themselves," "lacking in discipline and morale," "like children caught in a grown-ups' quarrel." Virtually every American in a position to influence U.S.-Lao relations between 1954 and 1962—presidents, cabinet members, military leaders, Foreign Service officials, aid workers, missionaries, editors, publishers, columnists, and reporters—drew from the same grab bag of pejoratives to characterize the people they professed to be helping.[23]

Had Americans not been so locked into their Kiplingesque conception of Laos, they might have been able to grasp a hard fact that, in retrospect, seems manifest: not *all* Lao were battle-shy; only the royalists were. The Pathet Lao fought with valor for years against better-armed opposition. The neutralists, too, showed pluck and resourcefulness; in August 1960, as Eisenhower's second term drew to a close, Kong Le and his single paratroop battalion seized Vientiane, which was not recaptured by Phoumi's American-trained divisions until December of that year. History indicated that the Lao did not have a congenital distaste for warfare; it was just those Lao asked to fight for Washington's puppet who threw in the towel. Yet Americans ascribed U.S. reverses in Laos to flaws in the Lao national character rather than to blind spots in U.S. foreign policy. When they stopped to ask themselves why neutralists and Pathet Lao performed so much better under fire than the RLA, a query they raised with remarkable infrequency before mentally sweeping it under the rug, the response was that the soldiers following Kong Le and "Red Prince" Souphanouvong were really North Vietnamese cadres in disguise.

To be sure, that charge had some merit. Control of eastern Laos was vital to Hanoi's long-term strategy of national unification. The Ho Chi Minh Trail ran through this territory, forming the principal supply route for the rebellion against Diem's government in Saigon, and the North Vietnamese politburo was not about to allow anyone to deprive it of a crucial logistic and tactical advantage. Hanoi therefore sent a delegation of military specialists to work alongside Pathet Lao forces in 1959, and gradually increased its commitment until, by the end of the 1961–62 Geneva Conference, there were around eight thousand North Vietnamese troops and twenty thousand auxiliary personnel in the northeastern Lao provinces of Sam Neua and Phong Saly. But—and this point bears emphasis—Hanoi did not take such measures until *after* Washington stage-managed the overthrow of Souvanna's neutralist government and its replacement by a rightist regime under Phoui Sananikone that, in the view of Ho and his associates, menaced the National Liberation Front's lifeline. Between 1954 and 1959, the North Vietnamese paid little attention to events across their western border; they were preoccupied with economic recovery and administrative

restructuring at home. Even during the succession of U.S.-sponsored conservative governments that followed Phoui's investiture, North Vietnamese
troops in Laos never rivaled the Pathet Lao numerically. Moreover, they had
almost no control over Kong Le's neutralists, the preeminent fighting units
in the kingdom.[24]

Beijing and Moscow likewise came late to Laos, responding to perceived
American attempts to establish a foothold, and their influence was always
exercised on the side of restraint. Far from encouraging Pathet Lao belligerence, the Chinese and Soviets made great efforts to resolve the Lao crisis
diplomatically before it escalated into region-wide hostilities. The opening
of archives in China and the former Soviet Union reveals that Mao Zedong
and Nikita Khrushchev both feared U.S. intervention in Laos. Mao saw it
as a threat to China's southern frontier, and had his representatives, chiefly
Foreign Minister Zhou Enlai, press the Pathet Lao to conciliate their opponents. China, Zhou declared, was willing to accept a neutral or even
"semineutral" Laos as long as it was free of American bases. Famine and
other disruptions caused by the Great Leap Forward left Chinese officials
loath to engage in foreign adventures, and memories of the Korean War
made the prospect even less attractive. Thus statesmen like Zhou recurrently
voiced their support for a settlement in Laos adhering to the terms of the
1954 Geneva Accords on Indochina: that is, a nonaligned Vientiane regime,
independent and sovereign, forbidden to join military blocs.[25]

Khrushchev, for his part, worried that events in Laos would wreck his
policy of peaceful coexistence with the West and divert resources from
more important regions. "I have not the slightest interest in this [Laos] affair," he told Mao, "because this affair itself is small, but there is much noise
around it." Unlike Washington, Moscow provided no assistance to Laos
until 1960, long after the Eisenhower administration had trained, equipped,
and funded a forty-thousand-man RLA. When Soviet aid did begin flowing, it went to Souvanna's government instead of the Pathet Lao, and it
was minuscule compared with the hundreds of millions of dollars spent by
Washington. From the moment Laos engaged his interest, shortly before
Kennedy's inauguration, Khrushchev was eager to take the kingdom out of
the East-West conflict by establishing a troika RLG comprised of centrist,
rightist, and leftist elements. He mused several times that he would even
countenance Lao neutralism weighted toward the United States.[26]

American policymakers, of course, were unaware of these top-secret remarks, but they ought to have been able to piece together enough bits
of information to conclude that the two communist superpowers did not

have designs on Laos. Khrushchev's statement to Harriman that there was "nothing really serious going on in Laos" and that Moscow and Washington ought to "ignore it" was hardly subtle, and the Soviet leader followed up that assertion by complaining that he did "not know all those silly Laotian names or the individuals to whom those names belonged." Chinese diplomats, though less transparent in their public oratory, tipped Beijing's hand through their actions. When, in early 1961, Cambodian leader Prince Norodom Sihanouk suggested an international conference to defuse the situation in Laos, Beijing endorsed this proposal and urged upon the Pathet Lao the acceptance of a cease-fire, even though Souphanouvong's forces were in a favorable position vis-à-vis the RLA at the time. Put simply, Pathet Lao and neutralist military successes prior to Kennedy's inauguration owed little to external communist meddling. Souphanouvong, Kong Le, and their respective partisans were patriots fired by ambition to free their country of foreign control. Washington's Lao ally had no corresponding stimulus.[27]

Why did Americans fail to comprehend this? Why did policymakers, pressmen, and other American observers cling to the caricature of the lazy, supine, timorous Lao when Lao military figures and civilians consistently rebutted it? How could Parsons sigh with bland assurance that "the unfortunate Lao are not a race of warriors" in the face of evidence to the contrary?[28]

There are, I submit, three explanations. The first relates to cultural differences, which did, and do, exist between Americans and Lao. For example— and here I hope I am engaging in the kind of responsible, non-essentializing generalization Andrew Rotter practices in his work on U.S.-Indian relations— Lao statesmen tended to embrace a code of performative masculinity that was less overtly aggressive than that subscribed to by American officials. They spoke softly, smiled even while being hectored, rarely interrupted a conversational partner, and never invaded someone else's personal space. Politicians like Souvanna did not believe that respecting these points of protocol put their manhood at risk, but Americans often misinterpreted Lao etiquette as evidence of effeminacy and lack of resolve. On other occasions, facial expressions, gestures, and body language that bore no relationship to battlefield performance or statecraft unwittingly served to bolster American views of the Lao as apathetic and infantile.

More important than false inferences drawn from Lao cultural characteristics, however, was the fact that Washington equated Vientiane's rational— indeed necessary—policy of nonalignment with appeasement, thereby investing the Lao with a range of values that no impartial observer could have attributed to them. As several scholars note, Laos occupied an unenviable geographic position. It was the Poland of the Far East, wedged between two antagonistic camps in a zone of great tension and pressure. Vietnam and China, historic enemies with populations incomparably larger, pushed against the kingdom's eastern and northern boundaries, while Thailand, also huge and allied with a capitalist superpower, threatened the western flank. It would have been impossible for Laos, under these circumstances, to adopt the pro-Western course demanded of it by Washington. Neutrality was the only option for Lao patriots seeking to keep their nation intact, independent, and at peace. Anticommunism would have sentenced Laos to balkanization and foreign control, a point underscored over and over by Souvanna and other members of the RLG. Yet the message never got through. Americans could not accept that leaders of a small, vulnerable country might be more concerned with their own national survival than with conforming to the geopolitical theories of John Foster Dulles. Washington thus construed the ill success of its campaign to make Laos a bulwark against red expansion as proof that the Lao were good-for-nothing naïfs whom the free world was better off without. In other words, Americans refused to recognize that the problem was "us," not "them." Norman Cousins, editor of the *Saturday Review,* eloquently expressed the frustration caused by this cognitive rigidity in a 1961 cover feature. "[I]f you want to get a sense of the universe unraveling, come to Laos," he wrote. "There is a tendency, in dealing with Laos, to develop a desperate passion for the recognizables. Out of the pounding confusion comes a groping for familiar notions of a world divided into just two camps, a world of good and bad, with blazing lights to distinguish between the two." Laos did not accommodate Washington's cold-war credo and paid the price in ridicule.[29]

Finally, institutional factors contributed to the persistence of American mind-lock. As shown in chapter 3, most U.S. officials assigned to Laos lived and worked in compounds boasting all the amenities of stateside upper-middle-class suburbia: schools, shopping centers, hospitals, churches, movie theaters, gyms, and other recreational facilities. Embassy personnel, aid workers, and military advisers saw little reason to venture outside their "Little America," and few did, with the result that they remained isolated from the host community. This had disastrous consequences. Given the immense distance, geographic and cultural, between Washington and Vientiane, senior U.S. policymakers were more dependent than usual on representatives "in country" to inform them of conditions on which to base an effective program. Statesmen like Rusk assumed that the "Laos" described in embassy cables and other correspondence from the field accurately reflected local realities, and they crafted policy based on that portrayal. But the compound-bound Americans in Vientiane never outgrew their initial derogative impressions of the Lao. Intellectually, they never left home. From air-conditioned office buildings and ranch-style houses, they poked fun at the shiftless natives and filed reports affirming American prejudices rather than accurately assessing local sensibilities and needs. Their self-segregation not only led to faulty policymaking; it alienated host citizens, who resented being treated as inferior. "Americans 'classify' themselves by living together on compounds and having so many places where Laotians cannot go," a resident of Luang Prabang complained in 1959. "They give the impression that they consider themselves superior to Laotians and do not like to associate with them." That impression was unfortunately true, and it would dog U.S. efforts in Laos from the beginning.[30]

A note on sources is in order. Some readers may take issue with the amount of attention I devote to press coverage of events in Laos. Despite works by Michelle Mart, Edward Said, Marda Dunsky, Mary Ann Heiss, John Foran, and others illustrating the impact of the American press on foreign policy, it is still not respectable in certain circles to assign mass media a role commensurate with that of geopoliticians, mainly because of the cause-and-effect question. Pulitzer Prize–winning reporter David Halberstam has famously called Henry Luce "at least as influential as the secretary of state," but historians cannot point to a specific order given by the cofounder, principal stockholder, and editor-in-chief of Time Inc. that led directly to a foreign-policy initiative. From this "no smoking gun" starting point, it is an easy next step to claim that the press just reports on policy while others make it. William Dorman and Mansour Farhang rebut this argument brilliantly in their study of U.S.-Iranian relations:

> [W]e believe the link between press and policy is enormously complex and subtle. We certainly do not mean to suggest that there is a simple cause-and-effect relationship. But if the press does not *make* foreign or defense policy, in some important ways it helps set the boundaries within which policy can be made. In this respect, the press is usually *affective* in the policy process rather than determining.

For Dorman and Farhang, *Time, Newsweek,* the *Christian Science Monitor,* the *Washington Post,* and other press organs foster a "critically important general mood," a "highly generalized *sense of things:* of what is required and what is not; of who is enemy and who is friend. The press sets the broad limits of our thinking about the 'other.'"[31]

That is what it did with respect to Laos. Publishers like Luce did not control U.S. policy, but they conditioned it, making some actions, such as supporting Kong Le, appear foolish, and presenting others as expedient, even essential. Kennedy, who read several newspapers every morning and cultivated friendships with many of America's leading correspondents, must have been aware of the journalistic establishment's negative opinion of the Lao. He must also have known that the media diet served up to Americans attempting to follow the Lao civil war ensured that few voters would object when he chose to extricate the United States from that conflict, even if his policy ran the risk of eventual Pathet Lao triumph. Laos was a tabula rasa experientially for Americans; they observed it through a lens ground and polished by the mainstream press, and the consensus media view as of 1962 was, in the words of the *Washington News,* that "no spot in Southeast Asia seems more hopeless."[32]

Ultimately, Kennedy reconciled himself to Lao nonalignment and set the machinery for compromise in motion. He did not do so, however, because he was more willing than Eisenhower to scale back the cold war strategy of global interventionism that projected American power into every inhabited latitude and time zone. Rather, he doubted the capacity of the Lao to fulfill Washington's grand design, and his pessimism grew out of convictions less noble than those cited by admirers. In addition, his prudent Laos policy, debatably the high point of his presidency, came with a hidden trip-wire. He did not believe he could retreat any further in Southeast Asia. If the North Vietnamese and Viet Cong pressed their advantage against the U.S.-sponsored Saigon regime, America would have to fight. By cutting his losses in Laos, Kennedy narrowed the range of options for himself and future presidents attempting to cope with Vietnam.

Chapter 1

# "A Long Country Inhabited by Lotus Eaters"

## Washington Encounters Laos

The three states of French Indochina—Laos, Cambodia, and Vietnam—stood on the threshold of a seemingly golden era as 1954 drew to a close. French defeat in the battle of Dien Bien Phu had ended the war between France and the Viet Minh and sounded the death knell of France's Southeast Asian empire. A multinational conference of communist and noncommunist powers in Geneva had worked out the details of a region-wide settlement: recognition of Laos and Cambodia as independent nations, withdrawal of all foreign troops from Lao and Cambodian territory, and partition of Vietnam until elections could be held to unify the country in 1956. The conferees had also established an international-control commission to oversee implementation of what came to be known as the Geneva Accords. While leaders of the various Indochinese liberation movements recognized that the accords were ambiguous in crucial respects, and while the refusal of the U.S. delegation at Geneva to endorse the settlement led some observers to predict that Western intervention in Southeast Asian affairs was far from over, millions of former colonial subjects celebrated their independence and looked with confidence to the future. "We were so optimistic," Lao politician Panh Ngaosyvathn recalled decades later. "Everything was in front of us. The country was peaceful, and we felt we could create the world anew."[1]

This was not the reaction in Washington. President Dwight Eisenhower declared at his weekly press conference that while he was "glad" the "bloodshed in Indochina" had come to an end, the accords contained "features which we do not like." Eisenhower and his advisers blamed French war-weariness and British pusillanimity for the free world's surrender at the Geneva Conference. As far as American policymakers were concerned, Paris's unwillingness to continue fighting and London's determination to appease China had allowed the Viet Minh to seize the northern half of Vietnam. Of equal importance, from the perspective of candidates in the 1954 off-year elections, was the conference's likely impact on American voters. The Republicans, having exploited the issue of "Who Lost China?" to win the White House and Congress two years earlier, now found themselves vulnerable to charges of having "lost" part of Indochina. Accordingly, no foreign-policy requirement was more axiomatic for Eisenhower and his party in the fall of 1954 than the need to prevent any more of the Asian mainland from retiring behind the iron curtain.[2]

One consequence of this imperative was that the Eisenhower administration began giving sustained attention to Laos and Cambodia for the first time. During the Franco–Viet Minh War, Washington's focus had been on Vietnam, site of most military engagements, but now American statesmen started to assess their prospects in all of France's liberated Southeast Asian colonies. They had little firsthand knowledge on which to base policy: the United States did not have permanent diplomatic representation in Laos and Cambodia, and the State Department maintained only one desk officer for all of Indochina. Nonetheless, after years of either ignoring these two states or conceptually conflating them with Vietnam, U.S. geopoliticians began to weigh their merits as cold war battlefields.

Probably the first government official to do this was Robert McClintock, chargé d'affaires at the American embassy in Saigon, who provided his superiors at State with a position paper titled "U.S. Policy for Post-Armistice Indochina" in mid-August 1954. McClintock believed Washington should "furnish... economic, financial, and military assistance to the three countries of Indochina," but advised that "this assistance should be conditioned by performance by the three countries." Some seemed apt to perform better than others. South Vietnam, for instance, was in "political chaos," and its army had "disintegrated as a fighting force." It required "strong leadership," or the "battle tested" communists in the North would impose their rule over the entire nation. "On the asset side," McClintock noted, "the Cochin-Chinese are a cheerful, *dolce far niente* people who are easily led and in fact prefer to have their decisions made for them." Thus, if Washington could nurture a pro-Western native strongman, South Vietnam might be saved for the free world. Unfortunately, the new South Vietnamese premier, Ngo Dinh Diem, struck McClintock as unqualified. He "has only one virtue—honesty," McClintock reported, "and is bereft of any practical experience." In comparing Diem's shaky government with the "monolithic" regime knit together by Ho Chi Minh above the 17th parallel, McClintock was forced to conclude that "the communist side has a decided advantage."

Cambodia seemed a sounder investment than South Vietnam. "The situation in Cambodia offers promise of success in resisting communist infiltration," McClintock wrote. "The people of Cambodia are homogenous, unified not only by race and language but likewise by the spiritual ties of Buddhism." They were also proven combatants: "It is noteworthy that the only place in Indochina when the Geneva Conference was in session where fire fights were won against the Viet Minh was in Cambodia." Cambodia moreover was "economically well off," with "vast rubber plantations," a "wealth of forest reserves," and a "fishing industry" that "makes available an extensive export...to nearby countries." In recent years, businessmen had begun to trade the nation's "export surplus for industrial commodities," which indicated that Cambodia was developing along liberal, capitalist lines and might soon present an opportunity for America's economic expansion. McClintock therefore recommended that Washington "go all out to enable Cambodia as a free, independent, democratic Southeast Asian country to...maintain its integrity against communism." In particular, McClintock counseled that a program in "psychological warfare" be inaugurated "to enlist the latent forces of the Buddhist Church." He felt that Cambodia was "preserved to some extent from the virus of communism by the moral precepts of the Buddhist religion," which, while not as militantly anticommunist as Americans might like, "at least exert a negative influence against communist penetration."

McClintock saved the worst for last. "Laos," he announced, "is a long country inhabited by lotus eaters." It possessed strategic value in that it could "interdict the most direct land route from China to the Gulf of Siam," but it represented no threat, or even an irritant, to its red neighbors. "From the aspect of penetration by communists," observed McClintock, "their greatest advantage is the indolence of the inhabitants, their political apathy, and their inability thus far to be counted as a military force." Laos had no industry or exports. Its population was "scattered over an immense area," and communication between provinces was slow due to the lack of roads, railways, airfields, telephones, and radios. It was financially in the dark ages. "[T]here is no one in Laos of native origin who knows anything about banking," McClintock sniffed. He did concede that "here, as in the case of Cambodia, an opportunity exists for strengthening the negative bulwark of Buddhism against communist penetration," but there were obstacles to any such campaign: "Laos offers a meager field for propaganda activity because of the illiteracy of the populace and the difficulty of reaching many Laotians at any one time by mass media." Given the nation's "slender human and military resources," McClintock declared, "Laos is a deficit country."[3]

McClintock's views did not strictly correspond to those of other mid-century American policymakers, who tended to be less sanguine about Cambodia's chances of repelling communist pressure and who found their doubts confirmed when Cambodian ruler Norodom Sihanouk announced his intention to follow a path of neutrality. Furthermore, as will be shown, the majority of American politicians, press lords, and pundits did not consider Buddhism even a negative bulwark against the red tide. Most important, key White House and State Department figures had greater faith than McClintock did in Diem's ability to build an anticommunist state in South Vietnam, and they would invest billions of dollars in the "Diem experiment," a commitment that marked the crossover point between advice and support and U.S. cobelligerency in Vietnam's civil war.

On one issue, however, McClintock and his colleagues were in agreement. To a man, they deemed Laos the least promising place in Asia, and perhaps on earth, to halt the march of communism. Apart from the logistical problems posed by a landlocked country with rugged terrain and almost no overland communications, Laos was unappealing in terms of what one U.S. diplomat called "the human material with which we have to work." American policymakers looked at the Lao and saw their own self-image reversed. "We are enthusiasts. We are doers," proclaimed Representative Walter Judd, one of Congress's leading advocates for an aggressive foreign policy. Confident, energetic statesmen like Judd were appalled by Lao fatalism and laziness. "Apathy is [the] general rule," McClintock reported shortly before the Geneva Accords were finalized. "Laotians merely wish to live and let live and have no . . . ardor." Left to their own devices, they would not resist a communist assault; they were more likely to sleep through it.[4]

Tellingly, the stereotypes invoked by McClintock in 1954 failed to evolve over time into more sympathetic understanding, despite the growth of the

U.S. presence in Laos and consequent opportunities afforded Americans to delve into the motives and objectives of their Lao allies. Greater familiarity only bred greater contempt. As late as 1958, the International Cooperation Administration, which supervised American technical aid projects in underdeveloped countries, complained about the "macabre inertness" of the Lao and admitted that "the United States would have no interest in Laos were it not for the cold war."[5]

But the cold war was the most important fact of American public life at midcentury, the rationale and justification for all U.S. foreign policy, and the Eisenhower administration viewed Laos as vital territory in the contest between communism and anticommunism. Thus, the dilemma Washington faced as it confronted Laos in the wake of the Geneva Conference was simple but daunting: How could the United States retain this country for the free world when it was obliged to work with such shoddy human material?

## *"Le Pays des Laos"*

The nation that American policymakers so disdained was one of the most ethnically and politically complex areas of Southeast Asia, and its chaotic history resists abridgement. To oversimplify for present purposes, however, we may identify the inception of the Lao *monarchy* as the point of origin of a Lao *state*. By that measure, Laos was over seven hundred years old when it became America's ally. The Kingdom of a Million Elephants had undergone stark transformations across the centuries, from regional hegemon to cluster of principalities to European colony, but Lao behavior, generally speaking, remained consistent. Contrary to the dismissive images promulgated by American journalists, academics, and diplomats, the Lao were a fighting people, ready to take up arms to defend their homeland. While Laos may not have been the Southeast Asian equivalent of Sparta or Prussia, it had a military record of which any country could be proud.[6]

In the mid-fourteenth century, Fa Ngum, a brilliant general, overcame tortuous geography and diverse demographics to forge a kingdom in the upper Mekong valley called Lan Xang. Fa Ngum is credited with introducing Buddhism into the territory; he commissioned the building of pagodas and monasteries, made Buddhism the state religion, and became a monk for a time. Yet Fa Ngum's destiny lay on the battlefield, not in the temple. His reign featured constant warfare, as he expanded his realm to the north and east and compelled the feudal rulers he thrashed to pay tribute. In his most celebrated exploit, he captured Phai Nam, a city protected by barricades of sharpened bamboo. Fa Ngum had the gold and silver in Lan Xang's treasury fashioned into arrows, which he ordered his archers to shoot at the barricades before feigning a retreat. When the defenders of the city saw this precious metal lying among the bamboo, they began cutting down the barricades to retrieve the arrows. As soon as they had cut a path through the bamboo thickets, Fa Ngum's army returned, penetrated the city, and sacked it.

Fa Ngum's successors were mostly men of peace, dedicated to consolidating what he had conquered. For three centuries, Lan Xang flourished. Strategically located at the crossroads for communications along the Southeast Asian peninsula, it developed an active commerce and became a center for arts and education. In 1563, the capital was moved from Luang Prabang to Vientiane, where it took its place among the marvels of the age. Travelers who visited Vientiane brought back stories of majestic buildings, monuments, and pagodas, including Pha That Luang, the "Great Sacred Stupa," with its fortresslike appearance and massive central tower surrounded by leaves of fine gold. They told of royal processions involving dozens of elephants covered with gilded draperies and precious stones, of two hundred blazing canoes descending the Mekong, of the river itself seeming to be on fire. Still, Lan Xang's crowning glory remained its army, one of the most formidable war machines in Southeast Asia.

The kingdom began to decline, however, in the mid-seventeenth century, as its neighbors launched repeated invasions. A series of wars with Burma (Myanmar), Siam (Thailand), and Annam (Vietnam) sapped Lan Xang's resources. Its borders contracted, and its national cohesion was undermined by quarrels among the ruling elites. In 1713 Lan Xang split into the three kingdoms of Vientiane, Luang Prabang, and Champassak. Neighboring powers moved in to exploit the situation, with Siam proving most successful. Bangkok extended its control over Vientiane and Champassak until they became, for all practical purposes, colonies.

Prince Chao Anou, ruler of Vientiane and a much-mythologized figure in Lao history, attempted to shake off the Siamese yoke by allying with Annam and staging a rebellion. He initially suckered the enemy: when his army met a larger Siamese force, he claimed that his troops were marching south to help their masters resist a British invasion; the Siamese lowered their weapons, and Chao Anou's men slaughtered them. After this promising start, though, the revolt collapsed. It lacked long-range preparation and was conducted on too broad a front. More important, the anticipated Annamite support did not materialize. Still, Chao Anou's army got within a three-day march of Bangkok before being routed in the battle of Saraburi, where the rebels fought with tremendous, even suicidal, valor. One of Chao Anou's generals, taken prisoner by the Siamese, refused to order his men to surrender. The Siamese had him staked to the ground and trampled to death by an elephant. After all the insurgents were dead or dispersed, Siam put Vientiane to the torch, destroying most of its houses and enslaving its population. Lao scholar Saveng Phinith writes that "the revolt by Chao Anou . . . is considered by all Lao as a high point of their history."[7]

At the time, however, it signaled the ruin of Lan Xang. Vientiane was in shambles, with just a few toppled spires to suggest the grandeur of the past, and Champassak was more firmly under Siamese control than ever. All that remained of Fa Ngum's empire was Luang Prabang. Even that kingdom did not enjoy territorial integrity; its eastern provinces fell to Annam in a series of border confrontations, and only the arrival of the French in the second half of the nineteenth century prevented its disintegration.

France had already laid claim to most of what is now Vietnam and Cambodia when it pressured Siam to remove its occupation troops from Vientiane and Champassak in 1893. The French proceeded to conclude a series of political alliances with the royal courts and highland tribal federations that consolidated the territories constituting present-day Laos. According to legend, the fact that Paris was able to assume command of this area without shedding a drop of blood was due to the efforts of one man, August Pavie, a civil servant who carried out a "conquest of the hearts," convincing everyone from rival monarchs to village headmen that Laos would benefit by coming under France's wing. Martin Stuart-Fox, one of the foremost authorities on Lao history, argues that while Pavie did prove successful in his campaign to acquire Luang Prabang through persuasion, France's procurement of Vientiane and Champassak came "more as a result of gunboat diplomacy than the winning of hearts." Nonetheless, the imposition of French control occurred with minimal carnage, a surprising development given the region's blood-drenched annals. According to one scholar, this was because "the people of Lan Xang, battered by generations of abuse at the hands of more powerful neighbors, showed little hint of their past military mettle, favoring instead compromise for survival." Whatever the reason for France's relatively painless takeover, the French moved swiftly to admit Lan Xang to the Indochinese Union, an administrative framework for French possessions in Southeast Asia, and set about surveying their new

domain. Cartographers drew up maps of the area, naming it, unimagina-
tively, "*le pays des Laos*"—the land of the Lao.[8]

Paris had high hopes for Laos. The Mekong River, many believed, would
provide a navigable route into southwestern China, where French goods
could be marketed to millions of consumers and China's resources could be
loaded onto French vessels, ferried downstream, and shipped to European
markets. Backers of the French Syndicate of Laos, mesmerized by visions
of a river empire, invested 100,000 francs in the venture, but they soon
discovered that the Mekong was cut by rapids and useless for commercial
travel. Laos did not have any gold or silver deposits either, and it was too
mountainous for plantations. Clearly, France was not going to extract great
wealth from this country of narrow valleys and precipitous slopes. But all
was not lost: the French needed a buffer to protect their Vietnamese hold-
ings from the British in Burma, and Laos would serve this purpose nicely.

As might be expected, few Frenchmen were eager to be posted to Laos.
The country never accounted for more than 1 percent of the total French
export trade from Indochina, and Paris tried to manage Lao affairs inex-
pensively. French administrators in Vientiane and Luang Prabang lived in
villas of modest proportions. They enjoyed none of the recreations available
in Saigon and Hanoi—and even, to a lesser extent, in Phnom Penh. No
wonder Laos was considered a dead-end assignment, and that France was
only able to maintain a staff of seventy-two officials there in 1904, while
the contingent in Vietnam numbered over forty thousand. No wonder, too,
that French rule rested lightly on Laos, as imperial functionaries adopted a
low-key attitude, conducted their administration through the Lao feudal
court structures, and either counted the days until their return to Paris or
surrendered to the temptations of opium, alcohol, and local women.

Since there were never many *colons* (white settlers) in Laos, and since the
Frenchmen who did reside there did not make harsh demands upon the
natives, rebellions were rare. They were not unheard of, however. An uprising occurred in southern Laos at the end of the nineteenth century, when
a Buddhist holy man called for independence. His followers overran several French garrisons, destroyed French property and crops, and conquered
almost the entire Bolovens Plateau before imperial forces reasserted control. In the insurgency's final act, two thousand rebels attacked the French
commissariat in Savannakhet and were gunned down en masse. Shortly
thereafter, rebels in Phong Saly Province flared up in an insurrection that
the French needed two years to quell. Muong Sing was next to raise the
standard of revolt; a guerrilla army inflicted heavy losses on French troops

and only capitulated after the French sent three military expeditions against it. Another insurrection swept across northeastern Laos on the eve of World War I, as rebels captured Sam Neua City, killed the French soldiers stationed there, and waged a no-quarter-given campaign in many provinces, some of which were wrested from French control. Add to these large-scale revolts lesser instances of violent opposition, as well as innumerable cases of passive resistance, and Laos hardly seemed to merit its reputation as the *enfant sage,* the "well-behaved child," of the Indochinese Union.

It might more properly have been called the abandoned stepchild. Paris did not even define Laos's legal status as a protectorate rather than a colony until 1941, the same year it recognized Sisavang Vong, ruler of Luang Prabang, as Lao monarch. The French supervised Laos as would an absentee landlord, leaving most of its population free to continue their lives as subsistence rice farmers in the plains or practitioners of slash-and-burn agriculture in the mountains. This approach proved a mixed blessing, for although the Lao were never subjected to the oppression suffered by the Vietnamese, their nation also never developed beyond its frontier status. While the French built railway networks, highway systems, administrative centers, hospitals, and schools elsewhere in Indochina, they ignored Laos. By 1940, there were only seven thousand primary school students in a country of over one million people, and not a single high school or university had been constructed. A few dirt roads were cut, but they were usable only in the dry season. Although the French did build one hospital in Vientiane and clinics in each provincial capital, this had virtually no impact on the state of Lao health care. Laos's infant mortality rate did not decline throughout the fifty-year French occupation.

World War II transformed the configuration of power in Southeast Asia and marked a watershed in Lao history. After the defeat of France by the Nazis in 1940 and the establishment of the French Vichy government, Vichy authorities relinquished control of Indochina to Japan. French personnel still held nominal command over the region, but real power was exercised by Tokyo, which soon controlled the British colonies of Malaya and Burma as well as Laos's neighbor, Thailand. The Lao, like other Asians, were impressed by Japan's victories over European powers, and Japanese rhetoric about Pan-Asianism and liberation from white overlordship found a receptive audience throughout Indochina. Nonetheless, it soon became apparent that the Greater East Asia Co-Prosperity Sphere touted by Japanese propagandists was really a plan to consolidate all the peoples of Asia into a bloc with Japan in control. Japanese occupation was more brutal than French colonial society, which explains, to some degree, why many Lao nourished feelings of affection toward the disempowered *colons*.

The liberation of Paris in 1944 and the overthrow of the Vichy regime prompted Tokyo to reevaluate its partnership with France in Indochina. If, as expected, a government headed by Charles de Gaulle came to power, the French puppets who had previously done nothing to interfere with Japanese programs might become obstreperous overnight. Consequently, as the Allies began rolling back Japanese gains in the Pacific, Japan encouraged local nationalist movements that could provide an alternative to the façade of French supervision. On March 9, 1945, the Japanese launched coups throughout Indochina, jailing French civil servants and soldiers and insisting that the various states declare independence from their colonial masters—meaning, in effect, that Laos, Cambodia, and Vietnam would accept Japanese sovereignty instead.

King Sisavang Vong then did an extraordinary thing. Alone among Southeast Asian rulers, he refused to obey Japan's edict, proclaiming that the offer of independence was hollow and that he preferred to await the Pacific war's outcome before making commitments with respect to his country's status. Crown Prince Savang Vatthana went further: he called for an uprising against the Japanese and promised severe punishment for any Lao who failed to participate. Many of his countrymen responded to this rallying cry. Lao soldiers joined with Free French commandos in the hills to carry out raids on Japanese posts. Prince Boun Oum, a future Lao premier, organized guerrilla bases in southern Laos, which disrupted enemy communications. Lao resistance fighters proved so effective that the British government decided to parachute weapons to them, and Paris commemorated their valor after the war by creating a special medal.

Tokyo, outraged at this display of defiance, sent a detachment of troops to Luang Prabang to kidnap the crown prince. Savang was taken into custody and spirited off to Saigon, while the king was held prisoner in his own palace. Under duress, Sisavang submitted to his captors, proclaiming, "Our kingdom has been delivered from French domination." Laos had become a member of Japan's new order. That order, however, was collapsing. The atomic bombing of Hiroshima and Nagasaki brought about Tokyo's surrender in August 1945, and Laos found itself with no settled identity. Was it now an independent nation? Would it revert to French control? Or would it occupy a halfway house between freedom and thralldom?[9]

The task of resolving this issue fell to three princes: Phetsarath, Souvanna Phouma, and Souphanouvong. All three were opposed to French colonialism, but each, as time would reveal, had his own vision of Laos's future. Each moreover possessed a distinctive temperament that may have been more important than political philosophy in shaping his career. Phetsarath, member of a collateral line of the Lao royal family and viceroy of Luang Prabang, was most clearly the product of an earlier time. A traditionalist, he envisioned Lao independence in terms of a return to the precolonial past. His brother Souvanna, by contrast, was a pragmatist, conscious of Laos's vulnerability, uninterested in abstract principles, determined to keep his country intact and at peace by conciliating the great powers that were shaping the postwar world. Souphanouvong, the younger half-brother of Souvanna, had compiled a stellar academic record in Paris during the 1930s and returned to his homeland already endowed with left-wing leanings, though it would take him a while to conclude that only an alliance with the Viet Minh could secure Lao independence. Flamboyant, militant, and fearless, he became known in the Western media as the "Red Prince."

Souphanouvong, Souvanna, and Phetsarath recognized that postwar conditions provided an opportunity for Laos to join the community of free states. Not only had the war loosened the shackles of French domination; it had stimulated the development of Lao nationalism, as many Lao, compelled by military exigencies to venture outside their villages for the first time, began to think of themselves as citizens of a country rather than members of isolated communities. Proud of their resistance to the Japanese, they formed patriotic societies, participated in mass rallies, and contributed to a renaissance of Lao literature, music, and dance. Lao statesman Sisouk Na Champassak exaggerated when he claimed that "the first awakening of a true Laotian consciousness dates from 1945"; nonetheless, Laos's wartime surge of jingoism was a powerful force for national liberation.[10]

Phetsarath capitalized on this sentiment, proclaiming that the declaration of independence delivered at Japanese gunpoint was still in effect, despite Japan's defeat. He also announced the formation of the Lao Issara (Free Lao) government to uphold that declaration. Joining Phetsarath in this new government were Souvanna and Souphanouvong, along with other nationalists representing a range of political beliefs. They ran afoul of Sisavang, who had reached an agreement with Paris days after the end of the war in which he accepted reestablishment of the French protectorate. Angered by Phetsarath's maneuvers, Sisavang dismissed him from service, which compelled Phetsarath and his followers to set up a provisional constituent assembly in Vientiane. When the king refused to recognize this assembly, it voted to depose him, leaving Phetsarath as head of state.

The two sides snarled at each other, neither willing to back down but both aware that civil war was not in the country's best interests. Finally, they reached a compromise whereby the king would be reinstated as monarch in return for royal endorsement of the Lao Issara government. Sisavang disingenuously affirmed not to have made any arrangements with the French invalidating the declaration of independence. Souvanna became minister of public works, and Souphanouvong took over the posts of foreign affairs and defense. While Phetsarath did not assume the premiership, the new head of government, Phaya Khammao, supported Phetsarath's anticolonial policy. Since the French were not yet ready to move back into Laos in force, the Lao Issara was able to preserve, for a brief period, the illusion that Laos was an autonomous nation.

That fantasy was cruelly dispelled in late 1945, when the French began to reassert their authority, moving up the Mekong valley and demolishing any Lao resistance they encountered. Souphanouvong led an outgunned Lao Issara force against French troops on the outskirts of the city of Thakhet, where, according to some accounts, the Red Prince walked up and down the lines, shouting encouragement to his men, as bullets whizzed around him. The Lao fought fiercely, but they could not block the French advance, and Souphanouvong suffered a gunshot wound while retreating. There were other last-ditch efforts in Savannakhet and on the outskirts of Vientiane, the administrative capital. On April 24, 1946, the day after Sisavang's re-coronation ceremonies, Vientiane fell. The Lao Issara cabinet fled across the Mekong to Thailand and established a government-in-exile. By late September, the French had retaken the last of Laos's provincial capitals and were in command of the country.

The Lao Issara kept up their fight for independence from their base in Bangkok, mounting raids on French outposts along the Mekong and endeavoring to gain international recognition as the real government of Laos, but it was a lost cause, and soon a schism split their ranks. Phetsarath and Souvanna concluded that total autonomy, at least in the short term, was unrealistic and that they needed to work out some accommodation with Paris if they were to play a role in running their nation's affairs. Souphanouvong disagreed, advocating instead that the Lao Issara merge with Viet Minh communists in an Indochina-wide campaign to expel the French. The Red Prince, who made his first contact with the Viet Minh around the time of Japan's capitulation, did not share the customary Lao antagonism toward Vietnam—his wife was Vietnamese—and he had been impressed by Ho Chi Minh when the latter granted him an interview in Hanoi. Souphanouvong saw Viet Minh assistance as indispensable in delivering his people from French domination; he was confident at the same time that he could prevent the Viet Minh from gaining unwarranted influence in a free Laos. These views so alarmed Phetsarath and Souvanna that they expelled Souphanouvong from the Lao Issara, whereupon Souphanouvong traveled to Ho's mountain hideout in North Vietnam to found a politico-military organization known as the Pathet Lao. While the group's manifesto made no mention of parties or ideology, few doubted its communist orientation.

Both the French and the remaining members of the Lao Issara had motivation to compromise by mid-1949. The French were floundering in their war against the Viet Minh, who appeared to be growing stronger day by day. In China, Mao Zedong's communist forces held the upper hand over Chiang Kai-shek's Nationalists; when Mao won the Chinese Civil War, the Viet Minh would gain an ally on their northern border and a seemingly inexhaustible supply of food, weapons, and manpower. French resources, meanwhile, were stretched to the limit, and colonial military commanders informed their superiors in Paris that it was essential to maintain a peaceful "rear area" if operations in Vietnam were to have a chance of succeeding. That meant France would have to appease Lao nationalists by complying with some of their demands. The French therefore offered the Lao Issara the opportunity to return home under an amnesty and promised to grant Laos greater latitude in foreign affairs. Sisavang and French president Vincent Auriol signed a General Franco-Laotian Convention that affirmed, among other things, that the "French Republic recognizes the Kingdom of Laos as an independent state." Souvanna and most of his colleagues found this sufficient. Tired of being frozen out of political life, they announced the disbanding of the government-in-exile and returned to Vientiane. Phetsarath wanted to hold out for more concessions; he remained in Bangkok until 1957, conferring leadership of the noncommunist Lao upon Souvanna.[11]

Despite the cooperation of Souvanna and other like-minded nationalists, France could not prevent its struggle with the Viet Minh from spilling over into Laos. In the spring of 1953, Viet Minh military leader Vo Nguyen Giap diverted two divisions to strike at French positions in northeastern Laos, and two thousand Pathet Lao soldiers fought alongside their Vietnamese comrades. The communists occupied the Lao border province of Sam Neua, established a rebel headquarters, and advanced upon Luang Prabang, at which point the U.S. ambassador in Saigon urged Sisavang and Savang to flee. Both refused; the king stayed in the palace, and the crown prince drove through the city's streets in an open car for all to see. Meanwhile, the Royal Lao Army (RLA), under French command, absorbed the full brunt of the communist assault. One Lao battalion stood in the path of a Viet Minh division as it charged toward Luang Prabang. Ordered to hold out for two weeks, long enough for reinforcements to be flown to the royal capital, the battalion stood its ground for an astonishing thirty-six days and fought to the last man. Ultimately, a combination of reinforcements and the early onset of the monsoon season, which mired the Viet Minh's supply lines, saved Luang Prabang, but the communists could not be dislodged from their stronghold in Sam Neua. At the end of 1953, they launched another invasion, pushing as far as Thakhet and again forcing RLA troops to pay a heavy price.

Observers at the time tended to dismiss the contest in Laos as insignificant compared with the events unfolding elsewhere in Indochina. While it is true that Laos did not experience warfare on the scale Vietnam did, the RLA suffered grave casualties: of its twenty thousand soldiers, almost three thousand died in combat, and this figure does not take into account the thousands of partisans who fought in irregular commando groups and were killed or wounded by the Viet Minh and Pathet Lao. Furthermore, it was principally to honor France's obligation to defend Laos, and also because French General Henri-Eugène Navarre thought he could lure the Viet Minh into attacking an impregnable base, that the French concentrated their forces at Dien Bien Phu near the border of northern Laos. The ordeal of the garrison in that valley ended the "first" Indochina War and ushered in the United States as France's replacement.

Less than twenty-four hours after the Viet Minh banner was hoisted atop the French command bunker at Dien Bien Phu, delegates to an international conference at Geneva began debating the future of Indochina. The Royal Lao delegation, headed by Foreign Minister Phoui Sananikone, was in a weak position. French representatives, although realizing that the pre–World War II status quo was irretrievable, often presumed to speak for their former subjects. More worrisome, from Vientiane's perspective, was the fact that the Viet Minh delegates insisted upon separate representation for the Pathet Lao; they even brought a communist Lao spokesman to Geneva to head the rebel delegation. Given Viet Minh battlefield successes and Paris's eagerness to negotiate peace at any price, it seemed that Phoui would have to accept the Pathet Lao on an equal footing with his own government.

This he refused to do. In some of the conference's most strident addresses, he declared that the Pathet Lao had been "fabricated lock, stock, and barrel by the foreign invaders" and that it would be "comic" to recognize Souphanouvong "as representing anybody." Phoui eventually won his point, thanks to American encouragement and the less than enthusiastic backing of the Viet Minh by China. The conferees acknowledged the Vientiane government's sovereignty in Laos, and they extended the same recognition to the Cambodian regime, despite the existence of a communist Khmer Resistance Government for whom the Viet Minh were mentors.[12]

The Royal Lao delegation performed adroitly, but Laos did not fare as well as Cambodia in the Geneva Accords. While the latter country emerged intact, in Laos the two northernmost provinces of Sam Neua and Phong Saly were set aside for regroupment of Pathet Lao forces until a settlement could be reached with the government. This was a blow to anticommunist Lao statesmen; the two provinces would provide the Pathet Lao a base area from which to wage political war, and their location was such that the Viet Minh could maintain contact with Souphanouvong and his followers. Nonetheless, Phoui accepted these terms, vowed to take steps to reintegrate all Lao citizens into the kingdom, and promised not to join any foreign military alliance, allow foreign military bases on Lao territory, or request military aid "except for the purpose of... territorial defense." The Vientiane government was not satisfied with the accords—it especially regretted the omission of details concerning *how* the Pathet Lao were to be reintegrated— but it took solace in the fact that Laos had come out of Geneva in better shape than Vietnam, which had been partitioned, and that despite the Pathet Lao regroupment zones, Laos had been confirmed as a unitary, independent country. Perhaps more important, Laos was at peace, a rare condition for this kingdom that had experienced so much war.[13]

As the foregoing—admittedly selective—outline of Lao history makes plain, there was no dearth of evidence with which to rebut the languorous cartoon of the Lao deployed by American policymakers in the mid 1950s. Laos was born on the battleground. The most revered Lao historical figures were warriors. Every major juncture in Laos's seven-century national existence, except for the transition from Siamese to French supremacy, had been distinguished by combat, and the Lao had always fought gallantly, whether they won or lost. It is true that Laos, a sparsely populated, polyethnic kingdom consisting of small communities in river valleys and among mountain peoples, took a long time to develop any sense of nationalism, and that the individuals who battled in Fa Ngum's and Chao Anou's armies and in uprisings against imperial powers did not do so in the name of an entity called "Laos"; they fought for their family, clan, village, or tribe—or they fought under compulsion. This is the case in many balkanized countries. The point is that they *fought,* and that no one familiar with the Lao historical experience could conclude that there was something uniquely nonviolent about the inhabitants of this kingdom. If the Eisenhower administration had not been so hypnotized by its impression of the Lao as anti-warriors, it might have noticed that Laos's national anthem is more pugnacious than America's (although it does not, like "The Star-Spangled Banner," mention rockets and bombs). The relevant lyrics are:

> Our Lao race had once known in Asia a great reputation.
> Lao people were united and loved each other then....
> They will not allow any nation to create unrest or to occupy their soil.
> Whoever wants to invade their country would find them determined to fight
> till death.[14]

**Figure 1.** Royal Lao Army soldiers prepare a mortar to defend the town of Vang Vieng, April 1961. Photographer/Artist: Rolls Press/Popperfoto. Getty Images.

## "Cheerful, Indolent, and Notably Unmartial"

Several historians have documented the lack of reliable information about Southeast Asia in the United States at the time of the Geneva Conference. Loren Baritz calls this "our impenetrable ignorance," and he, like most scholars seeking to apply cultural analysis to the study of the Eisenhower administration's Indochina policy, focuses on how Washington mishandled relations with Vietnam. Yet mid-1950s Americans' knowledge of Laos was even more limited, the available stock of stereotypes cruder and more contemptuous. Indeed, while the Vietnamese received shameful treatment in those few English-language books, magazines, and newspapers that acknowledged their existence, they seemed virtual paladins next to the Lao.[15]

No one made this point better than Virginia Thompson, an Asia specialist whose 1937 work *French Indo-China,* "the most comprehensive American study of Indochina before World War II" according to one diplomatic historian, remained a standard reference book into the 1960s. It anticipated Chargé McClintock's 1954 report by ranking the Indochinese in terms of their conformity to Western standards, finding, as did McClintock, that Cambodians scored highest. "They live frugally, eat abstemiously, and bathe frequently," Thompson observed. "Moreover, they are, unlike most Orientals, hard workers." The Vietnamese—or "Annamites," as Thompson called them—made a poorer impression: their "laziness" kept them in "chronic poverty," they lacked "the driving power given by strong desires," and their "famous tolerance" was really "dislike of effort." Still, they had more initiative than the Lao, whom Thompson dismissed as "hopelessly apathetic" and whose "extreme indolence" she attributed to religion and weather: "Partly it is because Buddhism has encouraged a life without violent desires, but it is also due to the climate which has conspired to reject effort and to encourage an immobile happiness."

In Thompson's view, these factors presented "insuperable obstacles to industrial and commercial progress" in Laos. The only hope for "future development" lay, ironically, with the Annamites whom Thompson elsewhere scorned. Compared with the "silly, lazy, and naïve" Lao, the Annamites struck Thompson as "somber" and "ambitious," and she identified Annamite immigration as the key to "economic betterment of the land." The Lao would be foolish to resist such interloping, in the event they were able to summon the energy to do so. "This evil is without remedy," Thompson wrote. "Rich, unoccupied land will inevitably attract an industrious and prolific people like the Annamites, who are able and willing to do what Laotians cannot and will not do."

Although Thompson deemed Laos the most "sluggish" and "insouciant" of the Indochinese colonies, she had to concede its attractive aspects. "There is almost no Westerner with soul so dead that he has not succumbed to the charms of Laotian music," she remarked. The "grace and elegance" of Lao sculpture enchanted her too, as did the "aesthetic appearance" of the Lao in general. Beyond that was Laos's "prevailing atmosphere," which made it seem "the simplest thing in the world to be happy." *French Indo-China*'s subchapter on Lao culture ended with a remarkable passage in which Thompson expressed something like longing for that culture while continuing to portray it as irretrievably stagnant:

> The country is an earthly paradise which offers a beauty and nourishment that demands no effort for its enjoyment.... Laziness is an idle reproach in a land where work would obviously make one less rather than more content. In fact, Laos is itself a passive reproach to the futility of Europe's bustling activity.... It is a museum-piece of earthly happiness, a reply to the West's gloomy disillusionment. Even the Civilizer, with all his utilitarian baggage, hesitates to trouble its idyllic calm.[16]

Like Thompson, Norman Lewis called Laos "an earthly paradise" in his travelogue *A Dragon Apparent,* the book that allegedly inspired Graham Greene to go to Vietnam (and then compose *The Quiet American*). Published in 1951, *A Dragon Apparent* traced Lewis's trip of the previous year through Indochina, where, among other things, he observed French pilots, equipped with American bombs, as they attempted to crush the Viet Minh insurgency from the air. Since Lewis spent the majority of his time in Vietnam, that colony received the most coverage; Cambodia and Laos got less. Lewis informed readers that the average Vietnamese "has a competitive soul, [and] is a respecter of work for its own sake." He also found the Vietnamese patriotic, "too civilized to spit at the sight of a white man," but seething with anticolonialist sentiment; even Lewis's rickshaw coolie in Saigon regarded him as a "foreign devil." While this attitude prevented Lewis from making any Vietnamese friends, it also commanded respect, and Lewis judged Vietnamese prospects for independence as excellent. Cambodia was a different matter. The Cambodians, although more affable than the Vietnamese, were hopeless soldiers, a shortcoming Lewis chalked up to Buddhism: "[W]hat could you expect in a country where every man-jack of them had done a year in a monastery, where they taught you that thou shalt not kill had to be taken literally?"

Cambodian pacifism, however, did not prepare Lewis for the Lao, who not only lacked any observable vigor but seemed to drain the strength from anyone coming into contact with them. "Laos-ized Frenchmen," Lewis remarked, "are like the results of successful lobotomy operations." The colony was "trance-bound," a big sedative, and Lewis felt himself falling under its influence. He experienced a "wasting away of the energy, and a seeping paralysis of the will." Every day brought an "increase in lethargy" until, after a month, "my strength had gone." Lewis was inclined to blame the climate, a "special kind of heat," which he imagined must have unmanned Laos's original inhabitants, those "mountain peoples" who, "attracted by the easy, abundant life of the hot river valleys," settled there long ago to enjoy "the formidable gift of leisure." Before long, Lewis speculated, "they lapsed into peaceful decadence, adopted religions which were suitable to their decline and which also fostered it, and became adepts of sleep." Whatever the reason for Laos's "lack of compulsion," Lewis could not wait to leave. He guessed that his French hosts' affection for the Lao and spiteful pronouncements about the Vietnamese hid deeper concerns. "[T]he French like the Laotians . . . because they do not fear them," he wrote. "They can relax their defenses in the comfortable knowledge that these are harmless and declining peoples." Colonialists who relaxed their defenses around the Vietnamese wound up dead.[17]

Other pre–Geneva Conference works on Indochina presented the same hierarchy, as Thompson's and Lewis's contemporaries in academe and journalism rated the Lao as the weakest, most servile, and most immature of Southeast Asians. They gave different reasons for Lao inferiority—one ventured, "The Laotian is cheerful and serene and contented, perhaps because of some strange physiology of his glands, of his bodily make-up, or of his environment, or all of these"—but none of their monographs repudiated or even complicated this caricature. Harold Coolidge of Harvard wrote, "The Laotians are a soft, quiet, contented race" who "hate . . . manual labor." Travel author Harry Franck thought them "the personification of laziness, . . . happy-go-lucky in their tropical fairy-land." Although Franck admitted that the Lao led "a visibly happier life than do our own serious and hurried people of the West," like Thompson he did not believe this life would endure. If Thompson envisaged the Annamites supplanting the Lao, Franck perceived a greater threat to the north. "[T]he beast-like pace of labor that prevails in China," he predicted, would overwhelm Laos's "Oriental leisureliness" as Asia modernized and intra-regional economic competition increased. Reporter Alan Brodrick, in his 1950 book *Little Vehicle: Cambodia and Laos,* also noted "how fast the life of this paradise" was "changing." Brodrick saw "modernizers"—including "Chinese sharp-dealers" and "Annamese shysters"—plotting to "make the Laotians sweat," a doubtful prospect since, he affirmed, the Lao were "the most contented people on this earth"; their "ideal in life" was "to chew betel, to drink rice-alcohol, and to sleep—they are very good sleepers." Asia's Henry Fords were going to have difficulty recruiting in the Kingdom of a Million Elephants.[18]

Perhaps the best summation of Western views of the Lao at the time of the Geneva Conference came from Bernard Newman, a novelist, historian, and journalist who covered the last act of the Franco–Viet Minh War in a breezy text titled *Report from Indo-China.* Newman flew into Luang Prabang before the communists launched their 1953 incursion, and he was astonished to discover that the royal capital "was defended only by a single company of Laotian infantry, no man of which had ever fired a shot in anger, or ever wished to do so." Interviews with Lao generals, cabinet ministers, and the king himself convinced Newman that "a less aggressive people it would be impossible to find the world over." The Lao, he told his readers, "are not a martial race: they do not interfere with others, and never did anyone any harm." As Buddhists, "they are forbidden to kill anything, even a fly." Furthermore, "they have no ambition." All they wanted was "to lie in the shade." In this regard, they were "quite different from the Vietnamese," whom Newman found "energetic" and "enterprising." Newman attributed the Viet Minh's failure to take Luang Prabang to a change in Giap's tactics rather than to RLA resistance, and he considered the communist conquest of Laos inevitable. Still, there was a silver lining: the reds, Newman argued, would live to regret their victory when Viet Minh "appeals for higher production" were "treated as comic" by the Lao.[19]

Readers disinclined to peruse book-length accounts of Indochinese history and culture could get their information in smaller doses from magazines like *National Geographic,* whose circulation skyrocketed in the Truman and Eisenhower years and whose mix of vivid photographs and melodramatic stories brought Africa, the Middle East, and other exotic locales into millions of American living rooms. While the number of *National Geographic* articles devoted to Indochina was scant, it increased during the run-up to the Geneva Conference, and the journal nearly always drew a contrast between docile Lao and assertive Vietnamese. In one photo-essay it took its subscribers on a tour "By Motor Trail, across French Indo-China," informing them that the Lao, "[p]leasant mannered and peace-loving," liked "few laws, light taxes, and much comfort," and that because "Laotians refuse to do coolie work and Annamite laborers are brought up from the plains," the Lao were obliged to "retreat before the Annamite settlements." The author of a 1950 pictorial described Luang Prabang as "Shangri-La," with a "misty, dreamy look," and noted that "the people seemed happy and carefree. I saw no serious-faced youngsters; I had seen many in Viet Nam." Less than a year later, *National Geographic* reported that the Lao had "escape[d] the worst aspects of Vietnam's fratricidal civil war" and preserved their "idyllic lives" amid communist-inspired violence to the north and east. "Certainly," the article concluded, "if smiles and hospitality are accurate evidence, then the Laotians are happy."[20]

*National Geographic*'s readers got their most extended look at Laos in September 1952, when the magazine ran a twenty-one-page photo story titled "Indochina Faces the Dragon," which assessed how "France and her former protectorates" were coping with the stresses of decolonization. Author George Long declared, "Laos is a land for lotus-eaters. . . . Life is simple, unhurried; siestas are long. What isn't done today may be done tomorrow." The "Laotians' favorite saying," Long observed, was *"Bau peniang*—'never mind,'" and their capital of Vientiane was "sultry" and "sleepy," typified by a "pedicab boy" whom Long saw "dozing in his vehicle near the market." Needing a ride, Long nudged the boy awake, only to receive a Lao response: "Slowly he opened his eyes, looked at me, shook his head, and closed them again. I should have realized—it was siesta time." Long found Vietnam's capital, Saigon, much livelier—it was a "teeming metropolis" where citizens "go to work early"—and the Vietnamese countryside just as bustling; he approvingly quoted a village chieftain to the effect that "We are trying to build a civilization in the jungle." The downside was that Vietnam was more violent than Laos, with "no absolute security anywhere" as French and Viet Minh soldiers killed each other by the thousands. Laos, by contrast, did not even suffer from petty crime. A judge in Vientiane informed Long, "I have so little work. The prison here, for all of Laos, has room for 800 prisoners. It now has 18." Americans thumbing through this piece doubtless found Long's portrayal of the Lao attractive, but they could hardly have viewed such jolly, idle children as the wave of the future in Indochina. Rather, like Thompson, Lewis, Newman, and other midcentury pundits, they probably anticipated the absorption of Shangri-La by its more diligent and warlike neighbors—in particular, Vietnam.[21]

The *New York Times,* America's newspaper of record, contributed to this impression with, among other things, a chain of adjectives strung together by Asia correspondent Peggy Durdin before the Geneva Conference began. "Laotians are gentle, uncombative, unassertive, unambitious, happy, lazy, hospitable, witty, artistic, fun-loving, and totally charming," Durdin reported. She did not consider them good candidates for Viet Minh indoctrination: "No concept would seem sillier to the average Laotian peasant than the 'nobility of work,' and no one more incomprehensible and ridiculous than a communist 'labor hero.'" Durdin pointed out that "there were many Vietnamese in Laos before the war" and that "Laotians didn't care for them. They were dour and unamusing, tough and industrious; they drove hard bargains"—most "un-Laotian." While the Lao "would rather not take sides in any dispute at all," she wrote, they "much prefer the French to the Viet Minh." Other *Times* features confirmed that "[t]o a much greater degree than the Vietnamese and Cambodians," the "Laotians appear generally satisfied with the amount of independence they now have within the French Union." Unfortunately for the West, that did not mean they would do battle to defend that independence. Joseph and Stewart Alsop, columnists for the *Washington Post,* warned readers in another pre–Geneva Conference piece that the "cheerful, indolent, and notably unmartial" Lao were unlikely to "put up much of a fight against Giap's hardened guerrilla veterans," a prediction seemingly borne out by the *Chicago Tribune's* portrayal of "Laotian Buddhists" bracing for a Viet Minh attack on Luang Prabang by "scattering holy water and sacred white pebbles" around the city's perimeter.[22]

There is no way to determine how much published commentary on Laos received the attention of American statesmen before or during the Geneva Conference; and even if one could establish that Secretary of State John Foster Dulles read every Laos-related article in the *New York Times,* it would still be impossible to gauge the influence those articles had in shaping his perspective on Indochina. What *can* be concluded, however, is that officials like McClintock sent their derogative views of the Lao to the State Department without fear of contradiction by any available English-language source. Had Dulles elected to supplement embassy dispatches with the expert analyses of Thompson or Durdin, he would have found nothing to challenge what his subordinates told him. Quite the contrary: the specialists made the same case in stronger terms. Laos may have been a paradise, but it was no battlefront, and the sovereignty conferred on it by the delegates at Geneva promised to be less of a deterrent to Ho Chi Minh than holy water and sacred pebbles.

## "We Can't Go On Losing Areas of the Free World Forever"

With France on its way out of Indochina, Washington hastened to fill the void. "The important thing from now on," Dulles told reporters, "is not to mourn the past but to face the future opportunity to prevent the loss in northern Viet-Nam from leading to the extension of communism throughout Southeast Asia and the Western Pacific." A month after the Geneva Conference adjourned, Eisenhower approved National Security Council Policy Statement 5429/2, which called on the United States to "make every possible effort, not openly inconsistent with the U.S. position as to the armistice agreements, to defeat communist subversion" in Southeast Asia. Washington's position as to the armistice agreements had been articulated by Undersecretary of State Walter Bedell Smith, head of the U.S. delegation at Geneva, during the conference's final session. Smith declared that while America could not endorse the Geneva Accords, it would "refrain from the threat or use of force to disturb them," meaning that overt U.S. military intervention in Laos, Cambodia, or the two Vietnams was out of the question.[23]

There were other ways to contain communism, however, and Washington devised two in the post-Geneva period: the Southeast Asia Treaty Organization (SEATO), which covered all Indochina, and the Programs Evaluation Office (PEO), which applied specifically to Laos. Both stratagems deepened America's Southeast Asian commitment, both entailed considerable risk of war, and yet both originated in the State Department rather than the Pentagon. Both, moreover, displayed America's cold war hypocrisy at its ugliest.

SEATO was a collective security arrangement conceived by Dulles and comprising the United States, Great Britain, France, Australia, and New Zealand, along with the only three Asian countries Washington could persuade to join: the Philippines, Thailand, and Pakistan. Dulles wanted an Asian equivalent of the North Atlantic Treaty Organization (NATO), which had proven effective in deterring the communists in Western Europe. He fell short of this objective: unlike NATO, SEATO had no standing military forces and did not require a response from all members if one were attacked; each nation merely pledged to "consult" in the event of aggression and "meet the common danger in accordance with its constitutional processes." The coalition was further weakened in Dulles's eyes by the fact that Laos, Cambodia, and South Vietnam could not become members. Those states had accepted an obligation at Geneva not to join military alliances, and Washington was loath to violate the letter of the Geneva Accords. Violating their spirit, though, was another matter. Dulles persuaded signatories of the SEATO pact to approve a protocol that extended the treaty's security provisions to Laos, Cambodia, and the "free territory under the jurisdiction of the State of Vietnam." While the "Indochina armistice created obstacles to these three countries becoming parties to the treaty at the present time," Dulles proclaimed, SEATO would "throw a mantle of protection over these young nations."[24]

Mysteriously, the young nations proved less than overjoyed. Laos in particular failed to respond with the gratitude Washington expected. "If SEATO came in," former Lao foreign minister Nhou Abhay complained, "there would be international war and this country would be the battlefield." Prince Norodom Sihanouk of Cambodia repudiated the protocol. Only South Vietnamese premier Ngo Dinh Diem accepted informal membership in SEATO, a gesture that, ten years down the road, would furnish justification for American military intervention to save South Vietnam. In the United States, the Senate ratified SEATO by a vote of eighty-two to one. No legislator pointed out that the pact was an attempt by Washington to subvert the Geneva Accords.[25]

The Eisenhower administration flouted the accords more arrogantly when it established the Programs Evaluation Office in 1955. Article Six of the Geneva settlement banned "the introduction into Laos of any reinforcements of troops or military personnel from outside Laotian territory." That seemed to rule out a U.S. Military Assistance Advisory Group (MAAG), which was Washington's customary method of managing foreign military aid programs. The administration thus had a problem: if American military personnel were not allowed in Laos, then who would prepare the RLA to fight communist guerrillas? The French? This was a possibility: the Geneva Accords permitted France to keep a fifteen-hundred-man military mission to train Lao troops, and thirty-five hundred men to maintain French bases in Laos. Throughout the Franco–Viet Minh War, U.S. military assistance had been administered by French personnel. This arrangement could have continued in the postwar years. But American policymakers were disgusted with the French, blaming them for the free world's reverses in Indochina and the unsatisfactory settlement at Geneva. Donald Heath, U.S. ambassador to South Vietnam, wrote Dulles in mid-1954 to argue that it was preposterous for Washington to pay French troops to train native anticommunist forces. "We are more and more convinced," Heath declared, "that to be really effective our aid must be channeled directly, ... and not through France." Any effort to create a strong Lao army would require American advisers, but Eisenhower wanted to station the requisite personnel in Laos while still appearing, for public-relations purposes, to respect the Geneva Accords.[26]

The State Department's solution was to set up an MAAG in disguise, a "civilian supervisory group" to "exercise appropriate control" of U.S. military aid to Laos. This new agency, the Programs Evaluation Office, was staffed by U.S. military personnel who had either recently retired or been given Foreign Service reserve officer rank to preserve the fiction that they were civilians. The PEO commander was a brigadier general of the U.S. Army whose name had been removed from the roster of active officers to conceal his status. PEO employees supervised the distribution of military assistance to the Royal Lao Government (RLG) and advised government officials on military matters, but they engaged in no formal training of Lao soldiers. France retained exclusive prerogative over training, while the PEO, technically, worked through the French military mission. The PEO did, however, train and equip the Lao police force, which expanded after 1955, and paid for the temporary reassignment of Lao officers to Thailand, where the Geneva prohibitions against American training did not apply. PEO members wore civilian garb, but this fooled no one; a reporter observed that their "slacks with loud Hawaiian shirts ... were as much of a 'uniform' as the khakis, patches, and rank insignia which they replaced." The State Department occasionally had to remind the military not to address messages to "MAAG Laos," a unit that, on paper, did not exist.[27]

SEATO and the PEO tied the United States more closely to Laos. There is no doubt that Eisenhower took this commitment seriously. As he warned the National Security Council toward the close of the Franco–Viet Minh War, if "Laos were lost," America was "likely to lose the rest of Southeast Asia and Indonesia. The gateway to India, Burma, and Thailand would be open." Eisenhower did not relish the prospect of fighting in Indochina— such a venture, he knew, would "absorb our troops by divisions"—but he believed that "some time we must face up to it. We can't go on losing areas of the free world forever." Nonetheless, Laos was just one of a raft of international headaches confronting Eisenhower as 1954 gave way to 1955: China began shelling the Taiwanese-held offshore island groups, South Vietnam descended into civil war when Diem attempted to consolidate his rule, and many parts of the developing world erupted into crises that demanded an immediate response. Eisenhower, spread too thin and inclined in any event to delegate authority, preferred to leave the day-to-day supervision of U.S.-Lao relations to subordinates.[28]

Unfortunately, these subordinates disagreed about what should be done to preserve American interests in Southeast Asia. Eisenhower's military advisers, especially the Joint Chiefs of Staff (JCS), were unwilling to dedicate resources to Laos. Still smarting from the stalemate of the Korean War, the chiefs advocated taking the offensive against Asian communism; they argued that instead of fighting peripheral wars that allowed the communists to pick the battlefield, America should strike at the source of belligerency in the area: China. Laos, Cambodia, and South Vietnam, the JCS insisted, merited only "limited support." Defense Secretary Charles Wilson went further; he recommended that the United States withdraw from Indochina because, as he put it, the situation there was "hopeless" and "these people should be left to stew in their own juice." The higher echelons of the Pentagon were not enthusiastic about either SEATO or the PEO, regarding the first as a commitment to resist aggression "in the locale where it occurs" rather than at its source and the second as a dangerous half-measure that left the French in control of U.S. military aid.[29]

So certain were the JCS that America should not be fighting communism in Laos, especially with the French as middlemen, that they resorted to bureaucratic foot-dragging. For months, they refused to estimate an optimum size for the RLA. This hamstrung policy, because the Mutual Security Act, which governed the distribution of foreign military assistance, required a JCS assessment before aid could be distributed. Charles Yost, America's first minister to Laos, grew irritated with the chiefs' obstructionism, and his annoyance turned to panic when Paris announced that it would stop payments to the RLA as of December 31, 1954. The government in Vientiane was incapable of paying the troops' salaries; independence had not altered the economic realities of Laos, whose citizens remained, for the most part, subsistence farmers. Yost got Lao premier Katay Don Sasorith to make a request to the United States for direct budgetary support, but the JCS still declined to gauge how many troops Laos would need and how much money would be required to fund them. Furious, Yost cabled Dulles that if Washington did not furnish aid immediately, it risked a "collapse of [the] armed forces." The administration managed to provide interim funding while State and Defense haggled over force levels, and the JCS, recognizing that the White House considered retention of Laos nonnegotiable, finally gave their recommendation as to the number of troops "required to maintain internal security." The chiefs stressed, however, that they did not offer this 23,650-man figure "[f]rom the military point of view" but for "political considerations." Their judgment that Laos was not the proper place to fight and that U.S. money could be better spent elsewhere had not changed.[30]

Eisenhower's civilian advisers were more militant when it came to the defense of France's former Indochinese colonies. America must "stand firm," Dulles proclaimed, "and, if necessary, meet hostile force with the greater force that we possess." There could be no more red territory on the map. Laos constituted "a front line of the free world," according to one State Department white paper. It was "a finger thrust right down into the heart of Southeast Asia," in the words of Assistant Secretary of State for Far Eastern Affairs Walter Robertson, and the fact that it was a small finger did not matter. *Any* concession to communism would encourage aggression. "The communists only respect strength and firmness," Robertson lectured the Lao king in 1956. "They exploit what they think is weakness, such as the peaceful desire to be friendly with all nations."[31]

Robertson may have been the most hard-line cold warrior in the administration. No one was more dogmatic in his refusal to recognize fissures in "monolithic" communism. In early 1955, Robertson informed a reporter that "the Chinese communists and, for that matter, the other Asian communists such as the Viet Minh, may have points of conspicuous physical difference from the Russians, but as communists they are all identical." British prime minister Anthony Eden felt that Robertson's approach to foreign affairs was "so emotional as to be impervious to argument or indeed facts." Nonetheless, as the State Department's chief Far Eastern policymaker, Robertson greatly affected Washington's perspective on Laos during the Eisenhower years.[32]

Another civilian hawk markedly responsible for shaping American strategy in this theater of the cold war was J. Graham Parsons, deputy chief of mission at the American embassy in Tokyo when the Eisenhower administration concocted SEATO and the PEO. Parsons became U.S. ambassador to Laos soon thereafter and eventually succeeded Robertson as assistant secretary of state for Far Eastern affairs. This career diplomat's philosophy, as far as Laos was concerned, was decidedly undiplomatic. In a typical cable to State, he averred that "no formula has the requisite chance of success for the

Laos situation that does not have as an essential ingredient the utilization of appropriate force to back up our position."[33]

When compelled to choose between, on the one hand, a reluctant JCS and Defense Department and, on the other, the saber rattlers at State, Eisenhower, a military man, sided with the civilians. Their views mirrored his own. Geneva had been a disaster that had consigned twelve million Vietnamese to communist slavery. The free world could not afford to yield more ground. Yes, Laos was a rotten place to fight, but it was where the reds had chosen to make their move, and America's duty was clear. Consequently, Eisenhower raised the legation in Laos to embassy status, making Yost Washington's first ambassador to Vientiane. He increased the number of PEO personnel and expanded their activities. Laos, which until 1954 had rarely engaged American policymakers as a separate country, now assumed a status disproportionate to its economic value. As far as Washington was concerned, this landlocked kingdom with no industry and few valuable raw materials had become a crucial barrier to red expansion.

The trouble was that the Lao did not seem to grasp this fact. A dominant theme of Yost's cables to State during the eighteen months he served in Vientiane was boiling frustration at his hosts' unconcern about the danger they faced. Even Laos's premier, Katay, could not get it through his head that the Pathet Lao were communists, preferring to believe, as Yost put it, that they were "wayward brothers" who would "return to the fold" if the government extended an olive branch. "I have for months been endeavoring to cure this delusion," Yost complained, but it appeared that the "only effective medicine will be sad experience." By that time, of course, it would be too late; Souphanouvong would control the country. And the problem went beyond Katay's blind spots. Yost fulminated against the "generally lackadaisical Lao outlook," which left the population "indifferent" to the "Red threat." "[W]e are most anxious to stiffen their backs," he declared. "We are engaged here in exerting daily pressure . . . to ensure that they be steadfast and courageous in the face of their powerful communist neighbors."[34]

Yet there was only so much that mortals could do. With limited resources and obligations all over the globe, plus a Congress demanding retrenchment in foreign aid, the Eisenhower administration was unable to commit American troops to Laos. Such escalation would moreover represent the sort of uncamouflaged infringement of the Geneva Accords that Eisenhower sought to avoid. Washington could contribute money, weapons, and advice, but the Lao would have to fight their own battles. "We can supplement," Dulles cabled the Vientiane embassy, "but we cannot supplant." No amount of American assistance could take the place of what Dulles termed "a spirit of resolution." America's other cold war Asian allies—the South Koreans, Nationalist Chinese, and South Vietnamese—had such spirit, and it impelled them to strap on sword and buckler when traitors posing as patriots tried to force them out of the free world pantheon and behind the iron curtain. Could Washington breathe this spirit into Lao politicians and military leaders, or would the Lao, in the words of one State Department official, "insist on committing what we consider political suicide despite U.S. advice and material support"? The twin challenges of making the Lao aware that there was a communist wolf at their door and galvanizing them to resist it framed America's relations with Laos throughout the remainder of the Eisenhower era.[35]

Chapter 2

# "A Soft Buffer"

### Laos in the Eisenhower Administration's Grand Strategy

In March 1958, Nationalist Chinese President Chiang Kai-shek hosted a meeting of U.S. ambassadors to Asian countries. The diplomats gathered in Taipei to evaluate America's Far Eastern policy, which had enjoyed smooth sailing since the death of Philippine leader Ramón Magsaysay the previous year. There had been no defeats or crises; indeed, events in Thailand, South Korea, and Indonesia indicated an upswing in the free world's fortunes, while Ngo Dinh Diem had pulled off what American journalists were calling a "miracle" by making South Vietnam a going concern. Secretary of State John Foster Dulles, who presided over the Taipei gathering, could survey the cold war's Asian front with optimism.

There was a soft spot, however, and it was contiguous to every country in Southeast Asia except Malaya. When the ministers at Taipei read their briefing books, they must have been appalled by the gloominess of the "Laos" chapter, as well as by the scornful tone author Patricia Byrne adopted. Byrne, the State Department's officer in charge of Lao affairs, began by noting that Laos appeared "more a liability than an asset to the free world." It was "the weakest and least stable of all of the states of Southeast Asia," it suffered from "the greatest economic handicaps," and its "minuscule elite" had not proven "equal to the task of... assuming the international responsibilities of a newly independent state." Most important, Byrne observed, was the fact that "[i]n its resistance to communist pressure, Laos has resembled nothing so much as a bowl of Jell-O." Byrne's forecast was dismal. "[I]t is hopeless to expect that Laos can in any way actively contribute to the defense of the free world," she wrote. "It is also hopeless to expect that Laos will stand militantly anti-communist with the West."

Having thus blasted the country in language atypical for diplomatic correspondence, Byrne explained why America had to stay in Laos anyway:

> Laos's positive value to us may be negligible, but its negative importance is great. A neutral but noncommunist Laos serves as a buffer between the communist bloc and the free states on Laos's borders. Its fall would remove this protection, give the communists direct access to Thailand and Cambodia across a long indefensible frontier, permit them to flank South Viet-Nam, heighten the threat to the rest of Southeast Asia, and cause loss of faith in the United States among the uncommitted nations.

In other words, Laos's importance was strategic and symbolic. If the communists overran it, they could use it as a springboard for further conquests, and its loss would mean psychological victory for Moscow in nations vacillating between communism and freedom. Therefore, Byrne declared, "the achievement of any Western success . . . demands our not conceding the field."

It was difficult to hold the field, though, when the Lao seemed bent on retreat. From Byrne's perspective, U.S. policy was handcuffed as much by America's Lao allies as by any communist intruder. The Lao, she noted, were timid and naïve: "they . . . fear offending the communists and mistakenly believe that 'neutrality' will earn them communist good will." They were capricious: "The Lao all desire to please everyone, which results in acquiescence in both Western and communist importunings." They had "scandalously misuse[d]" American aid. And they were easy marks for red propaganda, accepting the party line that the Pathet Lao were nationalists rather than "the tool of international communism." In all, America had been "sorely tried" even before the Lao National Assembly's recent approval of a coalition cabinet including Pathet Lao ministers. That "dangerous development," Byrne asserted, put Laos in a situation "horrifyingly reminiscent of Czechoslovakia and other once-independent states of Eastern Europe."

Given such a "formidable list of liabilities," how could Washington preserve Lao independence? "Our efforts in Laos have of necessity always been geared to the short-term," noted Byrne. "Our next target is again a short-term one: the winning of the May 4 elections." Twenty-one assembly seats were at stake in those supplementary elections, and the Eisenhower administration wanted every one of them filled by pro-Western candidates. "If the Pathet Lao win a significant number of seats," Byrne affirmed, "the communists would be on the way toward achieving their objective of taking over the entire country." Should the government capture a majority, "the communists would suffer a serious setback." Byrne was confident of the government's chances. "All agencies in Laos are working to assist conservative candidates," she reported. "Moreover, the government is determined to win, and has stated its intention to use 'black' methods if necessary."

Even a conservative sweep, however, would not solve Laos's problems. Byrne characterized the administration's Laos policy as a "holding operation" and admitted that "we cannot guarantee that continuing our support will keep Laos free." Nonetheless, "it provides our only hope of doing so." America continued pouring money into the kingdom because of "our awareness of the disastrous consequences for the free world position" if Laos succumbed to "communist bloc pressure," not because the Eisenhower administration expected Laos to start acting like "a country willing to protect its sovereignty." "There are situations in this world which we cannot control," contended Byrne, and one of them was "Laos's softness." In an appendix to Byrne's analysis, Thomas Corcoran, former U.S. consul in Hanoi, stated matters more directly. "[O]ur policy in Laos since Geneva has been to make that country a buffer between Chinese and North Vietnamese communist expansion and the adjacent free countries," Corcoran averred. "Since it has proved impossible to make Laos a hard buffer, we should now concentrate on making it, if possible, a soft buffer."[1]

Byrne's and Corcoran's contribution to the Taipei briefing book summarized the vicissitudes of U.S.-Lao relations from 1954 to 1958. When the "Indochina Phase" of the Geneva Conference began after the fall of Dien Bien Phu, the American diplomatic presence in Laos consisted of one Foreign Service officer who did his own typing, but the Eisenhower administration soon changed that. Along with establishing the U.S. Operations Mission (USOM) in Vientiane to administer economic assistance, Washington created a thinly disguised training organization, the Programs Evaluation Office (PEO), within USOM to handle military aid. A U.S. Information Service (USIS) unit, responsible for propaganda, also set up shop in the Lao capital, and operatives of the Central Intelligence Agency (CIA) began carrying out a variety of enterprises, from information gathering to providing arms. Arthur Dommen, the Saigon bureau chief for United Press International at the time, recalled how the "arrival in Vientiane of hundreds of Americans to implement this large program created a swarm of activity that caused no little astonishment."[2]

The activity never translated into progress. No matter what the Americans tried, conditions did not improve. The Royal Lao Army (RLA) remained, in the words of one observer, "worthless. Let a real war come and they'll all run for their villages." The civilians were hardly better. "They have no government seeking [to] vigorously defend [the] independence of Laos," snorted veteran diplomat J. Graham Parsons, "and they give little sign of forming one." According to the U.S. legation in Vientiane, the Lao premier "totally failed to show [the] expected energy," his advisers were "falling down on the job," and every day American officials "discover[ed] new fields in which the Lao are incompetent." After Washington raised its diplomatic representation in Laos to the rank of embassy, the tenor of on-site commentary grew more peevish. Cables in late 1956 lamented the "[v]agaries, inconsistencies, and about-faces" of the Royal Lao Government (RLG), called the premier a "pushover," and complained that the crown prince could have forced through some salutary legislation "if he'd had the guts." Eventually, Parsons, then U.S. ambassador to Laos, put into words what many of his colleagues had long since concluded. "I hope we can at least develop a country which, while it desires neutrality, will be as strong as possible and lean to us rather than to our enemies," he wrote. "This sort of buffer is about all we can reasonably expect, . . . and I venture [to] raise [the] question, what more could we really want of [a] country like this?"[3]

Parsons's cable marked the transition from what we may call Washington's "bulwark" policy to a less ambitious "buffer" policy. All attempts to institute in Laos what had been built in South Vietnam—or what Americans thought had been built in South Vietnam—had failed. Whereas Diem had managed to freeze the communists out of his government and whip the South Vietnamese military into an effective counterguerrilla force, the regime in Vientiane had welcomed Pathet Lao representatives into its cabinet and seemed incapable of fielding an army that stood its ground. Clearly, Laos would never be an anticommunist stronghold. The best Washington could hope for was a neutral Laos whose sympathies inclined westward, a weak client state supplied by free-world patrons rather than by the opposing bloc.

This was the Eisenhower administration's objective until the event spotlighted by Byrne in her report to the Taipei conferees. Lao and American

officials recognized that the May 1958 elections had the potential to determine future U.S. policy toward Laos. The elections were a crucial part of
the Royal Lao Government's program for national reconciliation, the first
campaigns in which the political arm of the Pathet Lao, the Neo Lao Hak
Xat (NLHX), would participate, and the twenty-one new seats would boost
National Assembly membership from thirty-eight to fifty-nine. More significantly, the seats would represent the heretofore Pathet Lao–controlled
provinces of Sam Neua and Phong Saly, along with other areas deemed
underrepresented. If conservative candidates won most or all of the seats, it
would deal a blow to Pathet Lao plans of seizing power through parliamentary means and strengthen American confidence in Laos as a buffer. But if
communists or neutralists did well at the polls, then Washington might have
to lower its already paltry expectations. As Eisenhower remarked while the
Lao were still casting ballots, "it would be a serious matter if any country
such as Laos went communist by the legal vote of its people." The shocking results of the elections sent U.S.-Lao relations into a tailspin and caused
several American policymakers to conclude that Laos, whatever its symbolic
or strategic value, might not be salvageable or even worth saving.[4]

### "Paralysis and Vassalage"

Charles Yost, former chargé d'affaires at the U.S. embassy in Bangkok,
arrived in Laos as America's first minister to that country in late 1954.
His accommodations befitted a hardship post. As he remembered fifteen
years later, he and his wife moved into a house "with no air-conditioners
of any kind, with leaking roofs and hordes of rats." When the USOM
staff showed up, they found their lodgings even more austere: for months,
they lived in a tent in a Vientiane pasture. From this inauspicious start,
the U.S. presence in Laos swelled, straining housing and other facilities.
Americans fought over rooms, furniture, food, and office supplies. They
wilted in the heat and became ill. A relief worker distributing medicine
to Lao villagers wisecracked, "There are only two kinds of Americans
in Laos—those who have amoebic dysentery and those who don't know
it." Unsurprisingly, the State Department found it difficult to entice
people to Laos.[5]

Those who did go were hardly advertisements for American know-
how. State relieved the first USOM director after doctors diagnosed him
as suffering from senility, and several of his subordinates had nervous

breakdowns—"a commentary on the difficulty of life in Laos," according to one embassy report, "but more on the caliber of the individuals." The Programs Evaluation Office in particular seemed to attract bunglers. Eight PEO members were fired before the organization even put down roots, some for drunkenness and the rest because they allegedly compromised security by having affairs with Vietnamese women. Thomas Unger, the first head of the PEO, served less than a year. While stationed in Vientiane, he shared a bed with his female secretary.[6]

Yost, at least, did not embarrass the Eisenhower administration. A diligent official, he worked himself to near-collapse during his term in Laos, enduring bouts of dysentery and losing over 10 percent of his body weight. Dulles wanted to turn Laos into what he called a "bulwark against communism," and Yost did his best to bring this about. He recognized that the odds were against him. State Department reports drawn up during the closing stages of the Geneva Conference low-rated the "combat effectiveness" of the RLA and fulminated against Laos's "political inertness." The CIA circulated a National Intelligence Estimate in November 1954 stating that the RLA had not "displayed a real will to fight" and was "incapable of defending Laos"; furthermore, the Lao population was "politically apathetic." Yost came to share these views, complaining to Dulles in a representative cable that "Laotians do not appear aware of [the] fact that [the] independent status now emerging implies responsibilities."[7]

The principal stone in Yost's path proved to be Katay Don Sasorith, whose appointment as premier coincided with the minister's arrival in Vientiane. Katay at first seemed pro-American—he had composed a tract entitled "Laos: Ideal Cornerstone in the Anticommunist Struggle in Southeast Asia"—but he alarmed the administration by trying to reach an agreement with the Pathet Lao as soon as he took office. His assurances that Prince Souphanouvong and the majority of his followers were not communists struck Yost as simpleminded or dishonest, a view shared by the National Security Council, which advised Eisenhower that the "situation in Laos continues to be alarming because of the soft attitude of the Lao government toward the communist Pathet Lao."[8]

Members of the International Control Commission (ICC) complicated matters for Yost when, in compliance with their mandate to ensure fulfillment of the Geneva Accords, they passed a resolution urging the RLG and the Pathet Lao to begin negotiations at once. It had been six months since the Geneva Conference adjourned, and the Pathet Lao had yet to be incorporated into the Lao national community. Souphanouvong still exercised dominion over Phong Saly and Sam Neua, having set up a de facto government there. The Geneva Accords stipulated that those provinces would come under Vientiane's jurisdiction by means of a negotiated settlement, but this was unacceptable to Washington if it meant the Pathet Lao received cabinet positions. Recent events in Czechoslovakia had convinced American policymakers that once communists were let into a government, they took it over: participation meant domination. This analogy ignored France and Italy, which remained U.S. allies despite communist membership in their governments, and it elided the differences between Eastern Europe and Southeast Asia, but it nonetheless exercised a powerful hold on the minds of U.S. statesmen. "We very much feared," Assistant Secretary of State for Far Eastern Affairs Walter Robertson declared in 1959, "that the same thing would happen to Laos as happened to Czechoslovakia." Yost made clear to Katay that future U.S. aid depended on the refusal of the RLG to enter into a coalition with the communists.[9]

How, then, was Laos to be unified? Yost advocated throwing down the gauntlet. He wanted Katay to demand the "immediate restoration [of] royal administration in [the] two provinces" without offering anything in return except guarantees of nonreprisal for past behavior. The Pathet Lao should be given "a few days to consider this proposal," and if they rejected it, the government should send in troops. Yost felt the RLA could overrun Phong Saly and Sam Neua, especially if it began operations before the rainy season.[10]

French military officials in Laos disagreed. They argued that the RLA lacked the ability to recapture the territory and that, besides, any attempt to do so would provoke intervention by neighboring communist countries. The French ambassador in Vientiane informed Katay that he could expect no help from Paris if the North Vietnamese or the Chinese stormed across Laos's borders. When the British ambassador seconded this message, Eisenhower wrote Prime Minister Winston Churchill an irate letter confessing his "bewilderment" at London's apparent belief that "communist aggression in Asia [is] of little significance." The president begged Churchill to recognize that "the time to stop any advance of communism in Asia is here, now." Churchill responded that "recourse to force" in Laos would be a mistake. Furthermore, even if the North Vietnamese and Chinese did not intervene, His Majesty's government doubted the capacity of the RLA to prevail.[11]

Such comments indicate that Katay's policy of negotiating with the Pathet Lao and reaching whatever compromises were necessary for integration was not the approach of a myopic appeaser. His methods were, moreover, in keeping with the provisions of the Geneva Accords, which Washington had pledged to respect. Indeed, it is difficult to see how Katay could have acted otherwise. As a patriot, he wanted his country unified, and he knew he could not restore Vientiane's sovereignty in the two provinces by taking up arms. His only option was to arrange some form of coexistence with the Pathet Lao—who, he repeatedly told Yost, were not communists. This may have been a naïve judgment, but Katay was conscious of Lao war-weariness; any premier who pushed his country into hostilities less than a year after the end of the Franco–Viet Minh conflict could expect to be turned out of office.

Katay emphasized this concern when he met Dulles in February 1955. The secretary visited Vientiane after the conclusion of SEATO council meetings in Bangkok, and he came armed with Yost's reports about the premier's "vacillation" in the face of Pathet Lao demands. He laid down the law to Katay, declaring that Washington "wished to help" but that U.S. assistance would only be effective if the Lao demonstrated the "will to help themselves." Making deals with Souphanouvong was no way to inspire American confidence. Katay protested that he needed to demonstrate to his people that the RLG "had exhausted every possibility for a reasonable settlement." There was a difference, he said, between "patience" and "weakness." Dulles saw no such distinction where communists were concerned. He reminded Katay that the SEATO treaty, although negotiated by a Republican administration, had been ratified by a legislature controlled by Democrats. This displayed America's "unity and purpose." Now Laos had to "show similar unity." Dulles delivered an identical lecture to Crown Prince Savang Vatthana. "The people of the United States are assuming very great responsibilities for preserving the independence and liberty of many countries," the secretary proclaimed. "They are doing so on the assumption that those people have an equal determination to defend their independence." If the RLG exhibited "resolution," American aid would keep flowing. But Vientiane could not expect Washington to subsidize activities contrary to free world interests.[12]

The next few months saw Katay execute a diplomatic tour de force in the teeth of American resistance and despite the withdrawal of French troops from Laos for service in North Africa. First, Katay's representative at the Bandung Conference of Nonaligned Nations secured verbal pledges of nonintervention in Lao affairs from China and North Vietnam. Then Souphanouvong agreed to postpone nationwide elections scheduled for August

1955 until December, which gave the government more time to counter Pathet Lao propaganda. The U.S. Information Service, although no fonder of Katay than the embassy was, concluded that he was the best of a bad lot and stumped the country for him with promotional gimmicks like *The Awakening,* a movie about a Pathet Lao soldier who changes his allegiance to the government. Mobile film units carried this drama and the instructional film *A Free Man Votes* to remote areas, while teams trained by the USIS distributed pamphlets and bulletins promoting conservative candidates.[13]

When the elections took place, Katay's National Progressive Party and Phoui Sananikone's Independent Party gained control of the assembly, capturing twenty-seven of thirty-seven seats. This was scarcely reflective of popular sentiment, given that Katay prevented the Pathet Lao from campaigning. He claimed that their candidates had missed filing deadlines and that the government could not grant them an extension, chicanery so blatant that Pathet Lao supporters boycotted the elections in protest. (Yost was not altogether wrong to call the premier "shifty and lacking in principle.") Still, Katay had scored a notable victory, and the ICC handed him another as the new year dawned; the commission passed a resolution calling for the return of royal authority in Phong Saly and Sam Neua.[14]

ICC resolutions were no substitute for men-at-arms, however, and the Pathet Lao, knowing they could not be dislodged, refused to loosen their grip on the two provinces. Katay's electoral triumph dissolved in factionalism. He had a falling out with Phoui, dissidents within his own party joined with opposition party members against him, and he failed to muster the constitutionally required two-thirds majority in the legislature to take control. Laos drifted, leaderless, for six weeks. Finally, Savang asked Prince Souvanna Phouma to form a government, and the latter scraped together enough votes on March 21, 1956. In his investiture speech, Souvanna called the resolution of the Pathet Lao problem the "most urgent question" facing his government. "No effort shall be spared," he said, to ensure that "negotiations with the adverse party" were "crowned by the loyal reconciliation longed for by all."[15]

The Eisenhower administration was unsure of what to make of Souvanna. Early assessments had been positive: a February 1955 State Department report described the prince as "one of the most able and competent officials in Laos," and American diplomats posted throughout Indochina echoed that verdict. But Souvanna's eagerness to cooperate with the Pathet Lao made American policymakers nostalgic for Katay. The fact that Souphanouvong was Souvanna's half-brother hardly raised the premier's stock in the United States, since familial ties between the two men seemed apt to facilitate a settlement. Washington's worst fears were realized when Souvanna invited the Red Prince to Vientiane, an offer Souphanouvong accepted. "Souvanna remains dangerously naïve not only about his own family but about [the] P[athet] L[ao] in general," Yost complained. Katay, whatever his shortcomings, possessed a "more keen grasp of realities than Souvanna."[16]

By early August 1956, Souvanna and Souphanouvong had, in principle, composed their differences: Souvanna agreed to permit the Pathet Lao to join his cabinet, and in return Souphanouvong promised to surrender the two northeastern provinces to the government; the Pathet Lao's political party, the NLHX, would receive the right to participate in elections, and Pathet Lao fighting forces would be placed under royal command. The half-brothers also vowed to pursue a neutral policy in international affairs. These were preliminary agreements rather than explicit plans, and political and military joint commissions still needed to work out the details, but Souvanna felt sufficiently sanguine to announce the "great news of the return of the Pathet Lao into the national community."[17]

The great news set off alarm bells in Washington. "We patently can no longer rely on friendly advice," observed Kenneth Young, director of the State Department's Office of Southeast Asian Affairs. Young deplored Souvanna's "weakness of character" and ignorance of the fact that "the communist interpretation of 'neutral'" meant "paralysis and vassalage." Days before Souvanna and Souphanouvong held their talks, Dulles delivered a commencement address at Iowa State College in which he stated the administration's views on neutralism in terms even stronger than Young's. "[T]he principle of neutrality," he declared, "has increasingly become an obsolete conception and, except under very exceptional circumstances, it is an immoral and short-sighted conception." Circumstances in Laos were no doubt trying, but, from Washington's vantage point, they did not rise to the requisite level of exceptionalism.[18]

Souvanna became America's bête noire after the August 1956 agreements. The Eisenhower administration would spend four years trying to install a Souvanna-free government in Laos, only to discover that this rotund, pipe-smoking prince was that phenomenon the poet Saxon White Kessinger famously declared did not exist: an indispensable man, the only Lao politician acceptable to right, left, and center. It proved difficult for any Lao government to survive without Souvanna heading it or controlling one of its ministries. Yost, who was close to the end of his service in Vientiane when Souvanna took office, did not have time to develop the rivalry with the premier that his successor did, but he witnessed enough of Souvanna's statesmanship to recognize that cold war concerns played no role; Souvanna did not subscribe to the two-worlds ideology that drove U.S. foreign policy and made negotiations with Souphanouvong unthinkable. "I hope I have sown some doubts in Souvanna's mind," Yost cabled Washington before returning home, but he was not optimistic.[19]

### "Lessons in the Way of the World"

By his own admission, J. Graham Parsons was an unlikely candidate to head the U.S. Embassy in Laos. "It seems that in certain respects the bottom of the barrel is showing," he joked to a friend. "My fluency in French is about the only reason I can assign for this development." He later admitted that even his French-language skills were "mediocre" at the time Eisenhower nominated him to replace Yost. Furthermore, his knowledge of Southeast Asia—"that exotic neighborhood"—was a "total void" he had never attempted to fill despite previous postings to Japan, India, and Manchuria. But Parsons did enjoy the support of Robertson, who wanted an arch–cold warrior on the scene in Vientiane. From Robertson's perspective, rigid anticommunism was more important than expertise, and Parsons had proven dependably hard-line. Eisenhower deferred to the assistant secretary's wishes and submitted Parsons's name to the Senate.[20]

News of his impending promotion alarmed Parsons, who would have preferred a European assignment. He did not welcome exile to what associates informed him was "the most difficult post in the service." At first, he half-hoped the nomination would be rejected, but a background check found no skeletons in his closet, and Capitol Hill confirmed him. Ellis Briggs, U.S. ambassador to Brazil, teased Parsons about Vientiane's "fascinating living conditions, by now no doubt complete with hot and cold running laotians [sic] padding about barefoot on teakwood floors and sweeping cobras under the dining room table." Other State Department officials remarked that the Laos job was a "challenge," a word that, Parsons sourly noted, came to be "synonymous with condolence." He took heart in the fact that at least he was going somewhere important. "Laos," he recalled, "had by then become a greater worry to Washington than South Vietnam, where, under Ngo Dinh Diem, real progress was being made." Parsons set sail for Indochina with his family in July 1956.[21]

A foul-up in the State Department's mail room led to Parsons's letter of credence being sent to Lagos instead of Laos, which meant the new ambassador could not present his credentials until mid-October 1956. Unperturbed by technicalities, Souvanna insisted on meeting Parsons right away and assured him that he would grant "provisional recognition" pending arrival of the mail from Nigeria. The premier was eager to explain why his efforts to negotiate a modus vivendi with the Pathet Lao did not signify that Laos was defecting from the free world. He was aware, he said, of the dangers posed by international communism. Furthermore, he knew that there was a small percentage of communists in the Pathet Lao. They did not, however, include his half-brother, who was a nationalist like himself. Souvanna argued that incorporation of the two northeastern provinces into Laos's national community was the surest way to guarantee that the communist minority there lost its influence. After unity had been achieved, he reasoned, the Pathet Lao would be "under parliamentary rule." If they obeyed the law, they could "do what they wanted," but if they tried to overthrow the government, they would be arrested. Souvanna said he understood that Washington sought the "maximum number [of] friendly non-communist countries," and that neither he nor Souphanouvong had any "quarrel with [the] U.S. position." On the contrary, they wanted to "be friends [with] both East and West." The RLG, Souvanna affirmed, would "follow [a] 'neutral' not 'neutralist' policy."[22]

While Parsons was unimpressed by this choplogic, and while he deplored the fact that "lady fingers and warm champagne" were served at the reception in Souvanna's office, he admitted that the premier was "gentlemanly" and "cosmopolitan"—the "most westernized" member of the RLG. The ambassador came away from this first encounter convinced that Souvanna was "equipped to lead his relatively backward people," if only he could be compelled to recognize the nature of the Pathet Lao. Like most Eisenhower-era pundits, academics, and geopoliticians, Parsons accepted the thesis that coalitions with communists were unworkable. He repeatedly invoked the 1948 Czech coup as a lesson of history. "After all," he noted, "if ... the experienced and sophisticated Czechs could not survive a coalition with the communists, how could the relatively helpless Lao?" Parsons also toed the Dulles-Young line on neutrality, affirming that it was "in the nature of militant communism that there is no such thing as a neutral."[23]

One of Parsons's first tasks was to persuade Souvanna to decline an invitation from Chinese foreign minister Zhou Enlai to visit the People's Republic. Laos had no formal diplomatic relations with its massive northern neighbor, and Washington wanted to keep it that way; if Souvanna went to Beijing, Robertson predicted, he would come under pressure from his hosts to make "concessions" that would "develop Chicom [Chinese Communist] influence and power within Laos." What if Souvanna permitted a Chinese embassy in Vientiane? A Soviet embassy would follow, and this would strengthen the Pathet Lao's hand. Accordingly, the State Department urged Parsons to "try to prevent" a visit to Beijing.[24]

Souvanna ignored American exhortations and decided to make the trip. In fact, he told embassy counselor Wendell Blanké that he might expand it into a goodwill tour, a "swing through Saigon, Phnom Penh, Bangkok... [and] Hanoi, if invited." Horrified, Parsons warned Souvanna that this gesture was "dangerous" and noted its likely impact on U.S. public opinion. A Souvanna–Mao Zedong summit, to say nothing of a Souvanna–Ho Chi Minh summit, would "make headlines" in America; it would affect Congress's "voting of funds for aid" and jeopardize the U.S. mission. Souvanna's claim that the trip was to be "purely [a] courtesy visit" did not mollify the ambassador or his stateside superiors. Dulles ordered Parsons not to see the Royal Lao delegation off when it left Vattay airfield for Beijing, a break with protocol not lost on the premier.[25]

The ensuing events were to be misinterpreted in Washington for years. American policymakers concluded that Souvanna's visits to China and North Vietnam proved he was either a communist or a fellow traveler, when they proved nothing of the kind. Sisouk Na Champassak, secretary general of the royal government under Souvanna and a staunch anticommunist, accompanied the premier on his globe-trotting and noted later that the Lao delegation did not seek aid from Mao or Ho, formed no "secret agreements," and adhered to a neutralist line. Souvanna went to Beijing and Hanoi, Sisouk recalled, to get Mao and Ho to commit themselves in writing to what their representatives had agreed to orally at Bandung: a policy of nonintervention in Laos's internal concerns. By securing that pledge, Souvanna hoped to undercut the Pathet Lao's bargaining power when it came time to translate the August 1956 statements of principle into a schedule for action—when, for instance, he and Souphanouvong decided such issues as whether integration of Pathet Lao forces into the RLA would precede or follow establishment of a coalition government. Given these objectives, the journey was a success, and it redounded as much to the benefit of the free world as to that of the communists.[26]

The Eisenhower administration saw matters differently. Dulles decried Souvanna's "one-way concessions," while Young considered the trip evidence of "Lao willingness to permit its [sic] independence to be subverted."

A dispatch from Beijing received at State depicted Souvanna truckling to the Chinese and gushing that his visit was the fulfillment of a "'lifelong dream.'" According to this report, Souvanna entertained ministers of the Chinese government by "performing a Laotian dance with sinuous competence" and "resembled a rabbit hypnotized by an enormous snake" when negotiating with Mao. Omitted were the terms agreed upon between the two nations, terms that revealed considerable Lao resistance to Chinese coercion. Mao and Zhou wanted to open a consulate-general in Vientiane, but Souvanna refused, claiming that Laos had not accepted a Nationalist Chinese consulate-general and that admittance of a Communist Chinese one would violate Lao neutrality. While Souvanna did promise not to allow American military bases on Lao soil, he persuaded the Chinese to drop their objections to "bases permitted under the Geneva agreements," meaning that French bases could remain. More significantly, Souvanna got the Chinese to join him in signing a declaration that stressed mutual respect for the principle of nonintervention.[27]

Souvanna was just as artful with the North Vietnamese. When Ho accused the Royal Lao Government of discriminating against his country by maintaining a diplomatic mission in Saigon but not in Hanoi, Souvanna pointed out that the Saigon mission had been established by the French before Laos became independent; Vientiane was therefore upholding the status quo, not displaying favoritism. Ho accepted this explanation and consented to sign a statement on noninterference similar to the document initialed in Beijing. The North Vietnamese voiced concern that the Pathet Lao would not receive a role in Lao affairs proportional to their numbers, but Ho did not pressure Souvanna to clarify any points of the August agreements with Souphanouvong, such as which ministries would be awarded to Pathet Lao politicians. For the most part, negotiations were cordial; many of the Lao and North Vietnamese statesmen had been college classmates under the French colonial administration and took the opportunity provided by Souvanna's visit to renew old friendships. On the eve of their departure, Souvanna and his colleagues were treated to an evening of Lao dances performed in Hanoi's municipal theater.

The Lao delegation returned home having given away nothing. Souvanna obtained the promises he sought. That the Eisenhower administration viewed these talks as a sellout reveals how little its judgment had to do with facts and how powerfully cold-war fears influenced U.S. policy decisions. Dulles cabled Parsons that "we may soon have to do something to show [the] Lao we mean business." If it took the "threat [of] withdrawal [of] American aid" to reverse Souvanna's "hazardous course," then Washington should be prepared to take that step. While the secretary believed there was "no need now [to] give up trying [to] keep Laos on [the] side [of the] West," he did not expect Parsons to work miracles. For the first time, he conceded the possibility that "Laos can serve as no more than [a] buffer."[28]

Souvanna's diplomatic peregrination in the summer of 1956 all but ensured that his relationship with the new U.S. ambassador would be difficult. Still, a more gracious lieutenant than Parsons—whom one co-worker described as "standoffish" and "arrogant"—might have managed the partnership to better serve Lao and American interests. "There very unfortunately developed an active dislike between them," recalled Christian Chapman, Laotian desk officer at the State Department's East Asian bureau. "It was a clash of policy, but it became personal." Parsons revised his initial assessment of Souvanna. The premier, he now concluded, was "vain, weak, and too readily influenced"; his arguments were "fatuous"; he was "playing footsie with his communist half-brother"; and he naively believed that Washington "would give him a blank check." Convinced that neutralism was synonymous with surrender, Parsons had no doubt as to where his own duty lay. "[I]t was my job," he later wrote, "to foil [Souvanna's] interest to bring the communist Pathet Lao into the Royal Government."[29]

Toward that end, he met with the premier almost daily, pounding on the same themes: only a pro-Western RLG could guarantee the country's independence; Pathet Lao control of even minor ministries risked a coup de Prague. "Round and round our arguments went," Parsons recalled. "He was wont to repeat that all Lao were brothers, ... that the integration of the Pathet Lao would be a genuine one—despite their control by Hanoi." Parsons found such assurances "galling, even infuriating." Blanké fed his boss's righteous indignation, and provided amusement at USOM cocktail parties, by composing a bit of doggerel "to be sung to the tune of 'Oh, Susanna'":

> Oh, Souvanna
> Oh, don't you cry for me
> 'Cause I'm gwine to old Vientiane
> And a coup there's gonna be.
>
> So reintegrate the Pathet Lao
> Make friends with Chairman Mao
> The French will call you hero
> As you unify the Lao.[30]

For his part, Souvanna resented being talked down to by someone recently arrived in Laos, unfamiliar with local conditions, and incapable
of distinguishing between advice and infringement on Lao sovereignty.
U.S. cultural attaché Perry Stieglitz, whose tour of duty in Vientiane
overlapped with Parsons's, thought the ambassador threw away any
chance of fruitful negotiations when he "tr[ied] to force his simplistic...anticommunism upon the foremost proponent of neutralism in
Southeast Asia." According to Stieglitz, Parsons never listened to Souvanna or considered him an equal; rather, the ambassador assumed "that
the head of the government of this little kingdom needed some lessons
in the way of the world" and proceeded to "lecture him." Souvanna endured the lectures, waiting for a chance to point out that, yes, it was true
that some members of the Pathet Lao were communists, but that they
numbered no more than two hundred people out of the five hundred
thousand inhabitants of Phong Saly and Sam Neua and that he could
not sacrifice the provinces to such a small group. Moreover, Laos, an underpopulated country with no industrial proletariat and no shortage of
arable land, was about the least auspicious place in the world for Marx-
ism to take root. Souvanna insisted that the Lao, including the followers
of his half-brother, yearned for one thing: national unification. In this
they mirrored patriots everywhere. "[T]ell me if there is any people on
earth who would shrink from consecrating its own unity," the premier
demanded. But Parsons's cold war certitudes were impervious to challenge, and the two men remained at loggerheads.[31]

Another ticklish issue between Parsons and Souvanna—not as urgent as
that of a coalition government, but serious nonetheless—involved irregularities in the U.S. aid program. As early as 1955, Senator Mike Mansfield
had toured Laos and reported that American aid had failed to generate economic development. The problem was the artificially high value of the kip,
the Lao currency unit. Under Washington's Commodity Import Program
(CIP), the Lao Ministry of Finance issued licenses to private merchants to
import goods, which were paid for in dollars and sold for kip; this arrangement was designed to prevent the inflation that would result if dollars were
allowed to circulate freely in the Lao economy. But the United States fixed
the exchange rate at thirty-five kip to the dollar, and a dollar was worth
over one hundred kip in Thailand, Hong Kong, and elsewhere. It did not
take long for opportunists to amass fortunes by buying America's aid dollars
from the Lao government at the legal rate and then selling them on the open
market, or by importing goods solely for transshipment to other countries.

During the first two years of the program, $24.3 million in imports was authorized and spent, but only $9.8 million worth of goods actually arrived in Laos, and these were mostly luxuries like jewelry and perfume. Investment in infrastructure was almost nonexistent. While Vientiane acquired a veneer of affluence, standards of living did not improve for rural Lao. Worse, the CIP led to graft, because import licenses became extremely valuable, and government officials demanded bribes before granting them.[32]

These foreign-aid problems did not attract much attention in Washington until after Parsons relinquished his ambassadorship in 1958 to become undersecretary of state, but several USOM officials recognized the potential for scandal early on and pressed the Royal Lao Government to institute reforms. Parsons himself called Souvanna on the carpet when he discovered that import licenses had been issued by the RLG without U.S. approval. The premier remained unflappable, declaring that he understood American concerns and would work to eliminate corruption. On the other hand, he argued, devaluation of the kip could cause unrest. He reminded Parsons that in 1953 the kip had been devalued relative to the French franc, to which it had then been tied, and hyperinflation had followed; if this happened again, it might undermine allegiance to the government among those city dwellers who formed the most dependable pro-Western bloc. Parsons's reply was another lecture. "I tried to explain to Souvanna the separation of powers in the United States," he recalled, "and that . . . the Lao must conduct themselves in such a way that the administration could persuade Congress to appropriate the American taxpayers' hard earned money." Souvanna, who was aware of the role Congress played in funding foreign-aid programs, listened and held his temper in check. The conference ended with the familiar lack of a meeting of minds.[33]

Savang, sensing the antagonism between Parsons and Souvanna and worried that it might prompt a shift in American policy, announced his intention to visit Washington in late September 1956. His timing was bad—Egyptian president Gamal Abdel Nasser had recently nationalized the Suez Canal, sparking a crisis that absorbed U.S. strategists' attention—but Robertson recommended that the administration receive Savang "in view of the delicate situation we face in Laos." Robertson speculated that the purpose of the crown prince's visit was "to counter the impression that Laos has turned to the communists." Savang did attempt to dispel that notion, assuring Dulles that his people were "opposed to communist dictatorship." Dulles replied that such fortitude had not been evident in RLG behavior. Washington, he argued, could not "replace the Lao will to remain free," and it was up to the Lao themselves to decide between "independence and alien domination." To Savang's protest that "[t]his choice" had already been "definitely made," Dulles replied, "Yes,...but in a rather weak manner." Soon after Savang's visit, State cabled Parsons a list of actions that would cause Washington to "reappraise its...policy toward Laos." Foremost among them was "P[athet] L[ao] participation [in a] coalition government."[34]

The ambassador relayed this message to Souvanna, who, sick of American bullying, exhibited a rare flash of anger. He threatened to resign before agreeing to the partition of his country. Souphanouvong and the majority of the Pathet Lao, he insisted, were "not communists and not under their control." Any program for unity would provide for the "unconditional restoration of royal authority in [the] two provinces and [the] complete submission of [the] P[athet] L[ao] to [the] RLG." He was no starry-eyed dupe; he acknowledged the presence of communists in the Pathet Lao. But he also understood that keeping Laos divided benefited the communists: it allowed them to disseminate propaganda among the people of Sam Neua and Phong Saly and continue playing by their own minority rules instead of obeying the national law. Incorporation of the Pathet Lao into a government of national union would reduce, not increase, the possibility of communist takeover. According to Parsons's cable, Souvanna "said with frankness and feeling that he had worked to [the] limit of his resources" and that "[h]e had now reached the point where he could go no further without American support." If Washington withheld its backing, "he would resign, and someone else—he did not know who—would have to take over."[35]

Parsons found the prospect of Souvanna's departure appealing, but Savang and other leading Lao figures told him there was no alternative to the premier. Only Souvanna could secure a two-thirds vote in the legislature. If he stepped down, Minister of the Interior Nhou Abhay predicted, it would be the "end of Laos." British and French representatives in Vientiane urged Parsons to support Souvanna, and Marek Thee, Polish delegate to the ICC, arranged a meeting with the ambassador to, as Thee put it, "impress upon him a view more true to Laotian realities." Parsons listened respectfully to Thee's presentation but paid no heed. "His mind seemed sealed off by deeply rooted preconceptions of world and local affairs," Thee noted. In this regard Parsons's mind was no different from that of his boss, Robertson, who remained opposed to a coalition. The Pathet Lao, Robertson proclaimed, were an "appendage of the Viet Minh," and Souphanouvong was "either a dyed-in-the-wool communist" or "so completely under their control as to make the distinction meaningless."[36]

Ultimately, appeals from the king and the crown prince induced Souvanna to stay in office, but his relationship with Parsons grew more dysfunctional. "I had perforce to oppose Souvanna at almost every turn," remembered the ambassador. "We used every tactic we could." He read the premier the riot act during meetings, encouraged rightist Lao politicians to attack Souvanna in the press, and advised Washington to delay its release of the Lao military budget. These machinations led to what Parsons described as a "distressing experience late one evening," when Princess Souvanna Phouma confronted him "practically in tears and, almost imploringly, asked why I had to thwart her husband." This "unusual tactic," added Parsons, "was unavailing."[37]

While Parsons schemed, however, the ICC kept the dialogue between the RLG and the Pathet Lao going. The mixed political and military committees that Souvanna and Souphanouvong had set up in August hammered out specifics for ending the Lao conflict, guaranteeing civil rights to Pathet Lao, and integrating Pathet Lao soldiers into the RLA. As 1956 drew to a close, the likelihood of a coalition government including communists increased, and the Eisenhower administration was forced to consider what its response would be if Souvanna called its bluff. Washington could not, as Parsons put it, simply "cut off aid," because American support was not "replaceable except by [the] Chinese Communists and [the] Soviet bloc." Denial of funds would result in the "most complete victory [the] communists could win here." On the other hand, the administration could not let Souvanna get away with ignoring its wishes. Eric Kocher, deputy director of the Office of Southeast Asian Affairs, noted that if Souvanna awarded ministries to the Pathet Lao and the United States did not respond, this would "giv[e] Souvanna the impression that our so-called 'firm' positions... need not be taken seriously." Kocher wondered if it would "not be the better part of wisdom for the U.S. to inflict some small hurt on Souvanna," a gesture that would "show our displeasure" but stop "short of cutting off aid."[38]

Unfortunately, no one could come up with a punishment to bring Souvanna to heel that would not operate to the advantage of Moscow, Beijing, and Hanoi. Some officials suggested that Parsons be summoned to Washington for consultations; recall of an ambassador usually preceded a shift in policy, and it might foster "fear among Lao leaders." Dulles, however, determined that Parsons could accomplish more by remaining in Vientiane and "demonstrat[ing the] seriousness with which we regard P[athet] L[ao] entry into [the] cabinet." On balance, that was all Parsons, or any other U.S. policymaker, could do: notch up American threats in frequency and tone. Meanwhile, Katay, serving as deputy premier, traveled to Washington in Savang's wake and was subjected to the same harangue his sovereign received. Dulles demanded a "manifestation of Lao will and backbone" and warned Katay that unless the Lao demonstrated this resolve, the U.S. Congress would ask why it should "waste money on people who will not help themselves."[39]


## "Worse than Expected"

As he had done when faced by the Chinese and North Vietnamese, Souvanna stood firm, refusing to allow his country to be treated as a pawn. He recognized that Washington held the purse strings and, to an extent, the whip hand, but he was diplomat enough to understand that the Eisenhower administration operated under constraints of its own, namely, the need to avoid sending soldiers to Southeast Asia. Eisenhower was the first Republican president in two decades, and a contributing factor to his election had been frustration with the Korean War. For him to have secured an armistice in July 1953 only to get the United States into another Asian conflict would cost him a great deal of support. This was why Eisenhower had been reluctant to use American air power to relieve the French garrison at Dien Bien Phu, and why he wanted to appear to be observing the Geneva Accords. Furthermore, as several historians have noted, Eisenhower was a conservative man who believed that his country could not sustain the military budgets of the Truman era without undermining the American way of life. His "New Look" foreign-policy doctrine was based on economy in defense, on deterring communist aggression through nuclear superiority, covert action, and security pacts instead of conventional warfare.[40]

Laos in 1956, however, did not appear susceptible to New Look solutions: nuclear weapons would be useless against the Pathet Lao; the CIA in Vientiane had yet to organize native counterinsurgency forces; and SEATO, unable to compel treaty members to respond to attacks, was a paper tiger. Most important, the RLA, despite being one of the highest-paid armies in Asia, displayed no eagerness to test its mettle against Souphanouvong's guerrillas. If the Pathet Lao tried to seize the country by force, royal troops would be hard-pressed to mount an effective delaying action, especially if Hanoi or Beijing became involved. The only way to prevent communist victory under such circumstances would be for America to commit its fighting men to the jungles, mountains, and plains of Laos, an undertaking Eisenhower knew would be unpopular politically.

Washington was thus as restricted in its choices as Vientiane, and the RLG's feebleness became for Souvanna a kind of diplomatic leverage. The Eisenhower administration dared not discontinue aid for fear that the RLG would collapse, leading to a communist takeover. American policymakers could not force Souvanna from office, because there was no one to take his place; were he deposed, lesser-known candidates would scramble to amass the necessary two-thirds vote, and the government would be paralyzed. Unless Washington was prepared to impose a pro-American regime upon Laos, which would compromise the United States' moral position in the world, or dispatch American troops to fight alongside the RLA, which would contravene the New Look and make it difficult for Eisenhower to protest Chinese and North Vietnamese violations of Lao sovereignty, the Americans had no alternative but to work with Souvanna and comply with his program to reunify his homeland.

Parsons acknowledged as much in a remarkable cable to State dictated after he and Souvanna spent the afternoon locked in debate. The "time may come," he noted, when Washington would face the alternatives of a coalition government or a "reappraisal [of] our policy." If the latter meant "withdrawal [of] U.S. support," it would be "tantamount to acquiescence in letting [the] communists win." That was out of the question. "Whether we like it or not," Parsons observed, "I do not see much chance of going back to [the] status quo ante Souvanna." Although he continued to believe that Pathet Lao inclusion in the RLG was "undesirable," he hoped the administration would not "commit us too inflexibly" and that State merely wanted to "avoid having [the] RLG believe that there is [a] possibility [that] we might at some time acquiesce in [the] inclusion [of the] P[athet] L[ao]." In other words, Washington should be prepared to bow to the inevitable, even if it never told Souvanna its position had softened.[41]

Parsons's pragmatism notwithstanding, the deal Souvanna sealed in late December 1956 raised howls of protest from the Eisenhower administration. Souvanna and Souphanouvong agreed to form a coalition government *before* supplementary elections and to change Laos's election laws to legalize the NLHX. The Pathet Lao would receive two ministries in an expanded cabinet, with Souphanouvong becoming minister of economic planning. (This meant the Red Prince would control the distribution of U.S. aid!) Souphanouvong pledged to transfer Phong Saly and Sam Neua to royal command and place his troops under RLG supervision, but only after the establishment of the coalition. Dulles, noting that the Vientiane government had "com[e] off even worse than expected" in this arrangement, proposed instituting a month-by-month allocation of American money. "We do not wish [to] deliver to [the] Lao [a] sum which could tide them over [for a] considerable period," he noted. From Washington's perspective, the RLG was on probation.[42]

Parsons and his associates in Vientiane lobbied for a toughening of the coalition terms. According to journalist Wilfred Burchett, Americans buttonholed every member of the assembly and threatened to stop aid if Souvanna's program was accepted. When the assembly adjourned on March 15, 1957, without ratifying the accords, Souvanna gave ground on a key point: integration of Pathet Lao troops, he declared, would precede rather than follow the formation of an enlarged administration. Souphanouvong countered with an amendment of his own: he wanted Laos to accept aid from China, which, he said, would confirm Vientiane's neutrality by "balancing" U.S. assistance—and which, of course, was unacceptable to Washington. The U.S. Embassy sent Souvanna a note reproving him for allowing the "future of the Kingdom of Laos" to be "dictated by dissident groups."[43]

With the RLG–Pathet Lao entente in disrepair, Souvanna reopened the assembly on May 11, delivering an address in which he attempted to mollify Souphanouvong and the Americans. He did not reject Chinese aid in principle, but argued that it would be premature given that Pathet Lao and government officials had yet to prove they could work together; he also criticized the Pathet Lao for continuing to skirmish with RLA forces despite the cease-fire. These comments were too wishy-washy for Dulles, who warned the premier, through Parsons, that the U.S. "Congress could only assume [that] Laos [was] not doing [its] utmost [to] preserve its independence."[44]

The result of American arm-twisting was a schizophrenic vote in the assembly on May 29 that plunged Laos into turmoil. When presented with the question "Is the assembly satisfied with the agreements signed between the royal government and the Pathet Lao?" the deputies voted "yes" unanimously. But they then defeated a motion to use those agreements as the basis for reunification of the country, and they voted "no" in response to the question "Does the assembly want the government to carry on with the policies outlined by the prime minister?" Although this was not a formal vote of no confidence, Souvanna chose to interpret it as one. He submitted his resignation to the king.[45]

This move surprised Washington, which had only sought to push the premier in a more anti–Pathet Lao direction. Parsons termed Souvanna's act an "unexpected debacle" and worried that the "result may be chaos."

When the crown prince selected Katay to form a new government, there were a few huzzahs from State, but most officials doubted whether the premier-designate could capitalize on the situation. Dulles noted that Katay had "disadvantages," chiefly the "dislike of him among other Lao politicians." Nonetheless, Katay was more willing than Souvanna to play the role of Washington's surrogate. During his recent visit to the United States, Katay had campaigned to make Americans forget that he too had tried to reach a compromise with the Pathet Lao. "I am proud to be labeled pro-American," he told guests at a Blair House luncheon. "Neutrality today is impossible." An impressed State Department official paid Katay the ultimate compliment, remarking that he was "developing into [a] second Diem." Although unwilling to go that far, Parsons reported to Dulles that Katay's "qualities contrast favorably with Souvanna's weaknesses."[46]

Katay proved more popular in Washington than in Laos, however, and he could not muster a two-thirds majority in the assembly, even after making Souvanna his foreign minister–designate. The crown prince then turned to leftist Bong Souvannavong, who likewise failed to secure investiture. Katay tried again and fell short again. Then Phoui Sananikone, whom Parsons considered more pro-American than Katay, went down to defeat. The farce continued for three months, with each of Laos's political personages taking his turn and demonstrating his inability to gain the requisite majority, until the crown prince begged Souvanna to resume command. On August 9, Souvanna presented himself before the assembly with the same platform that had caused his resignation earlier in the year. This time, he encountered little opposition, winning investiture by a comfortable margin. Any lingering American doubts about Souvanna's irreplaceability were dispelled.[47]

Impatient after the ten-week interregnum, Souvanna and Souphanouvong hurried to conclude their deliberations. They spelled out the terms of the 1956 agreement in greater detail, and the result was a compromise. Souphanouvong became minister of economic planning; another Pathet Lao politician, Phoumi Vongvichit, became minister of cults; but Katay and Phoui secured ministries, and, more important, the Pathet Lao had to return to royal control the administration of Phong Saly and Sam Neua before the new coalition could begin governing. Souphanouvong also had to surrender all arms held by the Pathet Lao and demobilize seventy-five hundred Pathet Lao troops; the remaining fifteen hundred were to be taken into the RLA. Souvanna pledged to appoint Pathet Lao civil cadres to suitable posts and recognize the NLHX as a political party. The two men set May 4, 1958, as the date for elections to the National Assembly.

The agreement favored Lao conservatives, not their opponents. While the Pathet Lao controlled two cabinet posts, the all-important ministries of interior, defense, and foreign affairs remained in royalist hands. The majority of Pathet Lao troops returned to civilian status after giving up their weapons. Souvanna accepted no aid from China, the Soviet Union, or North Vietnam, and no communist nation established a diplomatic mission in Laos. Souphanouvong fulfilled his part of the bargain on November 18 when he turned over the two northeastern provinces to Savang. The next day, the assembly unanimously approved the new government and broke into applause when the vote was announced. No reasonable observer could conclude that Souvanna had caved in to the communists. Rather, given the Pathet Lao's military advantage and the presence of China and North Vietnam on Laos's flanks, the premier had secured the best settlement possible—a fact recognized by most of the world's governments, which joined Souvanna's colleagues in applauding his efforts. The one harsh note was sounded by the U.S. State Department. In its official announcement, State declared, "A coalition with the communists is a dangerous line of conduct, for the history of similar coalitions elsewhere in the world reveals that they end tragically in penetration and seizure of the country by the communists."[48]

## "Through Lao Eyes"

Souvanna was disconcerted by State's fit of pique. At first, he decided to send Phoui to Washington to explain the advantages of Lao unity, but then changed his mind and elected to make the trip himself. This put the Eisenhower administration in an awkward position. As Robertson advised Dulles, "one of our problems will be to reconcile our giving him red-carpet treatment, which he is due, ... and our desire not to appear to endorse his hazardous policy of coalition." Ultimately, a fish-and-fowl compromise was crafted whereby Souvanna received the red carpet but State described his two-day stopover as a "business meeting" rather than an "official visit"—owing, department spokesmen claimed, to the "lack of time for preparation." Eisenhower moreover did not host a dinner in Souvanna's honor, as would have been customary. The president, his press secretary announced, was still resting after a recent NATO meeting. While this did not amount to an outright snub, Souvanna could hardly have failed to notice how it contrasted with the receptions he had been accorded in Beijing and Hanoi.[49]

Briefing papers prepared for Dulles before Souvanna's arrival described the premier as "tractable and easy to please," qualities that made him "susceptible to the ideas of those who oppose U.S. policy objectives." He was "probably aware of the communist character of the Pathet Lao," Robertson surmised, but he "steadfastly maintained" that they were "misguided nationalists who have now returned to the fold." The reason for this charade was obvious: "For him to do otherwise would make his coalition with the communists indefensible." Robertson felt that some "display of the seriousness with which we regard the situation is required," and he proposed that Dulles give Souvanna a "paper on communist takeovers in Eastern Europe." Perhaps the premier needed to be reminded of how Czechoslovakia went from democracy to a Moscow-controlled dictatorship in two weeks. "We are not certain that we can reach any kind of workable understanding with Souvanna," declared Patricia Byrne, officer in charge of Lao affairs, "but we wish to try to make of the visit more than an exchange of our respective viewpoints."[50]

The premier likewise sought genuine dialogue. He was sure that he could convince administration officials of the correctness of his policy if he could talk to them face to face. Parsons found him "full of easy confidence," "eager to meet key Americans," and "hopeful of reaching [an] understanding." "He believes he is right and we are wrong and that he can prove it to us," observed the ambassador. Contrary to State's portrayal of a compliant premier, Parsons advised Dulles that Souvanna could be "stubborn," noting that, despite U.S. opposition, "he has adhered for [a] year and [a] half to [a] consistent... plan." Souvanna's "bland" exterior concealed a strong will. Parsons urged the secretary to avoid being drawn into arguments about whether the Pathet Lao were communists; it would be better, he said, to proclaim that the "precautions we seek are in [the] interest of Laos regardless [of] who is right." Against Souvanna's wishes, Parsons accompanied the RLG party to Washington, writing years later that he was "endlessly amused by the incongruity of my little Lao friends from their sleepy rural capital whirling about in the big time of our nation's capital."[51]

However amusing or incongruous his presence might have been, Souvanna was not intimidated by the big time and came prepared for his meeting with Dulles on January 13, 1958. He first had to withstand another lecture, as the secretary expounded on the evils of "communist imperialism" and handed Souvanna the paper Robertson had drafted, commenting that it might provide "useful ideas" of the kind of tactics the premier should be on guard against if he wanted to save Laos from Czechoslovakia's fate. While admitting that Souvanna possessed "qualifications by which to judge the matter," Dulles emphasized the Eisenhower administration's own expertise, "from our world-wide experience in the way international communism operates." Souvanna's response struck an exquisite balance between servility and intransigence. Laos, he declared, considered itself "a child, especially in relation to the United States." He assured Dulles that he did "not misunderstand the communist danger" and that he would be "the first to fight the communists" if they attempted to seize power. In fact, the RLG had recently passed, at his behest, legislation "requir[ing] the death penalty for those defying the regime," which scarcely indicated subservience to Moscow. As for Eastern European coups, Souvanna doubted they were analogous to developments in his country. He contended that Poland, Hungary, and Czechoslovakia had become communist "because of the presence of the Soviet Army," not because they had coalition governments with communist membership. Laos was like Finland, he said; it existed "in close proximity to overwhelming communist force" and yet preserved its freedom. He moreover argued that communists represented only a fraction of the population of Sam Neua and Phong Saly. If the majority of the Pathet Lao had been communists, they would have "remained masters of the two provinces"; instead, they had "submitted to the government's authority." This confirmed their independence.

It was a trenchant plea, but it left Dulles unmoved. Washington could not, he said, "take much comfort" from the fact that the communist element in Laos was small, since communists always preferred to "operate from a minority position." Finland's retention of its liberty was indeed "one of the great achievements of modern times," but Dulles reminded Souvanna that it was "the exception rather than the rule." Whether Laos, lacking the "experience of Finland," could "match its performance" was an issue for Souvanna and his government to resolve. In any event, the Eisenhower administration, which was bearing the entire cost of the RLA and underwriting most of Vientiane's nonmilitary expenses as well, was "concerned about Laos" and believed it was "indispensable that something be done to remedy the situation." With that vague but ominous pronouncement, the meeting adjourned. Souvanna had made no more headway with Dulles in ninety minutes than he had made with Parsons in eighteen months.[52]

Subsequent conferences proved similarly counterproductive. Eisenhower met Souvanna the following morning and offered a few platitudinous remarks about how Americans were "interested in Laos's sector of the world" before calling in the press for photographs. Parsons then teamed up with

State Department officials to demand that Souvanna devalue the kip. Vice President Richard Nixon hectored the premier on Vientiane's "misuse of funds." Robertson warned—gratuitously, in light of the November 1957 accords—that any Lao "agreement to exchange diplomatic representatives with the communist bloc" would "put in jeopardy continued U.S. support for Laos." No record exists of Souvanna's luncheon meeting with CIA director Allen Dulles, but Arthur Dommen is almost certainly right to assume that the American "did all the talking."[53]

The visit was an exercise in frustration for Souvanna, who only managed to get his hosts to "see the situation through Lao eyes," as he put it, once: when he noted the likely impact of devaluation on the May elections. After a scolding by Gardner Palmer, deputy assistant secretary of Far Eastern economic affairs, Souvanna observed that "[i]n theory, devaluation is used to stimulate exports and to stimulate economic life in general." But conditions in Laos were unique. Given that the economy was "at scratch, with no production [and] no exports," devaluation would lead to an outcome "different from that which one would expect in theory." It would "disrupt the entire... social life of the country." Did the White House want to impose an austerity program on Laos that would cause dislocations of the price structure, foster resentment, and benefit leftist candidates when the Lao went to the polls?[54]

That question found its mark. Souvanna sensed Washington's anxiety over the looming elections, the first in which the NLHX would compete. No one knew how popular Souphanouvong and his party were, either in the two northeastern provinces or in other newly enfranchised areas of Laos. Americans had not concerned themselves with this issue in December 1955, because no voting had taken place in Sam Neua and Phong Saly, and the Pathet Lao had boycotted the elections. Now that the contest had moved from the battlefield to the ballot box, however, Washington had an interest in limiting NLHX gains. Robertson expected the NLHX to "bend every effort to increase their position" and insisted that "all ideas must, for the moment, be judged from the standpoint of impact before May 4." John Foster Dulles agreed. He assured Souvanna that monetary reform could wait until after the elections.[55]

Apart from this concession, Souvanna had nothing to show for his diplomacy. The visit concluded with stock ceremoniousness, as State released a communiqué "[r]eaffirming Laos's membership in the free world." Secretary Dulles, substituting for the president at a black-tie dinner, toasted Souvanna's "effort to resist totalitarian domination." "One might wonder at the close ties existing between two nations some 14,000 miles apart," Dulles intoned, "yet these bonds are strong." The secretary's words could not disguise the strains in the U.S.-RLG alliance.[56]

## "A Great Deal to Fear"

"The battle for Laos is on," proclaimed James Babcock, an official of the International Cooperation Administration sent to Vientiane in early 1958 to evaluate the USOM's progress. "At stake in an election to be held in May are twenty-one seats in the National Assembly." Like his superiors, Babcock understood that the elections could derail America's enterprise in Laos. They also, however, represented an opportunity: Washington had been unable to prevent Souvanna from taking Pathet Lao members into his cabinet, but if conservative candidates swept the elections, the premier's coalition plan could be nullified, because Laos's parliamentary tradition reserved cabinet posts for members of the legislature. Furthermore, as Kocher advised Robertson, a conservative landslide "might have repercussions outside Laos." "This is the first time a population formerly under communist control is being permitted to vote freely," Kocher noted, referring to the residents of Sam Neua and Phong Saly. "Should the people openly repudiate a communist candidate, the 'Lao formula' might set a precedent for the unification of other divided countries." It would moreover give the United States its greatest propaganda triumph since the Berlin Airlift.[57]

Robertson had laid out the administration's position when Souvanna visited Washington, declaring, "We assume . . . that leftist parties will be excluded from the government to be formed after the May elections if they win only a handful of seats." He promised Souvanna that America would do whatever was necessary to ensure a favorable electoral result. Along with furnishing cash, he said, "[w]e would be prepared to lend projectors, films, and mimeograph machines, arrange for the printing of posters, and provide other electioneering aids." State granted Parsons a "special fund" of $500,000 "to enhance conservative chances in [the] forthcoming election," and Souvanna was given to understand that this was only the beginning. Money was no object and matériel no matter when it came to keeping Laos inside the free-world gravitational field.[58]

Washington's deep pockets alone would not suffice, though. Success required sound strategy, and the Americans confronted a confusing political scene. Organized parties had only recently arrived in Laos. There were dozens of them, mostly centered on powerful individuals or families, and few had a firm agenda, although they readily adopted the ideology of their patrons. The major players on the noncommunist side were the Independent Party of Phoui Sananikone, the Nationalists under Katay, and Souvanna's Progressive Party. The leftists included the NLHX under Souphanouvong and the Santiphab, or "Peace through Neutrality" Party, run by Bong Souvannavong. Souvanna and Souphanouvong towered over the other figures in terms of name recognition. Katay, who had suffered a stroke, could do little campaigning. Phoui was the Eisenhower administration's preferred candidate, but State and the White House had learned that the best they could hope for was a Souvanna-led government that leaned rightward, perhaps with Phoui as second-in-command.

To achieve that goal, Washington had to avoid a split in conservative votes. Parsons got the party leaders in the pro-Western camp to agree to run only one person per contested seat, thereby pooling their votes and creating what the U.S. Embassy called a "National Front." This arrangement proved costly, as several candidates demanded bribes before withdrawing. There was little cooperation among Souvanna, Phoui, and Katay, who mistrusted one another and had difficulty keeping their followers in line. After a few weeks, the preelection agreement broke down and the number of office-seekers multiplied: by February there were eighty-five conservative candidates competing for the twenty-one seats. Meanwhile, the NLHX and Santiphab had put together a single slate of candidates, and their political cadres were hard at work in the countryside.

Some American civilian and military officials began to worry. "The U.S. has already expended over 130 million dollars in Laos," thundered Admiral Felix Stump, commander in chief, Pacific. "We run the risk of losing this investment if we lose Laos...as a result of [the] May elections." Stump insisted upon "bold action" to retrieve the situation. Parsons, unable to narrow the list of rightist candidates, tried another approach. He persuaded the White House to launch Operation Booster Shot, a village-aid program that flooded rural Laos with food, medical, and other supplies and financed the construction and repair of hospitals, dams, and schools. This $3 million operation was intended to redress the imbalance in U.S. aid, which had until that time been concentrated in the cities. Parsons felt that if the benefits of American assistance spread to the countryside, and if the RLG received credit, villagers would reject Pathet Lao claims that the government was not interested in them.[59]

Booster Shot looked good on paper, but it backfired. The projects covered by the program were selected, Bernard Fall observed, "more for their psychological impact than for their long-range beneficial effect," and some of them were downright silly, such as the air-dropping of leather shoes into remote villages where roads were nonexistent and rains turned the ground to mud for most of the year. While Washington wanted to minimize the U.S. role in Booster Shot and make it appear as though the RLG implemented the program, the Americans did not cover their tracks well. The planes that delivered goods to needy areas bore U.S. Air Force markings, and when State requested unmarked planes it was informed that there was not enough time to paint over the insignia. Civic-action projects that should have been the responsibility of the RLA were often carried out by Americans. The NLHX and Santiphab denounced Booster Shot as foreign interference in Lao affairs. They also—consistency not being an asset in politics—stressed its eleventh-hour nature and milked its few successes for counterpropaganda. "You see, little villagers?" read one broadside. "Now that your votes are precious to the government, you are being showered with gifts. . . . If the government is so rich that it can now give away these things to you, you can imagine how much the government has put away in its coffers for the past years, depriving you of your rightful share of American aid!"[60]

The program generated corruption, as candidates pocketed the money Washington gave them or used it to plug their respective parties instead of the national front. "We thought that politics is politics the world over," recalled a CIA operative, "so we tried to transplant Tammany." In this regard the Americans succeeded only too well. Party hacks like Independent Ngon Sananikone received lines of credit in cash or merchandise from the U.S. Embassy; they then whistle-stopped among their constituencies by pirogue, truck, or plane, showing movies, throwing parties with free drinks, distributing gifts, and exhorting everyone within earshot of their public address systems to vote Independent. At the same time, and often in the same areas, stumpers from the Progressive or Nationalist parties vied for the favors of the electorate, and the Eisenhower administration found itself paying candidates to run against each other. Even within the three main conservative parties there were factions pursuing their own interests and diluting the anti-NLHX vote. The rightists' attempt to buy votes, and the obvious part Americans played in their campaigns, alienated many villagers and made them receptive to NLHX agitprop.[61]

Parsons was still confident of victory. He assured a House subcommittee that "the results of the election will be such that only three or four out of the fifty-nine seats in the full legislature will be held by former Pathet Lao," and that, consequently, "when the present government resigns, as it is committed to do after the elections, a government may be formed which does not include communists." Some Americans thought the NLHX and Santiphab would do a bit better than that, but all expected the conservatives to win most of the twenty-one seats at stake. Howard Jones, deputy assistant secretary for Far Eastern affairs, predicted that the May 4 elections would "represent an important crossroad in Lao history."[62]

They did, although not in the sense Jones intended. When the vote was counted, the NLHX had won a stunning nine seats and the Santiphab four. Souphanouvong received more votes than any other candidate in the country. The news sent shock waves through Washington. Allen Dulles informed Eisenhower that there had been "significant communist success in Laos" and that while the NLHX and its allies would not control the assembly, they would "increase their power." The Eisenhower administration, Dulles said, had "a great deal to fear." With another round of elections scheduled for 1959, it now seemed to many American policymakers that Laos might go communist by a legal vote, the worst possible outcome from Washington's standpoint.[63]

Viewed objectively, matters were not as bleak as that. In fact, over 60 percent of the voters chose pro-Western candidates, while the leftists gained only about a third of the ballots cast. Lao election law, however, granted victory to the candidate with the most votes, regardless of whether that candidate had a majority, and conservative factionalism undermined the anticommunist effort. Unlike the NLHX and Santiphab, who were able to enforce a one-candidate-per-district rule, the rightists fragmented their electoral support by fielding so many candidates. Thus, although conservatives got 680,370 votes to just 256,010 for their opponents, the leftists won thirteen out of twenty-one seats in first-past-the-post voting. Even that strong showing did not signal Laos's imminent retirement behind the iron curtain. There were fifty-nine seats in the assembly, after all, with deputies unacceptable to Washington holding only thirteen. The Italian and French parliaments had a greater proportion of communist or fellow-traveling deputies relative to the majority, and no American policymaker was suggesting that Rome or Paris was on the verge of becoming another Prague.

Souvanna, although unhappy with the election results, understood that they did not change Laos's legislative balance and that, furthermore, their true importance lay in the fact that they marked the fulfillment of the pledges Vientiane had undertaken at Geneva: a government of national union had been established, and fair elections had taken place. Souvanna therefore requested that the ICC adjourn and depart. He also asked his American allies to recognize that NLHX and Santiphab successes did "not indicate a choice of communism by the Lao electorate but simply a protest vote against war and in favor of peace."[64]

Such level-headedness stood in contrast to the angst in Washington, where officials interpreted the election returns as proof that the Lao could not be relied upon even to establish a soft buffer against communist encroachment. Secretary Dulles lashed the RLG as "negligent, self-seeking, or worse." The Operations Coordinating Board admitted that the administration had been "shaken by the communists' show of strength," which it attributed to the "inertia and complacency which pervades conservative political circles." Parsons, who had just returned to the United States to work under Robertson as deputy assistant secretary of state for Far Eastern affairs, delivered the harshest verdict. "[O]nly [the] Lao themselves can save their country," he declared. "This, it seems, is the message which Laos's friends...cannot get across to them." As Parsons saw matters, the RLG had given "little evidence of putting [the] survival [of their] country...ahead of individual self-interest." "We do not wish to see [the] country slip away," he insisted, but the Lao needed to "understand [that] we are near [the] end of our tether."[65]

Washington's zero-sum view of the world, and the domestic political exigencies that made the loss of any nation to communism a liability, ensured that the Eisenhower administration would not let Laos slip away, no matter how disgusted policymakers were with Lao behavior. The 1958 elections, however, prompted a readjustment of U.S. policy toward Laos, one that increased the American presence in that nation and entailed a greater hands-on approach to civil and military affairs. While Americans were sensitive to communist charges of neocolonialism, and while they continued, at least rhetorically, to uphold the integrity of the Vientiane government, they wanted the crusade against red tyranny in Southeast Asia prosecuted efficiently. Hence, within the next two years they had founded a Lao political party of their own, headed by a strongman whose defining feature was his willingness to obey American commands; they had raised an army of mountain tribesmen who exhibited the initiative lacking in the RLA; and they had engineered a coup that plunged Laos into civil war.

Chapter 3

# "Help the Seemingly Unhelpable"

### "Little America" and the U.S. Aid Program in Laos

The August 1958 newsletter for the American Women's Club of Vientiane spotlighted several recent events, most prominently a community theater production of *You Can't Take It with You* performed at the mess hall of the United States Operations Mission (USOM) compound. "Bouquets should be tossed" to an "excellent cast," wrote the newsletter's anonymous drama critic. "The Mekong Players came into their own" with this, their second show, a "comedy in the old tradition of Joseph Jefferson." Singled out for "[s]omething special in the way of bouquets" was Alice Drew, a secretary in the USOM's procurement division, who, readers learned, "went through one rehearsal [*sic*] voiceless due to laryngitis." Drew's "stellar performance" helped make the play a hit, but other cast members received plaudits, too: "[T]here couldn't have been a better Donald than Charlie Searles (loved that Phi Beta Kappa key bit), nor a more likable curmudgeon of a Grandpa than Charlie Anderson." The actors' work was "pointed up by masterful direction" and "abetted by a set that smacked of Raoul Pene du Bois." While the reviewer acknowledged that "most of the audience had a nodding acquaintance with the piece that had been a highly successful Broadway show," this did not prevent them from enjoying "three evenings of fine entertainment—a very salable commodity in this community."

Wedding announcements followed the theater review, as the newsletter revealed that Miss Janet Bell and Sergeant William Wallock had exchanged vows on July 27 at the home of Mr. Rothwell Brown, head of the Programs Evaluation Office (PEO). A few days later, Miss Evelyn Suessenbach, wearing a "full skirted ballerina length dress" of "her own creation," married Mr. Myron Colony at Vientiane's Cathedral of the Sacred Heart. Since Miss Suessenbach's father could not make the trip from Peekskill, New York, to Southeast Asia, the bride was given away by Mr. Henry Hecksher, identified in the newsletter as "first secretary of the American Embassy" but really the Central Intelligence Agency (CIA) station chief in Laos. Additional "Social Notes" concerned the impending arrival and departure of USOM employees, the scarcity of greeting cards, and September's "sewing schedule." The newsletter also gave notice that "conversation coffee" would henceforth be held "on the first and third Wednesdays of each month" and that Mr. and Mrs. Kenneth Matthews had won the USOM bridge tournament.

Sewing, coffees, and card games were only a few of the activities American women in Vientiane could choose among that autumn. According to the newsletter, "career girls interested in an evening class of Interior Decoration" should "contact Sheila Faulkner for more details." Other classes included "Dress Design" and "Pattern Cutting." The USOM teen club needed chaperones. A workshop met "every day now at Bon Berget's," making decorations for the upcoming USOM bazaar. Several first-run movies had been flown in from the States: *Tennessee's Partner* (starring Ronald Reagan), *Never Wave at a WAC,* and *Sea Devils.* And, of course, there was "BINGO! BINGO! BINGO!" which featured "special prizes" that would be "on display later this month." Finally, readers were encouraged to begin preparing for the holidays, even though the fall season had just begun. After all, "a parcel mailed for delivery in the U.S. must travel halfway around the world," which meant that last-minute shopping was not an option. The USOM store had the situation well in hand: "Within the next two weeks you will be able to buy Christmas cards... with 'Season's Greetings from the Kingdom of Laos.' Better come in and order now!"[1]

Except for that last advertisement, a few references to Vientiane, and the term "Mekong Players," there was nothing in the newsletter to indicate its place of origin. The production headlined was of an American comedy, the names dropped in praising it those of an American actor and an American set designer. All the weddings listed were between Americans and, to judge by the newsletter, attended exclusively by Americans. The films shown were American films, featuring American stars, dealing with American themes. The social events involved American women getting together for the same functions they would have engaged in stateside. Not one Lao woman—or Lao man, for that matter—was mentioned. There were no announcements of excursions to Laos's historic or cultural sites, no discussion of the local residents' ways of life, no advice on how to establish friendships with the Lao. Nowhere was there any reference to the political warfare convulsing Laos. The newsletter captured in its five mimeographed pages the almost pathological insularity of the American community in Vientiane.

To be sure, the women's club represented an extreme example of this trend, for obvious reasons: of the almost one hundred USOM workers in 1958, fewer than twenty were female, nearly all of them secretaries. Their jobs kept them deskbound most of the day, unable to travel outside the confines of their offices. The other American women who lived in the USOM compound were the wives and daughters of mission employees. Unlike their husbands and fathers, they did not have a professional obligation to collaborate with the local people. Also, most of them had been socialized to accept a nuclear-family ideal that consigned women to the domestic sphere; it would have required courage for them to venture beyond their "golden ghetto." Add to these impediments a language barrier, and it is not surprising that they had little to do with the Lao.[2]

Unsurprising, but not inevitable. Donna Alvah has demonstrated that American women living overseas in the first decades of the cold war learned about and showed respect for the histories, cultures, and customs of host countries; indeed, they viewed themselves as "unofficial ambassadors" promoting international cooperation by conveying American benevolence and humility. While their efforts succeeded most often in places like West Germany, a "white" country where they felt ethnocultural solidarity with the inhabitants, there were also bridge-building attempts in Asia, Africa, and the Middle East as American women mastered local languages, enrolled their children in local schools, and otherwise tried to counter perceptions of Americans as arrogant. Such unofficial ambassadors could have exercised soft-power influence in Laos during the Eisenhower years, but members of the American Women's Club of Vientiane were more interested in dress design and bingo than in reaching out to host citizens.[3]

Their clannishness mirrored that of America's official representatives: the men and women who staffed the organizations administering American aid—the USOM, PEO, embassy, and United States Information Service (USIS)—and the CIA operatives who worked alongside them. Even by the standards prevailing at hardship posts, the U.S. population in Vientiane was solipsistic. Americans did not involve themselves in the host community. They rarely explored the countryside, exhibited no curiosity about local customs and folklore, and seemed not to care if they were making a positive impression on the Lao. Ensconced in compounds, they went about their business with scarcely any input from the people they were trying to save from communism.

When necessity compelled U.S. aid workers to interact with the Lao, they lectured rather than listened. Never did they treat local inhabitants as allies and friends, certainly not as equals, and they made no attempt to foster a sense of camaraderie, of working shoulder to shoulder in a common cause. In fact, they doubted whether the Lao could contribute anything to the struggle against communist encroachment. For the over two hundred American diplomats, military advisers, engineers, economists, teachers, and other salaried professionals—and their families—residing in Laos, the suffocating heat, mazelike terrain, and lack of overland communications posed less of a challenge than what J. T. Rimer of the USIS called "basic Lao psychology." "The very concept of giving aid, with implications of energy, drive, expansiveness, are [*sic*] sharply countered with the passiveness of the Lao," Rimer declared, arguing that progress in Laos would "necessitate considerable changes in their attitudes." A USOM employee stated matters more bluntly. "The Lao absolutely will not work," she wrote. "It's not in their nature." Long before the U.S. mission in Vientiane was at full strength, lower-, middle-, and upper-echelon officials concluded that the best they could hope for was that the Lao would stand aside while Americans kept the communist bear at bay.[4]

This attitude had consequences beyond antagonizing statesmen like Premier Souvanna Phouma, whose assistance Washington needed if Laos were to become anything other than a tottery stake in the free world's fence against communism. It gave the lie to U.S. claims to support democracy and equality. "The Americans have a lot of money," a Lao villager complained in 1959, "and they give it to the government, and the government must then do as the Americans order." Many Lao saw no difference between this arrangement and the colonial control relinquished by the French—except, perhaps, that Paris had been honest enough not to pretend that Laos was a sovereign state.[5]

American ignorance of and contempt for the Lao also wounded the Eisenhower administration in its most sensitive spot: the pocketbook. Since U.S. officials posted to Laos made no effort to understand the complexities of the country, they conceived and executed projects that did not work in a Lao context and that were extraordinarily wasteful and corrupting. "Dollar for dollar," a State Department representative told reporter Stanley Karnow, "it is about as bad a bargain as international aid money has bought." In mid–1958, a number of newspaper and magazine articles directed American popular attention to what journalists called "the mess in Laos," and the White House suddenly had a scandal on its hands that threatened to undermine its foreign aid program.[6]

Coverage of the maladministration of U.S. assistance marked the first time events in Laos received feature-story treatment from the *Washington Post, Time* magazine, and other major American press outlets. The resulting disclosure of abuses and irregularities made for "wacky reading," according to the *Wall Street Journal*. Americans learned that "Cadillacs, Buicks, and Fords" had been "imported by the dozen," even though Laos's main highways were "hardly more than jungle trails." Other items on Vientiane's import list for 1958 were "four and a half tons of feather dusters, 73 tons of sporting goods,... and thousands of dollars worth of costume jewelry." Meanwhile, plans to build a new airport, a ferry system, and mines to exploit Laos's coal reserves remained unfulfilled, the funds diverted into the pockets of "bigwigs." Even worse, the Royal Lao Army (RLA), whose salaries were paid by U.S. taxpayers, could not be "expected... to make any organized resistance at all if either the Chinese or the Viet Minh should intervene." An outraged Congress convened hearings to investigate why Washington had so little to show for two hundred million dollars spent in Laos. The surreal nature of the malfeasance and incompetence—one magazine called it "fairy-tale implausibility"—reinforced stereotypes of the Lao as improvident children and exacerbated the inclination, in some circles, to cut America's losses and abandon these hopeless people to their fate.[7]

## "Not a Question of Money but of Ideas"

By far the most incisive critic of the American aid mission in Laos was Joel Halpern, a young anthropologist fresh out of Columbia's Ph.D. program when the USOM hired him in late 1956. Halpern did not go to Laos with a chip on his shoulder. He was exhilarated by the prospect of spending two years in Southeast Asia. "I don't think there's anything like a perfect job," he wrote to his parents, but this came close. At twenty-seven, he was not ready to settle down. While admitting that "college teaching seems attractive," he saw little profit in "forcing knowledge into the heads of a lot of people who aren't much interested." He also disliked many of the features of Age-of-Consensus America. "At home, people seem to be all bound up in the pursuit of luxuries," he observed. "It seems really too bad that we have no frontier left." Indochina could be his frontier. "I am a field service officer with the Community Development Division of the International Coopera- tion Administration, working in Luang Prabang, royal capital of Laos," he proclaimed. "Does that sound good?"[8]

The USOM flew Halpern to India for a month to study American- sponsored village improvement as preparation for his assignment in Laos. His wife, Barbara Kerewsky, also an anthropologist, accompanied him. Com- munity Development Director Louis Miniclier agreed to put Kerewsky on the USOM payroll, reasoning that she had "assisted her husband in the past in field observations" in Alaska and Yugoslavia and that it was "important that she have as much background as possible in order to give her an in- formed interest in the work he is doing." This proved a wise investment— from the historian's perspective, if not from the USOM's. Kerewsky's letters home offer one of the best firsthand accounts of intercultural contact, or lack thereof, during the Eisenhower era.[9]

Halpern and Kerewsky arrived in Laos in January 1957, frazzled from their Indian itinerancy but eager to get to work. The scene that greeted them when their plane touched down did not inspire confidence. "The airport, if you can call it that, is an expanse of red dust outside of town," Kerewsky reported. "Off to one side is a shack. I don't mean a wooden building, but a one-storey dilapidated hut with box-like appendages built out from it. This is Vattay, Aerodrome de Vientiane, capital du royaume Lao." No one was on hand to meet the couple, but the plane's pilot sent a messenger to the USOM compound, and in a short while a jeep came to collect them. "Welcome to Laos, rectum of the universe!" the driver an- nounced. Kerewsky assured her family, "It's not nearly as bad as all that."[10]

It was unusual, however, and Halpern began to have misgivings even before he and Kerewsky traveled north to their post in Luang Prabang. Although he liked Vientiane, comparing it to "the frontier towns I saw in Alberta," he noticed that the Americans lived apart from the Lao. "Our American community is pretty self-contained," he observed two weeks after his arrival. The USOM compound was cordoned off by barbed wire, as was a "separate embassy compound made up of prefabricated aluminum houses." Americans flitted between the two compounds, and a third under construction, but most of them did not explore other areas of Vientiane, to say nothing of the provinces. "[I]t is possible, I think, to spend two years— the normal tour of duty—in Laos without ever really coming into contact with the people," Halpern noted. "This is made possible by the grouping of American colonies." In one colony, the USOM's, residents could avail themselves of athletic facilities, libraries, movie theaters, churches, an American restaurant, and a commissary supplying American food. They were not obliged, or even encouraged, to interact with the "natives." As a result, Halpern noted, "of the 200 Americans here, there is only one who can speak Lao to any extent, . . . so it is not hard to see how contacts are limited."[11]

Halpern found Luang Prabang more agreeable. Since the aid mission had yet to gain a footing in the royal capital, there was no sanitized environment for American personnel. Halpern and Kerewsky were the only Americans there for months. The house that the USOM leased for them was, in Kerewsky's words, "the most incongruous thing imaginable," a cream-colored stucco mansion built for colonial officials and in dire need of renovation. The shower lacked a drain; the doors opened only from the inside; and the ceilings "plop[ped] out in big pieces during the night." Every room was furnished with "a full complement of tropical accessories—spiders, gnats, red ants, bullfrogs." They had no privacy: "[T]he neighbors on one side are one meter away, and, on the other side, less than three meters." Many aid workers would have recoiled from this setting, but it was an anthropologist's paradise. Halpern discovered that he could do "casual ethnology simply by sitting at the open window," and Kerewsky was soon "circulat[ing] with ease among all levels of Luang Prabang society, from joining the neighbors under their stilt houses . . . to attending a soiree at the palace." "Really, this place delights me," she gushed. "It's not hard to understand the appeal tropical life had for [Robert Louis] Stevenson."[12]

The longer Halpern and Kerewsky worked in Luang Prabang, the more obvious it became to them that their situation was atypical, that, as Halpern put it, "unlike most Americans, we actually get to meet the Lao people." Kerewsky informed her family that "[i]n Vientiane, most Americans tend to stick together in their fenced-in compound. . . . Thank goodness we are spared that dull existence." At the six-month mark of their tour, the couple paid a visit south to the USOM settlement, where Kerewsky noted the "American ranch houses, with glass-walled living room, . . . fully-equipped kitchen and bathroom, sliding door closet and storage space, hot water heater, garage, [and] screened porch." The air conditioners prompted a twinge of envy, but overall she was unimpressed: "I'd still rather be in L[uang] P[rabang] in our funny square house, where at least I feel I'm living in Laos and learning something about my neighbors."[13]

Frustratingly, though, none of the information she and her husband collected seemed to result in effective community development projects. "I have an almost ideal set up from the point of view of a field anthropologist but a very poor one from the point of view of anyone 'itching' to get things done," Halpern wrote to a stateside colleague. By early March 1957 he had started to wonder "whether Washington knows we are here." He spent weeks in the field inspecting villages and passed along his recommendations to his immediate supervisor, Robert Minges, in Vientiane, but he received scant notice of any plans to improve the villagers' living standards. The USOM, he remarked, "acts as if we didn't exist."[14]

The few projects that were realized tended to be "one shot affairs," sloppily administered. When Halpern reported a need for farming tools in northern Laos, the USOM sent thousands of American-made axes and shovels to Luang Prabang, where a "stream of men, women, and in some cases children" came to collect them. Halpern observed that most recipients "wore wrist watches and other signs of city life"—indicating they were not rural dwellers, the target of the aid. They moreover did not know how to use their new tools, which differed from local agricultural implements. Because the USOM distributed its goods on a first-come, first-served basis, no Hmong, Khmu, or other non-Lao villager obtained assistance, and this confirmed beliefs that the Royal Lao Government (RLG) did not care about the welfare of minorities. American aid thus undermined national cohesion rather than enhancing it.[15]

Other initiatives suffered from a similar lack of planning. They took the form of giveaway projects in which the USOM provided villages with dams, wells, roads, and whatever else the authorities in Vientiane deemed appropriate. Rarely were villagers asked what their needs were. American contractors and third-country nationals from Thailand, South Vietnam, and Japan constructed the dams, dug the wells, and bulldozed the roads while the local residents—the people whom the projects were intended to help—watched. Having contributed no labor or capital, the villagers regarded these services as government charity, which, Halpern noted, could hardly lead to a sense of responsible citizenship. When he inquired why the USOM did not involve host nationals in its operations, he was told that the Lao lacked technical qualifications and that, more important, as one functionary explained, "Laos [*sic*] don't want to work." This presumption of indolence made the USOM loath to waste time instructing villagers on maintenance and repair, with predictable consequences. After a few months, the dams broke down, the wells ran dry, and rain washed the roads away, leaving local inhabitants back where they started—and resentful to boot, because the USOM had built up expectations the RLG could not fulfill.[16]

**Figure 2.** The opening of a dam project undertaken by the United States Operations Mission in Luang Prabang, 1957. Joel Martin Halpern Laotian Slide Collection, University of Wisconsin–Madison.

"[T]he situation is quite fouled up as far as getting a program going," Halpern wrote his father. "Basically, it is not a question of money but of ideas." Every day he spent doing fieldwork convinced him that the USOM "could use a lot of constructive scrutiny on the part of those who value the taxpayers' dollar." American efforts to win hearts and minds were failing. Villagers had many complaints. They wanted to participate in the development of their communities, and it irked them when they were not consulted about what kind of help they required. They deplored the absence of continuity in USOM projects. Why, they asked, did the mission not train local people to mend and preserve the public works bestowed by Washington? Why were there never any follow-up evaluations to determine whether an aid project had achieved its desired effect? The most frequent objection, recorded over and over in Halpern's notes, was that not enough assistance was reaching the countryside. "Yes, I know all about American aid," snapped the headman of a village on the bank of the Mekong opposite Luang Pra-bang. "It goes straight to the Big Palace, and what is left over trickles in to us." In another village upstream, a blacksmith remarked, "I once went to Vientiane and saw all kinds of equipment there.... This is American aid, isn't it? Then why don't we get any of it here in northern Laos?"[17]

Halpern empathized with the villagers, especially when he contrasted their plight with the profligacy of the administrative capital. "Vientiane, as far as I am concerned, is disgusting," he asserted in early September. "I feel this way for a number of reasons." First, "a good part of our aid is concentrated there and never gets outside the city limits." Second, even within those limits, the aid was misdirected: "There is an air-conditioned nightclub plus many other types of luxury consumer goods. Building is going on like crazy with absolutely no planning." Movie theaters, dance halls, and bars sprang up all over town, but there was no sewage system to dispose of the waste. Refuse collected in ditches covered by wooden planks. Five thousand broad-tailed automobiles jammed the roads, which could barely accommodate oxcarts. There were no sidewalks, but retail shops were stocked to their ceilings with Roy Rogers T-shirts, Colgate toothpaste, and Vicks inhalers. Black marketeering and smuggling were rife. Ministers who had previously lived in bamboo houses and ridden bicycles to work now owned European-style villas and Cadillacs. Other well-placed Lao enjoyed lifestyles that their official salaries could never have supported. The infusion of American funds had the effect not only of underscoring class differences in Vientiane but also of making the gap between city and province greater.

U.S. officials were undisturbed by this boomtown atmosphere because they were isolated from it. "Embassy people have prefabs with air con-ditioning and wrought iron furniture, while the USOM has 14 new houses... built very similarly to 'ranch houses' at home," Halpern fumed. "In either of these 'communities,' with your commissary food, you might as well be in the States." He witnessed a "good index of contact between the Americans and Lao" at a party thrown for Minges, chief of the Field Service Division, who had just resigned his post. Out of some eighty guests at the party, Halpern observed, three were Lao, two of whom "Minges did not know."[18]

To Halpern, the scatterbrained administration of U.S. aid, in concert with the lack of interaction between Americans and Lao, was playing into the hands of the communists, giving them issues on which to score propa-ganda points. He noted that much of Prince Souphanouvong's popularity derived from the fact that he and his followers refused to accept gifts from

Washington and lived among villagers. Meanwhile, the Americans' sequestration generated rancor among those Lao in sympathy with U.S. objectives. Sincerely anticommunist rural people and town dwellers saw the embassy and USOM as sanctums of privilege, off-limits to the native population. This cost America friends it could ill afford to lose.

Like many Americans during the post–World War II, pre–Vietnam War era, Halpern accepted without scruple the notion that the United States had an obligation to block red advances wherever they occurred, regardless of the strategic or economic value of the territory in question, and like many educated liberals he was frustrated by what he considered the Eisenhower administration's unimaginativeness when it came to dealing with the communist challenge in postcolonial areas. "Anthropologists could be of real help here," Halpern asserted, "but as far as I can see [the] USOM has never brought the use of social sciences into their operations." He was shaken by an encounter with Prince Phetsarath, Laos's elder statesman, who had just returned home after ten years of exile and who declared that, in his opinion, the greatest danger facing his country was not communism but the "corrupt" disbursal of foreign money, most of which disappeared in unsolicited projects carried out on a crash basis. Phetsarath appreciated U.S. aid, admitting that Laos "could not survive for long" without it; still, he advised the Americans to "see more carefully the ways in which it is used." Black-marketed luxuries were no substitute for health care and education when it came to persuading rural Lao to cast their lot with the West.[19]

After what he termed "eight months of inactivity," a frustrated Halpern went over the heads of his Vientiane superiors and wrote to the community development director, Louis Miniclier, in Washington. "I have now completed one-third of my tour in Laos and have done exactly nothing in community development," he declared. If an "active community development program" could not be put into effect in the Lao countryside, he recommended that "serious consideration be given to eliminating the Field Service." This would leave him out of work, but, as he wrote to his parents, "your little sonny boy has a conscience and I feel I should be attempting to do the job that it is costing Uncle Sam $10,000 a year to do."[20]

Halpern's letter to Miniclier earned him an admonition to "follow official channels" when discussing mission business. "I have absolutely no regrets," he noted. "My position is on the record." His correspondence with USOM officers in Vientiane grew more obstreperous. He reminded Robert Smither, Minges's successor, that "[f]requent attempts, via field observations

and interviews, have been made to determine and analyze village development and other needs in northern Laos." As far as Halpern knew, "none of
these efforts has resulted in the planning of any concrete projects." News
of the Soviet launch of *Sputnik* strengthened Halpern's conviction that his
country, swimming in money but bereft of ideas, was losing the cold war.
"I like to believe that when the challenge has been laid down our people
will rise to the occasion," he wrote, "but do we clearly realize that the
challenge has been laid down?...I think it will be an excellent thing if the
Russians soon launch another and bigger 'Sputnik' to jarr [*sic*] us out of
our complacency and make us see that world leadership does not consist
of Edsels, television spectaculars, Relax magazines, and frozen foods." This
was the lesson the bureaucrats in Vientiane could not seem to grasp. Out-
spending the communists and providing more consumer items meant nothing if American projects failed to meet local needs and American conduct
estranged the Lao.[21]

## *"Bo Pen Nyang"*

All the objections Halpern raised in 1957 would be put forward by more
prominent critics the following year, when the "mess in Laos" scandal
broke and *The Ugly American* rocketed to the top of the bestseller lists.
That novel, a publishing sensation, has been compared to *Uncle Tom's
Cabin* in terms of its impact on American public discourse. Authors
William J. Lederer and Eugene Burdick brilliantly exploited cold war
fears by dramatizing, in a series of cautionary tales set in the fictional
Southeast Asian country of Sarkhan, how the U.S. Foreign Service fostered the spread of communism. The diplomats and foreign-aid officials
portrayed in *The Ugly American* lived in compounds, isolated from the
world around them; they supported impractical programs that wasted
American tax dollars; they neither understood their enemy—having
never read the works of Mao Zedong—nor their allies, whom they held
in contempt. The free world's only hope lay in independent operatives like Homer Atkins, the ugly American of the book's title, whose
homeliness concealed his inner virtue and who, unlike the behaviorally
ugly organization men in their air-conditioned enclaves, recognized the
need to tackle Sarkhan's problems at the grassroots level. Atkins worked
alongside the residents of the village of Chang 'dong, befriending them,
learning their language, and helping them build a bicycle-based water

pump that did more to improve their lives than the highways and dams bankrolled by Washington. He thereby demonstrated how the United States could win the fight against communism in the third world. But time was slipping away. The Foreign Service needed fewer hacks and more Atkinses: resourceful professionals unafraid of getting their hands dirty. While Lederer and Burdick never met Halpern, their "factual epilogue" read like a paraphrase of his field notes, as they warned, "If the only price we are willing to pay is the dollar price, then we might as well pull out."[22]

*The Ugly American* made a number of valid points. U.S. Foreign Service personnel in Southeast Asia did lack language training and often offended host nationals with their arrogance. Many of the projects they approved were inappropriate, given conditions in the countryside. Nevertheless, as several historians have noted, Lederer and Burdick's jeremiad fairly pulsed with ethnocentrism. None of the Asians in *The Ugly American* displayed agency or independent thought, and the book's heroes, those "good" Americans who integrated themselves into foreign cultures and won converts for the free world, achieved this objective either through deceit—one American officer, upon learning that his Asian hosts believed in palmistry, pretended to read pro-U.S. military maneuvers off the premier's palm—or by tutoring the peasants as one would a child. Despite their demand for greater sensitivity to local history and customs, Lederer and Burdick's own understanding of the political situation in Southeast Asia was shallow; the solutions they proposed obscured the role of nationalism and reduced Asians to pawns. Similarly, Halpern's insight into the problems plaguing the aid mission in Laos did not prevent him from making statements about the Lao that echoed, to a degree, the sneers of USOM bureaucrats. That a sensitive, well-traveled man—indeed, a trained anthropologist—could record such observations indicates the power of those ideas, values, and prejudices that influenced American perceptions of Asia at midcentury.[23]

"I really think the Lao have some feelings—at least in some cases," Halpern informed his family as he approached the halfway point of his assignment. The son of Luang Prabang's chief of agriculture had died "the day before" of grippe, and Halpern noticed that the chief appeared "saddened, although even in this case his feelings were suppressed." Lao insouciance was a persistent theme in Halpern's notes and letters. "I think one of the big differences between Americans and Laotians is bound up in the word 'worry,'" he asserted. "[T]he local equivalent of 'Que sera, sera' is Bo pen

Nyang.... [I]t can have a great many meanings; the most common is that 'It doesn't matter.'" And as far as Halpern could tell, that idiom summed up the psychology of the Lao. Little mattered to them—or, rather, little mattered much. They could be momentarily dejected, apprehensive, or put out, but they did not exhibit potent desires or fears. Halpern ascribed the "lack of striving and strong competitive feeling" he found to "the Buddhist religion, which discourages these things," and noted that "throughout Southeast Asia much of the most profitable business is in the hands of the Chinese, who have quite a different philosophy." While he conceded the positive side of Buddhist sangfroid—"after all our worrying and ulcers we die in the end anyhow.... [A]m I beginning to sound like a Buddhist?"—it made implementing an aid program well-nigh impossible. The typical Lao villager was "not dissatisfied" with the status quo, he admitted. Americans might see untapped potential in Laos and hear Beijing's not-too-distant guns, but the villagers themselves were blind and deaf.[24]

At times, Halpern considered Lao complacency a greater obstacle to progress than the time servers in Vientiane. "I don't really think the Lao are much interested in community development," he wrote. "There is no 'covek mora da radi' ('a man must work') ethos here." Whereas in India he had witnessed "a definite will for ... development," the Lao were "mostly interested in having a good time." "[T]his is a recreation and ceremonially oriented society," he declared, noting that "one time a car failed to meet a visiting UNESCO delegation and the governor explained that it was engaged in transporting people to a boun [festival]," which Lao administrators deemed "more important." Although Halpern never expressed the scorn for the Lao shown in embassy cables and other official dispatches, familiar adjectives punctuated his commentary: "placid," "supine," "unresponsive," "lazy," "tranquil."[25]

Halpern's lapses, if they may be so termed, were minor compared to Kerewsky's. A gifted writer, Kerewsky enjoyed conveying her experience in Laos to family and friends. "Forgive my adjectives," she effervesced in one letter. "I frequently get carried away." Her descriptions of Lao culture and customs were more polished than the reports Halpern dashed off every evening, and were often funny; an account of graduation ceremonies at Luang Prabang's lone high school would have merited publication in *Reader's Digest* or a similar middlebrow journal. Yet the Lao Kerewsky portrayed bore no resemblance to the warriors who had held off a Viet Minh drive on Luang Prabang four years earlier. Instead, they alternated between two stereotypes, both derisive. When Kerewsky felt favorably disposed toward the

Lao, she depicted them as children of nature, unacquainted with modern civilization's rat race:

> Life seems something of an idyl [*sic*]; nothing very much concerns or bothers people. If something occurs to temporarily disrupt the tranquility, the reaction is "Bo pen yang—it really doesn't matter." The Lao, it would appear, are satisfied with life and have little desire to change it.... Nobody hurries, nobody bothers, and everybody has a toothy, betel-stained smile.[26]

Kerewsky wrote that she had been "annoyed, when in Washington, to read generalizations about Lao character," but that her stay in Luang Prabang had convinced her that "they are true, and that the generalizations indeed hold for almost anyone." *All* Lao were "smiling, carefree, lackadaisical," and their "life" was "a very simple thing—for food you catch a fish or open a coconut." Furthermore, they were the most peaceful people on earth: "Buddhism prohibits the harming or killing of any kind of life, and our Lao friends have cringed when we, unconsciously, have slapped a mosquito from our ankle." If they fell short as gladiators in the struggle against communism, they were nonetheless irresistible in their innocence and amiability.[27]

On those occasions when the Lao tried Kerewsky's patience, they became "lethargic Asians," immune to enlightenment, ungrateful for aid. "The Lao are very passive," she complained in early October 1957. "Sometimes I can't help wishing they would react, emote a little, even negatively, and I can't resist comparing them to the ebullient Serbs." The most disturbing event of her term in Laos occurred when she accompanied a U.S. medical team to the northern village of Nam Tha, which was "in the midst of a whooping-cough epidemic." "One child died," she wrote, "simply because the Lao do not hurry or get excited." The toddler "choked on phlegm, and if her father had walked quickly, instead of ambled, over to call Tan Mau (Mr. Doctor)," the physician "could have saved her in time." Instead, the father's lack of initiative resulted in tragedy. Such "crumbling nonchalance" left Kerewsky, as "a product of a goal-oriented society," mystified. She pitied the missionaries posted to Luang Prabang, because "the Lao do not react to prothelytizing [*sic*], just as they do not respond to anything."[28]

Aid workers fared the same. Kerewsky noted that if an American agricultural adviser demonstrated that a villager could "double his rice yield by using certain techniques," the Lao was "delighted," but not by the prospect of a surplus: "[N]ow he will only have to go to the trouble of cultivating half as much land." More time for sleep! No wonder, then, that "Chinese immigrants" outstripped the native population in earnings. They were "much more on the ball and aggressive," Kerewsky observed, and "their children seem inherently brighter."[29]

Many of Kerewsky's letters from Luang Prabang addressed "our only unsolved big problem, servants." "I didn't want to bring a good Vietnamese girl up from Vientiane," she wrote, "because I idealistically thought it would be just as simple to get someone here." She discovered, however, that housekeeping held little appeal for the locals, even if she was prepared to offer a salary several times larger than Laos's per capita income. The first candidate, a "coolie" named Saiiy, "lasted four days" before quitting. Then the head office in Vientiane dispatched a young couple who, Kerewsky noted, "whimpered like poor lost animals until we had to send them back." Next came Lon, who "learned pretty well" but whose work ethic was distinctly Lao. While Kerewsky "persuade[d] him to sweep outside and pump the water," he balked at washing the jeep: "[H]e said he was tired and it was too much work." Lon handed in his resignation before Kerewsky could discharge him. "All this is right in line in the land of Bo pen yang," she grumbled, where the "pace of life" was so "lethargic" as to seem "literally at a standstill."[30]

Exasperated, Kerewsky finally hired Le, a Vietnamese refugee from Hanoi. "[S]he retains the long black silk Vietnamese trousers and mushroom-shaped bamboo hat," Kerewsky noted. More important, "[s]he has the Vietnamese attributes of diligence and hard work." Anxious to spare other USOM recruits frustration, Kerewsky warned a woman preparing to join the American community in Luang Prabang, "The Lao will not work as servants, for it is not in their nature to follow fixed daily routines, so that is why we have a Vietnamese."[31]

Nearly all U.S. officials posted to Laos in the late 1950s shared the view that the Lao were workshy, and like Kerewsky they pointed up Lao stagnancy by contrasting it with Vietnamese drive. Franklin Huffman, an instructor with International Voluntary Services, recalled having to "segregate the English classes" he taught because "the Lao were very happy-go-lucky and laid back and never did any homework; the Vietnamese were bright and quick and worked hard and learned much faster than the Lao." They also had better heads for business, it seemed. "The Vietnamese were the entrepreneur class," asserted Yale Richmond, a public affairs officer with USIS. "All of the stores and little shops [in Vientiane] were either owned by Vietnamese, Indians, or Chinese. The Lao people were not entrepreneurs."

Leonard Bacon, deputy chief of mission in Vientiane, attributed the dissimilarity to environment, speculating that competition for scarce resources had bred in the Vietnamese, Indians, and Chinese a sense of industry and thrift, whereas underpopulated, provident Laos made no such demands upon its inhabitants. "Living is very easy for the Lao," affirmed Bacon. "They can sit under a tree and pick bananas as they fall, and that's all they need to do." Bacon found Lao phlegm as annoying as other Americans did, but he recognized that it also presented a deterrent to the communists, who, he said, "couldn't possibly get very far in Laos because the thought of working your head off for the government, or anybody, never occurred to anyone." Public affairs officer Gerard Gert was less sanguine, remembering, "When my colleague from Cambodia said the Cambodians suffer from an inferiority complex as compared to the Vietnamese, I got up and said, 'Well, my people in Laos, we don't have an inferiority complex. We *are* inferior to the rest of you.'" Gert conceded that this "was not nice to say about the Lao, but that's the way I often felt about that place. There was just so little to work with."[32]

These remarks give some indication of why Americans and Lao never developed a relationship based on mutual respect, and why Halpern's final reports from Luang Prabang were so despairing. Forced by a family illness to return to the United States, Halpern cut short his USOM career in 1958. "[T]he outlook for our program is not very hopeful," he wrote shortly before departing for home. "I honestly don't think anything is going to happen." As for Laos's "political situation," he admitted that "there is no use pretending it is good because it isn't." The "Commies" were in a better position to "take over this country" than had been the case a year ago. Halpern did not consider matters "hopeless," but he left Southeast Asia with a profound sense of disappointment, telling a missionary acquaintance, "I feel deeply my inability to do anything constructive for the people during my year in Laos." He would try to do more for them back in America.[33]

## "A Failure and Waste of Money"

By the fall of 1958, Halpern was, in his words, "settling into the academic life." He had accepted a position as assistant professor at the University of California at Los Angeles (UCLA), where he found the "routine of class work" a "pleasant experience." Although he planned to travel overseas again—"I'd be bored to death to spend the rest of my life in the States"—he began putting down roots. He "made the big leap" of buying a house and welcomed the birth of his first child. The University of California Press offered him a book contract. His days were filled with the junior academic's usual concerns: teaching, research, publication, and promotion.[34]

He remained interested in Laos, however, and the eruption of the U.S. aid scandal prompted him to write an essay that was first circulated by the Council on Economic and Cultural Affairs and subsequently appeared in *Practical Anthropology.* Titled "Economic Development and American Aid," the piece was so urgent in tone that Halpern opened it with a disclaimer, assuring readers that he considered "some type of aid program" for Laos "essential." Nevertheless, he declared, the present program was a "complete failure." Evidence for this conclusion was overwhelming: Pathet Lao gains in the May 1958 elections, the miserable performance of the RLA under fire, lack of long-term economic progress, and corruption on a scale so colossal it staggered belief.

Yet these manifestations of U.S. defeat were only symptoms of a deeper problem, which Halpern termed "Little America" and defined as "the intellectual culture of official American government personnel residing in Vientiane." It also included "American material imports which have made possible...a way of life fundamentally similar to that of middle-class government workers in Washington, D.C." Halpern noted that aid officials arrived in Laos ignorant of the country where they would spend the next two years. He and his wife had been able to transcend this ignorance because they had plunged into the lifestyle of Luang Prabang and been compelled to adapt to local mores, but the "overwhelming majority" of Americans worked within the confines of "barbed-wire compounds" in the administrative capital. They lived in "American ranch-style homes." They ate at "a restaurant serving only American food." Religious and recreational activities were "exclusively American," with aid workers worshipping at churches maintained by American missionaries, attending cocktail parties and other social events "within the American community," and keeping fit at "a swimming pool built exclusively for the use of American personnel." In short, Americans in Vientiane enjoyed "an existence completely independent of the local culture." Washington had spent millions to create a replica of an American suburb on the other side of the world.

The results were disastrous. Aid workers, comfortable in their oasis, never left it. They learned nothing about the "surrounding social and cultural matrix" and wrongly presumed that "American concepts apply" to the "way of life of the Lao." Fervent believers in the virtues of a consumer economy, they created an aid program in which the "most important activity" was "the one under which various goods are imported into the country." Commodities flooded Vientiane through the American pipeline, most of them "luxuries and not necessities": perfume, roller skates, motorcycles, and expensive cars. The assumption behind this cascade of trinkets was that the Lao, dazzled by American abundance, would cast their lot with the free world. Yet the strategy backfired, encouraging aspirations that were incapable of fulfillment and deepening hostility toward the RLG. U.S. munificence "accentuat[ed] social and class differences" in Vientiane, where, Halpern wrote, there had "never been really great differences in material wealth" before the Americans arrived. Even the premier had lived in a bamboo house, and vice-ministers cycled to work. By 1957, however, the economic, and therefore the social, distance between upper- and lower-class city residents was vast, the gulf between capital and hinterland unbridgeable. Villagers who saw or heard of Vientiane's array of goods and services knew that they could not afford them, and this, insisted Halpern, had political repercussions, making it "easier for local communists to increase their influence."

While Americans' reckless provision of commodities in Vientiane undermined the aid program, their public-works projects in the provinces were even more counterproductive. They did not ask villagers what kind of government assistance they wanted, presuming that local ambitions accorded with American objectives. U.S. technicians and third-country nationals showed up at a designated spot with their heavy equipment and built roads, dug wells, and constructed other village facilities. Then, Halpern noted, "[a]s far as they were concerned, the project was finished business." Was it, though? Since the USOM never conducted any opinion polls, Washington could not know if its activity succeeded in enlisting the support of the rural population. Were villagers grateful for the new road, well, or schoolhouse? Would they use these services? Did they even associate them with the United States? Often, the answer was no, and the USOM magnified its error by lack of long-range planning. Although crafting policy for an extended term was complicated, since the funds available from year to year fluctuated depending on congressional appropriations, there was no reason why the mission could not conduct post-factum reviews of its projects. Why not have technicians visit a village every few months after the donation of a well to ensure that it did not become polluted? Or, better yet, why not teach the villagers to clean the well themselves? That solution, so obvious, had few backers in Vientiane's air-conditioned retreats, where, as

Halpern recalled, "[m]any Americans connected with the mission claimed that it was difficult if not impossible to train Lao." Given such views, was it any wonder that villagers had no sense of participation in the national life? Laos would never become a viable state until Lao organizations—Lao-led, Lao-manned, and recognized as legitimate by the Lao—performed the same functions discharged by Americans. To treat villagers as passive beneficiaries of U.S. charity was to encourage dependence and replace one colonial master with another.

Halpern's suggestions for reforming the aid mission flowed logically from his analysis. Local personnel should be used in community development projects, he wrote. Continuity in operations was vital. Emphasis ought to be on the kind of U.S. aid supplied, not the amount of aid. The USOM must do things *with* local inhabitants, not *for* them. Halpern knew that "[m]any will scoff at these ideas and say they are impossible." He did not share this view, but if it was correct then Washington would be better off with "no aid program at all." "Little America is basically a failure and waste of money," he proclaimed. "Another alternative must be sought."

As Halpern noted in the preface, his essay was to receive "limited distribution" before publication "in the hope that it may elicit comments." That hope was fulfilled, although not, perhaps, as Halpern anticipated. Members of the American community in Laos, and officials in Washington responsible for shaping U.S. policy toward that country, responded wrathfully. USOM director Daly Lavergne found Halpern's piece "objectionable," Assistant Director for Economic Policy Monroe Burk thought it "tilt[ed] against windmills," and Miniclier, Halpern's old boss, sniffed, "You sound at times like 'one of the angry young men.'" Frank Corrigan of the USIS admonished Halpern for writing "with considerably more haste and indignation than scholarship" and dismissed his "little treatise" as "valueless," "ignorant," "shallow," and "dead as yesterday's news."[35]

The blandest reaction came, ironically, from the man with most cause to feel insulted. J. Graham Parsons had been U.S. ambassador to Laos during Halpern's term of service, and had returned to the United States around the time Halpern did to become deputy assistant secretary of state for Far Eastern affairs. Given that Parsons outranked all other Americans in Laos for the period Halpern examined, he might have taken the article as a calumny against "his" mission. Yet he dictated a pleasant reply. "I think we both realize the difficulties in trying to operate a really effective aid program in Laos," he declared. "However, the fact that Laos has remained on our side...is, I believe, a real accomplishment." Halpern should be aware, too, that reforms were under way: "A genuine rural and village improvement program is now being implemented in Laos, and we are hopeful of its salutary effects."[36]

The deputy assistant secretary may have expected Halpern, thus reassured, to withdraw his manuscript from publication. Since Washington already had matters under control, why disseminate an article that would create controversy? Instead, Halpern wrote Parsons asking for details. "I was very much intrigued," he said, by "your sentence" concerning advancement in the rural improvement program, and he wondered if it would be "possible for you to amplify this statement, or tell me where I could obtain concrete information on these matters."[37]

Parsons never responded. This was probably not a deliberate snub. He was just too busy during the final months of 1958 and all of the following year to maintain correspondence with a junior professor. The "mess in Laos" scandal, with its attendant headlines and congressional investigations, held the potential to kill the Eisenhower administration's projected foreign-aid package. Parsons and his colleagues at the Far Eastern desk were working sixteen-hour days to defuse the crisis, a crisis Parsons had done more than anyone to create. Although Halpern refrained from singling out Parsons by name, he would have been justified in holding him responsible for the grimmest defects in the U.S. aid program and asserting that Little America was, to a considerable extent, one man's psyche writ large.

## "The Ignominious Architect"

J. Graham Parsons dominated Laos policy for most of the Eisenhower years, first as ambassador, then as deputy assistant secretary, and finally as Walter Robertson's successor as assistant secretary of state for Far Eastern affairs. Rarely has a diplomatic actor been more miscast. Unacquainted with Lao political realities, incapable of viewing the alliance between Vientiane and Washington as anything other than a servant-master or child-parent relationship, Parsons caused havoc at every turn. Shortly before John F. Kennedy's ascension to the presidency, Lao premier Souvanna Phouma denounced Parsons as "the most reprehensible and nefarious of men, . . . the ignominious architect of [the] disastrous American policy toward Laos." This indictment was, in the main, deserved, although Parsons's superiors at State and in the White House bore their share of responsibility; despite complaints from the Lao government,

Washington kept Parsons in a position of authority—indeed, promoted him—during Eisenhower's second term. Whether because of presidential inattention, bureaucratic inertia, institutional loyalty, or because, owing to the paucity of Southeast Asia experts in Washington, there really was no one better equipped for the position, Parsons escaped censure, at least in American circles, until it was too late.[38]

Parsons's relationship with Souvanna, addressed in the previous chapter, was representative of the cultural tone-deafness he brought to his duties. If Charles Yost considered Laos backward and fatiguing, Parsons vaulted beyond such views into outright xenophobia. Laos epitomized everything he loathed: idleness, incompetence, squalor, and, above all, disorder. As functionaries who worked under Parsons in Vientiane noted, the ambassador prided himself on being "a real pro," a perfectionist who scrupulously observed standard operating procedures. He had spent two decades in the Foreign Service by the time Eisenhower tapped him for Laos, filling posts in Japan, Cuba, Italy, India, Nepal, and Canada, and his career represented a case of travel narrowing the mind. With each promotion, he grew more pedantic, preoccupied with process rather than content. He was a bureaucrat to the depths of his being. Because he lacked imagination and flexibility, he was comfortable with the black-and-white view of international relations promulgated by John Foster Dulles. USIS officer Perry Stieglitz remembered Parsons as "rigid in his convictions," certain that the world was divided into two blocs of nation-states and that "neutralism was synonymous with anti-Americanism." This perspective left Parsons ill-equipped to manage U.S.-Lao relations and ensured that, for two years in Vientiane and three in Washington, he would find himself alternately bewildered and enraged by Laos's refusal to follow the American cold war rule book.[39]

To begin with, Laos did not hang together as a state. "The nation to which I was accredited was hardly a nation at all," Parsons recalled. "[I]t was a geographic expression, . . . named for the principal ethnic component, the Lao." Yet that component made up only between 50 and 60 percent of the population. More people of Lao origin lived in Thailand than in Laos. A complete classification of the kingdom's ethnic groups had never been attempted, but there were over forty of them, some comprising only a few hundred persons, most "living in self-contained villages," as separate from one another as if they occupied different planets. With ethnic disunity came linguistic disunity: Laos was a babel of tongues; about twenty dialects were spoken in Phong Saly Province alone. Religion did not tie the country together, either; although the Lao constitution designated Buddhism as the state religion, animist beliefs were widespread, with every tribal cluster worshipping its own version of *phi*, spirits associated with natural phenomena. The RLG, for its part, provided no cohesion; fewer than 10 percent of Lao knew the name of their premier, and only one-fifth could identify the king, who had reigned for fifty-six years. Even Laos's borders were fuzzy, especially the Lao-Vietnamese boundary; during the period of French colonialism, Paris had never demarcated where one colony ended and another began. "[L]ittle landlocked Laos," Parsons declared, was "more a name on a map than an organized nation."[40]

It also seemed out of place in the modern age of superpower conflict. Parsons acknowledged that many nations lagged behind the West politically and economically, but Laos was "the most underdeveloped country I have seen," lacking everything that might be termed lack-able. Transportation was virtually nonexistent. Washington could not get assistance to those who needed it because of the absence of rail lines and paved roads. Anyone wanting to travel from Vientiane to Luang Prabang required "a four-wheel-drive vehicle, lots of time, no floods, and a tolerance for the unusual"; when Parsons made the trip, it took him two days, and his car nearly slid off the side of a mountain. Travel by plane likewise proved difficult, since most airports functioned only during the dry season. It was impossible for the government to communicate with far-flung provinces, because there were no telephones, television sets, or newspapers. There was moreover no industry. The economy was based on subsistence agriculture and bartering, and 80 percent of the population had never used the Lao currency. Laos exported nothing, apart from a pittance of coffee, tin, and tobacco. The illiteracy rate stood at near 90 percent, with little chance of dropping, and other indices of underdevelopment—infant mortality, illness, low life expectancy—were similarly off the charts. Parsons concluded that Laos was in the "fourteenth century," an anachronism blindsided by the contest between America and the Soviet Union. Neither communist nor capitalist, nor even feudal, it scarcely existed in twentieth-century terms: "No more obvious vacuum of power, no greater vulnerability, could be imagined."[41]

Worse than the dearth of national unity and the civilizational backwardness were the Lao themselves, "the frail and incompetent human material with which we had to work," as Parsons described them. Parsons was familiar with Dulles's vow to make Laos a "bastion of freedom," but he concluded days after deplaning in Vientiane that "it would be difficult to make Laos into a flea flicker." The problem was simple: most Lao were oblivious to the cold war, and those who were aware of it felt no obligation to choose sides, much less fight for a side. "Communism...evokes little comprehension," Parsons advised State in late 1956; this explained why "'Souvanna-ism' or neutralism" remained popular. The "naïve and weak" premier was typical of his countrymen, who, in contrast to the "ferocity" of the Vietnamese, "wished only to be left alone." They were "the least war-like, most passive of all of the components of the Indo-China peninsula," the ambassador proclaimed. Even had Laos possessed a coherent society and an industrial economy, it would still have been a miserable ally because of the population's moral obtuseness and pacifism.[42]

The trait that most rankled Parsons, though—if we may judge by the number of times he mentioned it in cables, letters, interviews, and a memoir—was "Laotian languor." "[T]he local people are extremely lethargic," he asserted, "and dealing with them is overly taxing to one's patience." Like his predecessor, Yost, Parsons had trouble adjusting to what he termed "fundamentally different standards of behavior." He lectured a reporter that whereas "Americans are a dynamic and energetic people," the Lao were anything but, and this made it "hard" to "transfer the American frame of reference...into the Lao frame of reference." Policymakers had to be aware, he said, of "the things that go wrong in Laos and have tradition-ally gone wrong: that for some reason they won't be able to move until tomorrow or the day after tomorrow, and when they do, there won't be as many of them or they won't be quite as energetic as had been anticipated." If the Lao were "charming" and "inoffensive," they were also "static" and "feckless," which meant that there was always a "gap between Lao words and Lao performance." The "natural bent of the Lao to take things easily" made them unreliable either on the battlefield or in the workplace.[43]

In chapter-length anecdotes that could have been written by a frustrated colonial plantation owner, Parsons's memoir conveyed his disdain for the people he had been sent to help. One chapter, "The Great Mango Caper," told the story of Peng, whom Parsons employed as a gardener but whose "skills and application to that role were as those of my first-grade grandson to those of a veritable Einstein." Peng was "Lao through and through, ami-able as most Lao are, and very fond indeed of mangoes." In fact, the "avail-ability of mangoes" in Parsons's garden was the "reason why he stayed with us,...because Peng was certainly not a convert to the market economy. Wealth did not interest him. Mangoes did." Every year, when "the mangoes began to ripen," Peng lay under a tree, "absorbing mangoes as they fell, the point of satiety seemingly never reached." Parsons indulged this behavior until the day when a cabin-sized refrigerated storage space was delivered to the garden and Peng, unaware that the "larder had for the first time been stocked to capacity with sides of beef, Virginia hams, [and] frozen vegetables," opened the door to luxuriate in the frosty air. "[A]s the door did not face the residence," Parsons wrote, "tranquil enjoyment was reasonably assured" and "Peng gorged, oblivious to all else." When Peng's consumption resulted in an upset stomach, he "departed with unaccustomed urgency, leaving the door still ajar" and the food spoilt. Parsons did not intend this vignette to call up images of shiftless field hands in antebellum proslavery literature or Hollywood icons like the pseudonymous character actor Sleep 'n' Eat, but he nonetheless drew upon a tradition of legitimating dominance by portraying nonwhite peoples as childlike, primitive, and unwilling to work except under coercion.[44]

The most revealing chapter, "Aid to Laos," dealt with Washington's gift of three fire engines to the Lao government, a gesture Parsons considered representative of "the socially useful, so we thought, 'projects' which . . . produced unexpected contrasts between American expectations and Laos [*sic*] realities." Parsons had recommended that Washington donate the engines because "the filigree of antique overhead wiring that laced central Vientiane" posed a fire hazard, but the Lao did not think in such pragmatic terms: "For the Lao, fire engines were good—bright, shiny, mobile . . . —and the impressive jet streams of water they produced were fun." The U.S. Embassy arranged a contest to find out which of three Lao fire companies could extinguish a blaze fastest. "No one in the diplomatic corps," recalled Parsons, "had ever seen the Lao, normally expert at conserving human energy, move so rapidly." Once the games were over, however, the fire companies dissolved; days later, when a house burst into flames, no one responded. "[W]e had reckoned without the Lao genius for doing what came most easily," Parsons noted. It turned out that the few firemen who still showed up for work were making extra money "nonchalantly delivering water to the house of a cabinet minister." Thus they and their vehicle were miles away from the station house when the fire alarm sounded. The punch line—or, as Parsons put it, the "ironic twist of fate"—was that "[t]he fire had been in the home of one Eric Faley in 'Silver City,' a cluster of prefabs constructed for the United States Aid Mission, donor of fire protection to the capital city." Readers could be expected to concur with Parsons's judgment that the aid program was striving to "help the seemingly unhelpable."[45]

This manuscript was never published, which was fortunate for the ambassador's reputation, but it explains, in large part, the failure of his mission. Specifically, it demonstrates why he devoted as much effort to creating a familiar, orderly environment in Vientiane's several American compounds as he did to achieving the aim of U.S. foreign policy. Appalled by the confusion around him, disgusted by Lao laziness, convinced there was little Washington could do, diplomatically at least, to save this misbegotten pseudo-nation, he withdrew into Little America, where he instituted a regime of structure and ceremoniousness that offset the perceived chaos of the host country. Little America was already established by the time Parsons took over from Yost, but the ambassador soon imprinted his button-down ethos on the facsimile of stateside suburbia that had grown up along the banks of the Mekong. Now, in addition to shielding its inhabitants behind barbed wire and double-pane plate glass, Little America became an organization man's finishing school, governed by a code of etiquette whose complexity rivaled that of Louis XIV's Versailles.

"Welcome to Vientiane!" opened the brochure that embassy and USOM employees freshly arrived in the administrative capital began receiving in late 1956. Parsons's signature stretched across the top of the first page, and his imprint on the succeeding text was unmistakable. There was not a word about Lao history, politics, customs, or traditions. The document focused on one subject, *"Protocol,"* which it defined as "good manners codified,... the ground rules for getting along in an official international community." Readers learned that the "basic principles of diplomatic protocol were laid down in an international congress many years ago." They were a durable part of Foreign Service culture. Parsons would tolerate no deviation from them.

"As first impressions are so important," the brochure read, it was essential to use the proper honorific when greeting a fellow American, particularly if he happened to be one's boss: "The Ambassador is addressed as 'Mr. Ambassador' or 'Sir,' not as 'Mr. Parsons' nor as 'Ambassador Parsons.' All communications are addressed to 'The Ambassador and Mrs. Parsons,' or, if for the Ambassador alone, 'The Honorable J. Graham Parsons,' or, if for Mrs. Parsons only, 'Mrs. J. Graham Parsons.'" The process of "getting acquainted," which might occur of its own accord elsewhere, required paperwork in Little America. For example, "[w]hen making a formal call, a married woman should leave one of her own cards and two of her husband's (e.g. one 'Mrs.' Card and two 'Mr.' cards, or one 'Mr. and Mrs.' card and one 'Mr.' card). Single women leave only one card, i.e., only on Mrs. Parsons." Invitations should be "replied to in the third person: 'Mr. and Mrs. John Smith accept with pleasure, etc.,'" and if the invitation came "by note," it "should be answered also by note, the name signed 'Sincerely, Mary

Jones,' never 'Mrs. John Jones.'" This last rule applied "to all correspondence, except that—in the case of business letters—the name '(Mrs. John Jones)' would correctly appear, in parenthesis [*sic*], below the signature." "Of course," the brochure observed, "formal acceptances should never be typewritten, nor should they be written on 'informals,' which are folded cards with the name on the outside. They should be hand-written on a plain sheet of your best notepaper."

Parsons required "all newly arrived employees of all agencies" to check in with him at his office, but he was a busy man and could not be expected to meet them individually. "[H]e likes to welcome new arrivals in groups," stated the brochure. "The initiative rests with you to contact the Personnel Officer as to date and time." Anyone who showed up alone or without having pre-booked his or her visit risked incurring the ambassador's wrath. Mrs. Parsons also received new arrivals, and the rules for paying respects were explicit: "All American women should call on the wife of the Ambassador within the first three days of arriving in Vientiane, by one of the following systems: a) leaving their cards at the Residence; or b) making an appointment via the Ambassador's secretary to call in person." Although Mrs. Parsons did not have "a regular 'At Home' day," she was usually "available mornings between 11 and 1, by appointment." Visitors were advised to be brief. "In general, you should not stay more than twenty minutes," the brochure counseled, "but, of course, if tea is late you don't drink it and run." Appropriate dress was indispensable: "[I]t is customary to wear a hat and gloves when paying your formal calls," Vientiane's steam-bath climate notwithstanding.

"Official functions" were tightly coordinated affairs. Parsons insisted upon punctuality. "When you are invited to the Embassy Residence," declared the brochure, "you should arrive 15 minutes before the appointed hour if non-American guests are to be present. . . . You should also not leave until all guests of other nationalities have gone." When, as was more common, the function involved only Americans, employees and their spouses still had to pay due deference to rank. "If the Ambassador and Mrs. Parsons are present," the brochure instructed, "you should remain until they have left the party." The yoke slackened for less formal events:

> At large cocktail parties, . . . you should, of course, arrive on time. After greeting your host and hostess, it is appropriate to greet the Ambassador and Mrs. Parsons. While at this post it is not required that you stay until the Ambassador and Mrs. Parsons leave, it is courteous to do so, if possible.

If you must leave before the Ambassador, it is also not required that you seek him out and say "good night," but, if convenient, it is again courteous to do so.

These points of propriety "may seem unimportant," conceded the brochure, "but foreigners overseas notice the relationship between members of the American community"—which was certainly true in Laos during Parsons's ambassadorship.[46]

Since Joel Halpern made only a few trips to Vientiane from his base at the royal capital, he was not prepared for Parsons's politesse and got off on the wrong foot with the ambassador when the two men met in early 1957. Halpern and Barbara Kerewsky flew south for a conference of American field representatives and took up temporary residence in the USOM compound. "We got a note one morning inviting us to lunch at the Ambassador's," Halpern wrote his family. "I told the servant who brought it that we would be delighted to come," assuming this was a suitable response. The next day, he reported, "we got another note from 'Peggy Parsons' asking us to please let her know if we could make it as she was waiting for our answer before inviting the other guests." Chagrined, Halpern sent a more "formal acceptance." The luncheon itself was awkward, beginning with "a problem as to whom [*sic*] shall go in first": Halpern made the mistake of entering the dining room before Parsons, which violated rules of precedence. He also slipped up "with respect to the seating" during the postprandial social hour. Returning to the living room after lunch, he sat down next to Kerewsky, whereupon the ambassador told him "in no uncertain terms" that "just wasn't done, sitting next to your wife." It bears note that, while the highest-ranking American in Laos scolded a subordinate on these matters, the spring session of the Lao National Assembly was drawing to a close without having ratified Souvanna's accords with the Pathet Lao. "Total turmoil engulfed Vientiane," reporter Bernard Fall remembered, "which, in Laotian politics, was the preface to a large-scale crisis"—although not one, apparently, on a scale comparable to disregard of embassy seating arrangements.[47]

The extent of Parsons's remoteness from popular sentiment in his host country became apparent on May 29, 1957, when he met Prince Phetsarath for an hour and a half at the U.S. Embassy. Phetsarath, described by one scholar as the "father of Lao nationalism," was a legendary figure. No politician spent more time touring the provinces than this sixty-eight-year-old aristocrat, whom Halpern accompanied on a four-day trip earlier in the year and judged "the most popular man in the country." "The people address him as 'King,'" Halpern wrote, "and behave toward him as they would toward the king." Many villagers believed the prince had magical powers, that he could turn himself into a whale or make bullets bounce off his skin. His return to Laos after a decade of banishment had been the cause of celebration, and King Sisavang Vong, recognizing the prince's following, had restored to him the title of viceroy. Souvanna, Phetsarath's former rival, now sought his elder brother's approval for RLG policies. While hardly a baby-kissing politician, Phetsarath was probably correct to claim in a 1957 interview, "No one knows my country better than I." Parsons could have learned a great deal about Laos from Phetsarath, had he been inclined to listen.[48]

He was not. The memorandum of the two men's conversation reads as black comedy. Phetsarath came prepared to discuss a subject of pressing importance: abuses in the U.S. aid program. Americans merited "thanks for their generosity," the prince noted, but the manner in which aid was administered aroused "hostile feelings among the people," because they could "see that it benefited only a limited few." Parsons brushed off these concerns and launched into a soliloquy that consumed the entire meeting. He began by warning Phetsarath that he would tell him things to which he "took exception." This was in the interest of "being frank" and ought not to be interpreted as "pretentious or rude."

First, Parsons wished Phetsarath to understand that, despite the "donor-recipient relationship" between the United States and Laos, Washington "did not want gratitude." It was "recompense enough" if American aid achieved its purpose. Nonetheless, Phetsarath should recognize that U.S. foreign aid bills had to run a congressional gauntlet. The Lao, Parsons observed, knew the West "only through France," which was unfortunate given that the "French system of government" differed from that of the United States. Parsons lectured Phetsarath on the distinction between a parliamentary administration, where "if government policy was not supported, it was the government which was defeated," and America's separation of powers, which left the executive in office even if the legislature rejected his policy.

It is inconceivable that a man of Phetsarath's intelligence could have been unaware of this information, but he listened composedly as Parsons chronicled his struggles with Souvanna, bemoaning the premier's inability to appreciate "the importance of congressional reactions." Capitol Hill was caught up in a "drive for economy," Parsons said, and legislators counted every nickel. Yet Souvanna insisted on bringing members of the Pathet Lao into the RLG, even though Parsons told him this would prompt Congress to ask "searching questions." The premier's bullheadedness had led to the present dire situation, in which many senators and representatives felt that U.S. money ought to go only "to those who were effectively defending their freedom" and that "aid should be denied" to nations like Laos, where "communists were being let into positions of power."

Another event had transpired that "could operate to the disadvantage of the Laos program," declared Parsons. "The visit to the U.S. of President [Ngo Dinh] Diem, who had succeeded against great odds in saving South Vietnam from the communists, had dramatized what resolute leadership could do." Diem's show of resolve made Souvanna look weak-kneed by comparison. "We admire greatly someone who has taken such a forthright line," the ambassador asserted, "and there is a natural tendency to wish to help first where the proof has been given that the communists would be kept out." If Diem could defeat Moscow's myrmidons in South Vietnam, why did the RLG embrace them in Laos?

To wind up what he admitted was a "too long exposition," Parsons assured Phetsarath that there was "nothing personal" in his remarks. Washington, he said, wished to "avoid meddling" in the affairs of a sovereign country. Nonetheless, Americans did "hope for governments that would be strong," and the only practicable course of action, as Parsons had been insisting since his plane touched down in Vientiane, was one of adamant anticommunism. "[I]n dealing with communists," he declared, it was "necessary to stand firm" and "expose their tactics before the bar of public opinion," in the expectation that "they would discover that it was in their interest to give way."

Parsons reported to the State Department that Phetsarath "listened to the foregoing with apparent interest and much more patience than I could have mustered." Thinking the ambassador had finished, the prince pointed out that he was "opposed to the communist ideology" and did not "favor it for Laos." He then tried to steer the discussion back toward the U.S. aid program. Parsons interrupted by citing one of Souphanouvong's recent speeches and arguing that its "criticism of the United States" was indistinguishable from that which Americans were "accustomed to hearing from Hanoi, Peking, and Moscow." The Red Prince was clearly "not neutral but a member of the communist bloc." Furthermore, said Parsons, it was pointless maintaining the charade that Pathet Lao troops would integrate into the RLA. Souphanouvong's forces owed their "origin to the Viet Minh" and their "support to... the Communist Chinese," and Parsons could not "imagine the Congress appropriating money to pay for communists." RLG statesmen had to defer to the "thinking in Washington," or they could find themselves cut off without a cent.

Phetsarath, whose nonverbal reaction to this harangue was not recorded but can be imagined, curtly replied that he was "sure that the government should make a very special effort to understand the American viewpoint." The prince then took his leave. "It is obvious that he needs a lot of educating," Parsons informed State. Nonetheless, the ambassador felt he had "contribut[ed] . . . to the process."[49]

This encounter epitomized Little America. It was a monologue. As had been the case in his confrontations with Souvanna, Parsons spelled out Washington's perspective on world affairs, presented nonnegotiable demands, and threatened to terminate aid if the Lao did not comply. Phetsarath barely got a word in edgewise. His lifetime of experience and role in the history of his nation counted for nothing, as the ambassador did not even ask him a question, much less solicit his advice. To Parsons, who had resided in Laos for half a year, Phetsarath was the one who needed "a lot of educating" about conditions in the country.

Since the ambassador refused to listen to him, Phetsarath took his concerns to the press, telling a French journalist, "The utilization of foreign aid is defective. It serves to outrageously enrich a minority, while the majority of the population remains poor." The prince said that mismanaged foreign aid "constitutes, in reality, the true danger of communism in Laos, because it will finish by creating discontent among people, who . . . will be easy prey for propaganda." Eleven months after this interview ran in *Nouvelles du Laos*, U.S. congressmen would be making the same argument, but the aid program scandal had yet to break by mid-1957, and Phetsarath's opinion carried no weight in Little America, least of all with the ambassador.[50]

Parsons's arrogance might have been less damaging to U.S. policy had his fellow administrators in Vientiane seen matters differently, but the record left by the embassy, USOM, USIS, and other American organizations indicates that the ambassador's views were, for the most part, shared by those officials whose authority approached his. They all regarded the Lao with a mix of irritation, condescension, and scorn untempered by empathy. Vincent Cillis, top U.S. adviser to the Lao National Police, noted in his 1958 terminal report that the Lao were "by nature somewhat indolent, perhaps due to the enervating climate, which reduces mental and physical vigor and produces a 'manana' philosophy." Whatever the reason, he observed, "[m]ost Laotians" were "indolent and unambitious." USOM deputy director Gordon Messegee complained in late 1957 that his biggest problem was "the ideology of the Lao people," which, he said, was not "in harmony with that required by a technical civilization." Messegee informed Robert Smither, acting chief of the field service division, that while Lao "tend to let matters take their own course, an industrial civilization requires people who are ambitious, . . . [who] make a virtue out of exactness." As far as Messegee was concerned, those requirements defined the antithesis of the host population. USIS leader Hank Miller's 1958 "Country Plan for Laos" bewailed Lao "[p]olitical naïveté" and unawareness of the "responsibilities of good citizenship." There were "no tested, articulate leaders" in the country, he noted, and citizens put no stock in "the value of 'self-help.'" Even the team of experts sent to Laos by the International Cooperation Administration in early 1958 to evaluate the aid program could not disguise their contempt. While much of their report was accurate and bracingly honest—they condemned the mismanagement of American funds and the "haphazard programming in the field"—they also described the Lao as "immature," "benighted," "unfamiliar with the twentieth century," and "not vigorous as to health." They were especially dismissive of Lao Buddhism, which, they claimed, "leads to the complacent acceptance of life as it is."[51]

Clearly, the attitudes Parsons brought to Laos were not idiosyncratic. They mirrored, if in exaggerated form, those of other cold warriors striving to inoculate the Lao against the communist virus, and, furthermore, they were consistent with the Eisenhower administration's approach to Southeast Asia. Robertson would not have stumped for Parsons to head the Vientiane embassy, and Dulles and Eisenhower would not have gone along with the assistant secretary's recommendation, had Parsons been a maverick. Parsons told the truth when, in later years, he explained to a journalist that "people other than me . . . deemed [Laos] to be strategically important." Those people—Eisenhower, Dulles, Robertson, and their policymaking peers—moreover had decreed as early as 1954 that neutralism was not an option for Laos, and they had expressed concerns about Lao irresolution long before Parsons took up residence in Vientiane. Stung by "revisionist historians" who "wrote as though it was I who originated the policy," Parsons protested that he was merely executing decisions arrived at in the White House and State Department.[52]

That claim was accurate to an extent—Parsons did not create the containment doctrine, the domino theory, or American intolerance of third-world neutralism—but it was also misleading and self-serving. It underrated the importance of ambassadors in the conduct of U.S. foreign policy. As Washington's highest-ranking official in Laos and, ostensibly at least, its most authoritative source of information, Parsons had the responsibility to advise his superiors of facts on the ground. His conceptual reduction of complex political and military events to the Orientalist equivalent of a minstrel show stymied his efforts and brought little honor to the country he represented.

## "The Mess in Laos"

If Parsons and other architects of U.S. policy disliked Halpern's limited-circulation critique of the aid program, they were beside themselves when they read the article that graced the front page of the *Wall Street Journal* on April 9, 1958. Under the headline "Living It Up in Laos," the piece told a story of ineptitude and corruption so shocking that it prompted two congressional investigations. Reporter Igor Oganesoff wrote with a pen dipped in gall. It was difficult for readers to determine what disgusted Oganesoff more, the waste of U.S. money or the people on whom it was wasted. Laos was "ecstatically drowning in American aid," Oganesoff observed, listing some of the items slated for import in 1958: "luxury cars," "French perfume," "fishing tackle," "thermos jugs," and "$11,500 worth of musical instruments." "Much of this stuff is unsaleable," remarked Oganesoff, "but it doesn't matter; the importers have already made their profits from foreign exchange manipulations."

Oganesoff then explained the dollar-kip exchange rate dilemma, in which Washington's Commodity Import Program operated on the officially pegged rate of thirty-five kip to the dollar while free-market operators in Hong Kong and Bangkok offered three times as many kip for the same dollar. "This sets the stage for fantastic profits," noted Oganesoff, as speculators either imported dollar-financed goods and exported them for sale elsewhere or, in some cases, bypassed Laos altogether and diverted the goods to another country after bribing customs officials to issue phony receipts. In fact, Oganesoff declared, entrepreneurs could make a fortune without selling anything to anyone: "A Laotian trader can buy 100,000 kip in the free money market for $1,000. He then applies for an import license for, say, $1,000 worth of building cement, but puts up only 35,000 kip to get the $1,000 from the government at the official rate. This leaves him 65,000 kip before he has even moved the goods." Small wonder he was laughing all the way to the bank.

Yet Lao venality and overvalued kip were not the only causes of the aid program's failure. Just as disastrous were the projects American officials implemented before determining their probable impact in a Lao environment. "ICA representatives still blush over the $27,000 tilapia project," wrote Oganesoff. "Local ponds were stocked with these imported fish. Then it developed that, while the local populace didn't like their taste, the other fish in the ponds did, and quickly gobbled up the entire supply." Efforts to crossbreed "meaty Berkshire hogs" with "the local sway-backed...Chinese hogs" also came a cropper as the new, improved swine proved unable to "withstand the rigors" of a tropical climate. Less bizarre, but no less costly gaffes included the 150-mile road from Vientiane to Luang Prabang, which opened for traffic in 1957 but soon became unusable because monsoon rains washed away stretches of improperly built roadbed and caused landslides. "No new roads are contemplated," Oganesoff observed. "Meanwhile, back in the countryside, the rank and file of the Laotians, a handsome dark people, live much as they have always lived, oblivious of U.S. help."

Even if the peasantry noticed the huge bureaucratic machine created by Washington to help them eliminate illness, ignorance, and malnutrition, they might not appreciate it. America's nation-building campaign was "bucking a strong tradition," Oganesoff contended. "The Laos [*sic*] people, by nature and their belief in ascetic Buddhism, are not prone to help themselves very much or to strive for material betterment." Oganesoff cited the same example Barbara Kerewsky had to prove his point: "Given fertilizer that will double his yield, the Laos [*sic*] farmer may simply halve his planted acreage." Moreover, "if a family member dies, very likely his plot of ground will be taken out of cultivation." This attitudinal predisposition was the biggest impediment Washington faced. Defects in aid program planning could be corrected, but the USOM could not so easily transform Buddhist sluggards into westernized go-getters.[53]

Oganesoff failed to reconcile his statements about Lao torpor with the cupidity of the administrative capital. If the Lao, as lazy Buddhists, did not value material trappings, then why were there more cars in Vientiane than there were miles of road in the country to drive them on? Why were previously penniless government officers living in $100,000 villas? Urban residents, at least, did not seem to be observing Buddha's rules. Few *Journal* readers noticed this inconsistency, though, and when "Living It Up in Laos" appeared in *Reader's Digest*, Oganesoff's exposé reached the largest magazine audience in the United States. It was a public-relations disaster for the Eisenhower administration, one that State Department officials, Parsons in particular, strove to contain.[54]

The just-appointed deputy assistant secretary of state ordered his staff to draw up a rebuttal of the *Journal* article days after its publication. He also wrote *Digest* editor DeWitt Wallace to complain that Oganesoff had presented "only one side" of the story in Laos. Surely the *Digest*, "in the interest of fair play," would consent to run a piece "setting forth in about the same number of words the other side." Parsons volunteered to write such an article himself. When the House Committee on Foreign Affairs began hearings on the U.S. aid program in Laos during the spring of 1958, Parsons defended American policy, arguing that even if the methods employed by USOM officials had not always been efficient, their impact had offset any waste. After all, Laos was still part of the free world. "[L]ots of things that were done in Laos were done for political policy reasons," Parsons declared, and to criticize the aid program because some money went awry was to miss the forest for the trees. Parsons admitted that there were "deficiencies" and "things to be corrected," but he assured the Subcommittee on the Far East and the Pacific that "we have been trying to correct them." He believed progress had been made, and predicted that the USOM would soon "arrive at a point where we can reduce the costs to the taxpayer."[55]

Parsons did not sway all the representatives. Subcommittee Chairman Clement Zablocki (D-WI) remarked, "There is no question but that the situation in Laos is a mess," while Leonard Farbstein (D-NY) accused the USOM of throwing American money "down a drain hole." But Walter Judd (R-MN), a former medical missionary in China and one of Congress's foremost authorities on Asia, stood by the deputy secretary. He believed Congress should give the USOM the opportunity to iron out its difficulties, and he advised his colleagues that the corruption disclosed by Oganesoff, while distressing, was common practice in the East. Ultimately, Zablocki moderated his criticism. Although the subcommittee issued a stern report, the chairman told journalists, "It is encouraging that there is no sign of fraud, malfeasance, or gross misadministration on the part of U.S. officials."[56]

The Democrat from Wisconsin would be unable to make this claim a few months later, when the *Reporter*, one of America's leading journals of opinion, ran a piece by Haynes Miller, an end-use auditor whom the USOM had fired in 1957. Miller had irritated his superiors by lodging repeated complaints about American complicity in the turpitude swamping Vientiane. He accused U.S. administrators of pocketing bribes for contracts, acquiescing in the delivery of defective equipment, and looking the other way as construction firms defaulted on agreements. He also issued memoranda that anticipated Halpern's 1958 broadside against Little America,

although he and Halpern worked in different areas of Laos and, by all accounts, never met. "I have not gone out at night with Americans, nor do
I voluntarily frequent the isolated, asceptic [*sic*] American enclaves," Miller
wrote in a representative dispatch to USOM director Carl Robbins. "I have
used my weekends and all of my vacation time to acquire some knowledge
of Laotian life, of the natural economy of Laos, of its peoples, and its cultures." The Lao to whom Miller spoke "have never been sought out and
asked for information and advice by any American except myself," and
what they told Miller convinced him that "the system presently in use" by
the USOM could only have "disastrous results." "It is my opinion, and the
opinion of every Laotian I know," Miller declared, "that the American aid
program has destroyed or is destroying whatever chance Laos may have had
to survive as an ally." For his trouble, Miller received a notice of termination
from Messegee, who cited Miller's "inability to adjust properly to the local
environment" as cause for his dismissal. Robbins and then-Ambassador Parsons filed a confidential report claiming that Miller displayed "signs of nervous disorder." The USOM did not even pay Miller's way home.[57]

After returning to the United States, Miller gave evidence to a number
of investigative groups and submitted an article titled "A Bulwark Built on
Sand" to the *Reporter*, which published it in November 1958. It dealt the
aid program another blow. Miller echoed Oganesoff's thesis, proclaiming,
"We have flooded a primitive country with money and goods it could not
possibly absorb and thereby created a situation in which corruption and
fraudulent currency exchanges have flourished openly." But while the *Wall
Street Journal* had portrayed U.S. aid workers as honest if bumbling, Miller
said that Americans succumbed to the lure of illicit profits as readily as the
Lao. Most U.S.-sponsored aid projects were "shot through with fraud," he
wrote, and he named names. Edward McNamara, chief of the USOM's
public works office, had accepted a bribe from Gerald Peabody and Willis
Bird of the Universal Construction Company in return for help in securing contracts and overlooking Universal's deficiencies in performance. Even
after the company failed to build a projected road and wrecked 40 percent
of the heavy equipment supplied by Washington, Peabody and Bird still
got "a contract to construct a ferry ramp and customs compound in Laos
at an exorbitant figure." Miller claimed that he had been "ordered to drop
my investigation of the possibly fraudulent aspects of Universal's activities" by USOM controller Harry Harting, who had a finger in the pie. He
also detailed a "pattern of job hopping," whereby USOM officials went to
work for private firms after participating in decisions to award those firms

contracts in Laos. Although Miller stopped short of accusing Robbins of fraud, the implication was obvious, and congressional critics would later voice that charge explicitly.

Miller also challenged Parsons's assertion that the aid program had made Laos more secure against communist takeover. He pointed to "last May's elections," in which the Neo Lao Hak Xat and Santiphab parties, "[c]ampaigning against the corruption of the pro-western candidates," won "a majority of the seats." Politically, Miller stated, U.S. policy had "served to strengthen the communist position." Prospects on the military front were equally dismal. Despite the fact that most American aid went to meet Laos's battlefield needs, the RLA was "unsuited to the sort of fighting it might be called on to do." It was a "motorized force" in a nation where there were "less than a thousand miles of roadway over which it can move in trucks." This left it "poorly adapted for guerrilla fighting." More important, its morale was so low that RLA soldiers had informed Miller that, in the event of Pathet Lao aggression, they "would take off their uniforms and return to their villages." The RLA, Miller observed, was "the only national defense force except our own whose budget is entirely underwritten by U.S. taxpayers," but Laos was no better prepared to defend itself in 1958 than had been the case in 1955. Instead, its vulnerability to Pathet Lao aggression had increased. There was, in brief, nothing good to say about the U.S. aid mission, and much to condemn. "It would be bad enough if the money had been merely wasted," Miller concluded. "The record to date, however, shows that our Laotian policy has demoralized our friends and strengthened our enemies."[58]

Miller's article enraged Parsons. The aid mission depicted in the *Reporter* could have been run by Boss Tweed. If Miller's charges were correct, then Parsons had either knowingly tolerated illegal acts or been so inattentive to the crookedness around him as to make readers question why he had later been promoted to a post where he was responsible for U.S. policy in the entire Far East. Furious, Parsons denounced Miller as a "paranoiac," an "unbalanced person," and a "zealot" who had been "fired for good reason." Eric Kocher, director of the office of Southeast Asian affairs, was less troubled by allegations of fraud than by the claim that American aid had achieved nothing positive. "[T]he over-all worth of the program must stand or fall on whether it is accomplishing U.S. foreign policy goals," he declared, and Laos had not retreated behind the iron curtain. That was sufficient return on investment. Two hundred million dollars was "insignificant if compared to the amount that would have been necessary . . . to support Thailand and South Viet-Nam defense forces if Laos were to have been abandoned to the communists." By ignoring that point, Kocher said, Miller had presented a "misleading treatment of the effects of the U.S. aid program." The *Reporter*'s executive editor, Philip Horton, found this argument persuasive and sent the U.S. embassy in Vientiane a quasi-apology, admitting, "We were not particularly happy to print the article, since the *Reporter* has always been a staunch advocate of the foreign aid program." Nonetheless, Horton wrote, "it is not in the public interest to ignore or to gloss over serious weaknesses of the program," and he believed the Miller piece was a "responsible piece of journalism."[59]

Congressman Porter Hardy (D-VA) agreed. A veteran crusader against what he termed "plush and frills," he had long sought to cut appropriations for foreign aid, and he had been dissatisfied with the work of Zablocki's subcommittee, feeling it had let American officials off the hook. Hardy launched a more extensive investigation into the Laos program in the summer of 1959. His Government Operations Committee held nineteen days of hearings, with testimony running to nearly one thousand pages, and Miller was a star witness. In addition to repeating the charges leveled in the *Reporter*, Miller declared that Parsons had personally asked him not to investigate the Universal Construction Company's conduct. He also claimed that Robbins twice offered to promote him to a higher-paying job, "with the implicit understanding that, of course, I had hushed." Other shocking disclosures followed Miller's testimony, as the committee learned that Carter de Paul, USOM director from January 1955 until July 1957, had sold his inoperable 1947 Cadillac for an inflated sum to the head of Universal, who displayed the vehicle in front of his Vientiane residence until it became "the subject of scornful amusement," whereupon he "cut it up with an acetylene torch and dropped it in the bottom of an abandoned country well." Edward Mc-Namara, USOM's former public works office chief, confessed that he had accepted $13,000 from Universal to make sure the company received a road-building contract; he had then turned a blind eye while Universal's operators bungled the job. Daniel Harkins, an ICA inspector who had been posted to Vientiane in mid-1957, revealed that Parsons and Robbins had filed their assessment "reflecting adversely on Mr. Miller's mental competence" without consulting with the embassy doctor, which violated mission code.[60]

One of the highlights occurred when the committee questioned Parsons. Hardy did not press the ex-ambassador on his relationship with Universal or his firing of Miller, but he got a rise out of him nonetheless by reminding him of testimony he had given to another congressional committee in May of the previous year. Right after elections had taken place in Laos, but before the results were known, Parsons had forecast a Pathet Lao defeat. Yet, Hardy noted, "the communists actually were pretty successful in that election, as I remember." How could Parsons, head of all American operations in Laos for sixteen months, have reached such an erroneous conclusion? Parsons resented Hardy's inference that he was out of touch with developments in his former host country. "I dare say that I have worried about Laos more than any man in this room," he spluttered. "And I am still concerned about Laos, still worried about the future of Laos." In a prepared statement read the following day, Parsons again justified the aid program on political grounds, affirming, "It would be contrary to the national interest of the United States to terminate our assistance to Laos, for... such termination would be tantamount to abandoning Laos to the communists." Yes, there had been some "shortcomings" in the management of American aid, but overall it had been successful, as demonstrated by Laos's continuing allegiance to the free world. In fact, Parsons told the committee, USOM officials deserved praise rather than blame: "The program was highly organized, remarkably efficient despite the difficult circumstances prevailing in Laos, and reflected, in my opinion, great credit on the personnel of the various participating U.S. agencies." Given the evidence uncovered by Hardy and his colleagues, this was an extraordinary pronouncement.[61]

The committee issued its report in mid-June 1959. It cleared Miller, who, the congressmen affirmed, had been "'railroaded' out of Laos because he was close to discovering the truth about Universal." Although the committee identified Robbins as "the prime mover in ousting Miller," it also noted that "Ambassador Parsons abetted this removal and lent it the color of his name and office." De Paul, McNamara, and Harting took their lumps, along with Universal's Peabody and Bird. Perhaps more satisfying to Miller than these paybacks was the fact that the committee accepted the larger argument of his *Reporter* article, declaring, "The aid program has not prevented the spread of communism in Laos." Pathet Lao victories in the May 1958 elections indicated that the program had "contributed to an atmosphere in which the ordinary people of Laos question the value of the friendship of the United States." The bribes, kickbacks, and speculation that "attended the aid program" gave "credence to the communist allegation that the Royal Lao Government was 'corrupt' and 'indifferent' to the needs of the people." Overall, Americans had received little of value for their tax dollars.[62]

Hardy was a dedicated public servant, and his probe accomplished its objective, as fiscal year 1959 aid to Laos was cut by a third from 1957 levels. The chairman's concern about waste, however, ought not to be confused with concern for the Lao, whom he scorned as much as his rivals in State did. One of the few points on which he and Robertson could agree was that the Lao were unfitted, as Robertson put it, for "our standards of democracy." Hardy assured the undersecretary, "Certainly, it would not be expected that the people of Laos have reached a point of political responsibility where they could exercise a degree of self-government which we consider our-selves capable of doing here." Congress did not "insist on pure democ-racy in a country like Laos," Hardy declared. They were even prepared to countenance a "military dictatorship," as long as American money was managed intelligently. When Charles Shuff, deputy assistant secretary for international security affairs, appeared before the committee to defend the aid program, Hardy concurred with his description of the Lao as "primi-tive." "I don't think we can expect them to grow up overnight," the chair-man observed. On the other hand, he dreaded the prospect of Washington becoming "permanently the fairy godfather of a government in Laos." He felt that policymakers were "inclined to use the fact that [the Lao] are underdeveloped as an excuse for doing too much for them," and he ad-monished Shuff that America could not "be too universal a Santa Claus." Elsewhere in the record Hardy referred to the Lao as lacking "political competence" and "developed intelligence" and questioned their capacity to "participat[e] in government, or... exercis[e] some voice in government, even remotely." This was not the kind of advocate Souvanna Phouma and Phetsarath looked for on Capitol Hill.[63]

America's mainstream media, which increased its coverage of events in Laos during the congressional investigations, mirrored Hardy's attitude by combining outrage at the misuse of U.S. funds with contempt for the men and women Washington was striving to protect. Tellingly, American magazines and newspapers placed most of the blame for what the *Wash-ington News* called "a record of corruption, ineptitude, and mismanage-ment... such as has not been heard of since the days of Chiang Kai-shek" on the Lao instead of on criminals like McNamara and Peabody. The *Wall Street Journal* suggested that the proper remedy for the "wasteful nonsense that went on in Laos" was "a show of willingness by the Laos [*sic*] govern-ment" to enforce "prudent administrative procedures." *Time* ascribed the aid program abuses to the fact that "[t]here are few more backward nations in the world" than Laos, a country populated by "jungle-dwelling, G-string clad tribesmen." Smugglers easily evaded "Laos's primitive customs guards," *Time* noted, and "Laotian officials, either out of confusion or collusion," allowed the aid program to become "a bog of misdirected effort, diverted profits, and squeeze." There was no mention of Americans' contribution to this bog. The *New York Times* gave an account of "graft on a big scale" in Vientiane, noting that "United States aid . . . has lined selected pockets to the bulging point." But the only pockets identified belonged to "a few Laotians"; American contractors and aid officials escaped censure. Moreover, the issue that really disturbed reporter Greg MacGregor was not corruption but the absence of local response to it. "Nothing approaching an austerity program has been seriously considered," he wrote. Rather, the Lao were "oblivious" of the scandal and "went languidly about their business."[64]

Columnists, less obliged than correspondents to strike a pose of journalistic detachment, vented their spleens. "Something will have to be done about Laos," wailed Raymond Moley of the *Los Angeles Times.* "This is too terrible to ignore." He called the aid program an "unbelievable mess," denounced its "inexcusable waste and incompetence," and demanded further congressional inquests "to clean up this sad piece of bungling." In terms of assigning responsibility, though, Moley named only one culprit: the Lao, a "people who are, to say the least, unaccustomed to independent administration of their affairs." Frederick Othman found the whole matter absurd. "I'm inclined, myself, to sympathize with the Laotians," he wrote in his weekly piece for the *New York World Telegram.* "All the millions we shipped to them turned out to be just money—a commodity with which they were unfamiliar—and no wonder they used it to light their cigars." Robert Ruark of the *Washington Daily News* was both irreverent and acrid, remarking, "Personally, I ain't lost nothing in Laos, and the more recent communiqués from the latest hotspot of red infiltration indicates [*sic*] that the Laotians share my disinterest." The average Lao, Ruark declared, "doesn't seem to care, or is unaware, of any red threat to their [*sic*] apathetic peace of mind" and "wouldn't know an ideology if it came up and bit him on his bare behind." While Ruark was "sore" about the "stealing [of] our dollars" by "grafters," and "inside boys," he thought the problem went deeper. "It seems a little silly of us to think about starting a war in a place where the people wouldn't know what the war was about," he declared, implying that even a flawlessly run aid program would founder under the circumstances.[65]

## "The Problems Remain Essentially the Same"

To Joel Halpern, rounding out his first year of teaching, the spate of Laos-themed articles was cause for both optimism and alarm. He rejoiced that popular attention had focused on defects in the aid program, but he felt that journalists and congressmen overlooked the principal reason for Washington's failure. None of the news stories or government reports addressed Little America and the extent to which it divorced Foreign Service personnel from life in Laos. As long as Little America existed, aid workers would continue to squander money on projects unrelated to the capacities of the host nation. They would also continue to insult local residents with their aloofness and furnish grist for communist propaganda. While censuring a few embassy and USOM reprobates might be emotionally satisfying, it would not keep Laos on the free-world side of the iron curtain. Neither would blaming the Lao for the consequences of America's diplomatic apartheid.

Anxious to find out whether the glare of publicity over the aid program scandal had prompted reform, Halpern leapt at the chance to return to Laos in the summer of 1959, when the Rand Corporation asked him to conduct a study of Lao elites. Unlike his earlier assignment in Luang Prabang, this errand kept him confined mostly to Vientiane, where, to his horror, he discovered that "the comments I made in my publication dealing with American aid are now more true than ever." On the outskirts of the city, he noted, "the 14-house [USOM] compound is now being expanded to 84 houses.... [T]he compound road and the accesses as well have been blacktopped and the whole place surrounded by a barbed-wire fence." Washington had approved funding for "a 24-hour-a-day chauffeur service to drive the Americans to the offices from their housing compounds or special hotels." Little America lacked only a moat to separate its occupants from the nation of their assignment.[66]

"[N]one of the basic ideas I mentioned in my report seem to have been fulfilled," Halpern wrote home to Kerewsky. "The problems remain essentially the same." Most USOM officials spent their time generating correspondence on organizational matters within the mission, attending committee meetings and conferences, providing services for fellow aid workers, and otherwise contributing to the self-perpetuation of Little America. Day-to-day interactions were almost exclusively among Americans and third-country nationals. "The lack of direct contact with local people ... cannot be stressed too highly," Halpern proclaimed. Little America's energies were directed inward rather than outward, and, hence, there was a "complete absence of information on the local culture and conditions of the country."[67]

This knowledge gap ensured that "American policy doesn't seem too much more enlightened than in the past." There were, as in 1957, complaints that U.S. assistance never reached the countryside, but now they were lodged by top RLG officials as well as by farmers. "American aid is very much appreciated in Laos," declared Tane Chounlamountri, minister of justice. "Only the way of its being done is often the cause of criticism." When Halpern traveled to a village six miles from Vientiane, the county administrator informed him that residents had received nothing from the USOM. "American aid can be good," he said, "but if it can help only the people in town, then it is not good." Other officials faulted the USOM for continuing its approach of implementing charity programs in which villagers did not participate. Minister of Fine Arts Bong Souvannavong had witnessed several USOM rural aid initiatives, and he dismissed them as "superficial." USOM workers and third-country nationals "went to the villages, gave things away, and then left," he recalled. "People did not really know what the program was all about." Such ventures had repeatedly failed to inspire loyalty to the RLG, but the USOM refused to benefit from experience. Its bureaucratic arteries rock-hard, it kept dispensing handouts and never assessed their impact on the rural population.[68]

By Halpern's reckoning, the Lao viewed Americans with greater antipathy in 1959 than had been the case two years earlier. They particularly objected to American self-segregation. Indeed, Halpern's interpreter compared Americans unfavorably in this regard with Laos's former colonial masters. There was "ill feeling because of the exclusive American compounds," he stated. "The French tried more to mix with the people." General Ouane Rathikoun of the RLA told Halpern that it was "essential for the American people to get to know the Lao and to show themselves." As many interviewees pointed out, the cocooning of USOM, USIS, and embassy workers made Pathet Lao populism look all the more attractive. Souphanouvong and his lieutenants had the common touch; they were close to the peasantry in their mode of life, they spoke the bread-and-butter language of everyday demands, and they had convinced thousands of villagers theirs was the only party fighting for redistribution of land and other reforms. One of the highest-ranking officials in the newly minted Committee for the Defense of the National Interest stated that, unlike USOM technicians, the "Pathet Lao stay in villages . . . where they work continuously." Americans, he said, should "imitate the methods of the Pathet Lao, and stay with the people." Holing up in compounds with commissaries and post exchanges was safer, but it prevented Americans from learning anything about the lives of the individuals they sought to influence.[69]

Halpern discovered that the Lao were as outraged by the frenzy of profiteering engendered by the aid program as were congressmen like Hardy.

Yet while stateside critics lamented the waste of taxpayer dollars, the Lao whom Halpern interviewed had different priorities. Maha Sila Voravong, Laos's foremost historian, condemned Washington for polluting his country's morality. "[A]ll the corruption, all the bad things, all the social conflict come... from the American aid," he declared. "Formerly, there was no stealing, cheating, or quarrelling," but U.S. lucre "caused differences in social classes." What Maha called "the time of dollars" had delivered Laos into the hands of Souphanouvong. "[T]he people here appreciate the Pathet Lao side, because the P[athet] L[ao] do not get rich like the people in the government," he said. "They aren't engaged in corruption and they don't receive the [American] aid.... Most of the people even in Vientiane appreciate the P[athet] L[ao]."[70]

Three months in the administrative capital convinced Halpern that Maha was right: even city dwellers took offense at the American assumption that a show of extravagance backed by dollars could buy anything, including friendship. Patriotic Lao were humiliated to see their leaders doing the Eisenhower administration's bidding in order to maintain the flow of aid. Honest Lao were mortified when their countrymen violated time-honored principles of conduct in a quest for easy wealth. "The P[athet] L[ao] have captured the hearts of the people," a student angrily declared. "They can't be won with money." Washington's aid program was like a mouse on a treadmill: the more Americans spent, the faster the wheel propelled them backward.[71]

Halpern returned from Laos feeling defeated. In 1957, he had believed the situation was retrievable, but now the rot had spread too far. No last-ditch effort would prevent the Pathet Lao from taking over the country. Washington might force them to pay a blood price, but, politically, the war was lost.

The paper Halpern prepared for Rand was not what the Santa Monica–based think tank was expecting. Nonetheless, given subsequent events in Laos and elsewhere, it must be judged one of the most piercing assessments of midcentury American foreign policy written by a contemporary. "After five years and the expenditure of approximately two hundred million dollars," Halpern wrote, "we have failed." America's "huge outpour of aid" had "caused hostility, ... even in non-communist quarters." Most of the money financed the pileup of unneeded consumer items in Vientiane and enabled a handful of Lao to live like Croesus. "Resentment is strong among the rural population," Halpern observed, "and the writer has been asked any number of times, 'Why is it that you Americans give all your money to the rich people who live in town and never think of us?'" That was a question American policymakers would do well to ask themselves, because in it lay the key to Pathet Lao victory. "The communist presents his life as one of sacrifice and self-denial for a noble end, arousing sympathy in his audience," Halpern noted. "This is particularly true since the Pathet Lao representative contrasts himself, a poor man, with the rich officials linked to the American imperialists." Such tactics had made Souphanouvong the most admired politician in the provinces, and his power base in Vientiane was growing as well.

If U.S. aid workers were unaware of these facts, it was because they lived in a bubble, "keeping each other busy with memoranda and cocktail parties." Halpern denounced Little America in the strongest terms. He said its "policy of exclusiveness" amounted to "racism" and was "hotly resented" by the host population. "Americans in Laos" had "no contact with the peoples of Laos." They exhibited no interest in local "history, customs, [and] institutions." Many of them "count[ed] the days until the end of their assignment and wonder[ed] how they ever came to be stationed in such a place." Worse, they "openly expressed" these views "in front of the Lao."

"Is it surprising," Halpern demanded, "that such an attitude, accompanied by the distribution of large sums of money, often leads to cynical corruption and embezzlement?" Why should Americans have expected a different response, since they had never shown any interest in Lao opinions or given the Lao anything to fight for? "What we have had to offer them has been largely a sterile form of anticommunism...and an abundance of material gifts," asserted Halpern. Souphanouvong had a cause, however repugnant, and he had been able to wrap it in the mantle of nationalism, whereas the RLG's agenda was manifestly set by Washington. Assuming that colonialism had ceased to be an acceptable relationship among peoples, as the Eisenhower administration never tired of proclaiming, the Lao had a right to expect more from the United States than a gaudier version of their lives under the French. They desired a broadly conceptualized vision of Lao independence, and, in Halpern's opinion, Washington had blown its opportunity to provide one. "Communism is above all a system of ideas that can best be met on the ideological level," he wrote. "Our ideas of individual liberty, political democracy, and the creative value of labor badly need redefining in the light of Southeast Asian cultures." But Americans would only redefine their ideas to meet Lao requirements if they got to know the

Lao, and this had never been the case. Souphanouvong therefore won the ideological battle. The USOM lost it by default.

Halpern concluded with an observation applicable not only to Laos but to all the nations of Asia, Latin America, the Middle East, and Africa that the Eisenhower administration sought to woo. "The points of view one hears so often in the United States to justify our military and economic aid programs are frequently anathema to the people for whom the aid is destined," he noted. "An example of this approach is the idea that we primarily wish to deny to the communists a strategic land." By framing U.S. objectives in this manner, Americans gave their allies the impression that they did not care about them as individuals or place any value on their countries except as chunks of territory that needed to be kept out of Moscow's grip. "The creation of a Little America in an alien cultural setting" only reinforced this impression, erecting "barriers between the Americans and the local population." It did not take long for the Lao to gather that these well-dressed white men and women behind barbed-wire fences "ignored or even reviled" the people outside. How did Washington expect "to inspire a real sense of partnership for the achievement of the goals which we share," Halpern asked, when the American aid mission operated under such Jim Crow conditions? Unless the Eisenhower administration eliminated Little America, as an institution and a state of mind, "what happened in Laos will also occur, with local variations," in other areas of the planet.[72]

The Rand paper was not published until 1990, by an obscure press in Virginia. At that point, Halpern was close to retirement, having taught at UCLA, Brandeis, and for two decades at the University of Massachusetts. He made light of his youthful efforts to change U.S. policy toward Laos—"I was full of beans in those days"—and rarely brought up the fact that history had vindicated his argument. During the late 1950s, he had been one of many Americans inveighing against the aid program, which, as Bernard Fall noted, was "probably the only aspect of the Laotian problem" to be "given some public attention." Halpern stood out among American critics, however, by refusing to settle for pat analysis. Unlike more prominent figures in Congress and the press, he understood that the difficulty went beyond itchy-palmed contractors or mercenary ministers. He moreover did not give in to the penchant, nearly universal among Americans, to seize on Lao incapacity as the reason for Washington's undoing. Rather, he assessed the situation with a keenness that belied his age and his generation, and he identified a different factor: the introversion and xenophobia of the American community in Laos. That he was unable to persuade superiors like Parsons to consider the possibility that American prejudice contributed to the erosion of support for the RLG indicates how unthinkable such notions were among U.S. policymakers during the Eisenhower years. Americans could see the mote in their ally's eye, but not the beam in their own.[73]

Chapter 4

# "Foreigners Who Want to Enslave the Country"

## American Neocolonialism, Lao Defiance

Vientiane would fall. Of that there was no doubt. General Phoumi Nosavan's men had American-supplied armored cars and tanks, gunboats and landing craft, artillery, mortars, rifles, and machine guns. U.S. helicopters flew above the advancing "Phoumist" army to direct its artillery fire. The soldiers defending Vientiane were outnumbered, according to a British diplomat, thirty to one. Worse, they had no armor. Phoumi hoped to take over the administrative capital without a fight.[1]

Quinim Pholsena, acting premier of the Royal Lao Government (RLG), refused to accommodate him. "Once fighting starts, it will go on until we are all dead," he told a reporter for the *New York Times*. "We will fight to the last drop of blood." Kong Le, the paratroop captain who would lead the defenders in battle, went on the radio to challenge Phoumi to a duel—just the two of them, man to man, to determine "who should be in control of Vientiane." He informed a Thai correspondent that his troops would "fight to the last" and would "save the last bullet for themselves." Phoumi's men were just as pugnacious. On the eve of hostilities, a Central Intelligence Agency (CIA) operative recorded one of them as boasting "in all seriousness" that he and his comrades possessed "a superhuman power which makes them immune to human destruction." They were "protected by special blessings of the Buddha," he said, and could stand up to the "enemy's weapons without being hurt." Their opponents, lacking "Buddha power," had no chance. "While [this statement] can be completely discounted as fantastic," the CIA man noted in his situation report, "it is one example of beliefs in [the] supernatural by the Lao."[2]

The prize for which Phoumi's rightists and Kong Le's neutralists fought posed daunting tactical challenges. Only a small part of Vientiane was laid out on the French rectilinear plan. The rest was a hodgepodge of wooden huts on stilts, brick houses, Buddhist monuments, and a few concrete buildings. Government offices, including the premier's house and the Defense Ministry, were dispersed in various sections of town. Coordinating attack or defense under such conditions would have tested the most experienced officer, and neither Phoumi nor Kong Le fit that description. The latter, however, had prepared well. From his command post at Wattay Airfield, two miles west of Vientiane, Kong Le had positioned machine-gun nests and snipers at key points along the city's main arteries, and a Soviet airlift of howitzers, mortars, and antiaircraft guns ensured that his men would be equipped with more than their usual light weaponry when the moment of decision arrived.

Phoumi had no strategy to speak of, relying, as always, on sheer weight and mass. Since he commanded a motorized army and there was only one road between Vientiane and his headquarters in Savannakhet, he would not be able to surprise the neutralists by striking from an unexpected direction. He did not need such ploys, though. His advantage in firepower made success certain. Besides, he expected Vientiane to be softened up, if not conquered outright, by the time his army arrived. Thai premier Sarit Thanarat, Phoumi's cousin, had imposed a blockade on the city, causing severe shortages of food and fuel. In addition, the Americans had suspended aid to the RLG and flown planeloads of Phoumist paratroopers to Camp Chinaimo on Vientiane's southeastern outskirts. These men would form the spearhead of the attack. Their commander, Colonel Kouprasith Abhay, bore a grudge against Kong Le and longed to see him dead. He anxiously awaited Phoumi's order to liberate the capital.

Fighting broke out on Tuesday, December 13, 1960, shortly after 1 p.m. It was siesta time, and the houses were shuttered, the streets deserted. Kouprasith's units, led by a tank and four armored cars, stormed down the road from Chinaimo into Vientiane. They met surprising resistance. Neutralist riflemen repulsed assaults against the police station and post office, and the Phoumists had to demolish army headquarters before its surviving defenders fled. The crash of shells and the rattle of machine guns resounded throughout the city. Citizens brave enough to steal a look outside could distinguish the adversaries by color: Phoumists wore white armbands and scarves; neutralists, red. For hours, "reds" and "whites" blasted away at each other, until, around dusk, Kong Le gave the order to fall back. His soldiers withdrew to the west and south, ceding control of the twenty-block downtown area, but they covered their retreat with a mortar barrage that knocked out one of the armored vehicles. Exhausted and bloodied, the Phoumists barely had time to enjoy their triumph, as Kong Le's men staged a counterattack after darkness fell. By dawn, they had retaken the center of town and driven the invaders back to Vientiane's eastern limits. The battle, it appeared, would not be decided quickly.

Both sides suffered killed and wounded, but most of the first day's casualties were civilian, as shells that missed their targets slammed into the surrounding wooden houses and shops, setting them ablaze and forcing their inhabitants into the street, where they were cut down by bullets and shrapnel. Those who could not escape the flaming structures burned alive. Fires swept through the brothels and opium dens along the Boulevard Lan Xang. The Constellation, Vientiane's only major hotel and the tallest building in the city, absorbed five direct mortar hits but remained upright, its guests huddling in the hotel restaurant.

This was only the beginning. The main body of Phoumi's troops had not shown up yet. They were still rumbling along the eastern road from Paksane, a town they had seized the previous week. Kouprasith was glad of their appearance on the afternoon of the fourteenth, because it seemed at that point as though he lacked sufficient strength to gain anything better than a stalemate. The neutralists, reinforced with arms flown into Wattay on Soviet planes, were holding their line even though the Phoumists poured out a ceaseless volume of fire. When Kouprasith tried to outflank Kong Le by sending gunboats up the Mekong to bombard neutralist strongholds from the west, he found that the captain had anticipated this move. Howitzers deployed near the river sent one boat to the bottom and the rest retreating downstream. Phoumi recognized that he had to cut off Kong Le's supply line. He ordered his cannoneers to take up positions on a rise near the National Assembly Building on the northeastern edge of town. From there, they began shelling the airfield. Kong Le responded in kind, his shells thudding down on Chinaimo. The two sides conducted an artillery duel that lasted for two days.

While shells whistled overhead, the Phoumists recaptured lost ground. Kong Le's men made the attackers fight for every block, but by evening the neutralists had been forced out of downtown Vientiane. Phoumi's tanks rolled through the streets, firing in all directions. Gunners shot up any house where neutralists might be hiding. They sometimes used civilians for target practice, and even opened fire on a hospital, ignoring the Red Cross flag it flew.

Shots from both sides ignited conflagrations in the poorest, most densely populated areas of town. Entire neighborhoods of thatched-roof shacks went up like tinder. "[I]t is the dry season," noted U.S. Ambassador Winthrop Brown, "and the buildings are very dry." Homeless, terrified people made their way to nearby fields and jungles, or to the bank of the Mekong in hopes of catching a ferry across to safety in Thailand. They carried whatever belongings they could rescue from the fire in carts, on bicycles, or in bundles at each end of bamboo poles. Black smoke hung over the capital in a stifling cloud.[3]

Representatives of Western powers stationed in Vientiane escaped the worst of the battle, but they spent some anxious hours. Shells fired from Kong Le's big guns landed in the compound of the French military mission. A mortar bomb exploded outside British ambassador John Addis's office window. Mervyn Brown, Addis's deputy, hid with his family in the garage beneath their house, which was, unfortunately, next to a road that the Phoumists used as a link between their forward troops and the base at Chinaimo. Kong Le wanted the road rendered impassable, and his gunners laid down a barrage that sounded to Brown like approaching doom. "[A] number of shells fell near [us]," he remembered. "As a former artillery officer, I was familiar with the principle of bracketing, and waited . . . for the next shell to explode on top of us." The projectile with Brown's name on it never struck.[4]

American buildings proved popular targets for the reds. Twenty-one were damaged, a few flattened. Large-caliber shells destroyed the second floor of the U.S. Embassy, and neutralists concealed in a nearby cemetery opened up on the ground floor with small-arms fire. Embassy counselor John Holt escaped disaster when a shell ripped through his office wall and plowed into an armchair where he had been sitting moments before. Neutralist shot and shell also damaged the compound of the United States Operations Mission (USOM), gutting several houses. A group of red soldiers fired a bazooka into a USOM apartment complex and took its inhabitants captive. One of the kidnapped Americans claimed after his release that the neutralists had threatened to kill him.

The din of battle subsided on the morning of Thursday, December 15. An undeclared truce caused by fatigue led many residents to assume that the fighting was over. Phoumi dispelled such notions by ordering another assault with artillery, tanks, armored cars, and infantry on foot, this time to be coordinated with a naval attack more powerful than the one Kouprasith had launched earlier. The operation began just before noon. Six gunboats and five landing craft, which the Phoumists used as gun platforms, chugged up the Mekong and pounded the retreating defenders with machine-gun and mortar fire. Phoumi's flotilla also seized an island opposite the center of town, where his men set up their guns and began mowing down red soldiers and civilians on the riverbank. Meanwhile, the armored vehicles pushed forward through the city, guns blazing, as the mass evacuation of the population continued. Phoumi and his aides flew into the battle zone by helicopter to view the combat. They never had the satisfaction of seeing Kong Le's men lose unit discipline, but the reds could not stem the white tide, pulling back to form a perimeter on Vientiane's western fringe. After a savage engagement, they abandoned even that, and by 4 p.m. Phoumi controlled the capital.

It would be more accurate to say that nobody controlled the capital, which did not have a working government. Vientiane had been largely destroyed. Almost every building in the city still standing bore shrapnel, machine-gun, and rifle bullet scars. Phoumi's and Kong Le's often random shelling had torn apart the power station and broken the water mains, leaving the city without electricity or water. There were not enough vehicles to remove the dead, and many bodies were cremated where they lay. Operating rooms functioned on a twenty-four-hour shift.

Phoumi's task was not complete, which meant that Vientiane's ordeal was not over. The general needed to capture Wattay and end the Soviet airlift of equipment. Kong Le, rallying his men at the airfield, vowed to "level Vientiane before giving it up." Red gunners released one final barrage of shellfire on the shattered, burning, rubble-strewn city. More flames. More buildings pulverized. More civilians streaming out of town clutching bundles. "It was cruel, indiscriminate warfare, pointlessly destructive of life and property," noted Michael Field of the *Daily Telegraph*. "Attackers and defenders were equally responsible. Kong Le seemed to be ending his turbulent rule in a Hitlerian *Goetterdaemmerung*. Phoumi was out to win, at whatever cost to the city and the people." As the Phoumist juggernaut closed in on Wattay, the neutralists withdrew northward into the jungle. They took their weapons with them. Although they had lost the battle, they were, in the words of Southeast Asia Treaty Organization (SEATO) chairman Pote Sarasin, "far from defeated." They would be back.[5]

For the next few weeks, Vientiane fought for its life. Lack of water caused a cholera epidemic. Teams of hospital workers went door to door to inoculate as many people as their stocks would permit. The central hospital, overflowing with sick and wounded, pumped water from the U.S. ambassador's swimming pool. Leaflets admonished citizens to only use water for drinking; cooking and washing would have to wait until workers repaired the pipes. Food was scarce. When Ambassador Brown tried to distribute bags of rice to the needy, a crowd of several hundred mobbed him, ripping the bags apart and fighting over the scattered grains. American, British, and French planes flew in shipments of food and medicine, but since the Phoumists had pitted Wattay's runway, the most modern landing strip in the country was unusable, and relief efforts made little progress. There was a "breakdown of law and order," observed the *New York Times*, as "the homes of well-to-do Laotians...were looted." Correspondent Jacques Nevard noted that some Phoumists were attempting to restore tranquility by administering on-the-spot justice. Most, though, concentrated on the task of mopping up stay-behind elements of Kong Le's army. They flushed snipers and saboteurs out of shops and homes and carried out a series of executions. Meanwhile, refugees began to filter back into what remained of their city.[6]

The battle for Vientiane was not, as politician Sisouk Na Champassak later claimed, the "bloodiest chapter" in Lao history, but it was sanguinary enough to persuade anyone not blinded by prejudice that the passive and indolent Lao, whose Buddhism allegedly prevented them from fighting, were every bit as capable of violence, cruelty, and heroism as other peoples. Over one thousand Lao were killed during the battle and many thousands wounded. Loss of property ran into the hundreds of millions of kip. Compared to the ruin that would be visited upon Laos in coming years, this destruction was negligible. Nonetheless, it marked a break from the course of peaceful neutrality set by former premier Souvanna Phouma after the 1954 Geneva Conference. Souvanna, in exile in Cambodia when the reds and whites devastated Vientiane, vented his rage to a journalist. Tellingly, though, he did not fix blame on either Phoumi or Kong Le. Washington, he said, was "responsible for the recent spilling of Lao blood." The "tragic mistakes of United States policy" had created "the present crisis."[7]

As was often the case, Souvanna understood matters better than the Americans did. The battle for Vientiane represented a failure of U.S. foreign policy. It had no redeeming features. Apart from the lives lost, bodies crippled, and property destroyed, it did not solve any of the problems plaguing Laos. Rather, it made the situation worse for virtually all parties involved, not least the United States. Kong Le, who had come to prominence as a neutralist, joined ranks with the Pathet Lao, believing that this was the only way to end foreign control of Lao affairs. U.S. support for Phoumi caused the Soviets, Chinese, and North Vietnamese to aid the Pathet Lao–Kong Le forces, which led to an expansion of communist influence in Laos. America's oldest European allies, Britain and France, objected to the Eisenhower administration's pro-Phoumi stance and refused to go along with a policy that statesmen in London and Paris felt could lead to World War III. Like the Australians, the Pakistanis, the Filipinos—indeed, like all SEATO members except the Thai—the British and French considered Souvanna the one man capable of keeping Laos whole and at peace. They therefore sided with the ex-premier in his denunciation of American actions. Finally, the clash that ravaged Laos's capital bound Washington seemingly beyond extrication to Phoumi—"our boy," in the words of Defense Secretary Thomas Gates—and ensured that America's nation-building enterprise would depend on a man with little popular support, few parliamentary skills, and the instincts of a gangster. U.S. diplomacy could scarcely have done worse.[8]

The train of events that culminated in the battle for Vientiane began two years earlier, when Washington tried to reverse the results of the May 1958 supplementary elections. As detailed in chapter 2, those elections saw left-wing candidates win most of the contested seats in the Lao Assembly, even though they gained only one-third of the popular vote. American policymakers, anxious to prevent future disasters at the polls, took a number of steps that violated Lao sovereignty. First, they created their own party to compete in local politics. They then used this party to undermine Souvanna, easing him out of office to make way for a premier who excluded the Pathet Lao from ministerial posts. After the new premier wielded plenary powers for a year, the Eisenhower administration underwrote a coup that resulted in an even more right-wing government, and when the RLG held its next round of nationwide elections, two of the major American establishments in Laos, the CIA and the Programs Evaluation Office (PEO), helped gerrymander the country to ensure success for conservative candidates. By any standards, American behavior was high-handed, a repression of indigenous nationalism.

Had the Lao been the docile, torpid creatures depicted in administration correspondence and U.S. newspapers and magazines, they would have borne this treatment without complaint. Yet the opposite was true. Kong Le's August 1960 revolt, in which his paratroop battalion seized Vientiane, made a mash of the caricature, as did Prince Souphanouvong's escape from prison and "long march" to Sam Neua. The defeats suffered by Phoumi's army at the hands of Pathet Lao units indicated his own ineptitude, to be sure, as well as the unsuitability of much of his equipment to Lao terrain, but they also showed the fighting spirit of the communists, who refused to accept a U.S.-Lao alliance that struck them as tantamount to imperialism. Although Americans had been involved in Lao affairs for six years by the time of the Phoumi–Kong Le showdown over Vientiane, they still refused to admit a sober truth knocking at the gate: unassertiveness was hardly a universal Lao attribute; it was only those Lao asked to fight for America's "boy" whose conduct under fire disappointed. Insensible to this fact and its implications, the Eisenhower administration pursued the same policy in 1960 as it had in 1954—albeit with more advisers, money, and weapons—and American officials continued to ascribe any setbacks to Lao ineffectuality rather than to flaws in Washington's approach. The result was a civil war that laid waste to Laos and redounded to the disadvantage of the United States.

## "New Faces"

Souvanna Phouma liked to call himself an optimist, and he had cause for optimism in the spring of 1958. Although candidates representing the Neo Lao Hak Xat (NLHX), the political arm of the Pathet Lao, had won nine out of twenty-one National Assembly seats at stake in the recent elections, and the Santiphab, or "Peace through Neutrality" Party, had captured four, conservative politicians still outnumbered leftists in the legislature. Only 32 percent of voters had cast ballots for the NLHX and Santiphab, hardly a red landslide. If the anticommunists had been able to unite behind one candidate per seat, they would have crushed their opponents. Communist influence in Laos remained slight, Washington's panicky reaction notwithstanding. More important, from Souvanna's perspective, was the fact that the country was unified at last, and the RLG exercised control over all twelve provinces. In return for being allowed to participate in the government, the Pathet Lao had agreed to hand over administration of Sam Neua and Phong Saly to Crown Prince Savang Vatthana and demobilize their armed forces, except for fifteen hundred troops who would be integrated into the Royal Lao Army (RLA). The "de facto disappearance" of Pathet Lao guerrillas, as stipulated in Souvanna's November 1957 agreement with Soupha-nouvong, more than offset the awarding of two cabinet posts to the

NLHX. Souvanna was confident he could hold those ministers in check, along with any left-leaning assemblymen. The task would require all of his political acumen, but he had met similar challenges before, and he was determined to keep Laos on a neutralist track. His nation, he proclaimed, would become "the Switzerland of Southeast Asia."[9]

To reassure Washington that there would be no repeat of the May 1958 electoral fiasco, Souvanna encouraged a coalescence of Laos's noncommunist political parties. He brought together Katay Don Sasorith's Nationalists and Phoui Sananikone's Independents to form the Rally of the Lao People (RLP), with himself as president, Katay as first vice president, and Phoui as second vice president. The RLP was a marriage of convenience, since Phoui and Katay despised each other, but it would avert the vote-splitting that had doomed the conservatives in the last elections. It would also control thirty-six of the fifty-nine seats in the assembly, enough to outvote the Santiphab and NLHX, although not enough to secure the two-thirds vote necessary to invest a government. While fragile, the merger signified progress, and Souvanna announced the RLP's appearance with a pledge to fight against subversion.

This was not good enough for the Eisenhower administration, which considered Souvanna, in the words of Secretary of State John Foster Dulles, "discredited if not suspect." Washington registered its dissatisfaction with the prince in two ways. At Dulles's behest, CIA operatives in Laos began an "intensive search" for "'new faces'... who have energy and courage." Dulles ordered the creation of a "new united party" that would "brand [the] NLHX as agents [of] world communism and unite in [an] effective struggle [to] defeat them." CIA station chief Harry Hecksher and his lieutenants wasted no time. Only four days after the RLP came into being, *Lao Presse* reported that 111 "merchants, industrialists, farmers, workers, intellectuals, police, [and] functionaries" had come together to form the Committee for Defense of National Interests (CDNI). Nearly all these men were under forty. They were, in the main, well educated. Unlike their elders, who either never went abroad or made infrequent trips to France, most CDNI members had traveled in Asia and Europe. Some had visited the United States. Indeed, the organization's ruling circle was not even in Laos when the CDNI was established. Sisouk Na Champassak, deputy representative to the United Nations; Kamphan Panya, ambassador to India; and Inpeng Suryadhay, director of the RLG's Information, Documentation, and Socio-Political Action Service, all proclaimed their allegiance to the CDNI via cable.[10]

Among these absent leaders was Colonel Phoumi Nosavan, who returned from officer training in France after the CDNI's inception. Like his cousin, Thai premier Sarit Thanarat, Phoumi was an autocrat, although he never articulated anything like Sarit's economic and cultural justification for one-party rule. He had no political convictions. His career path as of 1958 featured several shifts in affiliation and was consistent only in its opportunism. After serving in the French colonial administration during the early 1940s, he had opposed the revival of French overlordship and fought alongside the Pathet Lao. He then broke with the communists to join the pro-French Lao National Army. When Paris granted Laos limited independence in 1948, Phoumi advanced quickly through the ranks of the RLA, becoming chief of staff by the end of the Franco–Viet Minh War. He saw the U.S. mission in Laos grow from a dozen or so men billeted in tents to a Little America staffed by hundreds, and he recognized that the United States would replace France as the principal Western power in Laos. Aware that strident anticommunism played well among Americans, he tailored his rhetoric accordingly, denouncing Souphanouvong at every chance and proclaiming that Pathet Lao participation in the RLG would make Vientiane subservient to Hanoi. The tactic paid off, as Phoumi was one of a handful of Lao invited to tour military installations in the United States in 1957. CIA and Defense Department representatives were impressed by this young officer who seemed perfectly cast in the role of strongman. Stockier and more heavily muscled than most Lao, Phoumi had been an amateur boxer in his teens, and, as an acquaintance recalled, "he was as ruthless as his appearance suggested." In other words, he was precisely the sort of "new face" Dulles sought to throw the rudder around in Laos. While Kamphan and Sisouk had greater administrative experience, Phoumi took charge of the CDNI and became Washington's surrogate.[11]

The CDNI characterized itself in its founding documents as a civic group, not a political party, and pledged its support to the RLP. Yet the program put forward by Phoumi and his fellow "Young Ones" (*les Jeunes*) was more bellicose than anything Souvanna advanced, calling for opposition to communism and "reform of our public service." Sisouk remembered, "We were anxious to keep ourselves dissociated from the senior politicians, the 'Old Ones,' whom we held responsible for past errors." The "purpose animating our tiny group," he noted, was "to bring fresh blood to a nation governed... by remnants of the defunct colonial administration."[12]

Despite efforts by Sisouk and others to portray the CDNI as native-born, its CIA parentage was common knowledge in Vientiane. None of the CDNI men were wealthy, yet they seemed to have limitless financial resources. The weekly CDNI newsletter was printed on expensive glossy paper, while other Lao publications were mimeographed sheets. Phoumi, Sisouk, and other Young Ones rarely appeared in public unaccompanied by Americans. Their speeches read as if ghostwritten by Dulles. Although most CIA records for this period remain classified, officials in a position to know have confirmed the agency's role in shifting Lao politics rightward. CIA deputy director for intelligence Robert Amory admitted in 1969 that the CIA modeled the CDNI after Ramón Magsaysay's anti–Huk movement in the Philippines, itself a CIA creation. Even if, as Sisouk insisted, the CDNI had a spontaneous local origin, Americans appropriated the movement and turned it to their own purposes so quickly that it might as well have been conceived at Langley.[13]

Washington's second anti-Souvanna act was less imaginative than the launch of the CDNI, but its effects were as dramatic. The State Department finally did what it had long threatened to do: it withheld payment of the monthly aid disbursement to the RLG, citing corruption in the commodity import program. This pretext fooled no one. "The excuse was the need for monetary reform," recalled British deputy ambassador Mervyn Brown, "but the real reason was to force Souvanna Phouma out of office." Since the RLG's budget was dependent on American aid, the cutoff precipitated a financial crisis. It could not have come at a more inopportune time for Souvanna, who, according to tradition, had resigned after the May 1958 elections and been invited by the king to form a new cabinet. Normally a formality, this procedure now held the potential to wreck the coalition Souvanna had struggled to build. Members of the assembly who were alarmed by the aid stoppage began defecting. They signaled their intention to vote against Souvanna's investiture. According to one journalist, the CIA offered "$100,000 upwards" for every such vote.[14]

Sensing Souvanna's weakness, and possibly acting under American instructions, the CDNI pounced. Phoumi demanded eight of the twelve cabinet posts for his organization, an outrageous request given that the CDNI did not hold a single seat in the assembly. He also wanted the NLHX ministers expelled, along with old-line politicians like Katay. The CDNI's American backing obliged Souvanna to take these claims seriously, but he could not give in to them all without alienating many of his supporters. He proposed a compromise: he would award the CDNI minor ministries while retaining the more experienced administrators and a few NLHX department heads. Phoumi refused to accept this arrangement, as did the nine Pathet Lao assemblymen when they learned of it. They insisted that the CDNI had no right to ask for cabinet positions. Souvanna should form a government of national union, they said, which meant one comprising representatives of every recognized political party. The CDNI, untested in elections, must be excluded.

At this point Souvanna received assistance from an unlikely quarter. Horace Smith, who had succeeded J. Graham Parsons as ambassador to Laos, did not share either Parsons's low opinion of Souvanna or the CIA's regard for the CDNI. He was also troubled by what he termed an American attempt to compel the premier to "mold [his] cabinet more closely in accordance with our desires." This infringed on Lao sovereignty, Smith noted, reminding his superiors in Washington that "[t]he choice of ministers is for the prime minister to make." As for the CDNI, Smith doubted whether it was anything more than a privileged group out for its own interests. He saw no sign of popular enthusiasm for *les Jeunes*, and he worried that the CDNI was planning to "impose a military junta by force." It was "imperative to maintain maximum legitimacy in any effort to give Laos a strong government," Smith cabled State. Only the communists would benefit if American-sponsored agents violated "constitutional procedures." Undersecretary of State Christian Herter replied that the Eisenhower administration wanted to "obtain [a] new government of maximum effectiveness." He ordered Smith to "avoid taking [a] position directly opposed to [the CDNI] and in favor of Souvanna." As would become apparent over the next few months, the CIA's opinion carried greater influence in Washington than the ambassador's.[15]

Souvanna, his base crumbling, made several moves to the right. He proclaimed that he would exclude the NLHX from his cabinet "because I have doubts about their political views." He redrafted his planned investiture speech to adopt a stronger anti-communist tone. He even hinted that he might urge the legislature to outlaw communism. All this availed him nothing. When the new, expanded assembly was inaugurated, over one-third of the deputies voted to block Souvanna's reappointment. A second-chance vote saw the same result. Souvanna gave up, announcing on August 6 that he was unable to get enough assemblymen to support him and that he planned to take a rest from politics.[16]

Crown Prince Savang accepted Souvanna's resignation and asked Phoui Sananikone to form a government, a choice that pleased the Eisenhower administration. Head of one of Laos's richest families, Phoui was staunchly anticommunist. American policymakers recalled his spirited performance

at the Geneva Conference, where he had refused to grant Pathet Lao com-
missioners a status comparable to delegates from the RLG. Since then, Phoui
had held many cabinet positions, including defense minister and foreign
minister, and he had always followed a pro-Western line. Parsons remembered, "It was easier to feel that you had a meeting of minds with him than
of any other Lao of stature with whom I dealt." Phoui demonstrated how
well he understood Washington's mind after a legislative machine allegedly
lubricated with American money voted him into power. His government
would be neutral, he declared, but this did "not imply neutrality on the
ideological plane: we are anti-communists."[17]

The new premier was good as his word. Despite the electoral victories
by the NLHX and Santiphab, Phoui did not award ministries to members of
those parties. Conversely, the CDNI's nonparticipation in the elections did
not prevent Phoui from appointing four CDNI officials to cabinet posts: finance and economic affairs (Thao Leuam), foreign affairs (Kamphan), justice
and information (Inpeng), and youth and sports (Sisouk). Phoui drew the
line, however, when it came to Phoumi. Fearful of the colonel's ambition,
Phoui refused to let him head a department. This detracted only slightly
from the CDNI's triumph. Just two months after its foundation, the party
had become a force in Lao politics and frozen its rivals out of the administration. The RLP benefited as well. To avoid alienating former Nationalist Party
supporters, Phoui gave Katay two portfolios, interior and defense, which
placed him in control of the police and army. The remaining ministries went
to politicians under the premier's thumb. "I have selected members of political parties who desire to oppose communist expansion," Phoui explained.
"The policy of the government that I have formed is as follows: to oppose the
threat of this dangerous ideology." While Phoui persuaded Souvanna to lend
his regime a centrist gloss by becoming ambassador to France, the dream of
reconciliation Souvanna embodied was dead, as Katay showed when he initiated a campaign of arrests, beatings, and executions in the previously Pathet
Lao–controlled provinces of Sam Neua and Phong Saly.[18]

It was a testament to Washington's all-or-nothing approach to the cold
war that U.S. policymakers found these results dissatisfying. CIA chief Allen
Dulles described Phoui's government to the National Security Council
(NSC) as a "compromise cabinet" that constituted "neither a victory nor
a defeat for our side." Americans could take comfort in the fact that there
had been "no communist penetration of the new cabinet," he said, but an
RLG conforming to Phoumi's blueprint—that is, purged of "old figures"
and dominated by the CDNI—would have been better. Dulles felt that the

influence of CDNI ministers would not "amount to much" and speculated that a "military coup" might be required "to prevent a communist take-over." Phoumi was presumably thinking along the same lines.[19]

Phoui tried to convince the Eisenhower administration that such measures were unnecessary, that he, not Phoumi, was the strongman Washington needed. In no area did he signal the RLG's lurch to the right more starkly than in foreign affairs. "As far as peaceful coexistence is concerned," he announced, "we shall coexist with the Free World only." Three months after assuming office, he recognized Taiwan and permitted the installation of a Nationalist Chinese consulate in Vientiane. He also raised the Lao legation in Saigon to embassy status. These moves reversed Souvanna's policy of maintaining friendly but impartial relations with the communist and non-communist governments of China and Vietnam. Phoui further distanced himself from his predecessor by inviting Ngo Dinh Nhu, brother of South Vietnamese President Ngo Dinh Diem, to visit Vientiane without issuing a similar invitation to a North Vietnamese statesman. After his encounter with Phoui, Nhu informed U.S. ambassador Elbridge Durbrow that the present Lao government was the "best since independence." State determined that it was good enough to warrant a resumption of American aid.[20]

If Phoui's gestures earned him applause in Washington, they elicited protests from the Pathet Lao and from the communist regimes to Laos's east and north. The North Vietnamese in particular objected to the abandonment of Souvanna-style neutralism. Hanoi had begun infiltrating cadres and weapons into South Vietnam through paths in the mountains of eastern Laos, a route later dubbed the Ho Chi Minh Trail, and Phoui's truculent anticommunism seemed to indicate that he would use the RLA to choke off that supply line. Determined to prevent such a disaster, the Democratic Republic of Vietnam (DRV) opened an offensive on the Lao-Vietnamese border close to the 17th parallel. North Vietnamese soldiers fired on a Lao military patrol, prompting Phoui to complain that his country's territory had been violated. DRV premier Pham Van Dong countered that it was the RLG that had invaded North Vietnam. The situation escalated, with Hanoi sending two companies across the border. When Phoui demanded that these troops withdraw, Dong proposed that the International Control Commission (ICC) be reactivated to arbitrate the dispute. Phoui retorted that there was nothing to arbitrate; the DRV occupied Lao soil and must leave. Hanoi refused. Hostilities seemed imminent.[21]

With American approval, Phoui dug in his heels. On January 12, 1959, he appeared before the National Assembly to declare, "Our eastern frontiers are seriously threatened." Hanoi was massing troops for an attack, he said, and the RLG needed enlarged powers to meet the emergency. He asked for permission to govern for twelve months without recourse to the votes of the deputies, meaning, in effect, that the assembly would go into recess for a year. He also asked to form a new cabinet "for the purpose of greater efficiency." Souphanouvong inveighed against this "violation of democracy," but the legislature was caught up in the crisis atmosphere and granted both requests.[22]

Although Phoui emerged from the assembly session seemingly the most powerful premier in Lao history, his mandate was illusory. In exchange for their votes, he had promised ministries in his reshuffled cabinet to RLP politicians, a move that would have reduced CDNI influence. The Young Ones objected to this arrangement and threatened to resign. Phoumi went further, promising to stage a coup if Phoui did not form an all-CDNI government. Since Ambassador Smith, the voice of moderation in the American mission, was on vacation, the CIA had free rein to pressure the premier to accede to Phoumi's demands. Hecksher warned Phoui that the flow of U.S. dollars, only just renewed, could be halted in a heartbeat. Laos's survival was at stake, he thundered, and Washington wanted the toughest anticommunist elements in the country controlling the government, which meant *les Jeunes*. Parsons, now deputy assistant secretary of state for Far Eastern affairs, encouraged these strong-arm tactics. A beaten Phoui ultimately turned his back on his party, expelling the RLP from the government as he had done with the NLHX. He stayed on as figurehead, but all of his chief cabinet members were CDNI men. Historian Martin Stuart-Fox observes, "Their appointment was a triumph for extra-parliamentary forces,... and a corresponding defeat for democratic processes." The principal beneficiary of this triumph-cum-defeat was Phoumi, who became minister of defense and received promotion from colonel to general. "For the first time in years," Parsons crowed, "there is some reason to be encouraged by the trend of the situation in Laos."[23]

Parsons was wrong. The situation had, in fact, grown more ominous for Washington as a consequence of the RLG's swing to the right. While Phoui's claims of North Vietnamese aggression were overblown, civil war loomed much closer in early 1959 than had been the case six months earlier, for obvious reasons. Phoui had deprived the Pathet Lao of power that could be exerted legally. Government channels were closed to them. They had no representatives in the cabinet, and the assembly would not be meeting for a year. Furthermore, CDNI command of the army ensured that repression of

NLHX members and sympathizers would increase. From Souphanouvong's viewpoint, the Pathet Lao had no alternative but a return to insurgency. Although he professed to respect the November 1957 accords worked out with Souvanna, the Red Prince told Pathet Lao troops to delay integration into the RLA as long as possible.

Souphanouvong thereby brought about the free world's biggest embarrassment in Laos since the recent elections. Most Pathet Lao soldiers had surrendered their weapons a year earlier and gone back to their villages, but two battalions, totaling fifteen hundred men, remained combat ready, awaiting assignment to the national army. The battalions were encamped at separate posts, one in a valley south of Luang Prabang and the other in former French Foreign Legion barracks in the Plain of Jars. Their commanders proclaimed that they would not accept integration until certain conditions were met, chief among them that Pathet Lao units be permitted a ratio of officers to men in excess of the RLA's standard proportion. After weeks of bargaining, Phoui agreed to let the Pathet Lao retain 105 officers when they merged with the royalists. Pathet Lao spokesmen then claimed that the government's concession had not been made in good faith, that Phoui intended to nullify the officers' commissions by forcing poorly educated men to take qualifying exams they were bound to fail. Phoui, exasperated, announced that the clauses of the November 1957 agreements covering the integration of the Pathet Lao would be implemented on May 11, Constitution Day. All Pathet Lao soldiers who refused to accept membership in the RLA on that date would be considered rebels and treated accordingly.[24]

Given that the RLA had twenty-nine thousand men to the Pathet Lao's fifteen hundred, Phoui expected this edict to end matters. Yet when General Ouane Rathikoun, RLA chief of staff, arrived in the Plain of Jars with his retinue to preside over the integration of one Pathet Lao battalion, he received a surprise. The soldiers drew their guns and chased the general away, shouting taunts. Ouane flew back to Vientiane in a rage, ordered the RLA to encircle the two battalions, and proclaimed a twenty-four-hour "surrender-or-die" ultimatum. Thousands of government troops surrounded the two Pathet Lao camps. Officers from both sides tried to work out a compromise. For a while, it looked as though there would be bloodshed, but on May 17 the battalion near Luang Prabang accepted the government's terms, yielding their weapons and receiving RLA rank insignia.[25]

It was a different story in the Plain of Jars, where, Sisouk recalled, the "whole complex seemed more like a gypsy settlement than a military compound." During the eighteen months that Pathet Lao troops had been quartered there, they had been joined by their families and fallen into a life-style that, compared with previous deployments, was luxurious. Maintained at public expense, the barracks provided shelter. Wives and children went to market in neighboring towns. "If any training at all was going on," a reporter noted, "it was hardly ever visible to the naked eye." Yet discipline remained strong, and when RLA battalions formed a ring around the camp, the Pathet Lao commander, Cham Nien, was prepared. In compliance with Souphanouvong's orders, he dragged his feet during negotiations, drawing out the process until May 18, when he promised that his men would capitulate the following morning. Only a few diehards had to be persuaded, he said; everything would be squared away by sunrise. That night, however, as monsoon rains pelted the plain, all seven hundred men vanished, taking with them their dependents, arms, possessions, and livestock. They slipped through the government cordon and began a long-planned trek to the North Vietnamese border fifty miles away. When RLA soldiers entered the camp at dawn, they found it empty. Hundreds of American-made uniforms, provided by the government for the anticipated integration ceremony, lay folded and stacked in the abandoned barracks.[26]

News of the battalion's getaway stunned Phoui, who declared it an act of rebellion. He closed down the NLHX's newspaper and had all party members in Vientiane, including Souphanouvong, placed under house arrest. Ouane ordered roadblocks set up and paratroops dropped to bar the rebels' escape route, but Cham Nien outfoxed him, marching his men south instead of east while royal forces stumbled in the wrong direction. For a week, Cham Nien led the RLA on a merry chase. Weather and terrain worked to his advantage. The onset of the monsoon season and jungle cover negated the RLA's control of the air, making it difficult for government pilots to see the columns of retreating rebels. Roads became rivers of mud in which motor transports bogged down. The Pathet Lao were mostly able to avoid contact, but they ran into a royal patrol on occasion, and the resulting skirmishes spotlighted the communists' superiority. Despite being outnumbered and outgunned, they trounced their adversaries, often putting them to flight in minutes. By May 25, the rebels had crossed the border, and Ouane gave up pursuit.

What Sisouk called "the Plaine des Jarres incident" left the RLA's reputation in tatters. "Before 11 May," reported U.S. Embassy attaché John Holt, the royal army "was respected ... by [the] general population." No more. The escape of the Pathet Lao battalion had "disclos[ed] to friend and foe" the "appallingly low effectiveness" of government troops. Although the RLA had made headway in politics, it had failed in its principal task, and only "emergency aid" would prevent the communists from running circles around it again. Holt's stateside bosses concurred. Members of the Operations Coordinating Board were aghast that a force costing hundreds of millions of dollars could not even "control a small-scale internal security problem" and recommended that Washington find "means of improving the effectiveness of the Lao National Army through American participation in training." This would necessitate a violation of the 1954 Geneva Accords, which prohibited foreign countries from sending military personnel to Laos, but the Eisenhower administration was flouting the accords anyway with its PEO. A few hundred more "advisers" made little difference, juridically speaking, and, besides, the communists had broken the accords as well. If Washington wanted to keep Laos free, it had to take a greater hand in beefing up that nation's armed forces, even if this meant elbowing aside French combat instructors and assuming responsibility for the RLA.[27]

The Eisenhower administration had already prepared the ground for such a transfer of power when it sent Brigadier General John Heintges, director-designate of the PEO, to Laos in December 1958 to survey the situation and make recommendations. Disturbed by what he found, Heintges proposed an "increase in the number of American active duty personnel in Laos." The French, he noted, had reduced the size of their military mission, with a corresponding decline in the amount of tutelage they could provide to Lao units. America had to take up the slack. Heintges wanted a larger PEO staff, and he wanted it to do more than deliver equipment and offer advice. American officers, he said, needed to engage in training of the RLA and, if possible, accompany royal troops into the field. Ambassador Smith endorsed the "Heintges Plan," as did policymakers in State and Defense.[28]

There were two problems, though. The first—how to reconcile Heintges's program with U.S. pledges to respect the Geneva Accords—was easily overcome. As before, PEO personnel wore plainclothes and were, technically, civilians. Heintges himself was discharged from the service before succeeding Rothwell Brown as PEO chief. His subordinates, all retired veterans or younger men temporarily given Foreign Service reserve officer rank, addressed their commander as "Mr. Heintges." Washington thus stayed within the limits of the rules agreed on at Geneva, although Hanoi complained that the Americans had established a Military Assistance Advisory Group (MAAG) in all but name.

The second problem involved America's allies, not its enemies. Paris, Allen Dulles noted, was not "disposed to welcome a U.S. military training mission." Few prospects offended the French more than watching their influence supplanted by that of the Americans, and they were unlikely to cede training authority with grace, even though financial pressure had forced the government of Charles de Gaulle to scale back French commitments in Southeast Asia. The Eisenhower administration had to balance what Smith called the "need to avoid hurting French feelings" with the need for an enhanced U.S. military assistance program for Laos.[29]

Washington accomplished this through an agreement thrashed out between French and American officers during the first half of 1959. By its terms, U.S. "civilian technicians" would be under the "authority" of the French military mission, and all training plans would be drafted by Heintges and his French opposite number. Heintges, however, defined "authority" as "nominal control," and stressed that each contingent would maintain its "own line of command." Furthermore, while the French were responsible for "tactical training," Americans would provide training in "communications, motor maintenance, demolition,...and employment of U.S. weapons." That final stipulation was most significant. Since all new armaments issued to the RLA were American-made, U.S. instructors would be teaching the Lao to shoot, a prerogative previously reserved for the French.[30]

The Heintges Plan brought the RLA under American stewardship and marked a watershed in Washington's colonization of Laos as significant as the birth of the CDNI. Commensurate with its expanded role, the PEO's staff grew from 25 men in 1958 to 514 by December 1959. Additionally, twelve U.S. Army Special Forces teams set up training centers in Luang Prabang, Savannakhet, and Vientiane. Their mission was supposed to be covert, but a French communiqué announced their arrival, and the commitment of U.S. Special Forces only proved what everyone in Laos already knew: the Eisenhower administration had taken charge of the anticommunist effort and staked American prestige on its success.[31]

## "Unstinted though Largely Unrewarded Support"

While Washington made a mockery of Lao self-rule, Phoui continued his bid to persuade the Americans that he represented the free world's best hope in Vientiane. He issued a statement on February 11, 1959, that Laos had "completely fulfilled" its obligations under the Geneva Accords and was no longer bound by the limitations the accords placed on foreign military aid. Denouncing "certain powers... whose ideology is not shared by the Laotian people," he accused Hanoi of waging a "campaign" against his country, including the "occupation of its territory." In May, he established a secret intelligence organization to counter Pathet Lao propaganda. Such measures satisfied Smith and other civilians at the embassy and USOM, but Hecksher still preferred a Phoumi-led government, as did "Mr. Heintges," who determined after assuming his new post that the general was the only Lao tough enough to prevent Souphanouvong from taking over the country.[32]

Phoui got his chance to impress kingmakers like Heintges when the Pathet Lao renewed their rebellion in July 1959. Guerrillas armed with submachine guns struck villages in the jungles of Sam Neua and Phong Saly. It was the height of the rainy season, an unpropitious time for military operations, and royal troops defending the area were caught by surprise. They panicked at the sound of gunfire and abandoned their posts, leaving villagers defenseless. Eager to justify their flight, they reported a gargantuan enemy assault when they reached headquarters, which helped them save face but also convinced the RLG that the communists were trying to seize northern Laos.[33]

The government's response was swift. Phoui announced that this was no rebellion but an invasion, that the North Vietnamese had "stiffened" the forces assailing the former Pathet Lao strongholds. He proclaimed a state of emergency in five provinces, and then extended it to the entire country. The RLA's finest units sped north to expel the invaders. Phoui ordered Souphanouvong removed from his villa and thrown into a prison cell, along with fifteen other NLHX leaders. When news arrived in Vientiane that the communists had routed royal garrisons near Luang Prabang and Thakhet, Phoui sent a telegram to United Nations secretary-general Dag Hammarskjöld accusing North Vietnam of violating Lao territory and asking that a UN fact-finding mission investigate the matter.[34]

This move seemed to have its desired effect, as Pathet Lao guerrilla activity subsided over the next few weeks. In late August, however, the rebels began the second wave of their offensive. RLA posts along the Nam Ma River, a few miles from the North Vietnamese frontier, came under mortar attack. The defenders fled, limping into Sam Neua City days later with tales of Vietnamese battalions storming out of the morning fog and carrying all before them. Although the inaccessibility of the fighting area made it impossible for reporters to verify these stories—roads were washed out and airfields too soggy to land on—a number of American journalists accepted them as fact. Joseph Alsop of the *Washington Post* happened to be in

Laos at the time and wrote several columns detailing the "massive border crossing" in Sam Neua, "where the tragedy of Dien Bien Phu threatens to be reenacted." Phoui demanded that a UN emergency force be "dispatched at a very early date."[35]

Since there was no evidence of North Vietnamese participation in the attack, Phoui must have known that the UN would deny his request, but it was Washington he was counting on for help, and the Eisenhower administration did not disappoint him. Secretary of State Christian Herter, who had just assumed the top cabinet post upon John Foster Dulles's death, told newsmen he was "disturbed" by the communist offensive, called the situation "dangerous," and proclaimed that SEATO intervention might be necessary "before too long." The Joint Chiefs of Staff urged the president to establish an MAAG in Laos. State and Defense agreed to enlarge the RLA by four thousand men, to twenty-nine thousand. Eisenhower alerted American forces in the Pacific to stand by for action. The "crisis," one historian notes, "took on a life of its own," despite the lack of reliable information from the front.[36]

By early September, however, doubts emerged as to whether there had been a crisis at all. Hammarskjöld, though unwilling to become involved militarily, got the UN Security Council to form a subcommittee to investigate Phoui's charges. When the UN representatives arrived in Laos, they found Sam Neua and Phong Saly quiet and the RLG unable to furnish proof that North Vietnam had invaded the country. No Vietnamese prisoners had been taken, and the weapons captured by RLA troops could have been manufactured anywhere. Phoui protested that the invaders had withdrawn from Laos in anticipation of the mission's arrival, and that they had been clever enough to cover their tracks. This was part of the communist strategy, he said; DRV troops would be back as soon as the fact-finders left. The RLG produced eyewitnesses who swore that, in some places, four-fifths of the attackers were Vietnamese, but the mission refused to accept this testimony as conclusive. After spending a month in Laos and another month preparing its report, the UN subcommittee declared the "information submitted...did not clearly establish" DRV involvement. Hammarskjöld privately told Phoui to embrace the neutralism that had characterized Souvanna's government.[37]

The CIA and PEO, speaking through Phoumi, pushed Phoui in the opposite direction. Noting that the premier's grant of extraordinary powers would expire soon, Phoumi proposed revising the Lao constitution to develop what he called a "modified democracy" similar to the one in

Thailand. He wanted to postpone elections indefinitely and place executive authority in the hands of Savang Vatthana, who had just become king and who, Phoumi knew, supported the CDNI. Phoui thought this plan was preposterous, that it would lead to civil war. Smith agreed. He had never trusted Phoumi or believed the general headed a nonpartisan organization. The CDNI, Smith cabled State, was "an opposition party . . . seeking power for itself." It had, moreover, no constituency, apart from the army, and none of the major Western powers save the United States saw it as the answer to Laos's problems. Indeed, Smith's European counterparts in Vientiane advised him that Washington was making a mistake in sponsoring the CDNI, that it should have stuck with Souvanna. Now that that bridge had been burned, they noted, the worst thing the Eisenhower administration could do was encourage RLG bellicosity. Smith believed these views had to be taken seriously. Without "the benefit of solid British and French support," he argued, "we may soon see ourselves maneuvered into a position" where SEATO could not "keep Laos from sliding behind the curtain."[38]

Smith was vexed by the recent tide of events. A garrulous man who boasted that he could split bricks with his bare hands, he did not intend to play a supporting role to other American policymakers in Vientiane. Yet he could not control Hecksher or Heintges, both of whom favored a Phoumist regime and neither of whom had qualms about acting without ambassadorial concurrence. Hecksher in particular ignored the chain of command. The CIA had a separate communication channel to Washington, independent of the embassy, which enabled Hecksher to operate behind Smith's back and sabotage his policy. While Smith promoted the legal government under Phoui and tried to unify Laos's conservative factions, Hecksher made such unity impossible by exhorting Phoumi to hold out for CDNI control of the country. Hecksher enjoyed advantages in this turf war, since the CIA did not have to account for every nickel spent or worry about congressional watchdog committees. Thus, Smith complained to Parsons, the "assistance we have accorded [the] CDNI . . . far surpasses" that received by other Lao political groups. Small wonder Phoumi felt confident ordering the premier about.[39]

Phoui would endure only so much provocation, however, and by mid-December he had had enough. In a move that shocked the CDNI and its American backers, Phoui exercised his plenary executive prerogative, firing all CDNI ministers and forming a new cabinet dominated by the RLP. He also sided with the thirty-four assemblymen who voted two days later to extend the legislature's mandate in view of the impossibility of holding elections immediately. The assembly set April 3, 1960, as election day, a move Phoui's new cabinet approved. Phoumi screamed foul, but the premier had evidently decided that accommodation of the CDNI was more hazardous to his position than a clean break, even if dumping Phoumi offended some Americans.

Undersecretary of State Douglas Dillon cabled Smith the obvious question: Would Phoumi retaliate with "some form of coup"? The ambassador responded that this was "unlikely," but Heintges, better informed, told Smith that the CDNI "plan[ned] to threaten Phoui... with a bloodless coup" unless he resigned. Smith's request for permission to discourage the CDNI by cutting off aid prompted a meeting in the White House, where Parsons and Allen Dulles, both Phoumi supporters, laid out the predicament for Eisenhower. The president had not given much thought to Laos of late—crises in Cuba and Berlin had monopolized his attention—and he was unaware of the rift between CIA and embassy officials. He accepted his advisers' argument that "faced with this delicate internal situation," it was "best... to stand aside and let the Lao work out their own relationships." Calling such an approach "sensible," Eisenhower authorized State to turn Smith down.[40]

This denial did not sit well with the embassy. Smith sent a cable denouncing Washington's "unstinted though largely unrewarded support" of the CDNI and protesting the hijacking of American policy. The following day, when the National Assembly's original mandate was set to run out, Smith made another attempt to foil Phoumi, telling State that "[i]n view of [the] known close relations" between the CDNI and the CIA, no one would believe the Eisenhower administration could not have stopped a coup "if we had wished." By standing aside, the administration was in effect sanctioning the overthrow of an ally.[41]

*Les Jeunes* made their move around the same time Smith's cable arrived in Washington. It was, as Heintges had said, a bloodless coup, and a slow-motion one that took two weeks to play out. Police officers loyal to Phoumi surrounded the premier's house on Christmas Day and demanded his resignation while Phoumi and other CDNI officers met with the king, who was in Vientiane to open a special session of the assembly. Savang, torn between sympathy for the CDNI and respect for legislative procedures, waffled, and Phoui refused to step down. Phoumi thereupon fortified the guard around Phoui's residence with tanks. The CDNI placed public buildings in the capital under surveillance and stationed troops on the main streets. Smith for the moment followed orders, isolating himself in the embassy and refusing to assist either government or rebels. Things remained at an impasse until December 29, when Katay suddenly died. Although Phoui had never liked his former interior and defense minister, Katay had commanded the loyalty of most of the RLP and represented a counterweight to *les Jeunes*. News of his death took the fight out of Phoui, who submitted his resignation. CDNI soldiers occupied the ministries, the national bank, Wattay Airfield, and the radio station.[42]

With Laos on the cusp of dictatorship, Smith broke ranks, desperate to at least keep Phoumi from becoming premier. He knew Washington would not permit him to instigate any anti-Phoumi action, but he also knew that the other Western diplomats in Vientiane mistrusted the general as much as he did. He therefore approached British ambassador Anthony Lincoln and French ambassador Jean Gassouin and asked them to take the initiative. If they made a joint démarche to the king, and then requested that Smith, as American chief of mission, accompany them when they presented it, Smith's superiors could hardly object to his tagging along. Lincoln and Gassouin were agreeable, as was Australian chargé Richard Gardner, and the obligatory notes passed among them during the first days of 1960. On January 4, the four men met with Savang. Gassouin did most of the talking, imploring Savang to preserve due process and admonishing him that a "junta" would not receive support from many of the countries with which Laos maintained relations. It would be a mistake, Gassouin declared, for the king to name a military man, especially Phoumi, to head the new government. Smith, nodding in agreement, said little. Savang never knew that the American had stage-managed the whole affair.[43]

Smith's stratagem flirted with insubordination, but it worked. By presenting a united Western front to Savang, the ambassador painted American hard-liners in Vientiane and Washington into a corner: now, if they insisted on a Phoumi premiership, they risked alienating two of America's most important allies. The CIA and PEO backed off, and Savang asked rightist parliamentarian Kou Abhay to set up a caretaker government until the April 1960 general elections were held. It was a Pyrrhic victory for Smith, though, as Phoumi dominated the new cabinet. Kou, elderly and ill, posed little challenge to the general, who again became defense minister.

Hours after Kou's investment, Smith received a message from State noting that in view of the "propensity" of "Lao governments to focus on only one major problem at a time, it cannot be expected that this provisional government will do much beyond preparing for elections." That was fine with the Eisenhower administration. Policymakers remembered the

1958 electoral results and were anxious to avoid another left-wing triumph. Some suggested that the NLHX be barred from campaigning, but this idea was scrapped as counterproductive. Why give the communists a reason to portray themselves as victims? With Souphanouvong and other Pathet Lao leaders in jail, the NLHX had no prominent candidates to run for the fifty-nine seats at stake. As Herter pointed out, this left the party two alternatives: either "refusing to run" or "presenting their second team," both of which would benefit the conservatives while maintaining the appearance of fairness. Phoumi and his fellow rightists saw the wisdom in this argument and agreed to allow NLHX candidates to stand for office.[44]

They were leaving nothing to chance, though, and the degree to which they skewed the playing field shocked even veteran observers of politics in the developing world. First, they revised electoral districts to break up zones of NLHX influence. Then they persuaded the Lao council of ministers to approve a law that required runoff elections if no candidate received a majority on the first vote; this would solve the vote-splitting problem that had handed victory to the left in 1958. The government also changed its eligibility requirements. In order to campaign, a candidate had to come up with an election deposit twice as large as before. Furthermore, he had to meet minimal education standards by presenting an elementary school certificate. The NLHX was able to find just nine candidates with the requisite qualifications. None had a national reputation, and few observers gave them a chance to win.

The RLG entrusted the army with the task of supervising the elections, meaning that it left this responsibility in Phoumi's hands. He moved quickly to, in Sisouk's words, "establish a favorable climate" by launching Operation Cleanup, a psychological warfare program conducted in areas known to be sympathetic to the Pathet Lao. Tactics included the arrest, beating, and murder of suspected subversives. Phoumi also reduced the number of polling places, citing security concerns. Residents of villages without RLA protection had to travel great distances to cast their ballots, and many decided to stay home, which did not trouble Phoumi. He was interested in victory, not maximizing voter turnout.[45]

Americans sanctioned and abetted these tactics. PEO chief Heintges called Operation Cleanup "well devised" and "progressive," and made sure Washington underwrote it. State and the CIA gave the CDNI millions of dollars for propaganda and bribed leftist or independent candidates to withdraw. A U.S. Foreign Service officer told newsman Arthur Dommen that he had seen CIA agents distributing bagfuls of money to village headmen to buy votes. While some policymakers expressed concern that Phoumi might dispense with formalities and introduce military rule, like his cousin Sarit had done in Thailand, none objected to the travesty of democracy slated to occur throughout Laos in April.[46]

And *travesty* was the word for it, as the vote counts defied belief. In one district, a Pathet Lao stronghold, the NLHX candidate received four votes to his CDNI opponent's 18,189. Another NLHX candidate was also credited with four votes, even though he had five family members eligible to vote for him. Quinim Pholsena, one of the most prominent left-wing politicians in the country, lost by a count of 17,175 to 721, and the former Pathet Lao governor of Sam Neua went down to defeat 6,508 to 13. The margins in other districts were similar, with pro-government candidates garnering over 90 percent of the votes cast. One CDNI candidate got two thousand votes more than there were registered voters. All told, the CDNI took thirty-two of the fifty-nine assembly seats, and the RLP picked up the remaining twenty-seven. Not a single leftist candidate won, even in electorates that had returned NLHX members two years before.

The way seemed clear for Phoumi to assume the premiership. His party held a majority in the assembly, and under normal circumstances it would have been impossible to deny him this prize. Circumstances were hardly normal, though. Apart from the irregularity of the elections and French and British opposition, there was the fact that Phoumi did not head a political party. The CDNI had characterized itself in its statutes and manifesto as a civic group, which put it in a different category from the RLP and NLHX and made legislative representation awkward. Phoumi fixed that by changing the CDNI's name to the Paxa Sangkhom (People's Society) Party and proclaiming himself its leader. He then waited for Savang to ask him to assemble a cabinet. The king might have obliged but for an event that occurred in a prison camp on the outskirts of Vientiane exactly one month after the CDNI swept to victory.

## "The First Step of a Possible Communist Takeover"

A grim Allen Dulles informed the NSC on May 24, 1960, that Souphanouvong and twelve NLHX leaders had just escaped from jail, "probably by bribery of the guards." Matters were worse than Dulles imagined. Souphanouvong had in fact converted jailers at the Phone Keng Prison to the Pathet Lao cause. "I talked to them about the immorality of their bosses, . . . of the anti-patriotic attitude of those who sold themselves for dollars," the Red Prince later told journalist Wilfred Burchett. "Our interests were selfless, we were not out for personal gain." For months, "it was like talking to a brick wall. . . . But, gradually, one or two started to listen at the window." The sham elections of April bolstered Souphanouvong's claim that Laos had fallen into the hands of "foreigners who want to enslave the country." By late May Souphanouvong had won over enough guards to ensure that one night's entire shift was composed of "friendlies." The MPs supplied the NLHX leaders with military uniforms and weapons. Then both captors and captives fled into the darkness as a thunderstorm drenched the area, washing away any traces of their flight.[47]

The escape, Smith remarked, was an "unfortunate break" and earned Phoumi a "dressing down" from Savang, who designated rightist Tiao Somsanith to succeed Kou as premier. Members of the American mission were even angrier than the king. A PEO official noted that the "laxity of [the] guard placed over such important prisoners" was "shocking but not surprising." Phoumi tried to save face by apprehending Souphanouvong, but it was a lost cause, as the Red Prince defied expectations and did not rush to either Sam Neua or Hanoi. Instead, he embarked on a "long march" that took him to Pathet Lao–controlled areas in every province of the country. Although his stretch behind bars had weakened him, he and his followers covered hundreds of miles, sleeping in the open, eating lizards and bugs, trudging through jungles and over mountain passes, always one step ahead of the RLA. This mythologized event, Sisouk admitted, gave "new life to the rebellion." A skeletal Souphanouvong arrived in Sam Neua in early November, ready, despite his condition, to lead the communists in their next campaign.[48]

By then, however, the Red Prince had been upstaged by another rebel, the most fascinating figure in Lao's postcolonial drama. Kong Le caught everyone by surprise, including the PEO officers who paid him. Five feet tall, one hundred pounds sopping wet, and seemingly younger than his twenty-six years, the paratroop captain hardly met U.S. criteria for a conqueror. Americans who passed him on the street in Vientiane had no reason to give him a second glance, or even a first. He was a good soldier, popular with his men, but poor and uneducated, having dropped out of school to pursue a career in the army. His political views, insofar as he had articulated any prior to 1960, were pro-Western, although he disliked the abuses associated with the U.S. aid program and made a point of bicycling to work while officers of equal rank drove Mercedes-Benzes. He had served the RLG since the end of the Franco–Viet Minh War, and his battalion had engaged the Pathet Lao in numerous firefights, most recently in Sam Neua during the summer 1959 invasion. Although Phoumi considered Kong Le one of his better commanders, he never thought of him as a rival.

Yet Kong Le carried out the lightning-fast coup Phoumi could only dream of, taking power in Vientiane on August 9, 1960. His motive remains a matter of dispute—contemporary American pundits cited everything from communist indoctrination to a Napoleonic "runt complex," while recently a historian has speculated that Phoumi and the CDNI orchestrated the revolt only to have it blow up in their faces—but the simplest explanation, Kong Le's own, is most convincing. "I am tired of seeing Lao fight Lao," he declared. "The only ones to profit from this fratricide are the Americans." He believed that the civil war ruining his country was a result of external interference, and he wanted to end both the interference and the war. His coup was an act of pure, guileless patriotism. Neither superpower saw it coming, and it made the captain a legend.[49]

He chose the perfect moment to strike. The entire cabinet, including Phoumi, was absent from Vientiane in early August, having flown north to Luang Prabang to consult with Savang about funeral rites for his father. Vientiane's warehouses were filled with weapons delivered by the PEO. Since monsoon rains made overland travel impossible, the rebels did not have to worry about Phoumi's forces retaliating. The capital was defenseless. Still, Kong Le wanted to win without bloodshed, and that required preparation. Several days before the coup, he asked the Second Paratroop Battalion's PEO advisers to conduct a training exercise. How, he inquired, could eight hundred soldiers seize and hold a city, like, for example, Vientiane? The paratroopers jotted down notes while their instructors walked them through the necessary steps: secure the airfield, take over the radio station and post office, maintain central control lest your unit fractionate, and so on. Kong Le thanked the Americans for their wisdom and began readying his men.

The coup, which took three hours, was a tactical masterpiece. Kong Le's followers attacked before dawn, spreading out across town, each equipped with a transistor radio that enabled the captain, after the radio station fell, to coordinate their movements. The rebels occupied all strategic points, including the Chinaimo army camp downstream from Vientiane. They disarmed RLA infantry units and placed government officials under house arrest. After taking Wattay Airfield, they parked jeeps on the runways to keep enemy planes from landing. There was a skirmish at the home of the army chief of staff in which two guards were killed, but those were the only casualties, as the operation unfolded so quickly that royal troops and police had no opportunity to muster resistance. By 7 a.m., Kong Le was in control of the city. U.S. policymakers who questioned whether the Lao could execute complex military maneuvers had their answer.

The captain's first radio address to his "compatriots" fluttered many dovecotes in Washington. "We are disgusted with this civil war," he proclaimed. "It is made by a handful of people for foreign money." He asked "all foreign troops established on the national soil" to leave and promised to establish "a policy of genuine neutrality." His closing line—"I suggest that everyone now clap and cheer!"—was typical of his earnest, artless style, and the audience responded. All morning Vientiane residents came to the premier's house, where Kong Le had established his headquarters, to offer congratulations. Later, at a rally at the sports stadium, the captain's anti-Americanism became more pronounced. "It is the Americans who have...caused civil war in our country," he announced to a roaring crowd. He called upon Somsanith to resign, and thumbed his nose at the Eisenhower administration by asking Souvanna to assume the premiership. While he did not know Souvanna personally, he respected him as a politician "who is strong and honest."[50]

CIA agents in Laos, the first Americans to file reports on the Kong Le coup, were dumbfounded by the excitement he aroused. What was it about this man that struck a chord in people's hearts? Judging the captain by American standards of behavior, the agents found him not only ill-equipped to lead a national movement but downright mad. "Kong Le was nervous, jerky, and had [a] decided twitch...in [his] face," one report of a press conference read. "He appeared to be in [a] daze and [his] conversation was disjointed and rambling. He stared into space and appeared to be mentally deranged." The agent concluded that Kong Le must "drink or take dope, or else he is cracking under [the] strain." Another report noted that Kong Le had "broken down and cried" when criticized by Ouane. Back in Washington, Daniel Anderson, director of the State Department's office of Southeast Asian affairs, expressed concern about "the apparent emotional instability...of Captain Kong Le," and Undersecretary of State Douglas Dillon described the captain's "actions and words" as "dangerously immature and irrational." A lunatic, it seemed, had derailed U.S. policy overnight.[51]

Fortunately for Kong Le, the new American ambassador to Laos, Winthrop Brown, was the ablest official to fill that post during the Eisenhower years and less disposed than his colleagues to write the captain off. Brown, who arrived in Vientiane two weeks before the coup, had little opportunity to acquaint himself with the intricacies of Lao politics, but he learned fast. Within days, he was reporting to Washington that Kong Le's "vision of neutralism has ignited widely smouldering enthusiasm." The Lao wanted peace, Brown declared, and their reaction to Kong Le showed their "sincere belief that [a] more obviously neutral policy" could bring this about. Brown cautioned State against underestimating the forces Kong Le had unleashed. While the ambassador recognized the "danger [of] Laos going more centralist," he believed that "its doing so is to [a] significant degree in response [to] genuine and growing popular feeling...which we cannot ignore." Brown was certain that the coup had not been "commie" or even "politically inspired." It grew out of something more basic: "the hope of [a] peaceful reconciliation of [a] long fratricidal struggle." The Pathet Lao could, of course, "exploit" this hope, but only if Americans refused to recognize that Kong Le's program had "great pulling power, not only in Vientiane but throughout [the] country."[52]

This was not what Washington wanted to hear. Even worse was Brown's conclusion that Kong Le was right about Souvanna: the prince did seem to be the one person capable of keeping Laos noncommunist and at peace. "I must say I was very impressed," Brown recalled of his first meeting with Souvanna, who was in Vientiane at the time of the coup. "The impression I got of the man, as such, was that he had qualities of leadership." Brown also appreciated Souvanna's determination to follow parliamentary rules. The prince told Kong Le that he could not accept command of the country as a gift from a rebel chieftain, that the National Assembly had to agree to any change in regime.[53]

Accordingly, a quasi-legal meeting of the legislature took place four days after the coup and voted for a motion of no confidence in Somsanith. The deputies would have found it difficult to do otherwise, as the assembly building was surrounded by a crowd of over six thousand people screaming themselves hoarse and carrying banners condemning American policy toward Laos: "Yanks Go Home!" "PEO. GO. GO. GO," and "Down with U.S. Imperialism." One placard depicted Uncle Sam, his pockets bursting with dollars, being pursued by the virtuous peasantry. When debate took too long for some demonstrators, they broke into the anteroom, destroyed furniture and paintings, and seemed on the verge of overrunning the main hall. Finally, Souvanna appeared to announce the assemblymen's vote, at which point he was swept up by the crowd and carried in triumph through the city streets.

A delegation from the assembly flew to Luang Prabang the following morning to deliver their verdict to Somsanith, who resigned. Savang accepted the premier's resignation and called on Souvanna to form a government.[54]

Although Brown regarded these developments favorably, the various Washington agencies, in particular the CIA, were appalled. Allen Dulles informed the NSC that in light of Souvanna's "dealings with the Pathet Lao," it was his "personal view" that this was "the first step of a possible communist take-over of Laos." Dillon concurred, noting that "our first step should be to get rid of Kong Le," who was a "Castro communist-type individual." Were the RLA to confront him with "overwhelming force," Dillon suggested, he might "cave in," leaving Washington free to put together a new RLG. Dulles pointed out that, sadly, "the Lao are not much given to fighting." Since there were "few people of any courage" in Laos, whom could the Eisenhower administration trust to take the bull by the horns? The answer was obvious. Army chief of staff General Lyman Lemnitzer declared, "Phoumi should be brought toward Vientiane as rapidly as possible." The next day, the JCS recommended giving Phoumi whatever assistance he required to "regain control of the Laos government." Chief of naval operations Admiral Arleigh Burke thought matters would be cleared up quickly. "If there is bloodshed," Burke predicted, Phoumi "can win whatever fight may develop." And Burke did not foresee bloodshed. "The Laotians are a very friendly people," he advised Defense Secretary Thomas Gates. "They do not want to fight. There probably will be no fighting."[55]

Phoumi was one Lao spoiling for a fight. As soon as news of the coup reached him, he flew from Luang Prabang to Bangkok to meet with Sarit, who agreed to impose a blockade of all supply lines into northern Laos. This would close off cross-river traffic carrying food and fuel to Vientiane and, in time, starve the city out. Phoumi then traveled to his hometown of Savannakhet, headquarters of Military Region III of the RLA, where he proclaimed martial law. Radio transmitters supplied by the United States began broadcasting anti-coup propaganda, and planes flew over Vientiane dropping leaflets that informed residents they were living in a "communist hell." Phoumi assured his backers in Washington that his position was strong. He had the support of the commanders of four of the nation's five military regions—the fifth, Vientiane, was controlled by Kong Le—and Sarit was providing him with troops and artillery. A drive to liberate the capital would be a mere matter of marching.[56]

Brown opposed any such move. What the Eisenhower administration faced now, he argued, was a situation in which the "military force in Laos is largely on Phoumi's side" while the "legal and international right [is] on Souvanna's side." Washington's task was to "bring them together," since the "army needs legal government direction and [an] effective government needs [the] army under its control." Besides, none of America's allies except Thailand would support a Phoumist attack. Britain and France were certain to object, and the Australians had already advised Phoumi against violence. State went along with Brown for the moment, authorizing him to try to reconcile Souvanna and Phoumi but warning him that the administration would not countenance a government containing Pathet Lao representatives.[57]

Word that Phoumi's troops had captured Paksane, a town eighty miles southeast of Vientiane, helped persuade Souvanna that accommodation was essential. He flew to Savannakhet on August 23 to see the general, and the two men spent an afternoon in conference before announcing that they would convoke a meeting of the assembly at Luang Prabang, considered neutral ground, and form a coalition government. Six days later, the meeting began in the royal capital, and on August 31 the assembly approved a government headed by Souvanna, with Phoumi as deputy premier and minister of the interior. CIA officials attributed this arrangement to the "Lao disinclination to combat, natural tendency to effect compromise, and desire [to] live [an] easy life without unnecessary stresses." The new cabinet was weighted toward the right: there were several CDNI ministers, none from the NLHX, and Phoumi's brother-in-law became minister of communications and public works. Ouane, an archconservative, assumed Phoumi's old post at defense. Souvanna's only left-leaning appointment was Quinim Pholsena, who took over the information ministry. In all, Brown considered the outcome a triumph for his side and urged Washington to endorse it.[58]

Just as Souvanna appeared to have rescued Laos from catastrophe, though, his plans began to unravel. Whether Phoumi ever intended to abide by the agreement cannot be determined, but Kong Le gave him an excuse for reneging the day the government was announced. Furious that Phoumi had received a post, Kong Le went on the radio and demanded the general's removal. Souvanna forced Kong Le to retract this statement, but the damage was done. Phoumi, scheduled to return to Vientiane with the other ministers, flew instead to Savannakhet, where he told anyone who would listen that he could not enter the administrative capital without risking assassination. He formed a Revolutionary Committee led—ostensibly—by Prince Boun Oum, heir to the former king of Champassak in the southernmost part of the country. Boun Oum, like Phoumi, had a taste for power, but he lacked the general's vitality, preferring to idle away his golden years with a whiskey and soda in his hand and a pretty woman on his knee. "The fiction was that Boun Oum was the mentor," U.S. cultural attaché Perry Stieglitz recalled, "but of course it was the protégé who was completely in charge." When, on September 10, Boun Oum broadcast from Savannakhet that "we revolutionaries... hereby declare that we seize power," he was announcing Phoumi's bid to become dictator.[59]

Most American policymakers, including the president, welcomed this proclamation. Although Eisenhower had not been kept informed about events in Laos, he remarked during an NSC meeting that "we should support Phoumi," a view seconded by Dulles and Dillon. The JCS recommended "aggressive support of General Phoumi" and felt he should be encouraged to "liquidate [the] Kong Le coup group even at [the] cost of some bloodshed." Parsons believed the captain was overdue for a comeuppance. "If it were any other country but Laos, I would not be able to understand why Kong Le has not been eliminated," the undersecretary cabled Brown. "It seems to be a fact that the Lao hate to take resolute action." Now that Phoumi had bucked that trend, his stock in Washington rose, especially among hard-liners like Air Force chief of staff General Curtis LeMay, who growled during a State-JCS meeting, "What's wrong with telling Phoumi we will give him everything he wants?"[60]

Brown countered that a pro-Phoumi strategy was "unacceptable" in that it would "involve support [of a] group which has... abrogated [the] legal govt." For weeks, Brown waged a gallant but losing campaign to steer U.S. policy away from Phoumi and toward neutralism. This made him unpopular in some circles, he remembered, noting that Pentagon officials called him "that communist ambassador," but his defense of Souvanna persuaded Herter to strike a balance between the stateside hawks and the embassy. The secretary instructed Brown to ask Savang to create a new government led by some "respected figure" whom both Phoumi and Souvanna could live with. Phoumi would serve in the cabinet, and "Souvanna might have [a] position." Brown was further instructed to tell the king that Washington would suspend aid if the "situation does not appear to move toward [a] resolution." To Brown's protest that there was no statesman other than Souvanna who could "avoid being widely considered a Phoumi/U.S. stooge," Herter responded that he was "disturbed by [the] lack of understanding... between us." Souvanna's "softness in the face of communist pressure" made him an undesirable ally, the secretary declared, whereas Phoumi, whatever his faults, was "pro–U.S. and anti-communist." The choice of whom to support was therefore academic.[61]

While Brown stalled for time, Phoumi's men fought their first battle as rebels. The experience ought to have given them, and Washington, pause. Phoumi ordered two battalions stationed at Paksane to advance on Vientiane, but before they got fifteen miles out of town they encountered two companies of Kong Le's paratroops, who, although outnumbered four to one, routed the Phoumists and sent them fleeing south. Not only did Phoumi fail to reach the administrative capital, but he lost Paksane, which was overrun by the paratroops. Meanwhile, the Pathet Lao, eager to take advantage of divisions in the noncommunist forces, reoccupied Sam Neua Province. According to reports, the fifteen hundred Phoumist troops defending the province either ran away or surrendered before the first shots were fired.

These reverses, plus Souvanna's decision to pardon Souphanouvong for past offenses and begin negotiating with his half-brother, sent Washington into a panic. The JCS, with State and Defense assent, authorized Admiral Harry Felt, commander in chief, Pacific (CINCPAC), to provide Phoumi with the "necessary arms" to "prevent another defeat." Four days later, Washington suspended aid to the RLG, making it impossible for Souvanna to pay his troops or civil servants. Yet military equipment and money continued flowing from the United States to Phoumi via Thailand, and the base at Savannakhet grew larger and more modern. American advisers helped Phoumi's men build an airfield, where planes soon landed bearing gifts, among them C-ration boxes stuffed with U.S. dollars. As Phoumi's war chest filled, his confidence returned. Messages from Souvanna inviting him to meet and resolve the problems of the country were cast aside, unread. The Phoumists began preparing to descend upon Vientiane again, their ranks bolstered by former RLA troops who had defected to the rebel side in search of a paycheck.[62]

Brown thought the Eisenhower administration was courting disaster, and said so. "[T]here is now little or no chance [to] salvage [the] country...through Phoumi," he declared. If Washington wanted to recover "anything we care about from the present wreck," it should support Souvanna, who was the "only rallying point left." Showering the Phoumists with weapons and cash would fix nothing. "They have recently suffered both military and psychological defeats and have lost confidence in themselves and, probably, in their leader," Brown pointed out. Even if, "by some miracle," Phoumi managed to "reunite [the] country," he could do so "only precariously by force" and "invite consequences," like internationalization of the conflict, too hideous to contemplate.[63]

The soundness of Brown's counsel was borne out when Souvanna, broke and stranded in a capital running low on food and fuel, did what any leader would and sought relief elsewhere, announcing that he would be happy to accept Soviet help. Moscow agreed to ease Laos's economic distress in exchange for the establishment of diplomatic relations. Souvanna acquiesced, and the Soviet Union sent its first ambassador to Laos. "Had the Americans been our best friends, they could not have acted otherwise," gloated Aleksandr Abramov, the man chosen to head the Soviet Embassy in Vientiane. The reception accorded Abramov when his plane touched down at Wattay compounded the Eisenhower administration's discomfiture, as a crowd of over five hundred gathered to welcome the Russian diplomat. Girls offered him flower bouquets, Buddhist monks bowed to him, and two companies of RLA soldiers stood at attention. As Abramov inspected the honor guard, twenty-six of Kong Le's parachutists jumped in formation from a troop carrier overhead. It was, noted the *New York Times*, "a greeting fit for a chief of state."[64]

## "All-Out Civil War"

In early October 1960, State and Defense decided to send a mission to Laos to square the circle, or, as Herter put it, "to make a last desperate effort to work through and with Souvanna Phouma as the legal façade of legitimate government and at [the] same time supporting Phoumi and other anticommunist forces." Unsurprisingly, given that tangled elucidation, participants in the mission held different views as to its purpose. One, Assistant Secretary of Defense for International Security Affairs John Irwin, thought it was to find out what Phoumi needed to conquer Vientiane. Another, Vice Admiral Herbert Riley, chief of staff at CINCPAC, believed he and his associates were supposed to determine whether there were any Lao leaders with sufficient determination to resist the communists. But the most interesting construal was advanced by the group's leader, J. Graham Parsons.[65]

We cannot know why Herter selected Parsons to head this mission. The secretary must have been aware that Parsons, while ambassador to Laos, had bent every effort to thwart a coalition, and that as a result there was no love lost between him and Souvanna. Herter moreover must have remembered the hearings conducted by Congressman Porter Hardy's Government Operations Committee, in which Parsons had been humiliated while trying to defend the U.S. aid program. Why, in light of these events, Parsons was entrusted with an assignment so weighty is baffling, as is the fact that he was recalled from vacation on such short notice that he was unable to catch up on his papers. "I got a telephone call... and I was told they wanted me in Washington the following morning," he remembered. "I was to leave from Washington after lunch for the Far East." To do what? "[T]his trip came about by somebody's idea in Washington that maybe getting three of the characters most responsible and knocking their heads together, something good would come of it." Irwin and Riley, the military men, would handle Phoumi's and Kong Le's heads, while the diplomat Parsons was responsible for Souvanna's. Corporately, they were to "clear the air," "put the pieces together again," and bring about "a meeting of minds." Parsons admitted that the mission was not "well judged as to timing or preparation" and that he was ill-suited to lead it, "given my break with Souvanna," but he insisted in a 1969 interview that "there was no choice." Orders were orders.[66]

The Parsons-Irwin-Riley mission marked a nadir in U.S. policy toward Laos. Parsons arrived in Vientiane jet-lagged after his globe-spanning trip, having barely slept in three days. He was even less interested than usual in listening to Lao complaints. Souvanna welcomed the undersecretary at his office, where Parsons proceeded to lecture him on the "historical facts" of communism. "Communists are today's imperialists," Parsons proclaimed, citing events in Eastern Europe. The Pathet Lao did not care about "Lao independence." Rather, they were an "instrument of international communism and as such would never cease their efforts" to take over the nation. Souvanna needed to get it through his skull that Washington could not "support [a] government permitting [a] country to become communist-dominated." Parsons laid down conditions for the resumption of American aid. First, Souvanna must cease talks with the Pathet Lao. Then he must move his cabinet to Luang Prabang, away from the administrative capital's political ferment. Finally, he had to direct Kong Le and his paratroops to stop battling the Savannakhet-based forces. Souvanna refused to comply with these demands and denounced Washington for supplying a rebel army. The discussion ended in deadlock, like so many other encounters between Souvanna and Parsons during the latter's ambassadorship.[67]

Confronting reporters the next morning, Parsons fended off questions about why he was in Laos with an ambiguous "I came mainly to see my old friends." He also stated that he had "made no proposals," which was untrue, and that "the U.S. has always been willing to offer its support to countries which wish to maintain their independence." Souvanna held a simultaneous press conference at which he announced, "If U.S. aid is not continued, the Laotian government will get it someplace else." This was not a threat, just a fact. "[W]e don't want to have communism come to power here," Souvanna insisted. "If the Americans understand our position, that's all right. But if not—too bad." At a luncheon for Western diplomats later that day, Parsons complained about the premier's attitude, only to have British ambassador John Addis advise him to give Souvanna "all possible support," because "no other leader" could "save Laos." French ambassador Pierre-Louis Falaize concurred.[68]

Meanwhile, Irwin and Riley met with Phoumi at Savannakhet. They issued contradictory pronouncements, urging the general to join a "new anti-communist government" and at the same time telling him the Eisenhower administration sanctioned his march on the capital. Irwin pointed out that Laos's "unique political situation" put America in a "difficult position." Washington had "proper relationships with [the] Vientiane government," which had declared Phoumi a rebel, and therefore U.S. policymakers had to "exercise restraint." Riley noted his colleagues' hope that "this situation would soon change." After the formal conversation ended, the two Americans took Phoumi aside and expressed themselves more clearly. Washington had lost confidence in Souvanna, they said, and was counting on Phoumi to "clean up the situation." The general need not worry about money, weaponry, or advisers. While "for the moment" U.S. policymakers had to give mouth honor to Souvanna, "in [the] long run" they backed Phoumi "all the way." Remarkably, neither Irwin nor Riley cleared these statements with Brown or informed him of them later.[69]

Brown therefore felt he had defused the crisis when he got Souvanna to accept a compromise whereby Washington would recommence payment of the monthly cash subsidy to the RLG if the premier would allow Americans to continue delivering military aid to Savannakhet. Souvanna went along with this gentleman's agreement, but insisted that Phoumi use the aid only to fight the Pathet Lao, not neutralists. Money began flowing to Souvanna's regime again on October 18. The United States was now paying two opposing noncommunist factions.

Although this arrangement made no sense strategically, Brown hoped it would buy time for cooler heads to prevail, which it might have if Phoumi had not felt free to welsh on the deal. As far as he was concerned, Irwin and Riley had assured him that the Americans would support an attack on

Vientiane, and public statements to the contrary were just for show. Brown's bargain, consequently, meant nothing. Besides, how could the provision about not attacking neutralists be enforced once Phoumi had the necessary equipment? The general never considered abandoning his plans to take the capital, and neither did the CIA and PEO officers assisting him. Furthermore, Sarit, Phoumi's patron, was not bound by any settlement worked out by the American ambassador and refused to relax his blockade. Thai support for Phoumi grew more militant. Vientiane even began taking mortar fire from the Thai side of the Mekong. By the time Parsons, Irwin, and Riley returned home, having neglected to speak with Kong Le, the balance of forces in Laos had shifted decisively against neutralism.

It had shifted in Washington as well. At a joint State-Defense meeting on October 28, civil and military officials addressed what Undersecretary of State Livingston Merchant termed "the most basic issue: whether the United States should work through Phoumi or Souvanna." The premier had no advocates. Predictably, Parsons's voice was loudest in calling for new leadership. Souvanna, he asserted, "has done little…to help us." Kong Le was on the warpath, RLG–Pathet Lao talks continued, and every day the Soviets gained more ground. Since the British and French were sure to oppose a Phoumi government, Parsons suggested that Phoui Sananikone replace Souvanna and that Phoumi obtain a top cabinet post. After further discussion, the participants agreed that Washington should try to get enough assembly members moved from Vientiane to Luang Prabang to vote Souvanna out of office and install Phoui. Herter cabled Brown the change in policy that evening.[70]

Brown responded with a four-part telegram listing the defects in Parsons's plan. Savang hated Phoui, he wrote, and would not ask him to serve. In addition, Phoui could not get two-thirds of the assemblymen to vote for him. The "majority of [the] 45 deputies still in Vientiane support Souvanna," Brown noted. "Neutralist feeling [is] strong." Also, even if the king and legislature accepted Phoui, America's allies would not. The British and French viewed Phoui as "contrary [to the] best interests [of] Laos as well as [the] West." Finally, there was the fact that Phoumi had ousted Phoui in 1959, which made any partnership between the two men unfeasible. On balance, Brown argued, the Phoui solution was a nonstarter. He recommended instead that "we continue [to] pursue our present policy and…come to terms with Souvanna." State did not attempt to rebut Brown's points, but put its foot down in a cable issued after another interdepartmental conference. "We have no faith whatsoever in Souvanna Phouma," Herter asserted, "and believe he is taking Laos rapidly down [the] road to [a] P[athet] L[ao] takeover." The secretary directed Brown to "proceed immediately to plan and act on this basis," namely to work for Souvanna's deposal.[71]

Before Brown could begin planning and acting, he received word that an RLA battalion had just revolted, seized Luang Prabang, and proclaimed its allegiance to Phoumi. Souvanna absorbed another blow when three companies of militia sent by Kong Le to retake the royal capital defected to the Phoumists halfway along the march from Vientiane to Luang Prabang. Perhaps Brown would not need to do anything to effect regime change. The "skids appear to be getting under Souvanna," a CIA report observed, "although he will continue [to] resist this trend strongly."[72]

How strongly became apparent on November 16, when the premier told reporters that American assistance to Phoumi was "illegal." That afternoon, Souvanna's cabinet announced its decision to send "goodwill missions" to Beijing and Hanoi. Two days later, Souvanna met with Souphanouvong in Sam Neua. The half-brothers embraced on the balcony of the Red Prince's villa and agreed to form a coalition government comprising neutralists, Pathet Lao—and Phoumists. There was a catch, however: military officers could not serve as ministers, which meant the new cabinet would exclude Phoumi himself, although his followers might be nominated. Souvanna spelled out the terms of this agreement to Brown with what the ambassador described as an "air of [the] greatest satisfaction." Then he politely said, "I am going to have to ask you to stop all aid to Savannakhet." In his genteel way, he had thrown down the gauntlet.[73]

Washington's reaction was indeed to halt aid, but to Souvanna, not Phoumi. Herter advised Eisenhower, "We ought to take the wraps off Phoumi right away." The president agreed, remarking that a bonus for Phoumi's troops might be in order. They would get one-half pay up front, he said, and the rest when they "licked the other fellow." State cabled Admiral Felt, authorizing him to coordinate a CIA payment to the rebel soldiers and the "removal [of] any military restraints hitherto imposed by us on Phoumi." On November 23, Phoumi's army began marching toward Vientiane.[74]

The opening battle of this campaign took place at the Nam Ka Dinh River, where Phoumists outnumbered neutralists five to one. At first, it looked like a repeat of their previous encounter, as Kong Le's men drove the rebels back, but Phoumi moved up reinforcements and attacked again five days later, this time supported by planes belonging to Civil Air Transport, a proprietary CIA company. Over one hundred neutralists were killed or wounded in the resulting engagement, and the government troops retreated northward. Phoumi's forces crossed the river and advanced upon Paksane, which fell to the rebels for a second time despite Kong Le rushing several companies to bolster his front line. While these firefights unfolded, the first Soviet planes bearing food and fuel landed at Wattay Airfield, and Abramov promised Souvanna that heavy weaponry would soon arrive. Allen Dulles informed the NSC that the "situation in Laos" was "moving closer to all-out civil war."[75]

Brown thought so too, and he found the prospect deplorable. Apart from the "loss of Lao life," he cabled State, civil war might lead to a "situation of two governments with [the] U.S. supporting one and everyone else the other." The ambassador implored his superiors "not to allow us to be forced by one man's stubbornness into cutting our throats." State and Defense were just as adamant in their conviction that the present government could not be preserved. "Souvanna Phouma wobbles," declared Admiral Burke. "He is not even a weak reed but merely jelly." Parsons admitted that Phoumi lacked "political skills," yet insisted he had "that unique quality among Lao, namely decisiveness," and therefore deserved U.S. backing. Brown found himself, as he put it, with "responsibility but not authority," as State translated none of his recommendations into policy and he was reduced to the role of spectator in the tragedy playing itself out in his host nation.[76]

That drama took a bizarre turn on December 8 when Colonel Kouprasith Abhay, head of the Chinaimo army camp on the southern outskirts of Vientiane, staged another coup. Kouprasith had earlier pledged his fealty to Souvanna, but his sympathies lay with the right, and as Phoumi drew closer to the capital, the colonel switched sides, leading his armored squadron into town and proclaiming the neutralist government overthrown. His coup lasted less than a day. Kong Le's paratroops forced the mutineers back to Chinaimo, which became, in effect, an enemy base, and Souvanna, sensing he was no longer safe in Vientiane, handed over civil and military powers to RLA chief of staff General Sounthone Pathammavong and flew with most of his cabinet to Phnom Penh. He was not resigning, he proclaimed, just delegating authority "to assure security and the functioning of public services." Sounthone in turn passed the reins of government to the remaining cabinet members, among whom Quinim Pholsena established himself as acting premier. Meanwhile, Phoumi contacted Kouprasith by radio at Chinaimo and put him in charge of the assault on Vientiane.[77]

Savang then gave Phoumi his greatest victory to date by issuing a royal decree in which he asserted that Souvanna had "allowed communist organization[s] to usurp power." The king pronounced Souvanna's government dissolved and entrusted the Revolutionary Committee, headed by Boun Oum, with conduct of the kingdom's affairs. Washington promptly recognized Boun Oum's regime as the legal government. As if to demonstrate that he rather than Boun Oum called the shots, Phoumi did not even await instructions before ordering paratroops dropped into Chinaimo to augment Kouprasith's force. The colonel was going to need these extra men. Russian aircraft began arriving at Wattay with howitzers and mortars for the neutralists, and Kong Le made clear that he planned to expend every bullet. It was "better to die than to be slaves of the Americans," he told his followers. "Arise and kill the enemy."[78]

Vientiane braced for battle. Shopkeepers padlocked iron grills on their doors and windows. Residents whose houses had cellars crowded into them. Those less fortunate stacked bookcases, furniture, and mattresses against their walls to trap bullets and shrapnel. Brown instructed Americans to stay off the streets and had the wives and children of embassy workers evacuated to Thailand. Kong Le opened Vientiane's arsenal and distributed arms to anyone willing to fight alongside him. Quinim ordered the schools closed, announced a curfew between 7 p.m. and 6 a.m., and flew to Sam Neua to ask Souphanouvong for aid in resisting the Phoumists. The Red Prince promised to do what he could.

So desperate were Vientiane's defenders for support, and so compromised was Kong Le's original neutralism, that the captain welcomed communist assistance. "Soldiers of the Pathet Lao are here to help us crush the enemy," he declared to a Western reporter. From the perspective of U.S. policymakers, such remarks only proved that Kong Le had been a communist all along. Now that Hanoi and Beijing had "built him up as a martyr, as a hero," Heintges proclaimed, they were seizing their "golden opportunity" to "take over the government." Parsons made the same point more obliquely. The "old three-cornered situation," he observed at a State-JCS conference, was "giving way to a more obvious polarization."[79]

No high-ranking American save Brown recognized the extent to which Washington had created this polarization. The battle for Vientiane was the predictable result of two years of ill-managed policy that had, by the winter of 1960, left neutralist Lao patriots with a choice between surrender or an alliance with Souphanouvong. Kong Le chose the latter course, as would Souvanna when he returned to Laos in mid-1961 to begin his fourth term as premier. Before he—and a new American president—could revive the dream of Lao neutrality, however, Vientiane had to pass through its ordeal by fire.

"It really makes you sick to see this senseless destruction," Brown cabled Parsons on December 13, as the battle swelled and ebbed around the embassy grounds. Fittingly, both sides fought with American-made weapons. Kong Le's men had guns and ammunition provided by the PEO, and most of the military hardware they received via Soviet airlift had been captured from American-equipped forces during the Franco–Viet Minh War. The Phoumists, of course, were armed to the teeth with the best instruments of destruction America could supply. Neutralists wore red scarves to the Phoumists' white, an arrangement that some observers invested with symbolic significance but that no more reflected Kong Le's communist leanings than it did Phoumi's purity. The combatants simply needed some such manner of identification, since both sides wore the same American uniforms. While Parsons dismissed Souvanna's claim that Washington caused the battle for Vientiane and was responsible for the damage wrought, the prince sized up matters correctly. The Eisenhower administration had Lao blood on its hands.[80]

# Chapter 5

# "Doctor Tom" and "Mister Pop"

## American Icons in Laos

Thomas Anthony Dooley III and Edgar Monroe Buell never met, which was just as well. They would have found little to talk about. The St. Louis physician and the Indiana farmer moved in separate circles, even when they were both fighting to save Laos from communism. Dooley may not have been aware of Buell's existence, and Buell mentioned Dooley only three times in letters home, twice parenthetically and once with the earthiness that made him such good copy. "God[,] you will never know how glad I am I worked hard on this language," he noted after delivering supplies to a Hmong village. "Mr. Dooley wrote about the many dialets [*sic*], it was imposable [*sic*] to learn them. Hell[,] I have been everywhere he was and more to [*sic*] and can get by."[1]

The pugnacity of that remark, and the substitution of "Mr." for "Dr.," reflected Buell's awareness of the social gulf between himself and Dooley. Whereas the doctor had enjoyed a privileged upbringing and had attended Notre Dame and St. Louis University School of Medicine, Buell's formal education had ended with high school. The demands of keeping his family in food and shelter made further academic pursuits impracticable, and Buell often grumbled about "educated fools" whose "book learning" hid their lack of common sense. In an unguarded moment, he confessed to his daughter-in-law, "You have no idea how I wish I had a degree. Not that I need the education so bad, but the piece of paper. I have to prove everything I do." When, during the final months of his enlistment with International Voluntary Services (IVS) in Laos, Buell was in a position to give orders to men with "Dr. degrees," he gleefully reported this fact to the folks back in Steuben County.[2]

Dooley and Buell belonged to rival political parties. Although Dooley tried to remain above partisanship—"I am a doctor," he proclaimed; "I pull out tonsils and leave politics to others"—he made numerous statements suggesting that his sympathies inclined toward pro–Big Business Republicanism. In the premiere episode of his radio series *That Free Men May Live,* Dooley raved about the "splendor of a capitalistic system," and he informed readers of his first best-selling book that "only in a country which permits companies to grow large could such fabulous charity"—namely the medical supplies donated to him by Pfizer, Johnson & Johnson, and others—"be possible." Buell was a New Deal Democrat and proud of it, telling a reporter in 1962 that his "favorite Americans" were "Franklin Delano Roosevelt, Abraham Lincoln, and Will Rogers." "I hate to put a Republican in that group," he declared, "but, hell, Lincoln was a rural boy and he was everything every other American ought to aspire to be." John F. Kennedy's victory in the 1960 election delighted Buell, who could never bring himself to criticize the new president for missteps in Laos. He preferred to blame Averell Harriman, the multimillionaire roving ambassador charged with reconciling the Royal Lao Government (RLG), the Pathet Lao, and the neutralists. "Harriman is no dam [*sic*] good," Buell wrote to his children. "He just isnt [*sic*] a Dem."[3]

As with politics, so too with religion. The Catholic Dooley and the Methodist Buell were a study in contrasts. Dooley personified American Catholic anticommunism, and his faith was an integral part of his public image, as evidenced by the thousands of fans who, unsure of how to reach him, addressed their correspondence to "Dr. Tom Dooley, Saint Patrick's Cathedral, New York City." Historian James Fisher argues that Dooley "served as a bridge between the grim Catholic cultural politics of the McCarthy era and the tremulous euphoria witnessed by the end of the 1950s," when American Catholics, more politically powerful than ever before, moved from society's fringes to its mainstream. Dooley was a clean-shaven Joe McCarthy, a Catholic cold warrior minus the boorishness and class envy. He yielded to no one in his hatred of communism, which he denounced as a "ghoulish thing," yet he also projected a savoir faire that appealed to upwardly mobile Catholics eager to distance themselves from the urban parish. In his books, speeches, television appearances, and radio broadcasts, Dooley repeatedly affirmed that he respected Lao religions, was not a proselytizer, and had no intention of "making my happy little Buddhist monks into mackerel-snapping Irish Catholics." At the same time, he stressed the religious motivation behind his work in Laos. "Our faith, our Catholicism, does not belong to the sophisticated," he lectured students at a diocesan university. "Those of us in the Judeo-Christian philosophy understand that one of the highest purposes of man is the liberation of man from the bonds that bind him down." Buell had no patience with such Bible-thumping. A kind man, by all accounts, who went out of his way to help the needy, he preferred to keep his religious views private and expected others to do likewise. Days after arriving in Laos, he put his new job on the line by insisting that the IVS field manager stop singing hymns before each communal meal. "If you want to pray, do it silently," Buell snapped. "If I hear that pie-anna tune up one more time with a church hymn, I'm gonna throw it right out the goddamned door."[4]

Then there was the matter of physical appearance. Two more dissimilar-looking men than Dooley and Buell are hard to imagine. Handsome, tall, and boyish, Dooley cut a striking figure. "The doctor is more glamorous than most movie stars," gushed gossip columnist Vera Brown, and her colleagues agreed. They likened Dooley to Montgomery Clift, Fabian, and other box-office luminaries. Bill Dorr of the *Chicago Sun-Times* remarked, "The screen, when it undertakes to film—as it will—the life of Tom Dooley, will have to go some to dig up a leading man with more cinematic good looks and dynamic charm than Tom Dooley." Buell, by contrast, was nobody's idea of a matinee idol. Even his hagiographer, Don Schanche, conceded that "the most charitable description of him...would synthesize in the old-fashioned generalization 'homely.'" Pressed for detail, Schanche portrayed a small-bodied, bowlegged "runt of a man," with a "dour countenance, like a carved souvenir coconut." Beneath a brow "scarred and furrowed," deep "cheek-puffing lines dropped like parentheses from the sides of a pudgy nose to the down-slanting edges of his lower lip, and the flesh beneath his eyes was crinkled and baggy." When in 1956 Dooley blew into Laos amid much fanfare, he was twenty-nine years old and looked like a college sophomore. When Buell made his unheralded appearance in 1960, he was forty-seven and looked a decade older.[5]

Yet Dooley and Buell had qualities in common, among them courage and almost superhuman stamina. Both men labored under hazardous conditions—Dooley on "the very rim of Red hell," as he put it, five miles from the border with China; Buell behind enemy lines in Xieng Khouang Province—and both amazed co-workers with their ability to put in eighteen-hour days, seven days a week, for months on end. The latter trait was especially impressive given that both men suffered from illness while in Laos. Cancer struck Dooley shortly after he set up his third Lao hospital; it would kill him at age thirty-four, but it did not slow him down before that, as he treated countless patients and stumped the United States raising money for the Medical International Cooperation (MEDICO), an organization he had founded to combat disease in developing countries. Buell had to persuade his family practitioner to omit certain facts when filling out IVS's medical form, namely a stomach ulcer that caused the middle-aged farmer constant pain and a spinal injury incurred in an automobile accident that made walking difficult. Either of these ailments would have disqualified Buell from service, but the MD obligingly gave him a clean bill of health. IVS workers accompanying Buell on dawn-to-dusk quickstep marches between refugee villages never suspected that the man they had trouble keeping up with was sick.[6]

Dooley and Buell also both journeyed to Laos to escape something: in Dooley's case, a professional disgrace; in Buell's, a personal tragedy. After rocketing to fame with his book *Deliver Us from Evil*—a first-person account of the U.S. Navy's Operation Passage to Freedom, which transferred Vietnamese refugees south of the 17th parallel after the 1954 Geneva Conference—then–Navy Medical Corps officer Dooley seemed poised for a brilliant career in uniform, but the homophobia of the 1950s torpedoed this prospect. When an investigation by the Office of Naval Intelligence (ONI) revealed Dooley's involvement with a number of gay men, his superior officer encouraged him to resign "for the good of the service" rather than face court-martial. Dooley's mission of mercy in the Lao jungles was an attempt to salvage his reputation, providing a cover story for his departure from duty and building on the persona he had established in *Deliver Us from Evil* of an idealistic young man ministering to Southeast Asia's communist-threatened masses. Buell, for his part, applied to IVS after his wife died. Devastated by the loss, he sank into a depression that would not lift. "I got somethin' wrong upstairs," he confided to a friend. "It seems I just can't stop grievin'." To preserve his sanity, he resolved to put as much distance as possible between himself and home, and few places were farther away from Hamilton, Indiana, than Laos. Buell turned his farm over to his son Howard and began work as a sixty-five-dollar-a-month volunteer.[7]

The most important attribute Dooley and Buell shared was their identification, in American eyes, with the Kingdom of a Million Elephants.
Buell's associates at IVS and the Agency for International Development
called him "Mr. Laos," a sobriquet Dooley merited even more. Of the
thousands of U.S. representatives stationed in Laos from the time that
J. Graham Parsons began his tenure as ambassador until the conclusion of
the 1962 Geneva Conference, Dooley and Buell were the only two who
established a vivid presence for Americans attempting to follow developments in that country. U.S. officials like Parsons barely registered as individuals, and the Lao were an interchangeable multitude of lazy children.
Dooley and Buell, however, became icons, larger than life. Through their
achievements, and the publicity given those achievements in the media,
they brought Laos to the attention of Middle America.[8]

Dooley played a more calculated role in this process than Buell, who
lacked the doctor's ego and flair for self-promotion. "I'm merely a realist,"
Dooley told the *St. Louis Post-Dispatch*. "Look, you can't get the American
people interested in helping a country like Laos. Most of them don't even
know where it is. But you can attract them with a personality—meaning me." Buell would never have said, or thought, such a thing. Nonetheless, he furnished reporters with a human-interest angle as compelling as
Dooley's, and the articles featuring him as protagonist attracted the kind
of enthusiasm that feeds on itself. Americans previously indifferent to Laos
now wanted to read about it, because that was where Buell was waging his
campaign to save the hill tribes from starvation. Similarly, as publishers, editors, and producers were quick to recognize, the spectacle of Dooley curing
yaws and malaria in a bamboo hospital a stone's throw from China attracted
wider interest than any disquisition on Lao politics and history. "We all
thrill to the tale of a hero," noted one reporter after watching Dooley in
action. "Well, here is a twentieth-century one."[9]

Heroic tales featuring Dooley and Buell may have thrilled audiences,
but they were a poor substitute for reliable information, and they had the
consequence of investing these two men with the authority to define *Laos*
for millions of Americans. Again, Dooley exploited this authority more
opportunistically than Buell. The Hoosier wrote no books, went on no
speaking tours, hosted no radio shows, and often seemed embarrassed by
the attention he received. "I ain't unusual," he once said to a journalist. Yet
he cared deeply about the people he had been sent to Laos to help, and he
pleaded their cause to correspondents, embassy officials, and anyone else
who would listen. Unfortunately, the nature of his work, and the tendency

of the American press to prefer sensationalism to complexity, led to a patronizing portrayal of the Lao, who appeared as depthless objects of pity in
the news stories devoted to Buell. He was their protector, their source of
manna in the wilderness, and they were his wards, incapable of improving their own lives or even feeding themselves without his fosterage. By
depicting Buell in these terms, press organs like the *Saturday Evening Post*
reinforced the notion that the Lao lacked the brains or gumption to halt
communism's advance.[10]

Dooley likewise harped on Lao ineffectuality, usually with the intention
of bringing glory to himself. Whereas Buell allowed reporters to cast him
as knight-errant, Dooley required no Boswell. Even a positive review of
the doctor's second book chronicling his benevolent deeds among the Lao
noted the "top-heavy preponderance of Dr. Dooley's own personality"
and the "extraneous 'I' and 'we' and other egotistical references." Admirers
whose knowledge of the Lao crisis came solely from Dooley's writings and
public addresses saw it as a melodrama in which everyone except the star
was an extra. Indeed, as packaged by Dooley, Washington's anticommunist
venture in Laos depended on a lone physician faced with challenges on all
fronts: Pathet Lao terrorism, Chinese and North Vietnamese propaganda,
an uncooperative U.S. Embassy bureaucracy, and, worst of all, the underdevelopment and imbecility of his patients. "Sure, they are backward and they
are stupid," Dooley told radio listeners in 1957. "But they do want a better
life." His task was to persuade them that the free world, not communism,
offered the surest route to this future. He made it sound a hard sell, though,
because the Lao were so ignorant of great-power politics, so mired in their
stone-age civilization, and temperamentally so disinclined to improve their
lot that even the saintly Dooley often found himself at wits' end. This did
not augur well for Laos's chances of remaining free, since, as Dooley declared over and over, he was one of the only Westerners in the country who
understood its people. If he could not rouse them against the totalitarians,
then it seemed unlikely anyone could.[11]

Americans avidly followed the struggles of Dooley and Buell to preserve
Lao independence, but by 1962 some of them must have begun wondering whether such heroics were misguided. Would the free world lose anything of value if Laos went communist? Perhaps the dike separating the
superpowers would move a few hundred miles south and west, but the
United States would also have relieved itself of two million mendicants
who needed outsiders to teach them how to perform rudimentary tasks and
who disdained fighting, working, and thinking in equal measure. Did these

slugabeds deserve U.S. aid? Might not it be better employed elsewhere—like South Vietnam, where the residents showed some moxie? Rooting for Dooley and Buell did not imply high regard for the Lao. Indeed, the myths that grew up around these two American Samaritans derived a great deal of their power from astonishment that such efforts could be made on behalf of people so unworthy.

## "His Personal Brand of Goodwill"

When Leo Cherne, chairman of the International Rescue Committee (IRC), approached Tom Dooley about establishing a mission in Laos, the doctor could not spell that country's name. He transposed the vowels, rendering it "Loas" in letters to friends and family members. Never, throughout Operation Passage to Freedom, did Dooley express any interest in the kingdom bordering Vietnam, nor did he indicate a desire to return to Asia after finishing his tour of duty. The publication of *Deliver Us from Evil* and its rapid ascent on the best-seller charts made Dooley a hot commodity stateside. Reporters clamored to interview him. He lectured to packed auditoriums. The Junior Chamber of Commerce voted him one of the "Ten Outstanding Men of 1956." Had Dooley's bosses not initiated their probe, he would likely have gone on to become the youngest surgeon general in naval history.[12]

Those plans lay in ruins as of April 1956. After tailing Dooley for weeks, rifling through his briefcase, engaging him in leading conversations, and listening at hotel-room doors, ONI detectives confronted him with the evidence they had obtained. Dooley had no choice but to resign. He escaped public humiliation—the navy could not afford to make a spectacle of him, having awarded him its Legion of Merit—but the abruptness of his move to civilian status was bound to raise questions and eyebrows. Cherne's offer, therefore, came as a godsend. The IRC had been one of the most respected relief agencies in the world since its founding as a left-liberal organization dedicated to saving European Jews from Adolf Hitler's despotism. It had solidified its anticommunist credentials during the early cold war with fund-raising drives on behalf of East German victims of Soviet repression. Sponsorship by the IRC made Dooley's split with the navy look not only innocent but admirable. After all, the United States was banned under the terms of the 1954 Geneva settlement from introducing military personnel into Laos. If Dooley wanted to bring the blessings of American medicine to the Lao, he had to do so out of uniform. Seizing the lifeline Cherne threw him, Dooley announced his new calling to two thousand students and faculty at Notre Dame. He had left the military, he said, and was going to Laos under IRC auspices to work as "a doctor and missionary on Americanism."[13]

While Cherne thought he had pulled off a coup by recruiting Dooley, some IRC members were not so sure. Anxious to preserve their association's good name and tax-exempt status, they soon found out about the doctor's dishonorable discharge. IRC president Angier Biddle Duke worried that Dooley could prove an embarrassment. Diplomat Claiborne Pell concurred. Apart from the potential scandal posed by Dooley's sexuality, he noted, there were rumors in Washington and elsewhere that *Deliver Us from Evil* sacrificed accuracy on the altar of self-aggrandizement. Pell warned Cherne that Dooley was "motivated by a search for personal publicity" and that he might "bounce back on us." Gilbert Jonas, the IRC's principal fund-raiser, offered a more serious objection. Dooley, he said, knew nothing about Southeast Asia and did not care to learn. During a series of briefings, Jonas, who held a graduate degree in Asian studies, tried to bring Dooley up to speed on developments in Laos, but the doctor was a poor student, bored and distracted. He told Jonas that he could handle situations as they arose, and that good intentions were more important than detailed knowledge. Jonas concluded that the IRC was diving into a shallow pool.[14]

The mission statement for Operation Laos bore out this verdict. Even by the standards of what Danielle Glassmeyer calls "sentimental Orientalism"— the paternalistic assumptions that legitimated policies toward Asia in the Eisenhower years—Dooley's prospectus was noteworthy for its condescension and the extent to which it infantilized the Lao. Written in the first person, it presented Dooley and the three ex-navy corpsmen who would accompany him overseas as agents of progress, "light[ing] a few candles" in the Lao "darkness." "We want to be on the offensive for America," Dooley declared, "not just denying what the communists say about us, but doing something about it." What did he propose to do? The answer lay in his "equipment," which included "pharmaceuticals, vaccines, [a] portable tape recorder and sound tract [*sic*] movie projector, lots of baseballs, several Sears Roebuck catalogues, an accordion, and a bucketful of good will." Dooley saw the Lao civil war in public-relations terms. The communists were winning, he thought, because the peasants, benighted and superstitious, did not appreciate the benefits of American expertise. Evil men like Prince

Souphanouvong had given them a false impression, one that Operation Laos would correct. The modus operandi would be simplicity itself:

> [W]e shall leave the city and drive to a mountain tribe.... Then we shall throw a baseball around[,] play with the kids.... We shall show them our Sears Roebuck catalogue which will amuse all.... Then that night we will show them a movie, *Bambi, Fantasia, Snow White,* or another Walt Disney type film.... The following morning we shall say, "Look, we possess medicines that can cure your yaws, your congenital syphilis, your malaria, your trachoma. We possess a type of miraculousness! Let us help you."

This struck Dooley as a perfect antidote to red propaganda. "[W]hen the communists say that we are monster Americans," he wrote, "these tribes shall say, 'Why that is not true, we met some Americans and they were very nice.'" Used properly, Walt Disney, Sears Roebuck, and Terramycin would keep Laos in the free world. It was a matter of salesmanship.[15]

More remarkable than the manifesto itself was the response it drew from donors and the American press. Cosmopolites like Jonas may have cringed at Dooley's show-biz approach, but it worked—in the United States, at least. Over the summer of 1956, Dooley solicited contributions from private and corporate sponsors, receiving, among other things, $100,000 worth of antibiotics from Pfizer; a complete line of surgical instruments from A. S. Aloe; fifty "midwife kits" from CARE; portable stoves, sleeping bags, lanterns, and other gear from Abercrombie and Fitch; and a projector and movies from Walt Disney. He even strong-armed his erstwhile employers in the navy into giving him six months' worth of rations and agreeing to transport him and his crew to Saigon.[16]

As Cherne had anticipated, Dooley's leadership of Operation Laos ensured the mission extensive media exposure. Journalists could not get enough of Tom Dooley, jungle doctor. "Once again this blue-eyed Irishman with all the charm and guts of his ancestry is preparing to head for Asia to spread his personal brand of goodwill," declared the *Washington Daily News.* "Baseball, movie cartoons, and medicine—these will be simple but effective diplomatic tools." The *San Francisco Examiner* agreed, noting that Dooley's "biggest tools" would be "three Walt Disney films—*Fantasia, Bambi,* and *Snow White.*" "Here's a style of diplomacy the commies cannot submerge," wrote Bish Thompson of the *Evansville Press.* "I only wish a thousand Tom Dooleys were going out on their own to do this job." Dooley obligingly furnished reporters with pungent on-the-record remarks. "You might find this hard to believe," he told the *Los Angeles Mirror,* "but Mickey Mouse is too sophisticated for these totally innocent people. I'm taking only those films which tell the simplest story, like *Bambi*." When an interviewer asked whether the propaganda-battered Lao might react hostilely to an American mission, Dooley shook his head. "We'll command their interest with Donald Duck," he said, "and their respect with 'miracles' in medicine." Thus "armed with penicillin and confidence," according to the *Washington Post,* Dooley left for Laos in early August 1956. The *Oregon Statesman* wished him "Godspeed."[17]

Dooley's ego received further strokes during the two-month peregrination that followed. He accepted awards in Hawaii, Japan, Hong Kong, the Philippines, and South Vietnam before reaching Vientiane in late September. "Thoroughly enjoy being a 'cause célèbre,'" he wrote to his mother. "Every day there has been a ceremony in my honor." The reception in Saigon was especially rapturous. South Vietnamese president Ngo Dinh Diem, who understood the role *Deliver Us from Evil* had played in shoring up American support for his regime, greeted the doctor as a returning hero, volunteering his personal airplane to fly Dooley to refugee resettlement sites where he could bask in the adulation of people he had helped escape from tyranny.[18]

After such an experience, Vientiane proved disappointing. Dooley and his assistants arrived during the monsoon season and found the capital a sloshy bog. "EVERYTHING is flooded," Dooley growled. "We walk knee deep in water and mud most [of] the time." The Royal Lao Government (RLG) had arranged for Dooley's team to be housed in Vientiane's only hotel, described by the doctor as "crummy" and infested with "the most awful flies." Worse, the staffs of the United States Operations Mission (USOM) and the American embassy did not recognize that they had a superstar in their midst. USOM director Carter de Paul turned down Dooley's request for planes to transport Operation Laos's supplies from Saigon to Vientiane, and Dooley had to rely on the South Vietnamese Air Force. Then Parsons refused to permit Dooley to build his first clinic at Nam Tha on the China border, citing security concerns. The ambassador argued that Vang Vieng, a village halfway between Vientiane and Luang Prabang, would be a more appropriate site. "In retrospect," Dooley admitted two years later, "I'm afraid I disagreed with him... somewhat brashly." But Dooley, although leader of an independent mission, needed ambassadorial approval before the RLG's minister of health would sign off on the project, and he ultimately agreed to a "shakedown cruise" in Vang Vieng.[19]

By challenging Parsons, Dooley earned a powerful enemy. Parsons did not care how many fans Dooley had; as head of the U.S. Embassy, *he* was the top-ranking American in Laos, and he expected his orders to be obeyed. The resentment between the two men deepened in the weeks prior to Operation Laos's departure for Vang Vieng, as Dooley demanded commissary privileges, berated embassy mail clerks for losing his correspondence, and complained that no one in the American community had wished him luck. When the USOM deputy director told Parsons of Dooley's boast that "whether American officials here liked it or not, . . . everything he did was to receive publicity," the ambassador interpreted this as a threat and fired off a scorching memorandum to de Paul. "Dr. Dooley's troubles with American officials are of his own making," Parsons declared. "He has been rude, arrogant, and short-tempered." Parsons advised de Paul to keep "a detailed record of our dealings" with the doctor. "On the basis of past performance," he wrote, "I expect him to play fast and loose with the truth in print." Parsons also warned his State Department superiors to expect "sensational criticism of American bureaucracy in this country" when Dooley sounded off to the press. The doctor suffered from "emotional imbalance," Parsons informed Kenneth Young, director of Southeast Asian affairs. "I do not think that Dr. Dooley is the kind of person who can be satisfied."[20]

Parsons conceded, in a conversation with Premier Souvanna Phouma, that Dooley's mission "could serve to stimulate American interest in Laos." The ambassador proved right on this score. Although scholarly evaluations of Operation Laos vary widely—one historian praises it as a "miracle" that saved or improved many lives, while another denounces it as a "sham" designed to feed Dooley's ego rather than provide meaningful care—the mission increased awareness of Laos in the United States. Dooley was a peerless mass communicator, and he brought Laos to the attention of a huge audience of Americans who had never heard of, much less cared about, that distant kingdom before. Through a weekly radio show, two best-selling books, and periodic fund-raising tours, Dooley conveyed a vision of his host country that was both intelligible and engrossing. As early as August 1957, Parsons acknowledged that the doctor had "put Laos on the map back home."[21]

### "*Bambi* Has Conquered Laos"

Dooley's main vehicle for accomplishing this was his radio program, broadcast over KMOX, the midwestern pillar of the CBS network. *That Free Men May Live* aired every Saturday evening at 6:45 in more than twenty heartland states, providing what KMOX advertised as "dramatic descriptions of a medical-diplomatic mission to a people living under the shadow of communism." Conceived by KMOX general manager Robert Hyland and agreed to by Dooley almost as an afterthought, the show ran for nearly five years. It was one of the most effective propaganda initiatives of the cold war, ingenious in design and brilliant in execution. Whenever Dooley could spare a few minutes from work, he made reports on a battery-operated tape recorder. Then, as *Variety* magazine breathlessly noted, his recordings were "sent by various means of transportation from remote areas by foot, jeep, canoes, and finally to a coastal town," there to be "placed aboard an airplane and shipped directly to CBS, which has scored another first in this style of programming!" Millions of Americans spent part of their Saturday dinner hour learning about Laos from "Doctor Tom."[22]

The success of *That Free Men May Live* surprised even Dooley, who had no idea how large his following had become when he remarked at the close of one broadcast, "I certainly wish I had some hot chocolate." KMOX's mailroom was soon inundated with hundreds of cans of Hershey, Nestlé, and Swiss Miss mix. This unusual bond between radio personality and audience owed in part to Dooley's performative style. Unlike many commentators, he spoke extemporaneously. "I don't write out what I say to you," he confessed in late 1959. "Perhaps you regret this, but I just don't have time." His tenor voice and slight speech impediment—he had trouble with his r's—contrasted sharply with the polished elocution Americans were used to hearing over the airwaves. When he said "Laos," he took a hiccupping lurch mid-diphthong, so that it came out "La-ah-aos," and he often ended declaratory sentences with a rise in tone more appropriate to questions. Yet the quirkiness of his delivery worked to the series' advantage. Dooley was so obviously *not* a trained orator that he disarmed listeners and drew them in. *That Free Men May Live* had an intimacy that slicker productions could not match, and the narrative Dooley presented week after week—of American kindness overcoming disease, ignorance, and communism—packed a tremendous emotional wallop.[23]

Dooley's broadcast of December 15, 1956, was typical. He opened with a joke, noting, "I received a letter from someone who said that they heard me mention that if you put a pin through the globe at St. Louis, it would come out on the other side of the world right here in Laos. The person said they did that. I haven't felt anything yet, but keep trying!" Then he thanked various hospitals for their contributions to the Vang Vieng clinic and announced that his new "operating room" was "all set up now," although it would never meet "American standards" of hygiene. After mock-apologizing to his corpsmen for working them so hard, he introduced the subject of his talk, a "precious little girl" whose family lived south of Vang Vieng. She had been "horribly crippled with a massive infection of the leg" for two months, but her parents, terrified by communist propaganda, had refused to seek help from the American doctor. Finally, desperation compelled them to bring her to Dooley's clinic. At the touch of his scalpel, pus "absolutely poured out" of the girl's leg. "We excised the leg from the knee to the groin and drained out buckets," Dooley stated. Despite injections of antibiotics, the girl's fever grew worse. It seemed impossible that she could survive, but Dooley and his assistants would not give up. Voice cracking, Dooley described a two-day ordeal that pushed the Americans to the limit of their endurance:

> All the memories of our past years, all the hopes and aspirations for any future destiny, all our present thoughts seemed sharply focused on this little girl. All that God had ever given to us as men, in the faint breath of talent, was focused on this huge present. No time, no anticipation, no past, no word, no bright moments—just a little girl in a hut of a hospital in an ancient little kingdom. She was our patient, and she was our little girl.

After they bound up the girl's ravaged leg, they still had to attend to her "good" side, which was covered with pressure sores, the result of her having lain in one position for weeks. Infusions of saline and glucose staved off dehydration. Vitamins and protein powder bolstered the girl's strength. On the morning of the second day, her fever broke, and she began crying, "not from pain this time—no, this time she was crying for a little happiness." Between sobs, the girl mumbled *"Cop chai, cop chai, cop chai,"* which Dooley translated for his listeners as "'Thank you, thank you, thank you.'"[24]

Twenty-first-century college students are reduced to tears by a tape of this broadcast, which gives some indication of how potent its impact must have been in the Eisenhower era. Dooley's audience, weeping and reaching for their checkbooks, probably did not notice that he never identified the girl or any member of her family by name, or that the Lao themselves played almost no proactive role in this drama of suffering and deliverance. As depicted by Dooley, the villagers were so brainwashed that it took the threat of imminent death to motivate them to seek help; had they bestirred themselves earlier, a great deal of anguish could have been avoided. When Dooley recycled this story in his second book, *The Edge of Tomorrow,* he denied the Lao even a minimal contribution to the girl's recovery. Instead, he gave the credit to a USOM employee, who, he claimed, was traveling by jeep from Vientiane to Vang Vieng when he discovered the "nearly lifeless little body" in a dwelling alongside a jungle trail. The girl's "people," Dooley wrote, were "[i]gnorant and helpless" and "just left her lying in the hut." If not for the American's intervention, she would never have seen a doctor.[25]

Lao disinclination to "help themselves," as Dooley put it, was a recurrent theme in *That Free Men May Live.* "These people are good and they are gentle," he insisted, but "they live in an uncontrolled tropical environment that... is conducive to lethargy." Just as debilitating was Lao religion, which Dooley described as "sorcery," "witchcraft," and "necromancy of an intensity similar to the deepest reaches of dark Africa." In fact, he claimed, "the people of Laos are more philosophically resigned to fate. They become apathetic in the face of severe physical crisis." When ill or injured, "the Laotian resigns himself, and enters into meditation, and says to himself, '*Bo pen yang,*'" or "'I don't give a hoot.'" It was difficult, Dooley complained, to "get a man imbued in such an attitude... to hike three days overland to the white man's hospital." It was harder still to train his fellow Lao to care for him when he got there: "Why, I can't even get some of my nurses to kill a fly in the operating room because of their religious beliefs!" The *bo pen yang* ethos had "political implications" as well. "Laos, dreaming and dallying," was ill-equipped to bear up against the "loathsome system" poised to engulf it. "My people are just happy and contented," Dooley declared. "It is sadly pathetic, because these people do not realize that their territorial location makes them pawns in a godless game of conquest."[26]

Like many American talking heads, Dooley contrasted the "easygoing attitude" of the Lao with Vietnamese pluck, a contraposition lent greater authority by the doctor's experience in both countries. Although he professed to love all Asians equally and urged his listeners to "stop criticizing, condemning, and complaining about" them, he often wished the "flimsy" RLG would show some of the backbone exhibited across the border. "Vietnam, with Ngo Dinh Diem at the helm, has no queasy moments like in Laos," he said. "It has firm and solid leadership that is the best in Asia." He saluted Diem for throwing "caution to the four winds by saying, matter of factly, that there just isn't any room in this day and age for neutrality.... Bravo, President Diem! We need more like you in Asia!" Washington especially needed men like Diem in Laos, where the RLG was attempting to appease "the hideous godlessness of communism." According to Dooley, Souvanna and other Lao politicians believed that "they must adopt the role of neutral. . . . They do not feel, as Vietnam, for example, feels, that they can shake this stick at the monster that is surrounding them on all sides." Their timidity led them to embrace a neutralism that, in Dooley's eyes, leaned "close to being pro-communist," and the Lao citizenry were so nonchalant that they hardly noticed. "Most of the people don't even know this is going on," the doctor lamented. Attitudes were different in South Vietnam. While on a visit to Saigon in 1957, Dooley taped a group of Catholic refugees singing their national anthem and played it for his listeners, editorializing, "That was the music of the people of Vietnam. I like it very much. I think it is strong, militant, and powerful, and I believe that it shows these people as they are, a fine and sturdy race." The Lao seemed incapable of such music or such militance.[27]

As Dooley had promised while plugging his new civilian enterprise, Walt Disney figured conspicuously in Operation Laos, and some of *That Free Men May Live*'s most vivid episodes centered on how Dooley, via Disney, won friends for America. "We show the villagers a movie every other night," the doctor noted in a broadcast recorded at Vang Vieng. "We rig a sheet over the front porch, put the projector in the back of the jeep, . . . and we show them the Laotian Academy Awards. Tonight, we are featuring *The Big Bad Wolf*. We also have *Sinbad the Sailor, Little Black Sambo, The Headless Horseman, Bambi, Fantasia,* plus a few others." Dooley's "favorite seat" was behind the sheet that doubled as a screen, where he could "look at the faces of the hundreds of kids who sit there on their haunches. . . . The light, reflected into their eyes, is wonderful." The films lacked a "Laotian soundtrack," and Dooley had "decided against explaining" the movie plots, reasoning that it was better to "let the children build their own delusional castles. How they must dream after they see the love and lollypops, the sugarcane world of Disneyland!" Although listeners no doubt found Dooley's account heartwarming, they could not have viewed the wide-eyed innocents he described as America's first line of defense in Southeast Asia, and they likely conflated Lao "villagers" with "kids" as effortlessly as Dooley did. They moreover would have had difficulty picturing the sturdy South Vietnamese squatting in front of a makeshift screen, building delusional castles while Bambi and Thumper sang to them in English.[28]

Dooley's broadcasts, according to a State Department official assigned to vet *That Free Men May Live,* had a "literary style and could easily be put together in book form." The doctor did draw upon his program for the two best-sellers he wrote while on vacation from Operation Laos. Most of the vignettes in *The Edge of Tomorrow* and *The Night They Burned the Mountain* first appeared on-air, and while Dooley sometimes changed details to make a story more dramatic, his portrait of the Lao remained consistent. They were "a drowsy people," "tired-looking," "languid," "primitive," "anachronistic," "passive," "stupid," and "completely the victims of external circumstance." Dooley liked them—"Their simplicity is delightful"—but he was not optimistic about their capacity to thwart red expansion. "They have no idea of the rift the world has suffered," he wrote. "They understand nothing of the two camps of ideas, the God-loving men and the godless men." These were "big issues far beyond their knowledge." Furthermore, even if an American could get the Lao to comprehend the gravity of the global crisis, this would not change their nature. They were lovers rather than fighters. Chai, the native interpreter Dooley cast as his sidekick in *The Edge of Tomorrow,* was, readers learned, typically Lao in that "he would not kill anything." When patients paid "for an operation with a live chicken or duck," Dooley recalled, "Chai could not kill the birds for our dinner." What chance did such milquetoasts have against Ho Chi Minh?[29]

Reviewers never challenged Dooley's portrayal of the Lao. On the contrary, they commended him for performing an essential service. Peggy Durdin, the *New York Times*'s Southeast Asia correspondent, declared that Dooley, "through anecdote and an Irish gift for the felicitous phrase, brings the reader an understanding of Laotian individuals, their ways of living, their attitudes, beliefs, and superstitions." The *New Haven Courier* called *The Edge of Tomorrow* "an excellent travel book" that "deals with a section of the East that is not too very well known to the West," and the *Peoria Register* agreed that Dooley provided "a lucid picture of the culture of the land." For Frances Burns of the *Boston Globe,* Dooley's prose summoned "some of the magic of the tinkling windbells and clashing symbols [*sic*] of the Royal Kingdom of Laos,...eons away in time from us." Sales figures indicated that the public shared critics' enthusiasm: *The Edge of Tomorrow* sold more copies than *Deliver Us from Evil,* and *The Night They Burned the Mountain* spent twenty-one weeks on the *New York Times* best-seller list.[30]

Capitalizing on what his biographer terms "celebrity sainthood," Dooley made four fund-raising tours of the United States between 1956 and 1960. He promulgated the same message on each go-round, one that was effective in tugging at heartstrings and opening wallets but that also contributed to the perception of Laos as an unsuitable place to wage cold war. Occasionally, Dooley milked the subject of Lao torpidity for laughs, as when he told an audience in Nebraska about the "misguided American" who donated "a huge box of tranquilizers" to Operation Laos. "If I gave our rather languid Lao tranquilizers," Dooley quipped, "they would stand still." Dooley's speeches and interviews reprised the paternalism of his mission statement, depicting the Lao as children—he repeatedly called Laos the "Kingdom of Kids"—and lauding Disney cartoons as the ideal device for earning Lao affection. "When the sun sets in whatever village we are in," he boasted to a reporter, "we show a movie. Needless to say, *Bambi* has conquered Laos." *Snow White, Fantasia,* and *Dumbo* pulled off similar conquests, and Dooley claimed to have overcome the natives' fear of Western technology by giving unfamiliar items Disney names: thus his X-ray unit became "Pluto," his pickup truck "Dopey," and his three jeeps "Lady," "Tramp," and "Mickey Mouse." Dooley's assistant Teresa Gallagher revealed perhaps more than she intended about her boss's conception of the Lao when she listed the contents of a typical "Dooley kit" assembled by his

**Figure 3.** Dr. Tom Dooley playing with Lao children at his clinic in Muong Sing, March 1, 1960. Time & Life Pictures. Photographer: Don Cravens. Getty Images.

fan clubs in America and mailed to Vientiane: "a bar of soap, a face-cloth, a tube of toothpaste, some tissue, a balloon, a small light toy, a lollypop, and some socks." These are not tools one issues to people expected to man the ramparts of the free world.[31]

## "He Is the Stuff from Which Saints Are Made"

The outbreak of the "mess in Laos" scandal and the near-simultaneous publication of *The Ugly American* gave Dooley a chance to aggrandize his mission at the expense of Washington's aid program, and he lost no time exploiting the opportunity. Yes, he told reporters, William Lederer and Eugene Burdick were right: unlike the crew of Operation Laos, U.S. Foreign Service personnel in Southeast Asia lived in oases sealed off from reality by cocktail parties and PX supplies. "They don't understand the people they're supposed to be serving," Dooley claimed. "The people don't understand them either, and are mistrustful." He charged the Eisenhower administration with "pouring millions down a rat hole" and insisted, "We must operate at the village level immediately in practical ways that people can see . . . if we want them to like America." In a cover feature for *Modern Medicine,* Dooley complained that whereas he and his corpsmen "mixed as friends and companions with the people we are trying to help," USOM and embassy officials "wasted millions" by "condescendingly giving handouts" to Lao peasants who did not appreciate the favor. "I believe we have got to cut out this 'gray flannel suit' kind of diplomacy," Dooley proclaimed to the St. Louis Chamber of Commerce. "I believe that if we want to show Asia and the world what America believes in, it's going to have to be done at the level of the villagers, by individuals like you and me who get down there and sweat." Such comments served the dual function of infuriating adversaries like Parsons and confirming for Dooley's fan base that Doctor Tom, alone among American representatives in Laos, discerned the will of the people.[32]

Yet there was a schizophrenic quality to Dooley's criticism. While he could be merciless in denouncing "those air-conditioned silver ghettoes in Vientiane where the Americans practice their social incest," he also offered an impassioned defense of the aid program after the House Committee on Foreign Affairs exposed its abuses. "Every paper, every major magazine I pick up recently, seems to be attacking the administration of foreign aid here in Laos," he remarked in a November 1958 broadcast. He admitted that there were a "number of jackasses working for various U.S. government agencies...overseas," but he assured his audience that the "superb men" outnumbered them. "These men are fine men," he said. "They are honorable, dedicated, and enthusiastic men. There are a great many of them down in Vientiane...trying their darnedest to do a good job." And they were succeeding. Dooley told listeners that there had been "a great deal of improvement" in recent months and that "the situation here is tremendously brighter." The "first-rate administrators" in Laos were "in urgent need of some public recognition for their services," he declared. "Let's stop publishing every mistake they have made, never mentioning the good things that they do!" This appeal could have been scripted by Parsons—and, indeed, the former ambassador virtually restated it when summoned before Congressman Porter Hardy's Government Operations Committee in 1959.[33]

Dooley further betrayed his ideological kinship with Parsons by refusing to entertain the prospect of a neutralist RLG. His solicitude for Lao feelings was not evident when the vox populi made itself heard in ways that deviated from anticommunism. Souvanna's November 1957 agreement to unify the country by sharing power with Souphanouvong, applauded by the National Assembly in Vientiane, drew a reproach from Dooley, who announced that the "loathsome state of communism will now have part and parcel in the affairs of the whole kingdom." Dooley reacted much the same way to the August 1960 Kong Le coup, even though he acknowledged that the neutralist captain enjoyed considerable support. "Kong Le has definitely incited the enthusiasm of all of the people of Vientiane," Dooley told his radio audience. "The people of Vientiane are 100% for Kong Le." This did not prevent the doctor from calling Kong Le an "idiot," "without ability," who had "allow[ed] the dogs of communism to come in closer for the kill." Like most U.S. policymakers, Dooley was at a loss to explain Kong Le's accomplishment. "It is amazing that a few men could overthrow a government which has been supported by a tremendously generous flow of American dollars," he declared, adding, "However, Vietnam has simply been magnificent." If only Laos had a Diem to keep its idiotic—albeit popular—rebels in line![34]

Never, in the five years he worked in Laos, did Dooley object when American-backed strongmen subverted democracy. He endorsed Phoui Sananikone's decision to exclude leftists from his cabinet, despite the fact that the Neo Lao Hak Xat and Santiphab parties had won a majority of contested seats in the May 1958 elections. "Neo Lao Hak Xat," Dooley informed readers of *The Night They Burned the Mountain,* "is just another name for communism." Dooley moreover supported Phoui's seizure of power in January 1959, proclaiming, "Bravo for the Royal Lao Government in showing the Pathet Lao just who is giving orders in this country." The coup that toppled Phoui and placed the Committee for Defense of National Interests (CDNI) in control of the RLG also received Dooley's sanction, and he praised CDNI members like Phoumi Nosavan and Kamphan Panya as "dynamic" patriots who "have a deep and profound love of their country." He passed over their rigging of the April 1960 elections with a shrug: "Being military men, they can sometimes cut through the red tape and the kibosh that you get involved with in Asia." Phoumi was his favorite Lao leader, "one of my closest friends," "the only one who is pro-Western." The general's efforts to transform Laos into a dictatorship indistinguishable from Diem's South Vietnam impressed Dooley as honorable and necessary. "Democracy, as championed by the United States, does not translate well into Lao," he asserted. "Not yet." Statements like this indicated that Dooley's rivalry with Parsons had more to do with a clash of egos than difference in policy.[35]

The doctor and the ambassador were most clearly of the same mind in their oft-expressed impatience with the Lao. Why, both men wondered, was the local population so difficult to motivate? Why did the simplest tasks take forever to perform? This attitude came across more forcefully in Dooley's correspondence than when he spoke or wrote for public consumption. "Sometimes I feel like I will give you this whole country for ten cents," he fumed to Rose Gilmore, a reputed "fiancée" back in St. Louis. He hated the "ministerial *bo pen yang*" of the RLG, complaining to his mother about the "ceaseless delays" he had to endure before receiving supplies. "It is so difficult to work in Laos," he declared. The government's favorite word seemed to be "*muon,*" or "tomorrow," but "their tomorrow is not unlike *manana.*... They move in the most languid fashion." To Gallagher and the "Dooley disc girls"—secretaries who transcribed the messages he dictated onto discs—he seethed, "You have to absolutely 'fight' to do good here." Nothing came easily: "You don't just 'ask' for a plane. You ask, cajoal [*sic*], beat, demand, and beg." After hiring "a truck and coolies,... you ask them to be at the warehouse at 5 in the morning—so that they will be there at 6." Dooley acknowledged that many Lao were "willing to help me," but "it takes so much prodding, goosing, urging, gnawing, pushing, shoving, hollering, grabbing, etc., etc., etc." Laos's gestalt even seemed to affect machinery. On a flight to Thailand for provisions, Dooley noticed that the plane began "whizzing only when it got out of Laos." He empathized with an American medical student just arrived in Vientiane and not yet "accustomed to the slow ways of doing things." When the Lao "look at him with that languid, *bo pen yang* attitude," Dooley wrote, "Jerry is ready to hit them on the head." Doctor Tom might have forgiven him for doing so.[36]

Dooley was operating his third Lao clinic—at Muong Sing, five miles from the Chinese border—when a visiting physician excised a cyst from his chest and sent it to Bangkok for analysis. Reports that Dooley had malignant melanoma soon flashed to the United States, igniting a firestorm of publicity. Bill Cunningham of the *Boston Herald* bewailed "the tragedy that struck this dedicated young man just as he had his mission . . . really rolling." Another columnist noted that "[w]hat four years of hardship in a Southeast Asian jungle couldn't do to Dr. Dooley, cancer is doing." Dooley received letters of support from President Dwight Eisenhower, Vice President Richard Nixon, and other prominent Americans. He flew to New York's Sloan Kettering Medical Center for surgery, and then, still recuperating, began one of the most intensive lecture tours of his career, determined, as he admitted, to use his illness as a means of raising funds for MEDICO, the successor to Operation Laos he had founded in 1958. "A healthy Dooley used to get a $300 honorarium for a speech," he wrote to his friend, Father Matt Menger. "A sick one gets $1,000."[37]

This final circuit, a farewell to America and to life, marked the zenith of Dooley's popularity, as journalists struggled to outdo one another in heaping praise on the jungle doctor. "Some day Dr. Dooley's church will canonize him," predicted Ferdinand Kuhn of the *Saturday Review*, "for he is the stuff from which saints are made." The *Los Angeles Mirror* declared, "Dr. Tom Dooley, in spite of his personal battle with cancer, has done an unbelievable amount of good for humanity where humanity needed it most." Other reports were comparably panegyric: "Dooley is the most selfless man ever to come under my remote observation"; "He has become, to tens of millions, a living legend for his courage and his service to mankind"; "The world, 20–50–100 years from now, will have erected monuments, dedicated memorials, and instituted special grants and fellowships in the name of Thomas Anthony Dooley III." Dooley was written up in every major newspaper and magazine in the country. He appeared on numerous television programs, including *The Tonight Show, The Jack Paar Show, This Is Your Life,* and an ABC News documentary titled *The Splendid American.* Over five thousand fan letters per day poured into MEDICO's offices, ranging from artless tributes in crayon—"I think you are a wonderful person to be helping the poor people of Laos who need somebody to care for them like you are so much"—to calligraphic verse:

> I love the very words from you,
> That speak a heart of gold.
> I have just but to listen
> And on your ideals I'm sold.

Polls ranked Dooley third among the "Most Esteemed Men" in the world, after Eisenhower and the pope. Wherever he spoke, audiences spilled into the streets. Terminally ill people tried to touch him in the belief that he had Christlike healing powers. It was a remarkable display of quasi-deification, epitomized by a columnist who confessed her inability to do Doctor Tom justice. "I cannot write this story," she asserted. "No one can write the Tom Dooley story. You must sit there before him yourself.... You must have your heart penetrated with the intensity of his words." Thousands of Americans followed this advice during Dooley's last tour.[38]

"Blessed Thomas of Laos," as admirers had taken to calling him, died on January 18, 1961. Cardinal Francis Spellman, one of the last people to speak with Dooley, reported, "I tried to assure him that in his thirty-four years, he had done what very few have done in the allotted Scriptural lifetime." Nobody thought to question this claim. The magnitude of Dooley's accomplishment seemed self-evident. John F. Kennedy, inaugurated two days after Dooley died, moved quickly to award him a posthumous Medal of Freedom, and Congress gave the doctor the Medal of Honor "in recognition of his gallant and unselfish work ... serving the medical needs of the people of Laos." When Kennedy cited Dooley as the inspiration for the Peace Corps, he confirmed Doctor Tom's standing as one of the great Samaritans of the twentieth century, equal to Albert Schweitzer and Gordon Seagrave.[39]

Yet Dooley has not been treated kindly by historians, who point out that he established little that was lasting. Everything he built up fell apart after his death; in fact, on the day he died, one of his clinics was overrun by the Pathet Lao. MEDICO collapsed by 1962, its surviving remnants absorbed by other relief agencies. Dooley pioneered no revolutionary techniques in third-world health care. Although his philosophy of demonstrating

American goodwill through one-on-one philanthropic missions was co-opted by the Peace Corps and Volunteers in Service to America, these organizations rejected his disdain for massive foreign aid programs; there was no flowering of "small is beautiful" MEDICO-style enterprises in the Great Society 1960s. Moreover, as author-priest Andrew Greeley notes, "When Dooley died, a lot of people wept, but there weren't many who wanted to take his place." Dooley nurtured no heir. He was sui generis, and when he passed from the scene, his benevolent empire evaporated like the stain of breath upon a mirror.[40]

James Fisher, the foremost authority on Dooley's career, contends that the doctor's true genius lay in propaganda rather than humanitarianism. "[N]o American played a larger role in announcing the arrival of South Vietnam as a new ally whose fate was decisively bound to that of the United States," Fisher declares, noting that *Deliver Us from Evil* "quite literally located Vietnam on the new world map for millions of Americans." Several historians second this judgment. Often overlooked in Dooley scholarship, however, is the extent to which Doctor Tom also located Laos on the map for a mass audience—and announced its arrival with considerably less enthusiasm than he mustered for South Vietnam. As portrayed by Dooley, Laos was no ally but a dependent, a slow-witted if winsome foster child whom America could not abandon but who was unlikely to amount to much. "These pathetic little people, so gentle and peaceful!" Dooley wrote home from Vang Vieng in early 1957, and that summed up his view. While his affection for the Lao was unmistakable—it radiated from every page of his books and suffused every episode of his radio program—it was an emasculating, infantilizing affection that foreclosed the possibility of a genuine Washington-Vientiane partnership and made any notion of fighting communism in the "Kingdom of Kids" absurd. The Americans who gave money to Operation Laos and MEDICO after hearing Dooley on KMOX, seeing one of his televised appeals, or reading *The Edge of Tomorrow* or *The Night They Burned the Mountain* could not have believed that their contributions helped fortify distant barricades against red aggression. Rather, Dooley gave them the chance to play nursemaid to eternal children, to experience, vicariously, the gratitude of innocents cured of medieval diseases. That U.S. charity provided these simple souls with diversions like Disney cartoons and lollypops only made the exercise more rewarding. But few Americans were likely to confuse it with the deadly serious business of war. A combat zone was no place for *Snow White*. Tom Dooley's Lao could win American hearts, but not American respect.[41]

## "You Have Got to Love Such People"

Edgar Buell found out about International Voluntary Services in 1959, when one of the friends who called on him during the difficult months after his wife's death showed him an advertisement for the organization in a magazine. Buell was intrigued, but scoffed at the idea that IVS might have a place for him. He hardly fit the profile of a volunteer. IVS workers were college graduates, and many held advanced degrees. They ranged in ages from twenty-two to thirty years. Their jobs obliged them to be in tip-top physical shape. A middle-aged, chain-smoking widower who barely finished high school and suffered from ulcers and back pains was unlikely to be welcomed into their circle.

As time wore on, however, Buell's grief over the loss of his wife grew unbearable, and he realized that he needed a change of scenery. Why not apply to IVS? The ad said the group was looking for people to teach farming methods, and Buell had been farming ever since he could walk. He sent the forms and character references to IVS headquarters in Washington, along with a plea that the college requirement be waived. To his surprise, he received a positive reply. IVS, in the process of expanding its operations into new countries, was desperate for recruits and willing to bend the rules if it got volunteers into the field more quickly. Buell was hired as an agricultural adviser and informed that he would be going to Laos, a country he had never heard of. At first, he planned to quit the job after six months, figuring that would be long enough for him to get "right in the head" again. It was an inauspicious start to the career of a man whom reporter John Lewallen later dubbed "the most super-extraordinary IVS volunteer of all time."[42]

The briefing materials IVS issued to employees bound for Laos gave only a sketchy overview of conditions in that kingdom. Buell learned that his host nation was torn by civil war, but that he should not "confuse the situation in Laos with that in Vietnam." The Vietnamese fought with passion, whereas "typical Lao battles" between the RLA and the Pathet Lao were "largely bloodless." American volunteers did not have to worry about being killed or wounded. "We are able to travel throughout the country," Buell's prospective supervisor in Vientiane wrote to him, "and security has never been a problem." Backwardness was the real challenge. "Laos has the least developed economy of the three former Indochina states," Buell read. "There is almost no skilled or semiskilled labor available," because "the French did little to train Laotians." Worse, the Lao did not seem eager to improve their lot. An IVS brochure warned Buell, "One of the first cultural shocks for the newcomer to Laos is the apparent lack of initiative and industriousness on the part of many Lao people." The "immediate reaction" of many volunteers was to "lose respect for the Lao," which could "prejudice working relationships." Buell was told to guard against such attitudes, and to remember the golden rule of working in Laos: "Patience, more patience, and still more patience." After all, the brochure noted, "If the Lao were the way we want them to be, then we wouldn't have any reason for being here."[43]

Buell flew to Washington for an orientation session, which consisted mostly of role-playing exercises and admonitions not to proselytize among the natives. IVS executive director John Noffsinger reminded recruits that although the organization's founders had been religious men motivated by the Christian philosophy of service, IVS needed to abide by U.S. government rules to receive federal funding. That meant no missionary work. It also meant that volunteers had to be above reproach in their conduct. Foul language, sloppy dress, drunkenness, and the like were grounds for termination. Impressionable people all over the world would be seeing America through IVS, and Noffsinger wanted them to see America at its best. The director dropped his hortatory tone when he spoke in private to Buell, admitting that IVS had lowered the bar for the latest crop of volunteers. He advised the farmer not to worry about meeting unrealistic standards. While the organization normally required its workers to master local tongues within four months, Noffsinger said, "no one expects a man of your age to learn the language." "We've got a couple of good interpreters working for us," he assured Buell before sending him on his first-ever trip outside the United States.[44]

The journey to Laos lasted five days, and Buell's letters to his children from each stopover were filled with wonder. "I can't see how the Good Lord has put so much beuity [sic] in one spot," he wrote after a tour of Honolulu. Tokyo struck him as "one complete mad house,...little taxis all over, bicycles, lots of cars, the old type electric trains." Hong Kong was "unbelevable [sic],...strickly [sic] all orental [sic],...wish you could see it, the way the world is maybe you can." Vientiane made less of an impression. Buell described it as "a pretty nice place" with "homes on stilts." Some of his affectlessness resulted from jet lag, but it was principally due to the fact that, compared with the great metropolises of Asia, Vientiane was a modest riverside town. Also, like Dooley four years earlier, Buell had the misfortune to arrive during the rainy season. He was a better sport about Vientiane's cat-and-doggish weather than Doctor Tom had been, though.

"It is pouring now," he wrote, "but it is not as bad as it sounds, it is warm water, and . . . the natives need it for rice planting."[45]

After a day in the capital, Buell flew a hundred miles north to join his IVS team in the village of Lat Houang in Xieng Khouang Province near the Plain of Jars. He got along well with the other volunteers, all of whom were half his age or younger. Having grown up on a farm without electricity or running water, he did not mind the austere living conditions—workers shared a clapboard building and an outhouse out back—and he enjoyed his job teaching basic skills to the villagers: "how to saw boars [*sic*] straight, how to use soap and water, what it means to boil water, sanitation, how to better raise live stock." More important, he discovered that he had a facility for languages. Within weeks he was able to communicate not only in Lao but also in the dialects of some of the hill tribes who lived around the plain. Although he spoke these dialects eccentrically, employing turns of phrase that caused listeners to laugh, he managed to dispense with the services of an interpreter before anyone else could. "You know sometimes I have to pinch myself to make sure its [*sic*] me, being able to set and talk to these people in there [*sic*] own language," he marveled. His fellow IVSers were impressed. The aging rustic they called "Pop" went from being a curiosity to unofficial team leader.[46]

Buell's relationship with local residents was complex, more so than eulogists at the time acknowledged. On the one hand, he developed a profound fondness for the Lao, Hmong, and Khmu in and around Lat Houang, probably because they helped fill the emptiness left by the death of his wife. He was also touched by the gratitude they displayed. "Just a few days ago I gave a lady a few red kidney beans for seed," he informed his children. "She droped [*sic*] to her knees in front of me, bowed, clasped her hands in front of her and said Cop ji li, li always means very much, cop ji, Thank you. You know you have got to love such people." Buell would prove his love many times over the coming years. He practically adopted several Hmong children, spent thousands of dollars of his own money on the IVS program in Xieng Khouang, and often risked death to help refugees made homeless by Pathet Lao aggression. "Pop puts the rest of us to shame," a co-worker declared in 1962. "He has more courage . . . and more human compassion than any other man I have known." To judge by deeds, this was not hyperbole.[47]

On the other hand, there were echoes of the prevalent American hauteur in Buell's letters, expressed with characteristic inattention to rules of grammar, spelling, and punctuation. He was stunned at the primitiveness of Laos. "[T]hese people are not yet to the wheel age," he noted. "[T]hey never fix nothing, they just cant figure out why it broke. Truely I belive they are fine people but the most civlization they know is what the French have give them." He observed that most of his students "still think the world is flat and all there is to it is just there own little country, the only kind of people are the Lao." Thus, "they think when they see a white man, they just came from the sky." Buell accepted the popular portrayal of the Lao as pacifists, writing, "Lao people just wont fight. . . . When they [the communists] capture a town or villiage it is most always done without blood shead, as . . . there is one thing the lao people dont want and I am sure will never do is fight." To illustrate Lao timorousness, Buell reported how he and a co-worker approached "road guards" of the Royal Lao Army (RLA) and asked "them to let us see there guns." When the guards obliged, the IVSers pointed the weapons at their owners. "[Y]ou should hear them beg," Buell chuckled. "Can you imange an American outpost turning there guns over to a foregner[?]" Such behavior caused Buell to wonder whether there was anything Washington could do to prevent Laos's retirement behind the iron curtain.[48]

Yet Buell was a cold warrior, excited at the prospect of contributing to the free world's crusade against communism. "God knows we cant let them take all Asia, all Africa, then others," he declared. "It is our own freedom on the line as well." He got his first opportunity to be a hero six weeks after arriving at Lat Houang, when Kong Le carried out a coup in Vientiane and pitched the country into turmoil. The U.S. Embassy ordered the evacuation of all "non-essential" Americans from Laos, a command Buell's boss and most of his co-workers were happy to obey. Buell, however, offered to stay behind and keep the IVS program going. He still had much to teach the native farmers, he said. They had just learned to plant their seeds in rows, and he planned to acquaint them with the advantages of the steel-tipped plow. Besides, the elementary school that IVS was building under contract to the U.S. aid mission was only half finished. Dick Bowman, a veterinarian who had been working for IVS in Laos since 1959, volunteered to remain with Buell. The other team members caught a plane to Bangkok, where they joined over seven hundred other uprooted Americans to await the outcome of the crisis.[49]

What happened in the next few months at Lat Houang has been the subject of considerable exaggeration, but the facts are impressive enough. Buell and Bowman—isolated, except for the occasional mail plane—held the program together. Work on the school continued, as did development of an IVS-supervised model farm. Buell "borrowed" a bulldozer left in

Xieng Khouang Province by USOM technicians and enlisted enough help to lay twenty miles of road. When the Eisenhower administration, in an effort to pressure the RLG into solving its problems, suspended U.S. aid, funding for the IVS station ceased. Undeterred, Buell drove to Xieng Khouang City and persuaded the head of the Programs Evaluation Office (PEO) there to cash his personal checks. He then drew $7,000 from his retirement fund and used it to pay local construction workers and other aid recipients. "At present I am keeping our own IVS team in money," he wrote to his son. "And if I ever hear [of the bank] charging int[erest] on the money I will blow my stack. It is a small way Mr. 'Pop' and the Edon State Bank can help the Free World succeed."[50]

During this period, Buell made the most important contact of his IVS career. Mua Chung, a sixteen-year-old Hmong boy who worked as an interpreter for the Americans in Lat Houang, introduced Buell to Colonel Vang Pao, who, Chung announced, was the only Hmong officer in the RLA. Buell and Vang Pao exchanged pleasantries, but nothing came of their first encounter. The colonel was slow to trust foreigners. After a few more meetings, however, Vang Pao decided that this was an American in whom he could confide. He admired Buell's courage in sticking to his post and appreciated the farmer's serviceable, albeit quirky, command of the Hmong language. In early October 1960, he informed Buell that he had a plan. With the RLG paralyzed and a showdown looming in Vientiane between Kong Le's neutralists and General Phoumi Nosavan's rightists, Vang Pao expected the Pathet Lao to capitalize on the situation by allying with Kong Le. When they did that, he said, the long-simmering Lao civil war would flare up, and most of the fighting would take place in northeastern Laos, where Vang Pao and his people lived. Vang Pao did not expect the RLA to stop the communists from seizing the Plain of Jars. He believed most royal soldiers were poorly led and unmotivated. His men, though, were a different breed. Vang Pao told Buell that he intended to lead guerrillas loyal to him to preselected hill sites surrounding the plain, from which they could harass the enemy and choke off his supply lines. They would need supplies of their own, though, and this was where Buell came in. After he left Xieng Khouang Province and the area fell to the Pathet Lao, Buell could map out the locations of the Hmong guerrillas for the American military and arrange to have food, clothing, and weapons air-dropped to the resistance. If he did his job well, he and Vang Pao might save Laos.[51]

This was heady stuff for an Indiana farmer. Buell promised Vang Pao that he would not breathe a word of the operation until the time was right, but he could not resist hinting in letters home that "something is in the making." "I could tell you much, but you couldnt belive me," he wrote to his parents. "A few others and myself are doing everything we can to help these mountain people, who have chosen death to communism." Buell did not know that the CIA had been courting Vang Pao for almost a year, and he was unaware of the colonel's less savory qualities, namely ruthlessness bordering on cruelty and disregard for the truth. For Buell, there were no shades of gray in the struggle for Laos: America's enemies were pure evil, and he would join with Vang Pao to fight them.[52]

Meanwhile, he went about his activities at Lat Houang, directing construction of the school, giving agricultural advice, and even running the IVS medical station, which had been without personnel since the Kong Le coup. He had just finished delivering a baby when, on New Year's Eve, some Hmong friends alerted him that the Pathet Lao and the neutralists were about to overrun the village. Kong Le's troops, defeated days earlier in the battle for Vientiane, had withdrawn from the capital and linked up with Pathet Lao forces for a drive north. They intended to capture the old French military airstrip in the Plain of Jars and thereby give Soviet supply planes a place to land. Other Pathet Lao units, coordinating their movements with Kong Le via radio, marched southward from the North Vietnamese border. Lat Houang was trapped in a vise. Buell's friends told him that he had to evacuate immediately. He and Bowman caught a last-ditch flight out of Xieng Khouang. As they looked out the plane windows, they saw Kong Le's men approaching the runway. It was, Buell wrote his children, "the most memorable thing that has or ever will happen to me in my life." In fact, his adventures in Laos were just beginning.[53]

## "Sent from Above"

As soon as Buell and Bowman stepped off the evacuation plane in Bangkok, they were taken to see U. Alexis Johnson, American ambassador to Thailand, who questioned them for an hour and then sent them to brief civilian and military intelligence officials. Buell was not intimidated by the brass—"they are just people," he remarked—and his fresh-from-the-battlefront reports made a powerful impression. CIA operatives were particularly intrigued to learn of Vang Pao's plans to raise a guerrilla army, plans the colonel had not divulged to any other American. Pop Buell, it seemed, was an asset worth cultivating. The

CIA officer responsible for training the Thai national police, a Texan named William Lair, met repeatedly with Buell and urged members of the American community to treat him well. Buell received a commendation from the USOM director in Vientiane "for outstanding services rendered under emergency conditions," the highest award USOM could give a volunteer worker. Taking the hint, IVS doubled Buell's salary and promoted him to chief of party, with the understanding, as Noffsinger put it, "that this does not represent in any manner your true worth." Buell was moved by these tributes and eager for more action.[54]

After a few weeks of R & R, he returned to Laos with a new assignment. Lair, working through the Vientiane embassy, arranged to have Buell put in charge of a relief program to airlift supplies to the Hmong refugees. Colleagues informed Buell that the job would be dangerous, but he never considered declining it. "To me, that would be walking out on a man who was down," he wrote, "and Laos is down." For months, Buell threw himself into his work, loading planes with rice, salt, blankets, and other essentials and accompanying pilots on their runs through narrow, mist-shrouded mountain passes. He pinpointed the sites where Vang Pao's followers were likely to be, and soon discovered that there were more tribespeople displaced by the civil war than anyone had anticipated. Since they had left their farms unharvested, they were in danger of starving. Meanwhile, the Pathet Lao, supplied by the Soviets, had turned the Plain of Jars into an armed camp, which meant that Buell often had to fly through enemy fire to reach the settlements where the refugees congregated. He counted "12 holes in the plane" after one mission, joking that reports of a cease-fire in Laos were "untrue." Whenever he could, he personally inspected refugee enclaves. If the terrain was too rugged for the pilot to land, Buell parachuted to his destination, or he hiked from site to site, talking to the people and assessing their needs. Then he helped them clear a drop zone for the supplies he ordered on his transceiver. Within hours, the gunnysacks of rice, rolls of plastic for temporary shelters, and parachute-borne crates of medicine began descending from the sky.[55]

It was a hazardous business, and it took its toll on Buell. Sometimes, when fog and cloud cover made food deliveries impossible, he went hungry alongside the refugees in their camps, surviving on leaves and roots. He developed immersion foot during marches on muddy jungle trails. Leeches burrowed into the skin of his legs and groin. He caught pneumonia and nearly died. "I can't belive how well I stand up under it all, 7 days a week," he noted. "Determination, I guess, or something." All of the settlements he visited were vulnerable to Pathet Lao attack, and he frequently had to flee as the communists tightened their noose. After one predawn escape, Buell trudged for eighteen hours through a rainstorm with a baby on his back, leading an exodus of two thousand Hmong to the mountain retreat of Yat Mu, where, to his horror, he discovered another nine thousand emaciated people whose existence came as a surprise to the American mission in Vientiane. Bad weather prevented emergency airdrops for an agonizing eleven days, and Buell saw hundreds of refugees die of hunger, disease, and exposure. Dozens committed suicide by swallowing opium. By the time the clouds broke, Buell, normally a wiry 135 pounds, weighed less than 100. His report of conditions at Yat Mu persuaded embassy and USOM bureaucrats to expand the refugee relief program. "I have met with all the big shots since coming back [to Vientiane]," he wrote home. "Washington is using my word for supplying these people."[56]

Washington—or, rather, the CIA—was also using Buell for another purpose, one he acknowledged but preferred not to dwell on. America's secret war in Laos, the largest paramilitary operation in CIA history, is a thrice-told tale worth retelling here only to point out that while Buell never accepted a dime from the agency, and while his own activities remained strictly humanitarian, he did give information to CIA officials like Lair, who in turn saw to it that Buell had the planes and supplies he required to take care of refugees. The pilots who flew with Buell worked for Air America, a CIA-owned airline that provided support for agency operations throughout Southeast Asia. After Buell became famous, he furnished the CIA with invaluable cover, as he supervised a relief camp at Sam Thong in the mountains of Xieng Khouang while the CIA built its Laos headquarters at Long Chieng, six miles to the south. Sam Thong soon boasted a hospital, schools, and warehouses full of food, powdered milk, and farm implements, and the embassy in Vientiane regularly sent visiting congressmen, diplomats, and reporters to see the good work Buell was doing among the displaced people. Long Chieng, however, was off-limits to observers, for they would have recognized at once what it was: one of the biggest U.S. military installations on foreign soil, complete with a mile-long runway capable of accommodating jet fighters, a fleet of planes and helicopters, massive storage facilities, a bombproof CIA office, and a population of forty thousand Hmong soldiers. Historian John Prados describes Long Chieng as "the nerve center of the secret war." This huge intelligence-gathering and administrative logistics station never appeared on any map, but it directed Vang Pao's army during its campaign to keep the communists from conquering Laos. Although Buell rarely went to Long Chieng, he knew what was happening there, and he understood that he played a vital role in the CIA's operation. As paramilitary officers joked at the time, Buell supplied "soft rice"—that is, real rice—to the guerrillas, and the agency gave them "hard rice," meaning arms and ammunition.[57]

Buell was troubled by this arrangement, especially after it became clear to him that the resistance around the Plain of Jars was hopelessly outnumbered. As early as February 1961, he told his children that "north Laos is in my book gone." When Vang Pao's men were routed in an attempt to defend their base at Pa Dong, Buell praised the colonel's bravery but concluded, "it was like a Dwarf + a Giant." If the Kennedy administration did not want Laos to go the way of North Vietnam, it had to "get modern warfare in here." Why had America failed to send troops? Buell began to suspect that "some big Washington individuals" were less interested in "helping people and saving the Country" than in putting a gloss on a neutralist settlement that would turn Laos over to Souphanouvong. To make America's departure look less like a defeat, these "educated fools and ten cent millionaires" were willing to fight to the last drop of Hmong blood. "Oh I get mad," Buell fumed. "At times you just want to blow Hell out of things." Yet he had to keep his mind on the task at hand: feeding the refugees and providing basic necessities. At the eight-month mark of his tour in Laos, he reported that he had flown so many "missions up north" that "if I was in the airforce...I would have enough missions to be discarged and receive the distinguished cross Ha."[58]

These exploits eventually attracted press attention, and when a journalist from the *Saturday Evening Post* named Don Schanche asked to accompany Buell on a trip upcountry, the U.S. ambassador to Laos gave his assent. Schanche, who at thirty-six had already covered cold war crises on four continents, was unprepared for the physical ordeal of this errand. He waited with Buell in Vientiane for a few days, hoping the fog would lift from the mountains and permit them to deliver supplies, until Buell declared that he could wait no longer. The two men and their pilot, Bob Smith, flew out of the capital on a Helio Courier, a small plane designed for short takeoffs and landings. Buell advised Schanche to expect ground fire when they reached Pathet Lao territory. Visibility was near zero, and Smith had no navigational aids. Relying on instinct and memory, he guided the Helio through passes that left only a few feet of maneuvering room on each wingtip, and over plateaus where trees rose so high they scraped the fuselage. It was like riding a rollercoaster blindfolded. Schanche almost threw up on the control panel. After a bone-jarring landing in an encampment southwest of the Plain of Jars, Buell called in airdrops from a C-46 and announced that he and Schanche would walk to their other destinations.

Initially relieved, Schanche soon learned that this meant a week in purgatory. Buell arose before dawn every morning and demanded that they cover at least ten miles, up mountains and down, across valleys, along forest pathways obstructed by vines. The stubby little farmer never tired. When they reached a settlement, Buell took candy from his pockets and gave it to the children. Then he met with the *nhibons,* or councilors, to determine what the refugees at that location needed. He radioed this information to Vientiane and, for the remainder of the day, oversaw the delivery of food, medicine, blankets, and clothes. After nightfall, Buell assumed the part of rural family practitioner, drawing from his first-aid kit to treat minor infections and ailments. Sometimes the case was more daunting: a fractured eye socket, ruptured appendix, or gangrenous limb. Buell took it all in stride. If possible, he arranged to have the patient taken to Vientiane or Luang Prabang; more often, he dealt with the problem then and there, as when he grabbed Schanche's bottle of whisky and poured it on a tribesman's head wound before sewing him up.

When he had a free moment, Buell entered the temporary shelters, visiting with the families, discussing their situation, explaining why the United States was helping them. All the refugees, Schanche discovered, knew who Buell was, and they called him by the name favored by his co-workers: Pop. It was nearly midnight when Buell and Schanche sat down to dinner, an experience that made the day's earlier trials seem tame. Schanche found the native diet—congealed blood, fire-baked rats, and the like—repulsive, but Buell insisted that they eat it. If the Americans ate C-rations while the refugees had boiled animal entrails, he said, that would violate the bond of trust essential to his work. The Hmong put their faith in Pop because Pop lived like one of them; he ate their food, slept in their huts, and spoke their language. If Schanche was going to travel with Pop, he had to follow Pop's rules. Schanche forced down the grub and crawled onto a mat, dead tired. Buell had him up by 5 a.m., and another punishing day began. By the time Schanche returned to Vientiane, he knew he had a hell of a feature on his hands.

"An American Hero: The Exclusive Story of How an American Farmer Has Devoted His Life to a One-Man Crusade for Freedom and Democracy in War-Torn, Communist-Infiltrated Laos" appeared in June 1962. Too long for a single article, it ran in two parts in successive issues of the *Post,* and Schanche set the tone immediately by declaring that Buell's "efforts have already eclipsed the record of Dr. Tom Dooley." Buell, readers learned, was a "Johnny Appleseed of democracy" so devoted to the refugees that he spent "90 percent of his time living behind enemy lines." Since coming to Laos, he had faced peril almost daily. "He has been shot at, run out of villages by attacking communist troops, and exposed to a variety of diseases," wrote Schanche. "Radio Hanoi, the powerful communist propaganda voice of Southeast Asia, has…offered a $25,000 reward for his capture." But the Hoosier was unafraid. Schanche portrayed Buell humming *When the Saints Go Marching In* as he hiked through mountains "surrounded and shot through with communist agents."

As inspiring as Buell's attitude were the results he achieved. According to Schanche, Buell had "made the difference between life and starvation for 50,000 to 60,000 primitive Meo tribesmen"—*Meo* being the term then in use for people today known as Hmong. Although Buell received the "support of the Laotian government" and the U.S. Embassy, the "job of getting the supplies to the homeless, hungry Meo" was "largely his alone," and his success in this endeavor had done more to "sell America" than any of the multimillion-dollar development projects underwritten by Washington. Thanks to Buell, there were now sixty thousand people whom the communists could check off their list as beyond their reach. "Other Americans are sowing the seeds of democracy overseas," Schanche observed, "but in many travels to almost every part of the world I have never seen one who did it so effectively as Mr. Pop." The story was illustrated with photographs of Buell tramping along mountain trails, barking into his walkie-talkie during a drop, deliberating with village elders, and making the rounds among grass-thatched huts. In one image, Buell cradled a baby whom, the caption read, "he saved from his mother's near-miscarriage."

"An American Hero" was a paean to Buell and an affirmation of the *Ugly American* thesis that what the United States needed in Asia was more agents who represented its best national characteristics: egalitarianism, common sense, resourcefulness, generosity. Indeed, Schanche described Buell as a member of "that woefully small group of Americans celebrated by Eugene Burdick and William Lederer in their misnamed book *The Ugly American*, whose hero was not ugly, but splendid." Like Lederer and Burdick, unfortunately, Schanche exalted his hero at the expense of the Asians, doing *The Ugly American* one better by making Buell's refugees so dense, gullible, and troglodytic that even Lederer and Burdick's fictional Sarkhanese would have looked down on them. While "An American Hero" comforted readers with the message that not all U.S. initiatives in Laos were wasteful or unsound, it also offered one of the most patronizing depictions of an ally in cold war literature.

The Meo, declared Schanche, were "miserable people" who "live at the absolute bedrock of human existence." Their only hope of advancement lay in Buell, and they knew it, investing the grizzled farmer with divine power: "The legend of Edgar Buell is passed from mouth to mouth and village to village in northern Laos. They think of him as a god." Buell's "divine status with the Meo" was reflected in his nickname, which, Schanche noted, "has a godlike meaning. The Meo call him *Tan Pop*. *Tan* means 'mister.' *Pop*, in Meo, means 'sent from above.'" Schanche had witnessed one of Tan Pop's miracles "on a worked-out opium field high in the mountains." Before Buell arrived, opium had been "the only exportable cash crop raised in Laos," and the Meo had received abysmal reward for their labor, as "a batch that might sell for $100,000" in America brought the Meo "about one dollar." The tribespeople were unable to conceive of a way out of such exploitation until Buell told them about sweet potatoes. Wisely, he did not mention "moral considerations," since, Schanche remarked, "[t]he evils of opium's misuse in a civilized western society would be inexplicable to the primitive Meo." Buell kept it practical, pointing out that "sweet potatoes...would grow beautifully in the rich soil of the hills," they "would bring more money, and, besides, the farmers and their families could eat them." The village leaders to whom Buell made this pitch listened to him, as Schanche put it, "rapturously."

Tan Pop enriched the refugees' minds as well as their diets and bankrolls. "All of them recognize him as the man who brought education to the Meo," wrote Schanche. Pre-Pop, "there were no schools in Meo villages" because the RLG considered the tribespeople "unworthy of education." When Buell began working upcountry, he "sought to correct this tragic oversight," enlisting as teachers the "few tribesmen who...could read and write" and scrounging "writing pads, pencils, and chalk from everyone in Vientiane who owed him a favor." The RLG objected, proclaiming that teachers had to be certified and schools accredited by the Ministry of Education, but Buell told them to go to hell. The payoff was dazzling. "At present," Schanche reported, "Pop's school system includes twenty-nine one-room, dirt-floored schools." The heretofore "uncomprehending" Meo were at last receiving enlightenment, albeit at a kindergarten level. Small wonder that when Buell and Schanche visited a refugee camp where a man had just died of tuberculosis, the widow threw herself at Tan Pop's feet. "From the look of mixed grief and hope in her tear-filled eyes," noted Schanche, "I guessed she thought there was a chance that Edgar Buell could bring the man back to life."

The most extraordinary passage in "An American Hero" involved a party held in Buell's honor at a settlement near Long Chieng. Buell and Schanche squatted with the *Nhi Khon,* or local chief, and other notables around an urn in a hut "dimly lighted by rags dipped in animal fat." The urn was full of homemade rice wine, and guests drank through "long, thin bamboo rods, hollowed to serve as straws." After a few hours of chat interspersed with friendly reminders from Tan Pop—"If you do not plant the seeds and care for the gardens, you may end up picking rocks instead of food from your fields; you cannot eat rocks"—the mood grew somber. Schanche noticed that the *Nhi Khon* was asking something "with great feeling" and that Buell's face had become "taut with emotion." What did the chief want to know? Buell said he would interpret, but prefaced his translation with a disclaimer. "There's a lot they don't understand," Buell declared. "You've got to realize that the whole world, for these people, is no bigger than the distance they can walk." Then Buell listened for a few minutes to the *Nhi Khon* and turned his gaze back to Schanche:

> "I'll try to give this to you exactly the way he said it to me," said Pop. "Here it is: 'Before the trouble came, the Meo people not need help. When the trouble came, we heard about the Thing.' (He's got a picture of the United States and the United Nations all wrapped up in one big, good ball which he calls the Thing.) 'Until the Others (North Vietnamese communists) came, we could have beaten the Pathet Lao with our muskets and crossbows. But we kept on fighting them and we thought we were fighting for the Thing. We were told that the Thing would come to help us. But so far the Thing has not been much help. Now we wonder if the Thing will move us to another country where we can live in peace. Will it?'"

Schanche noticed a tear running down Buell's cheek. "You answer him," Buell said to the journalist. "I can't. That's what I thought the Thing was for too."

A more paternalistic portrayal would have been difficult for Lederer, Burdick, or even Tom Dooley to compose. The Meo came across, literally, as babes in the woods, defenseless against their own ignorance and the forces confronting them, dependent on an American for life itself and everything that made life worth living, so far behind the modern world that they did not have words to convey its splendor. Tellingly, Schanche shared Buell's pessimism about the ongoing civil war, writing, "Unless the United States changes its policy in Laos the communists are bound to take over." Tan Pop could not win this fight by himself. The Others were too strong, and the Meo lacked the resources to beat them back. If the Thing did not move beyond providing agricultural counsel, foodstuffs, and primary health care, Laos was doomed. "An American Hero" ended on a dismal note, with Buell admitting that the country would probably fall to the reds "in a few months" but refusing to lose hope. "I'm sowing seeds that, by God, someday is going to grow," he told Schanche before the latter bade him farewell. It was a poignant declaration, rendered more so because the soil in which Tan Pop planted his seeds seemed barren.[59]

Schanche's piece made Buell a celebrity. Soon, other magazines and newspapers came out with their own Tan Pop stories, advertising them with headlines like "Hoosier Farmer Braves Red Peril to Help Poverty-Stricken Laotians." "I am getting many letters of cong[ratulation]," Buell informed his son. "Many people are wireing and writing how they can help Mr. 'Pop.'" Having never sought notoriety, Buell was at first nonplussed, but he discovered that stardom had its perks; now he was able to bring attention to the plight of the refugees and compel previously unresponsive bureaucrats to support his relief efforts. He granted an interview to any journalist who requested one, and let some of the correspondents tag along on his settlement-hopping tours. "Took with me a big man from N.B.C. television, who took many shots of Mr. 'Pop' which by now should have bean on T.V. in the U.S.," Buell noted in late June 1962. "I think it was to be on the Today program by Chet Huntley.... [M]aybe you saw your Dad on T.V." Buell knew that many of the stories on him forsook subtlety for melodrama—he enjoyed telling newsmen that their reports were "a load of shit"—but from his perspective the benefits of being Tan Pop outweighed the drawbacks. Two years after arriving in Laos as a low-paid volunteer, he was the most famous American in the country. The *Indianapolis Star* saluted him for "carrying on the work begun by the late Dr. Tom Dooley," a compliment that, for Buell's contemporaries, was unsurpassable praise.[60]

After the Kennedy administration achieved neutralization of Laos in the fall of 1962, events in that kingdom faded from the headlines, but Buell's legend only grew more lustrous. He completed his term with IVS and became a representative of the Agency for International Development, which sponsored his work in the northern mountains. The U.S. embassy also employed him as a diplomat whenever friction arose between the hill tribes and the RLG. He would have various job titles over the years, but his mission did not change. "I am going to help these people survive in any way I can," he told the *Christian Science Monitor.* Tan Pop's crusade remained an irresistible news item long after Washington shifted its focus from Laos to South Vietnam. In 1965, the CBS series *Twentieth Century* aired "Hoosier at the Front," a half-hour story on Buell narrated by Walter Cronkite. Two years later, John Steinbeck extolled Buell in the pages of *Newsday.* "I think Pop is an example of how the ancient gods were born and preserved in the minds and the graven images of people all over the world," the Nobel Prize–winning author declared. "Remember, the story invariably goes—in olden times people did not live well as they do now and they practiced abominations. Then a stranger appeared and he taught us how to use the plow and how to sow and how to harvest. He brought us writing so we could keep records. And he gave us healing medicines to make us healthy, and he gave us pride so we would not be afraid." To Steinbeck, Buell proved that "there are still giants in the earth."[61]

Left unstated in Steinbeck's essay was a necessary concomitant: that for there to be giants like Buell, there still had to be pygmies in the earth; that the bearer of civilization needed blank-minded savages to uplift or the story lost its meaning. Although an incomparably better writer than Schanche, Steinbeck reprised the imagery of the *Saturday Evening Post* articles by figuring the Meo as children and Buell as their "Pop," a father figure who introduced them to rural economics, literacy, and as many other hallmarks of progress as their brains could absorb. This hero-tale, reminiscent of nineteenth-century manifest destiny narratives and subsequent "little brown brother" rationales for U.S. empire, made American readers feel good about themselves and their country. In all likelihood, most put it down eager to learn more about the midwestern farmer who had gone to the other side of the world to sow seeds of democracy. They could not, however, have imagined that Tan Pop or anyone else was capable of transforming Laos's tribespeople into gladiators. It was challenge enough to keep them alive.

Chapter 6

# "Retarded Children"

## Laos in the American Popular Imagination

"The typical Laotian, and most of the two million Laotians are typical, is probably the world's last un-angry man," editorialized Warren Rogers of the *New York Herald Tribune* in May 1962. "He is Puck and Huckleberry Finn, but without the guile those two were capable of. He loves gentle music and gentle games and is ever ready for a party. He hates to fight and will almost always refuse, and he loathes the thought of harming another living thing." Thus far, John Q. Laos seemed a capital fellow. Yet he had a flaw. "Such a man," Rogers wrote, "is hardly soldierly material."

This was a problem, because the cold war compelled Washington to try to make soldiers out of about seventy thousand Lao—forty thousand in the Royal Lao Army (RLA) and thirty thousand in the Lao National Guard. "It has been a harrowing experience," reported Rogers. "The Americans have been frustrated beyond words at the typical Laotian recruit's good-natured, happy-go-lucky incompetence in the simplest military arts." Even when the Lao "appeared to have grasped enough to face a test in battle," they kept "shooting at an angle of 30 degrees over the heads of the enemy." A glance at Lao history indicated that this dovishness was no recent development; the Lao had always preferred "partying to fighting" and had "submitted without fuss to foreign domination" whenever fate thrust it their way. What made the Lao so nonaggressive? To Rogers, the answer was obvious: Their "religion is the gentle creed of Buddha," and "Buddhism forbids the taking of any life."

Aware that his portrayal of the Lao would raise a question in readers' minds, Rogers preemptively asked it himself. Why were Pathet Lao guerrillas, mostly ethnic Lao, "so different from the Laotians they oppose and seem to defeat so easily?" Again, he had a ready response: "Chinese and North Vietnamese . . . have been working closely with them for years—cajoling, threatening, convincing, and, some say, doing most of the fighting." Any admiration for Pathet Lao military prowess was therefore misplaced; those who put steel in the spines of Prince Souphanouvong's men were infiltrators from neighboring communist countries. Rogers did not explain why Americans had been unable to pull off a similar feat with the RLA. He did, however, admit that Lao nonviolence might seem laudable in a different context. "If the rest of the world were like the Laotians, and the two million Laotians were its only quarrelsome inhabitants, perhaps life would be better," he mused. "But in the grim, bitter struggle between communism and democracy, there is currently no room for pacifists."[1]

This article summarized conventional wisdom about Laos in the United States at midcentury. Rogers was neither the most prolific writer on Lao affairs nor the most famous, but he touched on the main themes pervading American discussion of the Kingdom of a Million Elephants. He depicted the Lao as carefree and passive, paid them the backhanded compliment of acknowledging their bonhomie, underscored the exasperation of U.S. military advisers, refused to give the Pathet Lao credit for battlefield successes, and blamed America's difficulties in Laos on that country's principal religion. Nearly all of the English-language commentary on Laos published between the two Geneva Conferences—1954 and 1961–1962—made these points, although authors differed in terms of what they chose to emphasize and occasionally came up with a novel argument, as when a few newsmen ascribed Lao docility to too much sex. For the most part, however, Rogers's piece might as well have been the only source of information available to Americans seeking to follow events in Laos. Except for limited-circulation works from obscure presses, there was nothing more edifying to be found.

As detailed in the previous chapter, Tom Dooley and Edgar Buell dominated coverage of Laos during the Eisenhower and Kennedy eras, and Dooley became in effect the lens through which millions of Americans got their first look at that distant kingdom. No other "Laos hands" attained

Dooley's and Buell's celebrity status and presumptive expertise, but three came within shouting distance. Oden Meeker headed the Lao program of the Cooperative for American Relief to Everywhere (CARE) in the mid-1950s, during which time he published a book about his experiences and opined in the media. Father Matt Menger of the Oblates of Mary Immaculate (OMI) arrived in Laos the same time Dooley did and worked there for nearly twenty years, overseeing missions, writing newsletters, and serving as a quotable source for reporters; he also lectured in America on Lao affairs. Stanley Karnow, *Time-Life*'s chief Southeast Asia correspondent, wrote dozens of Laos-themed articles for the most popular magazines in the United States. These men provided Americans with detailed and sometimes moving accounts of the Lao civil war, thereby helping to construct a vision of Laos that Main Street could understand.

Yet the Laos they described was, for all practical purposes, identical to Dooley's: a land of feckless half-wits uninterested in standing up to the red scourge or even acknowledging its existence. "The Lao ... is not like a German," Menger informed *U.S. News & World Report.* "A German has a strong will." Meeker went further, declaring, "In Laos the Americans and their allies are faced with the problem of trying to instill a sense of economic and political urgency in a group of people who may well be the least urgent souls on earth." Many Americans reading these passages—and hundreds of similar passages in mainstream newspapers, periodicals, and other publications—must have concluded that Washington was on a fool's errand and that the United States would be better off permitting Hanoi and Beijing to swallow up their insouciant neighbor, whose "most striking characteristic," in Karnow's words, was "a lethargy so profound that it is almost spectacular."[2]

Political correctness, even of the Age-of-Consensus variety, did not permit pundits to advance explicitly racist interpretations for the phenomena they analyzed. At a time when Washington was striving to demonstrate to third-world populations the difference between the United States and the decolonizing powers of Europe, it would have been unthinkable for any member of America's fourth estate to invoke Rudyard Kipling and diagnose the debacle in Laos as a case of sloth and heathen folly bringing all Washington's hopes to naught. Nonetheless, despite the substitution of euphemism for slur, there was little in midcentury American reportage on Laos with which the poet of British imperialism would have disagreed (except perhaps on stylistic grounds). Journalists and editorial writers across America held the Lao in derision, scoffing at them with a brazenness—and a unanimity—that may have been unprecedented. When neutralist fugle-man Captain Kong Le complained in 1961 that "Americans have a 'master race' complex and regard Laotians as inferior people," he was more than half right.[3]

## "An Ingrained Sense of Fatalism"

CARE director Oden Meeker and Father Matt Menger, OMI, both en-joyed close friendships with Tom Dooley during the young doctor's crusade in Laos. Dooley liked the two men for different reasons. Meeker, cosmopolitan and waggish, knew Doctor Tom was no saint and prod-ded him not to take himself too seriously, an approach Dooley found refreshing after the public-relations schmaltz of his fund-raising tours. Menger, devout and earnest, considered Dooley a latter-day Raphael and fed his ego with praise. Both the relief worker and the missionary joined the doctor in propagating an image of Laos calculated to elicit American sympathy but also redolent of condescension. While Meeker and Menger were humanitarians acting on the loftiest of motivations, like almost every American posted to Laos they viewed the local resi-dents as naïfs whose claim on Washington's conscience was undercut by a maddening immunity to the stimulant of U.S. economic assistance and moral tutelage.[4]

CARE sent Meeker to Laos in 1954, after the fall of Dien Bien Phu. A rice-crop failure had caused famine conditions in the northeastern part of the country, and Meeker's job was to coordinate the delivery of food pack-ages from New York to Bangkok to Vientiane and thence to the jungle-covered peaks on North Vietnam's border. His account of this mission ran in the January 14, 1956, edition of the *Saturday Evening Post*. It had a jaunty, grin-and-bear-it tone, as Meeker related the difficulties of "getting our boxes of food into the provinces": uncooperative weather, shortages of gasoline, maps so out of date they were useless, and roads that could not accommodate motorized vehicles. A veteran CARE official who had su-pervised relief missions in French Guiana, Meeker was used to such irritants and treated them as routine. What he did not anticipate was the indiffer-ence displayed by the host population toward the food shortage, the disloca-tions caused by the just-completed Franco–Viet Minh War, or anything else that might "awaken" them from their "unique siesta." Daily life in Laos, Meeker noted, was "tranquility just this side of Rip Van Winkle." No one bustled. No one raised his or her voice. Everyone was "utterly charming" but also "dreamy," "lazy," and "slack," not so much unappreciative of U.S. aid as uninspired by it. "The Laotians are gentle people, content in their bamboo-and-thatch houses," Meeker observed. "They ask only to be left in peace." While Meeker found such an attitude beguiling—"all the dreaming corners of this magical kingdom" struck him as "touched with gentle fantasy"—it was not conducive to relief work. He concluded his *Post* piece by admitting "discouragement" at the meager results of CARE's foray into Laos but rationalizing, "The alternative was to wring our hands and not begin to do anything." Perhaps the next crisis spot would have a citizenry with more élan.[5]

By the time Meeker expanded his article into a book, *The Little World of Laos*, Pathet Lao activity had increased and the Eisenhower administration had escalated its commitment to the Vientiane government. Meeker therefore placed his magical kingdom more obtrusively within the context of the cold war, warning readers that American efforts to "create in Laos a nation strong enough to resist the... pressures across the communist frontiers" were likely to shatter on the rocks of a "Lao genius for passive resistance" that made "*manana* sound dynamic." The origins of this genius were obscure, but Meeker speculated that religion, "the gentle doctrine of Buddhism," was to blame. He cited a former colonial official who proclaimed, "When things go wrong, we Europeans and Americans take a combative attitude and try to redress the situation. But the Lao attitude is to withdraw, like a hedgehog. Because he is a Buddhist, he has been taught resignation, passivity, and to hope that the catastrophe will soon pass over." Or perhaps, Meeker ventured, "the fevers and the parasites" brought about by Laos's climate had "intensified the dreaminess for which the Lao are remarkable." Whatever the reason, these "dreamy, gentle, bucolic, nonaggressive people" were ill disposed to shoulder arms. "The Lao are still Lao," wrote Meeker. "They aren't really very angry with anybody."

Meeker did not advocate abandonment of Laos. Because he was fond of the Lao, he thought it "monstrous that these people are in danger of being turned into pastoral robots by their dedicated neighbors." But as someone who had spent time in Laos, he felt obliged to tell his fellow Americans what they were letting themselves in for. "American impatience to get things done," he declared, "is due for a workout in Laos, where the first two phrases a foreigner learns are *bo mi*, or 'there isn't any,' and *bo pen nyan*, which can mean 'never mind,' 'too bad,' 'it doesn't matter,' 'who cares,' and a dozen other things, all gently negative." Everywhere Meeker went in the kingdom, at all hours of the day, "it always seemed to be siesta time." Getting the Lao to "work at a faster tempo" was "like trying to nail jelly to the wall." Meeker recalled how, during his first trip to Vientiane, he had dropped off his shirts at a one-day-service laundry only to be told, a week later, that they were not ready. When he protested, the launderer yawningly declared, "You are too exigent, monsieur. You must be more supple." "What happened to that one-day service?" Meeker demanded. The answer was the same: "You cannot be too rigid, monsieur. You must be more supple." Even the army adopted *bo pen nyan* as an article of faith. Meeker noted that it was common for the bugler to "blow the eight o'clock reveille at nine-thirty," or to forget it altogether, predictable behavior in a nation where people were "more interested in decorating things with curlicues than in getting ahead in the world." To Crown Prince Savang Vatthana's boast that "in Laos no one ever suffered a nervous breakdown," Meeker offered the retort: "if anyone did, it would be foreigners in the country administering economic aid."

On balance, Meeker low-rated Washington's chances in Laos. The problem was not "the usual . . . frustrations which seem inevitable in trying to meet a deadline in these latitudes." Rather, it lay in the Lao themselves: "gentle, peaceful, innocent, charming, feckless, and makes-no-never-mind." Experience suggested that no matter what Americans did, the Lao could not be "fired with enthusiasm for the techniques of the Western world," for they were "docile in their acceptance of what this and future Buddhist lives may hold." Meeker consoled readers that the communists faced the same dilemma. "One can imagine the Vietminh's experts-on-loan, like their opposite numbers in the American foreign-aid programs to the south, muttering about the impossibility of getting anything done in Laos," he observed. "Certainly, the ineffable Lao seem unlikely material for rural Marxists." This was cold comfort, though, to a "transplanted American under pressure and in a hurry." While Meeker's breezy prose helped his message go down easily, *The Little World of Laos* was a depressing book that left no question as to which nation constituted the softest spot in the free-world perimeter.[6]

Matt Menger had graver doubts about Laos's future than his secular compatriots in the aid program. As a man of God, however, he was doubly committed to preventing a communist takeover. "We need a foreign policy whose sole criterion is 'right,'" he thundered to a reporter in 1962. "If communism is wrong—and it is, for it is atheistic materialism, and thus directly opposed to Christian democracy—let's stop it." Menger dealt in absolutes and held no brief for those who called for a coalition government in Vientiane. It "could never work," he insisted. "Imagine, if you will, the

United States ruled and directed jointly by Richard Nixon, Mao Tse-tung, and Indira Gandhi!" From his arrival in Laos in 1956 until his expulsion nineteen years later, Menger emphasized the same point: compromise with godlessness was as impossible as it was undesirable. Either Washington was on the side of the angels or it was not. The Lao were fellow human beings, sons of Adam and daughters of Eve, and Americans had an obligation to defend them against the unholy forces threatening their nation.[7]

By his own admission, Menger made little headway for the church in Laos. "[T]he Lao are extremely difficult to convert," he wrote in 1959 from his parish in Tha Ngon. Nonetheless, he drew encouragement from small triumphs—"I have four families 'on the doorstep,' with more to follow, I hope!"—and he raised enough money through mass mailings and lecture tours of America to finance the building of churches, schools, and orphanages in his adopted country. The strength of his faith gave him great energy and enabled him, like Dooley and Buell, to work longer hours under harsher conditions than most people could have endured. McGeorge Bundy, national security adviser in the Kennedy administration, assured one of Menger's supporters that "the president believes it should be a source of pride to all Americans that we have such men as Father Menger carrying on their vital work."[8]

Menger considered himself as much a proselytizer of modernity as Catholicism. Indeed, he thought the latter depended upon the former, because, in his view, Laos's economic and cultural impoverishment rendered its people susceptible to the "negative philosophy" of Buddhism, which in turn perpetuated the "stagnant environment" in which the Lao lived. "Buddhism," explained Menger, "is oriented to leaving the world," not acting in it: "To the Lao, death and the achievement of paradise are passive. . . . When a man attains a completely passive or negative state—no thinking, no desiring, no acting—he is considered perfect and thus, after death, will attain Nirvana." By contrast, if that same man worked to improve his circumstances, he ran the risk of reincarnation, the "sorrow of life after life" that Buddha forecast for all but the most meritorious. Was it any surprise that someone reared in such a doctrine hesitated to "discard his formerly passive role and exist as an active, contributing member of society"? Moreover, why should he take on a new role, when he had never witnessed progress? "Permeating this society has been an ingrained sense of fatalism, of being unable to change the world," Menger wrote. Most Lao were "content to lie dormant on the veranda, . . . waiting for the spirits to turn on the sun, turn off the rain." Menger believed that Laos would become fertile ground for the true faith when the Lao were convinced that their lot was not inevitable, that American aid could help raise living standards and expand intellectual horizons. Once given hope, predicted Menger, "they will not be content with the apologies or excuses of the past, but will demand...a better life than that so fatalistically accepted by their parents." They would also be prepared to receive "the saving waters of Christ's baptism."[9]

For all his drive, though, Menger often despaired of success. The Oblates of Mary Immaculate, he was wont to point out, were "specialists in difficult missions," and he had been given the most difficult of all. "Laos is a challenge unlike anything America has ever taken on," he observed. "She is a...slow-moving nation,...unwilling to recognize the tragic realities of today, and even less willing to sprint, as America would like her to do, into tomorrow." Americans needed patience, "the patience a loving mother would have for a slow-learning child," to engineer change in the Kingdom of a Million Elephants. Menger's account of his apostolate among the Lao was a two-volume howl of frustration leavened only occasionally by humor, as when he told of how a water buffalo destroyed the half-completed church at Ban Keng. That buffalo, sadly, exhibited more vigor than the natives did. In every village where Menger preached, he ran "smack into a wall of tradition, custom, and indifference" that nearly broke him. "I kept reminding myself to be charitable to these good people!" he recalled, noting that the average Lao was "not dormant by stubbornness or by choice, but because he knows no other way to live. He is like a child who must learn to crawl before he can walk." It was hard to be patient, though, with people lacking any "competitive spirit," people whose minds were "empty and vacant, shriveling from neglect." "The Lao have a gentle charm," Menger conceded. "But Laos must bring to this new era more than...the gentleness of a non-aggressive society." And Americans, like it or not, had to accelerate Laos's modernization. As Menger put it in a striking analogy, "Retarded children in the family of nations are a source of expense, aggravation, and embarrassment."[10]

When an American correspondent asked Menger if the Lao would "stand and fight" against communist invaders, he equivocated. "They will if they have to," he said, but then qualified his statement by acknowledging that the Lao had not shown much inclination to fight "in the past." "[T]hey do not have a strong dedication," he observed. "The Lao is a wonderful person. He is a hospitable, a gentle person. He loves to live and let others live. He does not like to fight." Noting the interviewer's puzzlement, Menger tried to clarify what he meant: "The Lao does not like to fight, but he will fight. He needs someone to go in and give him courage.... [U]ntil the United States has a firm, unified, constant policy in Laos, the Lao themselves do not want to fight, do not want to commit themselves, because they feel—they say, 'Why should we fight with the Americans against the communists?'" This testimony hardly bade fair to justify the millions of dollars invested in the RLA. What kind of allies were these, if they needed Americans to give them courage to fight for their own country? That a God-fearing cold warrior like Menger, who had spent six years in Laos trying to bring its people to Christ and save them from Marxist domination, could respond so desultorily to a direct question spoke volumes about the lack of American confidence in the Lao.[11]

## "Primitive Inefficiency and Shattering Inertia"

Menger and Meeker put themselves at the center of the story, which lent their accounts an immediacy absent from most coverage of Laos. Readers were invited to share the authors' frustration when American good intentions and material aid proved no match for Lao otiosity. As a professional journalist, Stanley Karnow rarely wrote in the first person, but this did not prevent him from depicting America's ally in terms just as unflattering. Shortly after he became Hong Kong bureau chief for *Time-Life*, Karnow penned "Tale of a Troubled Paradise," a piece that blasted the "primitive inefficiency and shattering inertia" of the Lao and asserted, "In Laos it is downright bad taste to work more than is absolutely necessary." Evidence of this lack of initiative was everywhere: "Years ago, someone ambitiously built a railroad station at the town of Savannakhet, but the railroad itself has yet to be started. The main highway...is paved for only eight miles....[Laos's] best hotel...is a dilapidated bungalow." No institution more perfectly reflected the nation's shortcomings than its army, which, Karnow noted, had recently captured a Pathet Lao battalion only to let the communists escape, unharmed. When asked to "explain how this had happened," Laos's defense minister had shaken his head and responded, "That is an extremely difficult question." Such attitudes contributed to a situation in which, by Karnow's reckoning, the communists had "only about 4,000 men" but nonetheless "held the initiative in both guerrilla and psychological warfare." Karnow did not attempt to reconcile his portrait of "affable, gentle, easygoing,...peace-loving Laotians" with the military performance of Souphanouvong's troops, other than to remind readers that "Pathet Lao fighters" were being "used as pawns by Ho Chi Minh and the Red Chinese." If not for these external sponsors of insurgency, he implied, the Pathet Lao would be as inept as the RLA. Karnow's article, illustrated with photographs of Lao playfully splashing one another at a water festival, ran in the September 7, 1959, issue of *Life*.[12]

A later *Life* full-page spread, "The Mess in Laos," saw Karnow tackle the scandal engulfing the aid program. "In Laos, U.S. money has been wasted, squandered, and mismanaged," he proclaimed. "But the real loss comes from Washington's insistence...[on] following goals and aims which the backward, imponderable little country could not possibly have achieved." American policymakers had tried to build a cold war stronghold in a "sleepy country whose people want little more than to be left alone in their paradise of poppy fields." The Lao were too "primitive" to "make responsible decisions, demonstrate sincere allegiance,...or react to standard programs designed for rational modern economies." And the RLA was simply a disgrace, "incapable of waging war." Karnow estimated that there were only a handful of royal troops "who *may* shoot back if assaulted." When he accompanied an RLA unit on a mission outside Vientiane, he found that their strategy consisted of aimlessly firing U.S.-donated howitzers into the jungle. "Enemy is out there somewhere," the commander said. This experience convinced Karnow that Washington faced a choice in Laos "between an inconclusive kind of war and an unsatisfactory kind of peace." He dismissed any notion of defeating the Pathet Lao as chimerical, not because American policy had been poorly thought out and implemented, but because the Eisenhower administration was compelled to work through the indigenous government and military, and nothing short of reincarnation would bring them up to the challenge.[13]

These broadsides were a warm-up for "Laos: Test of U.S. Intentions," a March 17, 1961, *Time* cover feature that publisher Bernhard Auer called "the only comprehensive story of Laos's history and current crisis that exists anywhere." In it, Karnow described Laos as "landlocked, lackadaisical, and so primitive that the currently favored adjective 'underdeveloped' would be an unwarranted compliment." The Lao, readers learned, were "charming, but, by Western standards, bone lazy"; they had "no zeal" and "no interest in fighting." While "in other backward lands" it was common to ascribe this trait to "malnutrition, liver flukes, and intestinal parasites," in Laos "lethargy extends to the highest rank of princelings, raised on French cuisine." Worst of all was the king, Savang Vatthana, who had "sunk into a torpor that could not be shaken by the fast-paced world around him." According to Karnow, Savang had once been a reformer, particularly with regard to education, but he had been unable to summon the energy to act on his progressive impulses and now considered them foolish. Karnow quoted Savang's rationale: "What is the point of sending children to school? We are backward, and whatever we do, we shall not rise to the level of other peoples." Such do-nothingness had not hurt the king's popularity. "Savang Vatthana is still widely loved by his countrymen," observed Karnow, "for the same phlegmatic qualities that make him the despair of foreign diplomats."

Other prominent Lao figures shared those qualities. Karnow depicted Souvanna Phouma "cultivating gladioli" in Phnom Penh during the battle for Vientiane and refusing to "define what he means by his doctrine of 'neutrality within neutralism' on the grounds that Laotians dislike precision." Boun Oum was "a sort of Buddhist Falstaff," praised by one of his supporters as "the most representative personality of the kingdom," which, Karnow noted, "means that he is excessively fond of drinking and wenching." General Phoumi Nosavan, the only "ambitious" Lao in power, had "trouble making his soldiers fight" and proved "embarrassingly unable to win any battles." With these men calling the shots on the pro-Western side of the Lao civil war, it was little wonder the free world was losing. As to why the rightists' adversaries fought so effectively, Karnow again evaded the question, except to note that the Plain of Jars was "crawling with Russian experts and Viet Minh cadres down to the gun-crew level." The intimation was clear: the Pathet Lao owed their success to foreign involvement. And the neutralist, Kong Le? He had "fallen under the thumb of the communists," asserted Karnow, and was a cat's-paw like Souphanouvong.

Karnow's portrayal of the RLA read as farce. "[T]he soldiers were small, laughing men, floppy as rag dolls in their outsized American fatigues," he reported. "They swam in mountain streams, stole pigs, [and] got drunk on rice whisky.... They disliked the idea of shooting at anybody with a rifle, since it is not permissible for any good Buddhist to knowingly kill another human being." In five weeks, the RLA had advanced "exactly eight miles" toward Pathet Lao units stationed in the Plain of Jars, and they showed no inclination to quicken their pace. "What could serious cold warriors do," Karnow asked, "with soldiers who set up tiny clay images of Buddha to shoot at,... [and] then deliberately missed?" The millions of Americans for whom *Time* was required reading doubtless asked themselves the same question.[14]

This article, one of the most sneering works of Orientalia produced during the cold war, was a digest version of a longer treatise that Karnow

completed but did not publish. While the book-length text never advanced
past manuscript stage, it merits attention for the scorn Karnow displayed
toward the Lao and the vehemence with which he made his case that hope
for a military solution to Laos's internal conflict was "a dream." "The Laotians themselves are, of course, incapable of waging war," he wrote. Despite
years of "bottle-feeding" by American advisers, the Royal Lao Government
(RLG) still lacked "discipline of any kind." From the "remote, torpid king"
down to the lowest civil servant "doz[ing] fitfully at his post," officials
"slept late," took "long lunches followed by siestas," and occasionally "visited their offices" for an hour or two—then it was time for "aperitifs and
lengthy dinners, with perhaps an excursion to a local cabaret for a nightcap."
However dire the crisis, there was "no sense of urgency, no hurry," as politicians "lol[led] around" in a "relaxed atmosphere." The government's "shyness of responsibility" enraged U.S. statesmen like Ambassador Winthrop
Brown, whom Karnow interviewed after an unproductive meeting with
Savang. "Don't ask me why the king is lethargic," Brown allegedly snapped.
"I'm not his psychiatrist."

Almost as infuriating as Lao laziness was Lao inconstancy. In terms of
choosing up sides in the East-West struggle, RLG members were will-
o'-the-wisps, given to "fuzzy qualifying expressions" best understood as
"attempts to fight off a flat, factual statement." Souvanna, wrote Karnow,
"vacillate[d] like a pendulum"; the king could "vacillate visibly before one's
eyes"; and former premier Katay Don Sasorith "simultaneously drifted off
in two opposite directions—as only a Laotian can do." Karnow did not
find this behavior surprising since, as far as he could tell, "there are practically no ideological notions in Laos, . . . nothing like a Left or Right." Such
concepts belonged to a mature society, and Laos was the opposite. The cold
war, along with the rest of the twentieth century, had passed the kingdom
by. "[I]f countries are products of their history," Karnow declared, "Laos
was not able to rise much out of the kindergarten class." Even in 1961, after
$300 million in American aid, there was "a medieval ambience to life and
love in Laos," and the pronouncements of John F. Kennedy and Nikita
Khrushchev seemed to bear as little relation to day-to-day events as Skybolt
would in twelfth-century Gaul.

Lao politicians made Karnow's blood boil, but they compared favorably
with Lao soldiers. "The care and feeding of this army," asserted Karnow, was
"as non-productive an investment as any imaginable." American officers
of the Programs Evaluation Office (PEO) were "doing everything but fire
the army's guns" for them while RLA troops "spent long hours leisurely

pausing for recreation" on their slow-motion advance to the front. Jerrold Schechter, a recent addition to the Vientiane press corps, marched with the RLA for a few days and remarked afterward to Karnow, "The countryside is so beautiful and the mountain air so refreshing, it's understandable why nobody wants to fight." Nobody in the free-world camp, anyway.

As in his shorter essays, Karnow did not entertain the possibility that the Lao opposing the RLA were motivated by patriotism or that their conduct under fire reflected innate courage and resourcefulness. He insisted that Souphanouvong was a North Vietnamese puppet, brainwashed and back-boned by Hanoi, and that the Red Prince's political life began when he was introduced to Viet Minh military commander Vo Nguyen Giap in 1950. According to Karnow, the two men met at Viet Minh headquarters on the border between China and Vietnam, where Giap "lectured" Soupha-nouvong for hours, "repeating Mao Tse-tung's homilies." Souphanouvong, Karnow wrote, was "spellbound as Giap spoke." Having "found his men-tor," he returned to Laos "filled with ideas and stereotyped slogans"—and, more important, with "Viet Minh instructors, arms, and money." From then on, Souphanouvong would be the "ostensible chief" of the Lao communist insurrection, but he danced to Hanoi's tune.

While Karnow acknowledged that Kong Le was no communist, he claimed that this did not matter; the "simplistic captain" had lacked "the faintest idea of how to proceed" after staging his 1960 coup, and the reds moved in to exploit his bewilderment. One fellow traveler, Quinim Pholsena of the Santiphab Party, "attached himself to Kong Le," "egg[ed] him on," and "helped him with his speeches," which amounted to "anti-American propaganda." By the time Kong Le ordered his men northward after the battle for Vientiane, he was in the communists' pocket, their "instrument," leading a "rebel army supplied by Russian arms and equipment [and] aided by North Vietnamese technicians." In Karnow's view, Kong Le and Soupha-nouvong had achieved command of the Plain of Jars not as a consequence of tactical prowess or inspirational leadership, but because communists from other countries were guiding their steps and galvanizing their followers with a bellicosity that Washington failed to instill in the RLA.[15]

## "So Much for So Little"

We cannot know how many pieces on Laos Karnow wrote or coau-thored, as *Time* ran nearly all its stories without bylines ("Test of U.S.

Intentions" being an exception), but Karnow was *Time-Life*'s Hong Kong bureau chief from 1959 to 1962, and the Hong Kong staff was responsible for covering developments in Southeast Asia. It seems a fair assumption, then, that he had a hand in most Laos-centered features during the period when Washington revised its policy toward Vientiane from firmness to flexibility. Although Karnow's pessimism deviated from the upbeat style normally affected by *Time* reporters, it was consistent with the magazine's treatment of Laos since before the 1954 Geneva Conference—a point that bears elaboration given that Henry Luce, founder of Time Inc., was one of the foremost advocates for an activist U.S. foreign policy in Asia. Indeed, several scholars hold Luce responsible for Washington's missteps in that area, including its support of Chiang Kai-shek in the Chinese Civil War, its quarter-century refusal to recognize the People's Republic after Chiang's defeat, its attempt to unify Korea under noncommunist auspices, and its intervention in Vietnam. According to T. Christopher Jespersen, Robert Herzstein, W. A. Swanberg, and others, Luce used his multimedia empire to shape public and official opinion about events in the Far East, convincing millions of Americans that a U.S.-sponsored Western, Christian, capitalist solution to complex local problems was not only possible but necessary. Herzstein argues that Luce had "a fervent faith in America's God-ordained mission in Asia."[16]

That faith, however, was not fervent enough to mandate defense of Laos. In contrast to his attitude toward other nations on the Asian mainland, Luce never considered Laos a domino worth propping up. Rather, he saw the former French colony as hopeless and believed Americans should wash their hands of it. While Luce wrote no memoir, and while biographers do not mention his views on Laos, those views may be inferred from his leading publication, *Time* magazine, which journalist John Kobler calls the "keystone of the Lucean arch." As numerous former employees have testified, Luce was obsessive about controlling the content of his periodicals and took liberties that would have horrified other editors-in-chief, such as altering correspondents' reports to the point where Time Inc.'s coverage bore no resemblance to what the reporters originally wrote. This meddlesomeness was particularly pronounced when the subject in question was one Luce cared about, and nothing engaged his interest more than Asia. *Time* would not have run a story on Laos or any Asian country that did not reflect Luce's viewpoint. To judge by the stories it ran, America's top press magnate thought the Kingdom of a Million Elephants was a pathetic joke.[17]

As early as 1953, *Time* portrayed Laos as "gasping on the mud-bank of its unpreparedness" while the Viet Minh bore down on Luang Prabang. King Sisavang Vong had been unable to get the "happy-go-lucky Laotians to mobilize," and the royal capital's only hope lay with a few thousand French troops airdropped into Sam Neua to "head off Giap's drive." *Time* credited Paris and the weather with saving Luang Prabang, affirming, "The only real opposition the communists met" came "from the French," while an early start to the "summer monsoon" turned roads into "rivers of mud" and caused communist supply lines to become congested. In *Time's* account, not a single Lao opposed the Viet Minh, and the magazine barely mentioned Laos in its coverage of the Geneva Conference, which it considered "communism's greatest victory since China fell." The only reference to the Lao delegation at Geneva came in a gloomy piece on the final hours of bargaining, with *Time's* anonymous author observing that "the Lao delegates were already in bed" when French premier Pierre Mendes-France and the British, Soviet, and Chinese foreign ministers drafted the Geneva Accords. Apparently, the negotiators decided that "to get them [the Lao] up would mean more delay," and that expedience was paramount. Therefore, at Mendes-France's suggestion, they completed their work and told the Lao "about it in the morning"—by which point the die was cast. Phoui Sananikone's defense of his nation's interests as head of the Lao delegation went unacknowledged. To *Time*, the Lao were bystanders at Geneva, victims of negotiations conducted over their heads.[18]

Laos did not improve in *Time's* estimation during the post-Geneva period. Readers discovered that the kingdom was "the least of the three nations carved out of French Indochina," a "lotus land" in "habitual half-slumber" whose "sleepy government" never "stirred itself to anger." The Pathet Lao had no indigenous support, being a "Viet Minh appendage . . . trained, supplied, and controlled by . . . Viet Minh troops masquerading as Laotians." Souphanouvong toed the party line "because he fears his domineering communist wife," who was Vietnamese. *Time* reported that the Red Prince "even washes his wife's underthings in the family washtub 'because she likes me to,'" an image that emasculated Souphanouvong and underscored his subservience to Hanoi. Pro-Western Lao leaders were similarly reduced to caricature. According to *Time*, Katay spent his days in Vientiane's nightclubs, "watch[ing] the dancing girls"; Souvanna walked about the capital "arm in arm" with Souphanouvong, "sipping champagne"; the "petulant," "tut-tutting" Prince Phetsarath vegetated "in luxurious exile in Bangkok"; and the "aging, gout-crippled" king, who had "never openly fought for independence from the French," summed up Laos's dilemma with the remark, "My people do not know how to fight; they know only how to sing and make love." *Time* took him at his word. "[T]he unwarlike people of this Buddhist kingdom," it asserted, wanted to "relapse into their old hedonist ways" after independence rather than "face the grim reality" of communist expansionism. American officials would have to think hard about whether "the pleasure-loving Laotians" were worth a conflict with Beijing or Moscow, and the evidence, as filtered through *Time*'s prism, indicated otherwise.[19]

Tellingly, *Time*, that champion of global intervention, predated the White House in its willingness to accept Lao nonalignment, declaring in September 1959, "Scarcely any country on earth is less fitted to serve as a pivotal point in the struggle against communism than Laos, a land of blue mountains, green jungles, and affably unambitious people." The magazine attributed Lao "gentleness" to the "prevalent Laotian faith of Buddhism, with its strong emphasis on harming no living creature," although it allowed that disease might also play a role, as "[m]alaria, yaws, gonorrhea, and kwashiorkor... are common." Whether doctrinally unmanned or too sick to fight, the Lao displayed a notable "lack of aggressiveness." Follow-up features belittled "primitive, soporific Laos," where "heavy-lidded politicians" preferred "the comforting sound of temple bells to the strident sounds of war"; the "bland, tired-eyed premier" could not "tell a red from a banyan tree"; and the "lackadaisical Royal Army" showed no "intention of attacking." A year before Kennedy assumed the presidency, *Time* determined that there was "little profit" in "trying to make a free-world bastion" out of Laos.[20]

The sequence of coups and countercoups that shook Vientiane in 1960 inspired some of *Time*'s most withering articles. When Phoumi overthrew Premier Phoui Sananikone, the magazine was cautiously optimistic, hoping the general could bring order to Laos, which, it observed, had "been wrestling for years with corruption, chaos, and communism—and an amiable indifference to all three." Readers were advised not to overrate Phoumi's triumph, though: it was "a *coup d'état* Laotian style and not on the South American level," meaning that there had been "no bloodshed." After Phoumi "disastrously flunked" several military tests, *Time* disowned him. He was such a poor commander, it reported, that his men not only "abandoned their stations before a terrorist hove in sight"; they left behind "weapons, ammunition, and trucks" for the enemy to collect. If Phoumi was the best of the pro-Western candidates for leadership, then Washington might as well admit defeat. "The U.S. has spent more than $300 million trying to shore up Laos," *Time* complained. "In few areas of the world has the U.S. spent so much for so little."[21]

Kong Le's seizure of Vientiane jolted *Time*, as it did every element of the American press, but the rebel captain received slight credit for his triumph. As far as *Time* was concerned, "the only solid accomplishment" of the coup was "to demonstrate how few men are needed to capture a capital city in sleepy Laos." More ominous was Kong Le's transfer of power to Souvanna, who *Time* thought would "lead Laos into neutralism in favor of the reds" because he believed that the "Pathet Lao will call off their guerrillas if only somebody will talk to them nicely." Alas, this approach had domestic appeal since, *Time* noted, "Laotians are fuzzy thinkers, when thinkers at all."[22]

As Vientiane fortified itself for battle in the final weeks of 1960, *Time*'s cutting edge grew sharper. It portrayed Souvanna awakening one morning, "his head still dizzy from ceremonial quaffing of a strong rice spirit," to find the royal capital in enemy hands. His reaction was that of a coward and spoiled child. He "blamed all his troubles on the U.S.," *Time* reported, and fled the country. Souvanna's successor, General Sounthone Pathammavong, continued the RLG's downward spiral. After taking command, he gave his people what *Time* called "some inscrutably Oriental advice," purportedly declaring, "Do not bruise lotus blossoms; do not muddy clear waters; do not anger frogs; do not harm little frogs." Americans accustomed to hearing Churchillian rhetoric from military leaders could be expected to roll their eyes.[23]

*Time*'s account of the three-day struggle for Vientiane, while extensive, lacked the gravitas normally accorded such an event. The tone remained flippant—"War is not in character for Laotians, a gentle people given to indolence, rice wine, and frequent Buddhist festivals"—and the most vivid image barely hinted at Vientiane's human suffering: "At a temple, 100 monks in saffron robes fluttered about like a flock of birds." Although *Time* acknowledged that Lao were killed, it placed the number at a much-too-low two hundred and depicted the fighting as a child's game. "Desertions were commonplace and simple to effect," it noted. "A soldier of uncertain mind had only to change the red arm band of the Kong Le faction for the white band of General Phoumi." This was not exactly Manila 1942 or Seoul 1951—or even Saigon 1960, where South Vietnamese President Ngo Dinh Diem's crushing of an attempted coup received more somber treatment in *Time* than did the nearly simultaneous and bloodier battle for Vientiane.[24]

Unlike some U.S. policymakers, *Time* saw no reason to celebrate Kong Le's defeat. Its first report on the new Phoumi–Boun Oum government exuded contempt, as it described Boun Oum as a "plump sybarite" who "demonstrated the qualities that make Laotians the despair of Western diplomats." The prince's "favorite companions turned out to be not candidates for the cabinet but girls from the Vientiane dance hall." Phoumi was scarcely better, showing "no more zeal than any of his predecessors" for facing down the communists. "Seldom had the winds of war blown about such artless heads," *Time* quipped, and then posed a crucial question: Although Phoumi had been "described as a 'strongman,'" was he "strong enough or determined enough to battle the Pathet Lao into submission?" The magazine concluded that this was "doubtful." In fact, the inability of *any* Lao statesman to serve free-world ends had been a constant *Time* refrain since the mid-1950s.[25]

When Kennedy began making noises after his inauguration about safeguarding Lao self-rule, *Time*, for once, proved disinclined to charge at the sound of the trumpets. "For the new administration as well as the old," it observed, "Laos offers the unattractive choice between a difficult peace and an impossible war." Victory with such allies was out of the question. Dwight Eisenhower's attempt to "make primitive Laos 'a bulwark against communism'" had failed "because of the reluctance of the Royal Laotian Army to fight," and Kennedy confronted the same problem. Lao soldiers, noted *Time*, were "even more inept—but less savage—than the Congo's," only interested in "saving their skins... until the rest of the world got them out of trouble." PEO advisers stationed in Laos did not attempt to conceal their low opinion of the RLA when interviewed by *Time* correspondents. "This is war, dammit," one colonel fumed, "but the Laotians are just not willing to risk getting killed." To the suggestion that a cease-fire might give the RLA a chance to improve discipline, another U.S. military official sourly responded, "They've been observing a ceasefire for some time now, anyway." *Time* doubted that the RLA could "win a battle anywhere in Laos" or that Americans would ever succeed in "teach[ing] the Laotian army how to fight." This did not mean that all Southeast Asia need fall to red tyranny, though. "[U]nlike the Laotians," *Time* pointed out, "the Vietnamese fight the communists and fight them well."[26]

## "Put Iron into Chocolate Soldiers"

Historian John Foran dubs *Time* "the most influential popular press outlet of the day," which may be an exaggeration but which testifies to the media power Luce wielded. Magazines and newspapers below—and above—*Time* in the American press hierarchy echoed Luce's judgment on Laos, either out of obeisance or, more likely, because their views coincided with his. The Lao whom readers encountered in mainstream journalism were quintessential anti-warriors, "pacifist Buddhists who frequently make jokes about how their country has never won a war," in the words of the *New York Times*. Apart from occasional praise for Lao "friendliness" and "good humor," American press organs had little positive to say with respect to the Lao, and their criticism often verged on contumely. Standard qualifying terms included "indolent," "sleepy," "stagnant," "passive," "languid," "unassertive,"and "drowsy"—adjectives unlikely to inspire confidence. "In Laos not even the fighting cocks are bloodthirsty," declared the *Saturday Evening Post*. "They wear no spurs and do not fight to kill." The *Washington News* claimed that Laos had been "conquered, if that is the word, once by a lone Frenchman....If the Laotians cared, there is no record of it." *National Geographic* was unsure "if this little world of gentle people will ever learn to cope with its new reality of grenades and machine guns." The *Wall Street Journal* did not think so. "Even with a great deal of U.S. help, they [the Lao] exhibit scant will to fight," read a March 1962 editorial. "In such circumstances, it is a real question whether we could save Laos no matter what we did."[27]

One of the earliest multipage articles devoted to Laos in a prominent American magazine was "Land of Leisure," which *Holiday* ran in 1956. Author Santha Rama Rau warned readers planning to travel to Laos that "Laotians are not particularly ambitious, and this is probably harder than anything else for a visiting westerner to understand." She did not know if the "Laotians' unhurried life" was a result of "malnutrition" or "plain indolence," but they clearly "prefer to watch other people exert themselves." Even the prospect of war did not ruffle their "*sang-froid*." According to Rama Rau, when the Viet Minh advanced on Luang Prabang in 1953, "city life continued as usual," with "children playing," "Buddhists priests washing their saffron robes," and most residents "simply sitting and watching the world go by." Although this seemed "an exasperating attitude for a nation that shares its borders with two communist regions," Rama Rau had to admit it was an attitude that "disturbs only the foreigners." The Lao were not losing any sleep. *Holiday*'s most concrete piece of advice for tourists followed logically from this portrayal: "[I]f you want to get anything done in Laos,...you must hire Vietnamese."[28]

The *Providence Journal* sounded the same theme in 1959 when it tried to explain why "American hustle to bring progress to this lazy land...has failed to have much impact on the fun-loving, unambitious people." Reporter David Lancashire argued that the Lao "frown on hard work" and were loath to emulate the example of eager-beaver Westerners sent to assist them. "During the recent communist offensive," wrote Lancashire, "lights burned nightly in the American aid offices,...but Laotian military headquarters closed for weekends and Buddhist holidays, and regular three-hour noon siestas prevailed." Lancashire described "an American financial expert work[ing] long hours" in a "hotbox office at the Laos national bank" while native "bank employees sat idly flipping elastic bands at lizards scurrying across the ceiling." Readers could be forgiven for concluding, along with the *Washington Post*, that the United States was "galloping off on a white charger to save people who don't want to be saved."[29]

At least, the Lao did not seem willing to fight for their salvation. R. H. Shackford, billed by the *Washington News* as "one of America's outstanding foreign correspondents," affirmed that "Laotian soldiers often resemble Ferdinand the Bull, who wanted only to smell the flowers." *Newsweek* depicted RLA troops in Vientiane enjoying a "water festival" even though a column of communist guerrillas was "poised on the southbound highway, just 75 miles from Vientiane itself." Despite this threat, the only RLA belligerence was directed heavenward: "When 'the big toad swallowed the moon' (the Lao explanation of an eclipse), Lao soldiers opened up with machine guns, shooting them into the sky to frighten the toad into disgorging the friendly moon." America's aim in Laos, *Newsweek* pronounced, was to "convince the Laotians that the rebels make a more important target than the moon." Anyone who needed such points spelled out belonged in playschool, not a war zone. "Fundamentally, it is a matter of the Laotian attitude—the absence of a strong popular desire for freedom plus the will to fight for it," declared the *Washington Star.* "In such a situation, even with the best of intentions, there is not a great deal that friendly nations can do to help." Certainly, those nations would be reluctant to send their citizens to fight alongside the Lao.[30]

Media accounts of the RLA in action rendered the prospect even less inviting. "Two hundred million dollars' worth of military aid has not made government troops capable of vanquishing the jungle-tough rebels," understated the *Christian Science Monitor* in early 1961. In fact, those troops seemed more likely to vanquish themselves: the *New York Herald Tribune* portrayed RLA soldiers as so incompetent they forgot where they planted

American-supplied land mines and wound up "blow[ing] their own feet off." According to the *New York Times*, "The typical Laotian soldier is a laughing young peasant who...abhors killing....He sings, dances, and plays music at every break as his 100-man company moves toward the front, often with a plucked jungle flower sticking out of the muzzle of his ill-kept rifle." The performance of such mooncalves under fire was predictable. "There has never been a real battle," declared the *Washington Post*, "just a series of 'fadeouts.'" The *Wall Street Journal* lambasted Washington for spending over $50 million per year on "an ineffectual army of 70,000 that has racked up a consistent series of panicky retreats."[31]

This obloquy again begged the question, bluntly phrased by the *New York Herald Tribune*, of "why the other side seems to have the will to fight while we [American-backed forces] do not." Washington had supplied the RLA with enough arms to subdue its adversary, and royalist forces were superior in numbers to the Pathet Lao and the neutralists. Yet every time there was a skirmish, the RLA lost. What magic did the other side have that enabled it, in the words of Associated Press correspondent John Roderick, to "put iron into chocolate soldiers"? Drew Pearson of the *Washington Post* felt the contrast was overdrawn. "The Russians are having just as much trouble trying to turn the pro-communist rebels into savage jungle fighters" as the Americans were having with the RLA, he wrote. "Russian technicians are reported returning from the front frustrated and disgusted." Their efforts bore fruit, though, and America's did not. Why?[32]

The *Baltimore Sun*'s Mark Watson offered the most thoughtful explanation, one noteworthy for its refusal to claim that the Pathet Lao were really North Vietnamese in disguise. He conceded the homogeneity of both pro- and anti-American armies—"There is little difference in their ethnic qualities"—and argued that the enemy's X factor was an "incentive" that "has apparently been developed in the Pathet Lao soldiers as much as has their present sense of combat discipline." The communists who controlled northern Laos had "implanted in the occupants of that area a readiness and a competence for fighting," while the "government forces, armed by the United States,...have shown no such zeal, and attained no such success." Watson knew that *incentive* was a fuzzy term that did not suggest a solution to America's predicament, but he observed that "without it, the two people are practically indistinguishable—as indisposed to fighting as to excessive working,...and with no such vigor as drives, say, a farmer living in Maine." If Washington wanted the RLA to exhibit New England–style resolve, asserted Watson, it needed to find what the communists had found: a motivational key, a "political objective which inspires the will to win." Guns and money were not going to keep the nation free.[33]

Like *Time*, America's other media heavyweights contrasted Lao stagnancy with Vietnamese dynamism. *Newsweek*'s dismal account of the RLA partying "While Laos Burns" featured a sidebar that praised "tough President Diem" for mastering "the tactics that defeated the communists in Malaya." Diem's "military campaign against the guerrillas," readers learned, had "become increasingly effective." The *New York Times* flatly stated that "the people of Laos lack the resolution of the Thais or the free Vietnamese." Another *Times* feature declared, "Laotians are uninterested in political or ideological conflict and, in contrast to the Vietnamese, will not fight." Robert Shaplen of the *New Yorker* visited Laos's administrative capital in 1962 and was struck by the indifference to communist aggression, commenting, "In South Vietnam, where the wartime austerity of the Diem regime has imposed itself on all forms of social life, one can feel the tension in the air, but here in Vientiane the Lao wouldn't dream of letting their pleasures be constrained by the issues and crises of the day." Although Shaplen liked the locals' "accommodating ways," he preferred to share his foxhole with a Vietnamese. Had he been in a position to advise Kennedy as to which Southeast Asian country represented a better investment of American tax dollars, there is little doubt what his recommendation would have been.[34]

## "A Buddhist People Who Don't Want to Fight Back"

America's ministers of information advanced four theories to account for Lao unassertiveness. By far the most common explanation blamed Buddhism, "with its prohibition against the taking of life," according to *New York Times* correspondent Peggy Durdin. *Newsweek* noted that "Laotians, being Buddhists, are notoriously unwilling to fight," and in a separate article described the Lao as "liv[ing] the quiet, indolent life their Buddhist religion commands." To Chester Morrison of *Look*, the reason why Washington had been unable to create a viable Lao army was clear: "The people of Laos are Buddhists. Buddhists don't kill people. And as the communists keep saying, you can't make an omelet without killing people." Veteran newsman Keyes Beech, while less likely to misquote Stalin, drew the same conclusion from "the matchless mess we have made in the kingdom of Laos." Despite millions of dollars in aid, the RLA "couldn't fight its way out of a pillowcase," Beech wrote in the

*Saturday Evening Post.* "As good Buddhists, Laotian soldiers . . . generally aimed high and expected the other fellow to return the favor." The only solace American advisers could take in "the Laotian's childlike evasion when faced with the serious business of killing" was the "thought that their communist counterparts were probably faced with the same problem." Whichever side taught its Lao proxy to shoot low would win.[35]

Other newspapers and magazines joined in the Buddhist-bashing. "Laotians are a people who do not want to fight [and] are so deeply Buddhist they abhor killing of any kind," declared the *New York Herald Tribune.* The *Washington Star* informed readers, "The royal Laotian soldier's lack of eagerness for fighting stems from . . . his Buddhist religion." *Time* ridiculed the Lao for their "Buddhist horror of going to extremes," which caused them to have "no interest in fighting" and ensured that the RLA's idea of an "advance" was not "a push, drive, Panzer, or pincer movement—just a leisurely walk through the jungle." Henry Luce's other publishing sensation, *Life*, ran a ten-page feature that portrayed the "unwarlike Laos [*sic*] army . . . collect[ing] brass shell casings and melt[ing] them down to form statues of Buddha." The *Washington Daily News* observed, "The Laotian army is opposed, as are all Buddhists, to killing people," and the *Denver Post* ascribed the free world's string of reverses in Laos to the fact that Washington was allied with "a Buddhist people who don't want to fight back."[36]

The second explanation for Lao submissiveness emphasized physical rather than philosophical determinants. Of course the Lao did not fight, this argument ran; they were too ill for combat. Tom Dooley's broadcasts and publications did much to buttress this theory, as nearly all the Lao he dealt with suffered from disease, and he described their plight vividly for his listeners and readers. "Sick call yesterday was about 100 people," he announced in a 1960 episode of *That Free Men May Live.* "The usual round of wretchedness, the usual meager handful of trembling bones, the raucous coughs. . . . We have the complete run of sickness—everything that they have in the book and then a few more!" Although hospital patients could hardly be considered representative of the Lao population, America's prestige press often portrayed Laos as a nation of invalids whose physical unsoundness made the simplest tasks exhausting. Lao water was "full of parasites," noted *Time.* The "majority" of Lao were "undernourished," according to the *Washington Star. Life* proclaimed that the Lao had "ailments ranging from bad teeth to tuberculosis and from dysentery to deafness," and the *New York Herald Tribune* declared, "Diseases long since stamped out in developed societies plague the Laotian and shorten his life span." Two articles in the *New York Times* stressed health factors in explaining why the Lao were "unaggressive and passive." In addition to the "Buddhist emphasis on contemplation and fatalism," the *Times* reported, "United Nations experts... attribute much of the Laotians' relaxed attitude toward life to poor health and disease," especially to "infection by intestinal parasites." Not only was the Lao spirit averse to battle; the flesh was infirm.[37]

Reporters dissatisfied with the first two explanations commonly cited a third reason for Lao reluctance to wield the sword: the absence of any feeling of national unity. According to this argument, Laos's tortuous terrain, scarcity of overland communications, diversity of people and languages, and scattered population made genuine patriotism impossible. The Lao had no sense of being part of a sovereign country, and therefore were unwilling to fight to defend that country against communism. "Laos is not a nation, as the term is generally understood," declared the *Saturday Review*. "Some of the mountain tribes are not only cut off completely from the outside world; they are hardly aware of the existence of tribes less than fifty miles away." The *Washington Post* noted that most Lao "do not even know they are citizens of a country known as Laos." *Time* thought nationhood was too sophisticated a concept for the inhabitants of this "land of love and laughter": "90% of all Laotians," the magazine reported, "think the world is flat—and populated mainly by Laotians." No wonder they had difficulty conceiving of a world divided into two hostile blocs![38]

Another notion that received a surprising amount of play in the American media held that promiscuity sapped Lao martial spirit. This theory was for the most part inferred rather than asserted, but the passages devoted to Lao sexuality in publications like *Time* and *Life* were invariably accompanied by accounts of the RLA's bungling performance, and the connection was difficult to miss. For example, the same *Time* cover story that ridiculed RLA soldiers as "small, laughing men" who "dislike the idea of shooting at anybody" also described Lao "fertility rites... when the men wave bamboo poles topped with phallic symbols and copulating puppets and the girls look on and giggle." In another feature, *Time* noted that "a 17th century Dutch visitor... complained that he could not stroll at night in Laos because of the 'horrible fornications' all around. Things have changed very little." The magazine then proceeded to deplore "the lack of aggressiveness among Laotians" and remarked that "many of the Laotian army's men are still incompetent." *Life* devoted considerable space to discussing the "Laotians' amiable attitude toward sex," revealing that Lao "festivals... are not complete without love courts" where native girls "wait in 'sacred groves' to bestow themselves on any passing male, strangers included." Perhaps this was why the "Lao army, kept alive by U.S. aid, is not in good shape."[39]

One of the most remarkable sex-themed articles concerned the Lao elections of 1958, which saw communists increase their number of assembly seats. In its postmortem on this foreign-policy disaster, *Time* explained the result by noting that "the day before elections was *Balung Fai*, the annual spring Fertility Festival." Everyone in Vientiane, even "the most respected males," had been "out from dawn to late at night, ... carrying phallic symbols, hoisting up bamboo poles atop which puppets were shown in the act of sexual intercourse." And that was not all: "French postcards were pinned on men's sleeves, and men dressed up like women submitted to mock rape while the women stood by giggling." The next morning, the Lao staggered to the polling stations and voted red. Readers could draw their own conclusions.[40]

Tested against the evidence, none of these theories held water. Buddhist troops were as gallant and bloodthirsty as non-Buddhist troops. To note the most obvious example: at least 80 percent of North Vietnamese soldiers were Buddhist, and this did not prevent their being superb fighters. Neither did disease, which was a constant problem for the North Vietnamese army, as it was for the Viet Cong in South Vietnam (and as it has been for virtually every fighting force in history). No Eisenhower-era American who recalled the bravery of the Japanese in the Pacific War or of the Koreans half a decade later ought to have assumed that Asian armies lost combat effectiveness when soldiers got sick. Americans should have been equally unimpressed with the argument that national disunity led to military nonperformance. The United States' own revolution demonstrated that a dispersed population, functioning regionally and locally and lacking common traditions and institutions, was capable of defeating the superpower of the age. Finally, if sexual excess made someone an indifferent cold warrior, then John F. Kennedy's presidency was difficult to explain.

American press coverage of Laos at midcentury reflected correspondents' prejudice more than it accurately chronicled developments there. To be sure, had the reportage been first-class, it would have tested a reader's staying power. As Deputy Undersecretary of State U. Alexis Johnson remembered, Lao politics were "fiendishly complicated." Phoui, Phoumi, Phouma—who could keep the dramatis personae straight, much less untangle the shifting alliances and remember all the coups? *Time-Life*'s portrayal of Laos was easy to understand, and the blasts loosed by Karnow, Meeker, Rama Rau, et al. were entertaining if not instructive. Also, it must be noted that except for a few months in 1958, 1961, and 1962, Laos did not receive headline/cover-story treatment in the American media; other crises dominated coverage, and Laos was relegated to the back pages. Yet the cumulative effect of hundreds of articles and editorials stressing Lao sluggishness, backwardness, and disinclination to fight was to foster a misleading and derogative image of Laos that influenced the attitudes Americans developed about that country.[41]

The *Wall Street Journal* captured the essence of this image more succinctly than most when it responded to charges that the Kennedy administration's posture at the 1961–62 Geneva Conference on Laos amounted to a sell-out of an ally. "In order for there to be a sell-out," the *Journal* declared, "there must be something to sell out. That was the case with Czechoslovakia in 1938, a civilized people who emphatically did not want to be delivered to Hitler, which is what Britain and France did at the Munich Conference. But Laos is an almost completely different matter. There the majority of people seem to have little interest in whether they live under freedom or communist tyranny." Americans reading this passage could scarcely have avoided asking themselves: If the Lao do not care, then why should we? The United States had mounted a global response to the Soviet challenge—forming myriad treaties and coalitions, stationing troops on every continent, imposing record taxes to pay for a military-industrial complex, pouring billions of dollars into foreign aid—and all Washington asked of its allies was that they show some degree of gratitude and pull their own weight. Laos's response was a languid rebuff. What advantages did America derive from protecting this sinkhole? Why not let it retire behind the iron curtain? The reds deserved no better.[42]

# Chapter 7

# "No Place to Fight a War"

## Washington Backs Away from Laos

John F. Kennedy may have decided against U.S. military intervention in Laos before his April 27, 1961, meeting with congressional leaders, but that encounter set the new policy in stone. Like many landmark exchanges of the Kennedy administration, it was impromptu. Kennedy hated former president Dwight Eisenhower's regimented way of arriving at decisions, preferring a more freewheeling approach that, he felt, saved time and encouraged innovation. Thus, when the National Security Council (NSC) presented its report on Laos on the morning of the twenty-seventh, Kennedy impulsively asked that prominent legislators be summoned to receive the same intelligence. Deputy Undersecretary of State U. Alexis Johnson, who was present, recalled, "A very considerable number of congressmen from both Houses, representing most of the committees and most of the shades of opinion, were ushered into the room." Although Chief of Naval Operations Arleigh Burke, an Eisenhower-administration holdover, found Kennedy's inattention to procedure irksome, the president wanted to know how much congressional support he could count on if he put American troops into Laos. "I would say that the NSC meeting terminated in the formal sense," Johnson noted, "but [the congressmen] blended right into it." In fact, they did more than that, haranguing Kennedy and his military advisers for an hour and making plain the extent of hostility on Capitol Hill toward the Lao.[1]

Key administration figures at this ad hoc executive-legislative conference included the president, Vice President Lyndon Johnson, Acting Secretary of State Chester Bowles, Secretary of Defense Robert McNamara, National Security Adviser McGeorge Bundy, and Admiral Burke, deputizing for General Lyman Lemnitzer as chairman of the Joint Chiefs of Staff (JCS). From the Senate came Majority Leader Mike Mansfield (D-MT), Minority Leader Everett Dirksen (R-IL), Majority Whip Hubert Humphrey (D-MN), Foreign Relations Committee chairman J. William Fulbright (D-AR), Armed Services Committee chairman Richard Russell (D-GA), Styles Bridges (R-NH), Bourke Hickenlooper (R-IA), and Leverett Saltonstall (R-MA). House Speaker Sam Rayburn (D-TX) was the highest-ranking representative in attendance, followed, in order of seniority, by Carl Vinson (D-GA), Charles Halleck (R-IN), Robert Chiperfield (R-IL), Leslie Arends (R-IL), Thomas Morgan (D-PA), and Carl Albert (D-OK). All told, nearly thirty men crowded the cabinet room to discuss the situation in Laos, and not one was optimistic.

Kennedy set the tone by reading aloud a recent cable from Winthrop Brown, American ambassador to Vientiane, who requested intervention by the Southeast Asia Treaty Organization (SEATO) to halt a communist advance on the Lao capital. The president also read portions of a Radio Beijing broadcast demanding "the withdrawal of U.S. military personnel...from Laos" before the Chinese would agree to negotiate over the kingdom's future. Bowles reported that U.S. efforts to obtain a cease-fire had been ignored by the Pathet Lao as they overran Royal Lao Army (RLA) positions in Sala Phou Khoun and Vang Vieng. At Kennedy's request, McNamara offered a gloomy assessment of "our military capabilities" in Laos, noting that it was the "opinion of the Joint Chiefs of Staff that if United States forces became engaged...and the North Vietnamese or Chinese communists came to the aid of the Pathet Lao, we would not be able to win by conventional weapons alone." Washington might have to supplement its ground troops with nuclear missiles to keep Laos out of communist hands. Even that scenario was "based on the premise that our landing would be unopposed." If the reds tried to prevent the insertion of U.S. soldiers into the Plain of Jars, the result could be a bloodbath.

The president further stressed deployment difficulties, quoting a JCS estimate that "the communists could put into Laos five men to our one," which made U.S. victory in a limited war unlikely. America would moreover be fighting alone, since its chief SEATO allies, Britain and France, were "unwilling to do anything at least until Vientiane fell," by which point "there would be no sense in intervention." Should policymakers in London and Paris change their minds and agree to come to Laos's aid earlier, Kennedy asserted, the free world still faced long odds. Westerners in Southeast Asia would always be outnumbered, and sending troops to Laos would reduce the strategic reserves available for crisis spots like Cuba and Berlin. Bowles added that the Chinese had "stated they would enter Laos if we did." Kennedy then asked the assembled lawmakers for their views.

Unsurprisingly, the congressmen rejected intervention, but their verdict had little to do with the logistical issues the briefers had raised. Indeed, Russell snapped, "Logistics be damned!" What was important, in his opinion, was that America fought "where we have an ally that will fight for himself," and that did not appear to be the case in Laos. Russell, leader of the southern Democratic bloc, called Laos "an incredible fantasy." He advised the president to "write Laos off." Burke was appalled. A firm believer in the domino theory, he argued, "[I]f we don't help the Laotians now, the [South] Vietnamese will give up, the Thais will find an accommodation with the communists, and it will only be a matter of time until the gradual erosion of all Southeast Asia takes place." Russell responded that he did not advocate surrendering all Southeast Asia, just Laos. "If you think Thailand and South Vietnam will fight," he said, "let's put our troops in Thailand and South Vietnam and take our stand there."

Dirksen agreed with his Georgia colleague. "[T]hese people [the Lao] have no fighting heart," he declared. "They do not want to kill each other, and there seems to be no fighting heart present." The senator referred to the "low casualty rates" suffered by the RLA in battle to underscore his point. Burke countered that "no one *wants* to fight," but the question was where America was going to draw the line "if we don't fight here." "Where do we fight—in India? Iran? Or where?" the admiral demanded. Before anyone could answer, Burke noted, "With respect to the fighting qualities of the Lao, it takes a long time to train troops, and we have not had that time. The [South] Vietnamese and the Thai are very good fighters." Burke meant by this to illustrate the positive results that American training could produce, but Bridges interpreted it as evidence that Washington ought to "stay out of Laos." Like Russell, he contended, "[W]e have to take a firm stand somewhere, but not... where the people won't fight for themselves." Hickenlooper concurred, stating that while he "liked the idea of our taking a stand in Thailand and South Vietnam," Laos was "no place to fight a war."

There was some discussion about America's hesitant SEATO allies, the risk of igniting war with China, and the utility of nuclear weapons in a Southeast Asian theater. The topic that pressed the congressional leadership's emotional buttons, though, was Lao reluctance to fight, or what Mansfield termed "Laotian values." Mansfield summarized the views of his fellow legislators when he said that he had been "thinking about Laos for a long time" and that "the worst possible mistake we could make would be to intervene there." America's seven-year effort to erect a Lao levee against the red flood had been a washout, he observed: "Hundreds of millions of dollars have been spent and we have nothing in return." Now the hawks wanted to risk nuclear holocaust over the same people who had failed to make constructive use of American aid. The "whole thing" struck Mansfield as "fruitless." He went so far as to blame Washington for exacerbating the Lao civil war. Why, he asked, "have we increased our airlift" to General Phoumi Nosavan's RLA forces "while a ceasefire is being considered?" McNamara protested that "[a]ny government in the area has to be based on firm military control" and that the Royal Lao Government (RLG) needed "supplies to control the country militarily." Mansfield's reply was a snort. He had it on good authority, he said, that supplies were "stacked up all over the place" in areas under Phoumi's control. RLA troops had all the weaponry they could possibly use. They just had no interest in using it, and never would.

Bowles, one of three participants in the meeting who took notes, informed Secretary of State Dean Rusk that evening that the "congressional group...seemed strongly influenced by [the] general impression among them that [the] Laotians [are] unwilling to fight for [them]selves." As he saw it, there was "complete unanimity...among all" that "we should not introduce U.S. forces into Laos," no matter what the "consequences to our position" in Southeast Asia might be. Kennedy did not explicitly endorse this verdict, but he did not repudiate it either, and he seemed to fall in with the legislators when he urged everyone to keep their discussion confidential because the "only card" Washington had to play in the Laos crisis was "the threat of U.S. intervention and the uncertainty of the other side in this regard." It would "weaken our position," he said, if "the other side felt that we had reached a decision not to intervene." The president's phrasing was significant: rather than denying that such a decision had been taken, he merely asked those present to behave as though none had been.[2]

Years later, Deputy Undersecretary Johnson designated this "crucial meeting" as the "turning point on Laos." April 27, 1961, he told an interviewer, was "the date on which, really, the die was cast." From then on, "it was quite clear in the minds of all of us that, whatever happened, we were not going to militarily intervene." While Johnson admitted that Kennedy did not promise the congressmen anything, he remembered coming away from the meeting "with a sense of a fairly momentous policy decision," and this was doubtless the impression Kennedy intended to leave. Never keen on the prospect of sending American soldiers to Laos, the president now knew that senior Democrats and Republicans in Congress shared his distaste.[3]

The momentous policy decision Johnson sensed was a cap rather than an about-face. Kennedy had not reversed his predecessor's course so much as set a limit on it. All the programs Eisenhower initiated in Laos continued after April 27, and it was fifteen months before the contending Lao parties and their great-power sponsors could agree on terms for a neutralist government under Prince Souvanna Phouma. During those months, headlines in the United States repeatedly warned that the Lao civil war might escalate into a global confrontation. Kennedy's public posture was belligerent, as he upgraded the Programs Evaluation Office (PEO) in Laos to an overt military mission, threatened large-scale deployment, and refused to rule out the possibility of using nuclear weapons. Privately, however, he had resolved upon a diplomatic solution, even if that meant allowing Pathet Lao membership in the RLG. Bundy considered the president's ruling equivalent to "an operational rejection of the domino theory."[4]

In a narrow sense, Bundy was right. The neutralization of Laos did violate Eisenhower's simile, which left no room for unaligned countries. Yet there was a difference between operational and ideological rejection. As numerous historians and biographers have shown, Kennedy accepted the deterministic philosophy of geopolitics handed down by earlier presidents. Two months before his death, he responded to television anchorman David Brinkley's question about "this so-called 'domino theory'" with an emphatic "I believe it." If South Vietnam "went," he said, this would "give the impression that the wave of the future in Southeast Asia was China and the communists. So I believe it." Kennedy increased the American presence in South Vietnam for the same reason Eisenhower had: to prevent the fall of that country from leading to a ripple effect of communist takeovers in neighboring countries. Furthermore, Kennedy had no intention of scaling back Washington's commitment to defend as much territory as it could from red aggression. He was as dogmatic a cold warrior as Eisenhower had been, reluctant to distinguish between vital and peripheral interests and insensible to the fact that there were areas of the world where the East-West struggle was irrelevant. His assent to Lao neutralism did not grow out of a nuanced foreign-policy doctrine or recognition of American limitations. And he definitely did not choose the diplomatic path in Laos because he had greater respect for Lao opinion or sovereignty than Eisenhower did. Just the opposite: policymaker disgust with the Lao intensified after Kennedy assumed office. The president and his advisers reached new heights of arrogance when they wrote and spoke about the Kingdom of a Million Elephants, with Ambassador John Kenneth Galbraith conveying the administration's scorn most memorably in May 1961. "As a military ally, the entire Laos nation is clearly inferior to a battalion of conscientious objectors from World War I," Galbraith cabled the president from New Delhi. "We get nothing from their support, and I must say I wonder what the communists get."[5]

Kennedy wondered the same thing, and this dubiety underlay his lack of enthusiasm for intervention. Laos, he concluded within his first four months as president, was an expendable domino, one that required so much effort to prop up and yielded so little reward for the effort that it would only weaken whichever bloc it joined. It was more deadwood than ballast. The wisest move was to cut it loose. Then, perhaps, it might preserve neutrality. Failing that, it would be as big a headache for Moscow and Beijing as it had been for Washington.

### "They're Just Not Very Vigorous"

By the time Eisenhower turned over the White House to Kennedy, the situation in Laos had escalated from a back-burner issue to one of the most dangerous crises of the cold war. America's support of Phoumi had internationalized the conflict, prompting the Soviets to aid the anti-Phoumi factions and throwing rebel captain Kong Le into Pathet Lao leader Prince Souphanouvong's arms. The Phoumist capture of Vientiane solved nothing, as Phoumi was unable to deal a deathblow to his opponents. Instead, the neutralist–Pathet Lao coalition consolidated its power in northern Laos, establishing a base area linked with North Vietnam and using Soviet assistance to transform the Plain of Jars into a stronghold. Stalemate ensued, with neither adversary willing to negotiate. "[W]e left a legacy of strife and confusion in Laos," Eisenhower wrote in his memoir. "This I regretted deeply."

Yet Eisenhower did not seem to understand why his administration's actions had led to this result. He maintained that Washington had followed the "correct policy" in "supporting the Boun Oum government" and did not say what Americans might have done differently. Such vagueness was unsurprising. Until the battle for Vientiane turned Laos into the hottest flashpoint in the developing world, Eisenhower paid little attention to events in that country and left the direction of U.S.-Lao relations to subordinates. Debate over Laos in the Eisenhower administration seldom rose above the assistant secretary level, and those officials, J. Graham Parsons foremost among them, who crafted Laos policy had a quick response to complaints that Washington had failed to cultivate a stable, pro-Western RLG. The United States did all that was humanly possible, they insisted, but the Lao were beyond help; their torpor and feeblemindedness defeated America's best efforts. On those rare occasions when he addressed himself to the Lao civil war, Eisenhower echoed this view, usually merging it with domino-theory ratiocination about how Laos, its inadequacies notwithstanding, had to be defended. Two weeks before the end of his administration, he remarked to Secretary of State Christian Herter that "if it weren't for the neighboring countries and the effect on them, we ought to let Laos go down the drain."[6]

Kennedy had assailed Eisenhower's handling of Laos during the 1960 presidential campaign. His main criticism was that U.S. aid had gone disproportionately to the RLA while failing to develop the Lao economy, and he promised a more efficient disbursal of taxpayer dollars. Never did he claim that Washington was backing the wrong horse in Phoumi or that a political solution built around Souvanna might be better. Although he made a number of statements to the effect that he regarded neutralism as "inevitable" for some "underdeveloped countries," he applied this principle chiefly to Latin America, where protests against U.S. hegemony were front-page news. When it came to Southeast Asia, the Democratic candidate sounded like former secretary of state John Foster Dulles. Washington, he proclaimed, "cannot allow Laos and South Vietnam to fall to the communists." After the votes were in and his victory assured, Kennedy began studying Laos in depth, realizing for the first time how bad conditions there were and admitting to aide Theodore Sorensen, "Whatever's going to happen in Laos, . . . I wish it would happen before we take over and get blamed for it." Kennedy considered Laos "the worst mess the Eisenhower administration left me." That mess would dominate his agenda in early 1961.[7]

While Kennedy assumed greater hands-on control of the policymaking bureaucracy than Eisenhower exerted, his initial moves with respect to Laos seemed to promise continuity rather than disjuncture. Inauguration day fell on a Friday, and the new president instructed an interagency Laos Task Force to meet over the weekend to draft a report outlining options and proposing strategy. He placed Parsons in charge of this group, a logical choice given the latter's years of involvement in Lao affairs but also one that ensured that the paper Kennedy received Monday morning contained nothing new. It opened by bemoaning the "internal situation in Laos, which makes the general populace and even large segments of the army apathetic toward the course of events." Washington needed to "stiffen the Laotian military," the report declared. Kennedy should assign "[f]irst priority in personnel, equipment, and funds" to Laos and demonstrate "our determination not to permit [the] overthrow of [the] Lao government by armed bands." And by *Lao government* the task force meant Boun Oum, not Souvanna. The "Boun Oum government" and its "Phoumi forces" were the "only Laotian leadership presently available to give cohesion to the forces resisting a pro-communist takeover," Kennedy read. A Souvanna-led coalition remained anathema, tantamount to the "loss of Laos" and a prelude to "Southeast Asia being captured by the communists." The task force advocated several measures to prevent that calamity: expansion of the PEO, establishment of a U.S. "support group" in Thailand, and improvement of the airlift delivering supplies to Phoumi's men. "It must be made clear that we do not intend to permit the bloc to take Laos," the report concluded. Diplomacy, although useful, ranked below cold steel, for if the communists "succeed militarily, there is no necessity for them to negotiate."[8]

Kennedy reviewed this document at his first White House conference on foreign policy. He did not approve all of the task force's recommendations, but he agreed to most of them, notably an augmentation of the airlift, and he showed little interest in negotiating with the Pathet Lao until Phoumi had improved the RLA's battlefield position. At another meeting two days later, Kennedy affirmed his resolve "to try by all means to sustain the government" in Laos and ordered JCS chairman Lemnitzer to prepare a memorandum "bringing out what, if we were to decide to commit American troops to Laos, we could do in the way of a buildup in 30 days." Lemnitzer, a hawk in the Dulles mode, was pleased to see Kennedy taking such a hard line.[9]

The president found that line challenged, however, when he spoke with Ambassador Brown, who had been summoned home from Vientiane for consultations. As detailed in chapter 4, Brown had consistently opposed the Eisenhower administration's pro-Phoumi policy and declared himself in favor of Souvanna and neutralism. This made him persona non grata to

Defense Department and Central Intelligence Agency (CIA) officials and limited his influence with Eisenhower, but Kennedy, one historian notes, "always wanted to hear about crises from the men on the spot." He therefore insisted on a report from Brown as soon as possible. The ambassador, having never met Kennedy, was uncertain what to expect when he arrived at the White House on February 3. Although Deputy Special Assistant for National Security Affairs Walt Rostow assured Brown that the president was "a wonderful listener," Brown never imagined that his presentation would have the impact it did.[10]

Kennedy got right down to business, asking, "What kind of people are these people—Souvanna and Souphanouvong and Phoumi and the king and Kong Le?" Brown responded, "Well, sir, the policy is—" He got no further. "That's not what I asked you," Kennedy interrupted. "I said, 'What do you think, *you*, the ambassador?'" Brown then became, as he remembered, "exceedingly indiscreet and said a great many things which were critical." Phoumi, he declared, was "overrated," a "poor politician" who was not even "all that good a general." Boun Oum was a "Lao Falstaff." As for King Savang Vatthana, Brown considered him a "total zero," a "weak man" who "cried several times when he talked to me." Brown held no brief for Souphanouvong, but he thought Washington had misjudged Kong Le and Souvanna. The rebel captain was a "patriot, not a communist," and the neutralist prince was the "one person in Laos who could be a unifying force." No one else possessed "the necessary attributes of popular appeal and diplomatic experience"—certainly not Phoumi or Boun Oum.

The president's interest in his opinion surprised and delighted Brown, who was used to being ignored. "I told him exactly what was in my heart," the ambassador recalled years later. "I had the feeling that I could say anything I wanted and it would be like the confessional." He expressed his "very low opinion of the Laotian army," which he described as a "feeble lot" plagued by poor morale and commanded by officers unfit to "lead a platoon around a corner." The Eisenhower administration had put "too great a faith in the capacity of the Laotian forces to be a good soldier [*sic*]," and this had caused statesmen to adopt policies that failed in their objectives. It was "not realistic," Brown proclaimed, "to expect that . . . any satisfactory solution of the problem" could be "found by purely military means."

Inadequate government and an army without "staying power" were, in Brown's view, symptoms of a larger problem: "the extraordinary poverty of the human material with which we had to work." Here the ambassador's report shifted from an assessment of personalities and events to a condemnation of Lao culture, suggesting how much the former depended on the latter and revealing that Brown, for all his courage and discernment, was a man of his time, scarcely immune to the bias through which midcentury American policymakers apprehended the Lao. "They're charming, indolent, enchanting people," Brown noted, "but they're just not very vigorous." Brown believed that most Lao favored nonalignment—"to the extent that there were thinking Laotians about these problems," and "there weren't too many of them." The Lao, he said, felt that "if they could establish a neutral position, . . . all these problems would go away and they would be left alone to be peaceful." While Brown was as frustrated by this attitude as any American—he called it "hopeless"—that was where the Lao stood, and six months in Vientiane had convinced Brown that Washington's only chance of holding Laos together and keeping it noncommunist lay in Souvanna's brand of neutralism.

By the time Kennedy stood up to indicate that the meeting was over, Brown had spoken for nearly an hour. He left thinking that his words had had an effect on the president, a judgment seconded by White House special assistant Arthur Schlesinger Jr., who recalled Kennedy musing afterward over lunch, "I don't see why we have to be more royalist than the [Lao] king." At the same time, Kennedy stressed the need to prevent a "communist takeover" and insisted, "We cannot and will not accept any visible humiliation over Laos."[11]

Three days after Brown gave his briefing, Phoumi began a campaign to retake the Plain of Jars that made the ambassador look like a prophet. Although the Phoumists outnumbered the Pathet Lao–Kong Le forces sixty thousand to eighteen thousand—and despite American logistical assistance in the form of aircraft, trucks, and PEO officers permitted to accompany RLA units into battle—Phoumi's men advanced very slowly toward the plain from Vientiane and Savannakhet, halting at any hint of resistance. "Phoumi is stuck," the Laos Task Force reported to Kennedy. The reason for his caution became clear when, in early March, some Pathet Lao troops launched what Rostow termed a "probing offensive" that caused the RLA to fall back "[w]ithout much fight." Major General Chester Clifton, military aide to the president, noted that Phoumi's soldiers did not even stand their ground long enough to see the enemy. They "folded," he said, "on account of some unobserved artillery fire which fell in the area and scared them to death." Clifton advised Kennedy, "No Laotians want to shoot each other. They cannot look down a rifle barrel and shoot another

Laotian." Kenneth Landon of the State Department's Division of Southwest Pacific Affairs was more concise, remarking, "The Lao will not fight."[12]

Kennedy responded to this setback by moving in two directions simultaneously. On the firm side, to let the reds know they could not intimidate him, he approved an increase in aid to Phoumi: bombers, transport aircraft, helicopters, and pilots. He also agreed to enlarge the U.S.-equipped Hmong army in northern Laos by one thousand soldiers. Most provocatively, he sent five hundred marines to the Thai-Lao border and ordered the U.S. Seventh Fleet, stationed at Okinawa, to steam southward to assist in the defense of Laos. Rostow, tapped by Kennedy to brief newsmen on the administration's plans, gave a fiery backgrounder that led the *New York Times* to conclude that Kennedy was "determined to take whatever steps are necessary to save Laos from communist domination."[13]

The president made some maneuvers on the diplomatic front as well, instructing Rusk to inform the Soviets that if the Pathet Lao consented to a "de facto cease-fire," Washington would agree to multinational negotiations over Laos's future. The likeliest venue for such bargaining would be Geneva, where Moscow and London could reprise their roles as co-chairmen of a conference on Indochina. Kennedy moreover proclaimed himself willing to countenance a reactivation of the International Control Commission (ICC) tasked with implementing the original Geneva Accords. He even posed a question that would never have passed Eisenhower's lips. Told during an interdepartmental meeting that none of America's allies except Thailand and South Vietnam supported Boun Oum, Kennedy asked, "[S]hould we let the communists into the [Lao] government?" He received no definitive response, and the participants moved on to other matters, but by raising the possibility of Pathet Lao membership in the RLG, the president signaled an erosion of Washington's hawkish Laos policy.[14]

Kennedy alternately flourished the mailed fist and the velvet glove in his March 23, 1961, televised press conference, a compelling piece of political theater marred only by his mispronunciation of the name of the country under discussion. (To Kennedy it was "Lay-oss.") The conference took place onstage in an auditorium at State Department headquarters, and the props were three six-by-eight-foot maps of Laos illustrating the progressive stages of communist expansion since August 1960. On the first map, Pathet Lao–controlled territory, shown in red, was a few stains near the North Vietnamese border; the second map, representing Laos at the time of Phoumi's capture of Vientiane, had much more red; and the third, dated early 1961, looked as though the northern half of the country had been dipped in blood.

"I want to make a brief statement about Laos," the president said. "It is, I think, important for all Americans to understand this difficult and potentially dangerous problem." Kennedy noted that in his final conversation with Eisenhower before the presidency changed hands, "we spent more time on this hard matter than on any other thing." Since then, Laos had been "steadily before the administration as the most immediate of the problems that we found upon taking office." Holding a pointer and gesturing toward the maps, Kennedy said that they demonstrated "efforts by a communist-dominated group" to "take over" Laos, and he ascribed Pathet Lao success to "support and direction from outside." Soviet planes, he declared, had been "conspicuous in a large-scale airlift into the battle area," and a "set of combat specialists, mainly from communist North Vietnam" were fighting alongside Souphanouvong's men. Having accused Moscow and Hanoi of intervention, Kennedy softened the charge by allowing that American behavior might have given rise to suspicions that Washington was bent on securing more than "a neutral or independent Laos." He wanted to allay such fears: "Our support for the present duly constituted government is aimed entirely and exclusively at that result." Kennedy's phrasing elided the issue of what the duly constituted government was—and of why so many nations considered Souvanna the premier rather than Boun Oum—but his tone was conciliatory.

Then he grew stern again, demanding that there be "a cessation of the present armed attacks by externally supported communists." If the Soviet Union and North Vietnam did not call off the dogs, "those who support a truly neutral Laos will have to consider their response." No one, Kennedy proclaimed, should "doubt our resolution on this point." Yet Washington's steadfastness did not imply belligerence, as "we are earnestly in favor of constructive negotiation... which can help Laos back to the pathway of independence." Kennedy observed that the British government of Prime Minister Harold Macmillan had recently proposed a cease-fire in the Lao civil war, to be followed by negotiations leading to the withdrawal of foreign forces from the kingdom. Washington viewed this plan favorably, the president said. "We are always conscious of the obligation which rests upon all members of the United Nations to seek peaceful solutions to problems." Kennedy's peroration was equal parts bugle call and peace pipe:

My fellow Americans, Laos is far away from America, but the world is small.... The security of all Southeast Asia will be endangered if Laos loses its neutral independence. Its safety runs with the safety of us all.... [W]hat we want in Laos is peace, not war; a truly neutral government, not a cold war pawn.... We will not be provoked, trapped, or drawn into this or any other situation, but I know that every American will want his country to honor its obligations to the point that freedom and security of the free world and ourselves may be achieved.[15]

Kennedy biographer Richard Reeves claims, with too much assurance, that the president's speech marked a new departure in U.S.-Lao relations: "What he had done in public was to downgrade U.S. policy from supporting a 'free' Laos to accepting a 'neutral' Laos." In fact, the address could be interpreted different ways, which was Kennedy's intention. For the hawks, there was a promise to defend Laos against communism; peace advocates could take heart in the president's willingness to settle the dispute diplomatically. The administration forged ahead on both tracks, military and political, over the following days. Kennedy flew to Key West to confer with Macmillan, and the two men announced their agreement on the need for a cease-fire and a conference, but the president also got the prime minister to guarantee British support for SEATO military maneuvers in Laos if they became necessary. Meanwhile, Rusk, at a SEATO meeting in

**Figure 4.** President John F. Kennedy's press conference on Laos, March 23, 1961. Time & Life Pictures. Photographer: Paul Schutzer. Getty Images.

Bangkok, sought a commitment from treaty signatories to safeguard the Boun Oum government, although he knew this was unlikely. The French representative, loath to involve his country in another Indochina war, was certain to decline, and other conferees appeared similarly unenthusiastic. While two days of lobbying by Rusk bore meager results—only Pakistan, Thailand, and the Philippines pledged troops for intervention—the secretary did manage to toughen the language of the final communiqué so that it sounded like an ultimatum: "[I]f... there continues to be an active military attempt to conquer Laos, members of SEATO will be prepared to take whatever action may be appropriate." Upon his return to Washington, Kennedy had a private talk with Soviet foreign minister Andrei Gromyko, after which he allowed aides to leak the news that although the two men had reached "no agreement" on Laos, the "objectives of both sides appeared similar."[16]

The president sent mixed signals to journalists when questioned about Laos. Chalmers Roberts of the *Washington Post* came away from one interview certain that Kennedy was about to plunge America into war. Kennedy "said that if he had to go in and if it meant that he would be around only one term, nonetheless he would do it," Roberts remembered. All this was stated "in a highly convincing manner." In another exchange, however, the president told Roberts that "to get a coalition government would not be a bad thing." After all, he argued, there had "been Pathet Lao in the government before, and you, the press, ought to point that out." During an April 6 backgrounder at the State Department, Kennedy expressed frustration with the RLA, complaining that Phoumi's army "has not maintained the fighting with the vigor we might have hoped. . . . Supply is not the problem; the Pathet Lao fight with more vigor." He nevertheless affirmed that the United States would intervene to shore up the Phoumists if they appeared on the verge of defeat.[17]

Such statements suggest that Kennedy had not made up his mind about Laos and wanted to leave himself room to maneuver as events dictated. He may also have been trying to keep his adversaries off-balance. In any event, the closest he came to announcing an overhaul in Washington's Laos policy during the first hundred days of his administration occurred when he removed Parsons from involvement in Southeast Asian affairs. Parsons had long coveted a European post, and Kennedy obliged him, nominating the veteran diplomat to head the U.S. Embassy at Stockholm. The Senate confirmed the nomination despite Parsons's well-documented difficulties with what he called "my little old friend, the Kingdom of Laos," and

Walter McConaughy, another hawk, took over the top job in the Far Eastern bureau. Career intact and bound for greener pastures, Parsons did not
escape his boss's reproof. At a White House lunch attended by Parsons in
late March 1961, the Swedish premier asked Kennedy what he thought the
most pressing problems facing America were. "Well, Mr. Prime Minister, of
course there is Laos," Kennedy replied. "Laos is a great problem." Turning
to Parsons, he said, "Perhaps I shouldn't talk about Laos, because the greatest expert on Laos in our government is sitting just two, three places down
from me, and I ought to be pretty careful." The guests laughed, and Parsons
acknowledged Kennedy's praise, not expecting a sting in the tail. "You
know, he *is* our great expert on Laos," the president added, "and perhaps
it's for that reason that I'm sending him to you as ambassador to Sweden."[18]

## "A Gutless Group"

Mid-April 1961 saw the administration absorb its worst foreign-policy
defeat. Operation Zapata, the failed U.S.-sponsored invasion of Cuba by
fifteen hundred expatriates trained by the CIA to overthrow Fidel Castro's
government, was an embarrassment for Kennedy and shook his faith in the
American military establishment. According to several of the president's
advisers, the Bay of Pigs fiasco caused Kennedy to develop doubts about the
Pentagon's plans for intervention in Laos. Sorenson has famously recounted
Kennedy declaring months after the *Cuba libres* were routed, "Thank God
the Bay of Pigs happened when it did. Otherwise we'd be in Laos by now—
and that would be a hundred times worse."[19]

Kennedy's Cuban misadventure undoubtedly did make him more cautious when it came to dealing with international crises. Yet his first post-
Zapata action in Laos was an advance rather than a retreat, as he authorized
increases in military aid to Phoumi, notably the transformation of the
PEO into a Military Assistance Advisory Group (MAAG) similar to the
one Washington had established in South Vietnam. This initiative did not
change much in practice—the PEO had been functioning as an MAAG
since its establishment under Eisenhower—but Kennedy hoped it would
have a psychological impact on RLA troops, who, Rusk noted, "are not
among the stoutest of heart, at best." Abandonment of the PEO's civilian
façade had the added benefit of liberating Kennedy from any obligation
to abide, even insincerely, by the 1954 Geneva Accords. The day following Castro's triumph at the Bay of Pigs, PEO personnel donned military

uniforms and began calling their commander "General" instead of "Mister." MAAG chief Brigadier General Andrew Boyle announced that U.S. advisers would go to the front lines with RLA soldiers if necessary.[20]

These gestures seemed to bear fruit, as Soviet premier Nikita Khrushchev, possibly worried that humiliation in Cuba might lead Kennedy to do something reckless in Laos, informed the White House that Moscow supported a cease-fire between the RLA and its opponents. Shortly thereafter, Gromyko joined British foreign minister Alexander Frederick Douglas-Home in appealing for a cease-fire and the restoration of the ICC. Kennedy kept his options open and his powder dry. He listened respectfully to Lemnitzer's proposal for an invasion of Laos by 140,000 men, and he maintained a straight face when the JCS chairman told him, "If we are given the right to use nuclear weapons, we can guarantee victory." Not until the above-mentioned meeting with congressional leaders on April 27 did the president appear to rule out military intervention, and even then his verdict was inferred rather than explicit.[21]

A number of factors pushed Kennedy away from the battlefield and toward the conference table. The reluctance of SEATO members to participate in any joint offensive to save Phoumi ensured that Washington would be shouldering the free world's burden in Laos virtually unassisted, which would mean heavy troop commitments, high casualties, and a depletion of U.S. reserves needed to deal with aggression elsewhere. Also, Kennedy's decision not to send American soldiers to help the Cuban refugees stranded at the Bay of Pigs set a precedent that limited his freedom of action in Southeast Asia. Since he had refused to intervene against Castro ninety miles off the coast of Florida, how could he justify dispatching thousands of troops to Laos? Logistical concerns, to be sure, weighed on Kennedy's mind. Laos was a poor locale for the employment of modern conventional forces. It was far away and landlocked. It had only two usable airstrips even in good weather. There were few roads. The climate fostered tropical diseases like malaria, amoebic dysentery, and hookworm. War in the mountains and jungles of Laos was a specter to trouble the sleep of any American commander.

Most important in persuading Kennedy to neutralize Laos, though, was the belief that the Lao were incorrigible pacifists who, in the words of the Laos Task Force, "demonstrated little desire, willingness, or ability to defend themselves." Everything Kennedy read or heard confirmed this image. The CIA calculated that the communists could defeat the RLA within two weeks because of the latter's "military impotence." A National Intelligence Estimate deplored the "ineffectiveness of the Laotian army, . . . its lack of motivation and will to resist." JCS assessments were equally dour. According to the chiefs, "Phoumi's forces demonstrated... a strong tendency to retreat or abandon [a] position in [the] face of relatively light pressure." Former president Eisenhower, while convinced that a pro-Western Laos was essential to America's security, voiced his disrespect for Lao martial skills when members of the Kennedy administration sought his advice. In one top-secret discussion, Eisenhower remarked that "obviously, the Laotians didn't like to fight." In another, he referred to the RLA as "a bunch of homosexuals."[22]

"'*Toughness,*'" British journalist Henry Fairlie observes, "was one of the most prominent words in the vocabulary of the New Frontier; perhaps no other quality was so highly regarded." The RLA's manifest lack of that quality elicited a torrent of abuse from the Kennedy White House. "I think that trying to turn the two million people of Laos into battle-hungry Turks was never likely to succeed," Bowles noted after a fourteen-nation conference on Laos opened in Geneva. "We spent $300 million in this country trying to buy an army... of people who don't know how to fight and don't want to fight." McNamara observed contemptuously that when RLA "forces were defeated, it was the Laotian generals who were the first to leave" the field. Schlesinger asked why Americans should "fight for a country whose people evidently could not care less about fighting for themselves," and Sorenson argued that a "bastion of Western strength on China's border could not be created by a people quite unwilling to be a bastion for anyone." When Kennedy expressed concern about the impact of a neutralized Laos on voter opinion, Undersecretary of State George Ball assured him, "[T]he American people would understand we cannot prop up a country if they won't fight themselves." Tellingly, Ball, praised by Vietnam War historians for his insight and iconoclasm, displayed neither of those qualities in commenting on the Laos crisis. To him, it was "a piece of Graustarkian *opéra bouffe*" that proceeded "with the pace and gentility of a cricket match," a "shooting war" in which "little actual shooting was ever heard" and the Plain of Jars remained "untouched by blood" because the RLA, "though incompetent as a fighting force, was unexcelled in fast retreat."[23]

The New Frontiersman who took greatest offense at the RLA's want of fighting spirit was Rusk, normally a taciturn man but outspoken on this score. "[O]ne of our great difficulties in Laos has been that the government forces have not been very effective," the secretary testified before the House Foreign Affairs Committee. "A relatively small engagement causes them to withdraw rapidly. They have supplies, they have equipment, they have apparently everything they need but any serious will to fight." Rusk regretted that the Lao fell so short of the standard set by America's other cold war allies. "In Greece and Korea [the] people gave us something to support," he said. "If Laos shows no interest, U.S. arms cannot import freedom into an indifferent country." Two months after Kennedy's inauguration, Rusk informed the president that "we could not guarantee the steadfastness of any Lao, even Phoumi." Although RLA soldiers were among the highest paid in the world, Rusk observed that Phoumi had been unable to light a fire under his men and that the United States "missed having government troops who were willing to fight." When the RLA commander visited Washington in June 1961, Rusk spoke to him with what the secretary himself described as "a frankness which went beyond traditional diplomatic practice." "If the U.S. is to call on its young men to go and fight to defend the freedom of another country," Rusk declared, "it must be quite certain of the desire of that country for freedom." Consequently, Washington had to be "certain that the will to defend freedom...exists in Laos," and such certainty required more evidence than had been "apparent" of the "readiness to accept sacrifice on the part of the Laotian people." Time did not soften Rusk's opinion. In his 1990 memoir he noted that the Lao, "a gentle people with little interest in killing each other," once "left a battlefield to attend a water festival."[24]

Kennedy's military advisers exceeded their civilian counterparts in heaping scorn upon the Lao. Brigadier General William Craig returned from a tour of the front lines in northern Laos to denounce the RLA as "totally ineffective," "grossly inferior," and prone to "bug out" under pressure. "Leadership is of poor quality," Craig proclaimed, "and motivation and discipline are lacking." Lemnitzer expressed his frustration in an outburst indicative of the hubris that characterized U.S. policymaking during the post–World War II, pre-Vietnam era. "We made good soldiers out of the Koreans," he said. "Why can't we make good soldiers out of the Laotians?" MAAG commander Boyle complained that RLA troops had "no stomach and no real capability" for battle, that they "put on track shoes" and were "ready to break and run at [the] first indication" of the enemy's presence. Major General Reuben Tucker, Boyle's successor, sent Washington a choleric report after a joint RLA-MAAG mission to repel Pathet Lao attacks on a provincial capital, raging that the Americans "had to make all the attempts to defend Ban Houei Sai" because the "Royal Government troops supposedly assisting them are worthless." To prove his point, Tucker noted that "when a Royal Government squad was detailed to defend the airstrip, it was later found swimming down in the river!" Tucker warned Kennedy that if he sent U.S. troops to protect the Lao government, "American blood would certainly be spilled for a gutless group." Kennedy was so impressed by Tucker's cable that he kept a copy to show guests at the White House cocktail hour. "You want to read something fantastic?" the president asked, withdrawing the document from his jacket pocket and reading it aloud.[25]

The Laos Task Force, Kennedy's principal source of information on the Kingdom of a Million Elephants, was consistently Cassandrian, especially after Parsons yielded the chairmanship to Deputy Assistant Secretary of State for Far Eastern Affairs John Steeves. No one in this group could find anything positive to say about the Lao, and their papers must have left Kennedy wondering whether to laugh or cry. "Despite the magnitude of our aid program and the large number of Americans working with the Lao," the task force reported in a typical memorandum,

> we did not succeed in developing any real sense of motivation among these people. We did not take sufficiently into account the political immaturity and administrative incompetence of the Lao. We generally assumed that the Lao were vitally concerned with the communist threat and were eager to preserve their country's independence. Instead, we find ourselves dealing with an almost total lack of political motivation. We have spent large sums to support the Lao army and employed a large force of Americans to assist in its training, but we have not instilled into the armed forces the necessary discipline and will to fight.

The "extraordinary handicaps" under which Washington operated led the task force to throw up its hands. "Time may have run out for the U.S. in Laos," it noted, "and we may never have an opportunity for a fresh start in that country." After reading commentary like this, would any president have welcomed a second chance?[26]

Kennedy did not. By late April 1961, he had decided to alter the Eisenhower-Dulles policy toward Laos. Even though some officials in the Pentagon, CIA, and his own cabinet held out for intervention, the president concluded, in Bundy's words, that "such a conflict would be unjustified, even if the loss of Laos must be accepted." Kennedy approved military measures across the Lao border in Thailand, but these were designed to strengthen the West's bargaining position at the conference table, not to obtain a Pathet Lao surrender. As would be the case with Berlin and Cuba, the president chose compromise over combat. Unlike those crises, however, the Lao civil war did not terrify Kennedy with the prospect of nuclear apocalypse. He just did not see anything worth fighting for.[27]

## "Less Than Perfect Solutions"

"Laos is a funny country," editorialized the French journal *Combat*. "It has got a funny king and a funny ceasefire; and there are funny negotiations going on at Geneva. And tomorrow, if peace were to come from them, it would be a funny peace." American delegates to the second Geneva Conference on Indochina were not laughing. They knew their country negotiated from a posture of weakness. Phoumi's men had not won a battle since taking Vientiane. The Pathet Lao controlled more of Laos than had been the case at the time of the first Geneva Conference, and Souphanouvong had only agreed to accept his Soviet patron's call for a cease-fire because an early onset to the monsoon season made guerrilla operations difficult. Had the rains not slowed the Pathet Lao offensive, Bowles observed, the conference would have been "little more than a communist victory celebration." Some of Kennedy's advisers thought that was what it amounted to anyway. Of the fourteen nations represented at Geneva, only three—the United States, South Vietnam, and Thailand—backed Phoumi; the rest were in favor of a Souvanna-led regime, which, as far as cold warriors like Rusk were concerned, differed only in name from a red satellite. "Commies at Geneva are full of confidence," reported the secretary, who headed the U.S. delegation. "They are purring like cats."[28]

Despite the RLA's recent string of defeats and the lack of support for Phoumi, Rusk began the conference defiantly, announcing that Washington would accept neither a government headed by Souvanna nor a three-party coalition of Phoumists, Pathet Lao, and neutralists. He also objected to the seating of a Pathet Lao delegation; the Boun Oum government, he insisted, was the only authority with the right to speak in Laos's name. This was a bluff, but Rusk did not want to give the impression that the Americans had come to Geneva hat in hand. Georgi Pushkin, leader of the Soviet delegation, sidestepped the issue of what kind of Lao government would emerge at the end of the conference and declared that three Lao parties should receive seats: the Phoumi–Boun Oum group, Souvanna's neutralist faction, and the Neo Lao Hak Xat (NLHX), the political wing of the Pathet Lao. Rusk gave ground on Souvanna, affirming that a neutralist delegation could sit as an equal with Boun Oum's representative, but he refused to permit

the NLHX to enjoy the same status because, he said, that would consti-
tute American recognition of communist membership in the RLG. Debate
continued for several days, until Kennedy broke the deadlock by ordering
Rusk to consent to seating all three factions as "individuals" rather than
"delegations." Then, by prior arrangement, Rusk turned the U.S. delegation
over to Ambassador-at-Large W. Averell Harriman and returned home.[29]

Harriman was in many ways ideally suited to fight America's corner.
One of the "Wise Men" who implemented containment at the start of the
cold war, he brought over thirty years of diplomatic experience to Geneva,
and his résumé included tours as U.S. ambassador to Great Britain and the
Soviet Union. His work ethic was legendary. Although verging seventy in
1961, he put in sixteen-hour days and ran his younger staff ragged. Moreover, as biographers have noted, he did not suffer from the McCarthyite
astigmatism that afflicted many officials in the State Department. Recognizing that not all communists were alike, he treated them as human beings
instead of robots, which enabled him to deal effectively with diplomats
from iron-curtain countries. While a tough negotiator, he was not rigid,
and he believed it was his responsibility to tell his superiors the truth, however unpalatable. (The fortune he inherited from his railway-tycoon father
made such forthrightness easier.) Beltway insiders initially considered him
too old to find a place in the youth-oriented Kennedy administration, but
he impressed the president with his shrewdness, and Kennedy made him, in
effect, the White House's point man on Laos.[30]

Kennedy's instructions to Harriman before the latter left for Geneva
could not have been clearer: "I want a negotiated settlement. I don't want
to put troops in. It's your problem. Work it out." Harriman obeyed. "Having chosen the conference route," he cabled U.S. ambassador to Thailand
Kenneth Young, "we must accustom ourselves to accept less than perfect
solutions." The U.S. delegation would accept several such solutions over the
next fourteen months, as Harriman single-mindedly pursued his objective.
He encountered resistance from the Pentagon, the CIA, and the Far Eastern bureau at State, but he prevailed, obtaining for Kennedy an agreement
that established a neutralist regime under Souvanna and allowed the United
States to withdraw its military personnel from Laos. Most scholarly treatments of the 1961–62 Geneva Conference sing the roving ambassador's
praises. One historian contends that "Harriman worked a series of near-
miracles at Geneva."[31]

Without question, Harriman was the conference's catalytic figure. He
took charge of his delegation right away, cutting the staff by two-thirds and

threatening to resign when State protested. He also fired his deputy, whom he considered too hawkish, and replaced him with a young Foreign Service officer named William Sullivan. Told that Sullivan lacked the seniority to serve in that position, Harriman directed everyone who outranked Sullivan to return to Washington. Kennedy approved Harriman's orders, with the result that by late May 1961 the U.S. delegation was, in the words of one of its members, "a lean and hungry team." More substantively, Harriman perceived at once that Moscow did not want war over Laos and was willing to seek an accommodation. He was not so sure about Hanoi or Beijing, but he felt that he and Pushkin could come to terms and, over time, steer the other delegates in the direction of peace. Ultimately, he proved to be right. That the major powers and bordering countries agreed to a pact guaranteeing Laos's neutrality was in great measure Harriman's accomplishment.[32]

Yet his diplomacy had an ugly side. Like the New Frontiersmen three decades his junior, he held the Lao in contempt, rarely soliciting their opinion and often disparaging them. According to Thailand's King Bhumibol Adulyadej, the roving ambassador did not treat the Lao "even as children, but as [a] master treats dogs." Harriman rivaled Tucker in his disdain for the RLA. Every time the enemy "appeared in the field," he declared in a representative cable from Geneva, "the Lao forces facing them fled in terror." He told Senator John Sparkman (D-AL) that "Lao don't know how to fight," noting that it was considered an "improvement" when RLA battalions who had previously "dropped their rifles and run like rabbits" in the face of Pathet Lao aggression remembered to "take their weapons with them" while retreating. "It's tragic," he remarked. "It makes you sick." None of the major Lao political figures impressed Harriman: Souphanouvong was "a card-carrying communist," Savang "a very weak reed," and Kong Le "a stupid little fellow." Echoing Brown, Harriman found Souvanna "the only man who can hold the country together," but that did not mean he thought highly of the prince. After one meeting, Harriman reported that Souvanna was either "naïve" or "willfully deceptive" in his "absurd self-confidence" that he could keep Pathet Lao ministers from trying to take over the RLG. "Souvanna seems to need some concerted effort[,] especially on [the] part [of his] Western friends[,] to . . . give him [the] facts of life about Russian tactics," Harriman asserted. Without such an effort, Souvanna would succumb to "complete dependence on [the] Pathet Lao."[33]

The Lao leader whom Harriman disliked most, though, was Phoumi, and he spent the greater part of his sojourn in Geneva trying to bring the general into line. If some American policymakers still regarded Phoumi as "our boy," Harriman never thought of him that way, nor did he subscribe to the view that Phoumi's participation in the RLG was essential if Laos was to remain noncommunist. Roger Hilsman, director of the State Department's bureau of intelligence and research, aptly titled the section of his memoir dealing with the Geneva Conference "Phoumi versus Harriman." From their first encounter, the two men hated each other, with Phoumi realizing that Harriman was willing to destroy him in order to extricate the United States from Laos and Harriman understanding that the general prized his own career above the best interests of his country. The issue that divided them was the makeup of a coalition government. Phoumi wanted to be premier, or at least to control the ministries of defense and interior. Harriman deemed this impossible, since the Pathet Lao would never let such crucial positions go to their enemies. Phoumi's refusal to accept a smaller role in a Souvanna-headed RLG struck Harriman as selfish and counterproductive. "The more I see of Phoumi, the less I trust him as [the] U.S. chosen instrument to carry out faithfully our agreed policies," Harriman declared. "We will simply have to determine for ourselves whether Phoumi is in fact negotiating in good faith."[34]

Harriman swiftly concluded that he was not, that on the contrary he was "dragging his feet with regard to formation of a government" and "stand[ing] in the way of achieving the president's objectives." The Phoumists boycotted the Geneva Conference because the Pathet Lao had received a seat. Separate and simultaneous armistice talks between representatives of the "three princes"—Souvanna, Souphanouvong, and Boun Oum—at the Lao village of Ban Namone saw Phoumi's proxy veto any proposal for a coalition that did not reserve top ministries for rightists. When, at the urging of Washington and Moscow, the three princes themselves met in Zurich at the end of June to iron out their differences, the best they could do was agree that Laos should have a tripartite government; they failed to determine who would be premier, or how cabinet posts were to be allocated. Harriman blamed the Phoumists for the stalemate, fuming, "It is fantastic that General Phoumi, who is entirely [a] U.S. creation, should be permitted to dictate American policy."[35]

Aware of Harriman's opposition and anxious lest the ground be cut out from under him, Phoumi tried to force Washington's hand. In October, he launched a series of probes into Pathet Lao territory and received a bloody nose for his efforts, as the communists drove the RLA back from the Kam Mon Plateau. Following the example of previous right-wing Lao leaders, Phoumi cried wolf, charging that Chinese and North Vietnamese troops had routed his men, but Harriman was having none of it. The general wanted to scuttle the negotiations, he told Kennedy. Experience had convinced Phoumi that if hostilities were renewed, Washington would throw its support behind him. Harriman suspected that some Americans were encouraging Phoumi in this delusion; he identified Jack Hazey, the CIA's liaison to Phoumi, as the likeliest culprit. Hazey was promptly recalled from Laos, and Harriman scored another victory in the "Thanksgiving massacre," when Kennedy made major changes in the State Department. One of the victims of this massacre was Assistant Secretary for Far Eastern Affairs Walter McConaughy, a Phoumi backer. Kennedy fired McConaughy and offered his job to Harriman, who was happy to accept.[36]

Harriman now resolved, in his words, to "put the screws on Phoumi." He advised Kennedy to suspend the cash grants the general needed to pay his troops. Kennedy agreed, and the $4 million in monthly economic assistance was cut off. Non-cash aid, meaning military equipment and training, continued, for the president did not want the RLA to collapse, but the sanctions weakened Phoumi and made him desperate. He complained to Ambassador Brown that Washington did not "understand the realities of internal Lao politics" and that if he acceded to Harriman's demands his countrymen would consider him "the slave of the Americans." Brown replied that the Kennedy administration held Phoumi responsible for the failure to establish a coalition government. As if to confirm this statement, during the first three months of 1962 each of the U.S. departments and agencies represented in Laos replaced its pro-Phoumi officials with personnel in favor of neutralism.[37]

Phoumi's supreme humiliation at Harriman's hands came in March, after the roving ambassador flew to Bangkok and convinced Thai premier Sarit Thanarat that his cousin needed to lower his expectations. Harriman told Sarit that a Souvanna-led RLG with neutralists controlling the major ministries was the only alternative to protracted warfare; maybe Washington could arrange for Phoumi to receive a deputy premiership, but that was all. Sarit, while disappointed in the new American policy, did not want to jeopardize Thai-U.S. relations by seeming to abet the general's uncooperativeness, and he consented to accompany Harriman to a meeting with Phoumi at Nong Khai, a Thai village just across the Mekong from Vientiane. There, Sarit took pains to preserve Phoumi's dignity. He did not look directly at the general and spoke in a low voice, explaining that Harriman was right, a negotiated settlement would be to everyone's benefit, and it was Phoumi's duty to serve in a government of national union headed by

Souvanna. When Sarit had finished, Phoumi responded by listing, at some length, the reasons for his refusal. According to Arthur Dommen, a journalist with years of experience in Southeast Asia, "the general's speech was the necessary prelude to his acceptance without loss of face of Marshal Sarit's advice." Harriman, however, would not be put off. He interrupted Phoumi, shouting that he was finished unless he got behind a coalition. "The entire world is agreed that Souvanna Phouma is the only possible person to lead a government," Harriman declared. Phoumi had "lost the war." He was "not going to be the person in control," and only his "stubbornness" kept him from recognizing this. "The time to decide is now," thundered the roving ambassador. If Phoumi did not "accept the solution we have proposed," the result would be "the destruction of Laos." U.S. Embassy chargé d'affaires George Roberts, who took notes on the meeting, called it a "harrowing session" in which Phoumi had "tears in his eyes" and looked as though Harriman had struck him "across the face with a baseball bat."[38]

A conference the following day in Phoumi's Vientiane office was even worse. Harriman berated Phoumi and his entire cabinet. "You, you, you, you, you, you, and you," he snapped, pointing his finger at each man across the table in turn, "I say you are driving your country to disaster. . . . We will not let you blame this on the United States. You are doing it to yourselves. If you have no courage to follow the path of negotiation, then it is better to step aside." Unmentioned in the memorandum of this conversation, but recalled by Harriman's interpreter, was a threat: should the civil war resume, the ambassador allegedly warned, "You bastards will have to swim that river out there, and not all of you guys are going to make it." The interpreter remembered Harriman speaking "with a directness and even brutality" that surpassed anything he had previously encountered in diplomatic circles.[39]

Phoumi indeed bore responsibility for obstructing the peace process, and his wings needed clipping, but one doubts that the roving ambassador would have read the same riot act to a European statesman, or even to a representative of another Asian country. Harriman's harangue testified to his disrespect for the Lao and smacked of the worst excesses of Parsons's ambassadorship. Phoumist spokesman Sisouk Na Champassak found the spectacle odious. In a press conference the following day, he objected to Harriman's "vehement tone," which, he said, "did not seem designed to persuade" because it was "very close to an ultimatum." Harriman fired back by telling reporters that all fourteen nations participating in the Geneva Conference agreed that Souvanna should be premier—a falsehood, given the South Vietnamese delegate's mistrust of the prince—and that Phoumi was delaying a settlement by his refusal to yield the defense and interior ministries. Harriman also announced that military aid to the Phoumi–Boun Oum faction might be discontinued along with economic aid if the rightists did not moderate their stance.[40]

This approach, apart from being insensitive, was ineffective, as Phoumi lapsed into sullen silence. Harriman had to inform Washington that "all our heavy artillery appears to have failed in moving Phoumi." The only softening of the rightists' position was an agreement by Boun Oum, apparently at Phoumi's direction, to participate in the Geneva Conference, but this was a cosmetic victory for Harriman. Once seated, the Phoumist delegation repeated its mantra: Souvanna was not a true neutralist and his control of defense and interior would be the opening wedge for a communist takeover of the country. Chester Cooper, Harriman's staff assistant, remembered Phoumi's representatives as having "little interest in the proceedings" and noted that a "member of the American delegation, for his many sins, had to spend a considerable amount of time wet-nursing them."[41]

In the end, it was the Pathet Lao, not the Americans, who made Phoumi change his mind. Still believing he could get the U.S. military involved on the ground in Laos, Phoumi reinforced the RLA garrison at Nam Tha, a village fifteen miles from the Chinese border. MAAG chief Boyle advised Phoumi not to do this, observing that it was certain to provoke the Pathet Lao or the Chinese, but that was precisely why the general sent additional men to that vulnerable northern town. If the communists took the bait and initiated a full-scale assault, he calculated, Kennedy would have no choice but to commit troops to prevent Laos from being overrun. By early May, there were five thousand RLA soldiers in Nam Tha, making sorties into the surrounding Pathet Lao–held hills. Souphanouvong's forces, at first unresponsive, finally attacked. They seized the nearby airstrip at Muong Sing, through which Phoumi had been supplying his troops, and laid down a mortar barrage on the garrison. Nam Tha fell in six hours. The American team of military advisers had to be evacuated by helicopter. According to Boyle, the RLA "gave a better account of themselves than during any previous engagement," but it was not good enough, and it ended disastrously, with two thousand Phoumists surrendering to the enemy and three thousand fleeing in panic across the Mekong, a retreat of over one hundred miles.[42]

The Kennedy administration did not react to the capture of Nam Tha as Phoumi had hoped. Although Kennedy ordered three thousand U.S. troops already stationed in Thailand to move to Udorn, thirty miles from the Lao border, he told journalists that the purpose of this gesture was "to help ensure the territorial integrity" of Thailand in case the Pathet Lao were tempted to exploit their defeat of the RLA by invading neighboring countries. "[T]here is no change in our policy toward Laos," the president said. Phoumi had played his last card and lost. He sent a cablegram to Souvanna informing him that he could appoint his own followers to head the ministries of defense and interior.[43]

This breakthrough, alas, did not signify that a settlement was in the offing. Americans in Geneva and Vientiane discovered that the three princes had their own timetable for negotiations. Souphanouvong, Souvanna, and Boun Oum, with Phoumi in tow, began a series of meetings at Khang Khay on the Plain of Jars, where the acrimoniousness of the previous months seemed forgotten and a festive atmosphere prevailed. Souvanna passed out cigars. Boun Oum brought champagne and endured good-natured ribbing about his weight. The men bargained for a few hours a day, at most. Paul Gardner, a U.S. consular official in Vientiane, remembered two things from this period: "an intense interest at the White House and the lackadaisical attitude of the Lao." One morning, he noted, "the negotiators didn't show up at the meeting place," and an American sent to track them down "found them in a restaurant drinking and telling dirty jokes. They had simply decided they didn't want to negotiate that day. They wanted to party instead." Harriman quipped to reporters that the negotiations were "rocking along in good Lao fashion" and complained to Rusk about being "'Laos-ed' up here for so long." Cooper, restless after spending months on the shores of Lac Leman, told a *New York Times* correspondent that Harriman should buy Laos and let everyone go home.[44]

While the princes and the general conducted their leisurely public diplomacy, Harriman confirmed an agreement he and Pushkin had made in private months earlier. The Russian diplomat, as eager to avoid war as his American counterpart, had suggested that the Soviet Union "police" the communist bloc insofar as Laos was concerned, while the Geneva Conference's other co-chairman, Great Britain, assumed responsibility for nations in the noncommunist bloc. Moscow and London would thereby ensure observance of the yet-to-be-finalized Geneva Accords. Harriman thought this an excellent arrangement, but he recognized its potential explosiveness, and at the conclusion of his cable to Washington recounting the Soviet proposal he noted, "Request no other discussion of this conversation with foreign governments." Some allies—Ngo Dinh Diem, for example—might not take kindly to an American making such a deal without consulting

**Figure 5.** A break during negotiations between leading Lao statesmen, Khang Khay, June 7, 1962. Left to right: Prince Souphanouvong, Prince Souvanna Phouma, Prince Boun Oum, General Phoumi Nosavan. Bettmann/CORBIS.

them. Nonetheless, Harriman believed Pushkin's formula would compensate for weaknesses in the accords, and he considered it the cornerstone of any durable neutralization of Laos. He therefore confronted Pushkin after Nam Tha's fall to insist that the Soviets do a better job of controlling "their" Lao. Pushkin replied that Phoumi had only himself to blame for the fiasco, a point Harriman was half-inclined to concede, and the two men renewed their pledge—the so-called "Pushkin-Harriman understanding"—to keep members of their respective blocs from violating Lao nonalignment.[45]

Not until July 23, 1962, did the foreign ministers of the fourteen nations represented at Geneva sign the Declaration on the Neutrality of Laos, wrapping up one of the longest conferences in diplomatic history. Laos's new provisional government was a mosaic. Seven of the cabinet posts went to neutralists, four to Phoumists, and four to Pathet Lao; the remaining four were held by so-called "Vientiane neutralists," meaning conservatives who had no love for Phoumi. Souvanna, of course, became premier—and defense minister as well. Phoumi and Souphanouvong became deputy premiers, each with the power to veto cabinet decisions. (Boun Oum obligingly went into retirement.) The Laos Accords required foreign military forces to leave the kingdom within seventy-five days and declared that Vientiane would establish diplomatic relations with all nations, regardless of their forms of government. At Diem's and Sarit's insistence, the signatories promised not to "use the territory of the Kingdom of Laos for interference in the internal affairs of other countries." The ICC was responsible for supervising the cease-fire and otherwise implementing the accords, but, as Harriman acknowledged, no one expected it to be effective. In one of the American delegation's most significant concessions, the roving ambassador had agreed that the ICC should be governed by the rule of unanimity, which enabled the communist commissioner to prevent investigation or punishment of Pathet Lao aggression. If the Pushkin-Harriman understanding proved a dead letter, there would be no enforcement mechanism to compel compliance with the accords.[46]

Harriman was tough-minded about the treaty it had taken over a year to cobble together. Asked by a colleague how the conference had gone, he replied, "About as badly as I expected." To him, the accords were "a good bad deal," less important in terms of what they portended for Laos than what they meant for Washington. Kennedy had given his roving ambassador explicit orders: obtain a settlement; permit me a graceful exit. Harriman fulfilled his task. When the ICC reported that only forty of the estimated ten thousand North Vietnamese troops in Laos had left the country by the end of 1962, Harriman advised Kennedy to let this violation of the accords pass. To respond by sending U.S. soldiers would solve nothing, he argued, and it would give Hanoi a pretext for escalation. Washington should abide by the Geneva agreement even if the communists did not; maybe this would cause fair-weather allies like Souvanna to see the light. Kennedy required little persuading. Having finally disentangled America from Laos, he was unlikely to plunge back in. He turned his attention to South Vietnam, where prospects looked brighter despite the arrival of thousands of communist troops via the Ho Chi Minh Trail—or, as some hawks soon took to calling it, "the Averell Harriman Memorial Highway."[47]

## "Vietnam Is the Place"

Kennedy's initial foray into summitry overlapped with the commencement of the Geneva Conference, and it was instrumental in convincing him that his decision to seek a negotiated settlement to the Lao civil war had been the correct one. French president Charles de Gaulle hosted three days of meetings with the U.S. president in late May–early June 1961, during which, in addition to discussing reorganization of the North Atlantic Treaty Organization (NATO) and France's development of an independent nuclear capability, the two men talked about Southeast Asia. Kennedy then traveled from Paris to Vienna for a conference with Khrushchev, who was, it seemed, ready to challenge the cold war status quo everywhere from Berlin to Saigon. Diplomatically, the Paris and Vienna summits were polar opposites: the former warm and extravagant, the latter acrimonious and hair-raising. The only feature they had in common was their shared verdict that, in Kennedy's words, Laos was not a country "worthy of engaging the attention of great powers."[48]

De Gaulle rolled out the red carpet for Kennedy, welcoming him at Orly Airport under a display of fifteen French and fifteen American flags. As the two heads of state rode in a motorcade to the Quai d'Orsay, Parisians lined up ten deep along the streets to gawk and cheer. There were white-tie dinners at the Elysée Palace and Versailles's Hall of Mirrors, a special performance by the Paris Opera Ballet, and other entertainments designed to emphasize the closeness of the Franco-American alliance. Kennedy and de Gaulle met six times during the visit, each talk lasting over an hour. Neither man said much that surprised the other. Kennedy knew de Gaulle was going to propose giving NATO a three-power directorate of France, Britain, and the United States, and de Gaulle knew Kennedy was going to say no. The French president knew the American president was going to ask him to have faith in the U.S. nuclear deterrent, and the American president knew the French president was going to demur. They smoothed over these disagreements with flattery: Kennedy called his host a "great captain of the West" and quoted passages of de Gaulle's autobiography from memory; de Gaulle toasted Kennedy's "intelligence and courage." The visit was a public-relations triumph. Both presidents were pleased.[49]

One of the few exchanges that flirted with spontaneity occurred on the first day, when Kennedy raised the subject of Laos. In an attempt to separate himself from Eisenhower's policy, he admitted that "the United States has made mistakes in the past." Nonetheless, he observed, "there exists a commitment" to defend noncommunist Southeast Asia, and he had to take this commitment "into account." The important question, from Washington's perspective, was "what to do at the conference in Geneva." Did de Gaulle have any suggestions? De Gaulle did, agreeing with Kennedy that past U.S. policy had been flawed because the Eisenhower administration had labored under "the unfortunate illusion that Laos could be made into something strong." This was preposterous, de Gaulle insisted: "Laos is an unhappy country with no unity, either political or national; it is, in fact, a nonentity which cannot be built up into anything at all." The general recommended that Kennedy make a virtue of necessity and support a Souvanna-led RLG that "will include communists but will not be fully communist."

At the time de Gaulle said this, the U.S. delegation at Geneva was still officially anti-Souvanna, but Kennedy anticipated Harriman's later advice. Souvanna "may be the best available solution," he noted, "even though obviously he is not a very good one." Nonetheless, Kennedy worried that the "collapse" of the RLA would make Souvanna a "prisoner" of the communists, to which de Gaulle replied that, given Western backing, the prince "might be able to push [the communists] farther away," albeit "not very far away." While de Gaulle painted an unattractive picture of Souvanna's neutralism, Kennedy did not seize on this as a reason to press for another premier. Instead, he acknowledged again that his predecessor's approach to Laos had been "unwise." The issue went beyond Laos, however. If the "solution to the Laotian problem is a communist one," Kennedy said, there would be "grave repercussions" in South Vietnam, Cambodia, and Thailand. Kennedy wanted to know "how to disengage in the best possible way," that is, without creating a chain reaction of falling dominoes throughout the region. De Gaulle once more offered no easy answers. He understood the difficulties Washington faced, he declared, but France's own experience in Indochina indicated that the "best thing to do is to encourage neutralism, . . . even if that neutrality is only more or less genuine." He commented that he was not advocating this approach for all of Asia. "The question is quite different in regard to India and Japan," he said. "These are important countries and real countries. They deserve that efforts be undertaken on their behalf. . . . The same thing cannot be said about the countries of Southeast Asia, which are not realities but only nebulous or legalistic entities."

Kennedy finally asked de Gaulle directly what France's response would be if the Pathet Lao took over Laos. De Gaulle answered with equal bluntness: "France would not intervene." Rather than expressing disappointment at the general's attitude, Kennedy stressed tactical considerations. If Souphanouvong and his mentors knew "we would not intervene," he pointed out, "then there would be no reason for them to seek any agreement acceptable to us." He therefore believed the Western allies ought to "hold the threat of an intervention in order to bring the Chinese and the Soviets to an agreement." De Gaulle concurred that "we should try to keep the opposition guessing." Kennedy needed to be aware, though, that qualified neutralism was the optimal outcome in Laos. "The only card for the West to play is that of Souvanna Phouma," de Gaulle insisted, adding that he was "under no illusions" as to the prince's "worth." Kennedy reiterated his concern that a Pathet Lao triumph would cause "weakness" in the noncommunist states of Southeast Asia. At the same time, he professed to be "extremely reluctant to think of an intervention in Laos."[50]

De Gaulle had given Kennedy several opportunities to strike a hawkish stance, and the latter had declined. As in his conference with legislative leaders one month earlier, Kennedy avoided making any declaration forswearing the use of force to resolve the Laos crisis, but by allowing de Gaulle's pessimistic claims to stand unchallenged, he implied that he and the general were of like mind. They did not discuss Laos again, an indication that the matter was closed. At de Gaulle's behest, the two men kept the content of their talks confidential, and aides merely informed the press that "a fundamental agreement exists." Despite this lack of detail, the *New York Times* editorialized that Kennedy's "diplomacy has shown positive results."[51]

The Vienna meeting with Khrushchev was a different matter. This summit, the most frightening of the cold war, has received extensive attention from journalists, biographers, and historians. Its images and rhetoric are part of Kennedy lore: Khrushchev barking at the president in the U.S. Embassy garden; Kennedy, off his game, fumbling for a response; the two men exchanging barely civil toasts over the imperial dishes of the Habsburgs; Kennedy calling Khrushchev's Berlin bluff with the retort, "It will be a cold winter"; an exhausted Kennedy confessing to friends afterward, "He just beat hell out of me." While the Cuban Missile Crisis is generally regarded as Kennedy's finest hour as president, Vienna ranks alongside the Bay of Pigs as his worst.[52]

Often overlooked in accounts of this conference is its one bright spot: Laos. After spending the afternoon of June 3 trapped in debate with Khrushchev about the relative merits of communism and capitalism, Kennedy decided to stick to concrete issues during the evening discussion. He led off with Laos, admitting, as he had with de Gaulle, that "U.S. policy in that region" had "not always been wise." Laos was "unimportant from the strategic standpoint," he said, but Eisenhower had made a commitment to it, and the new administration could not renege on that commitment without upsetting America's other Southeast Asian allies. Kennedy wanted to "find a solution not involving the prestige or the interests of our two countries," and he felt this could be attained through a "neutral and independent Laos" on the model of Cambodia and Burma. He asked Khrushchev what his view was. The Soviet leader, in contrast to the bluster he had shown earlier in the day, replied that he held "the same view." He said that North Vietnamese soldiers were not assisting the Pathet Lao, which was false, and accused Washington of overthrowing Souvanna in 1960, which was true, but his tone remained moderate and the topic did not seem to pique his emotions.

He grew agitated, however, when the discussion turned to Cuba. Kennedy's attempt to disarm his rival by conceding that Washington had "made a misjudgment" at the Bay of Pigs backfired. Khrushchev interpreted it as weakness and launched into a diatribe about how America was on the wrong side of wars of national liberation, "holy wars," all over the globe. Cuba, Iran, Spain, Algeria, South Korea, Pakistan, the Congo—everywhere "U.S. policy is that of support for colonialist powers." Changing the subject, Khrushchev raged against U.S. and NATO bases surrounding the Soviet Union and demanded to know why, if Kennedy was so troubled by a socialist Cuba off America's shores, he saw nothing provocative about stationing Western troops in Turkey. He also said that if he, Khrushchev, ran China he would have "attacked Taiwan a long time ago." When Kennedy suggested that free elections in Poland might turn out the communist regime, Khrushchev exploded. Poland had a fine government, he bellowed. "Its election system is more democratic than that in the United States." What happened in Poland was none of Kennedy's business, and it was "not respectful" for him to comment on another county's internal affairs. Shaking his fist, Khrushchev berated the president until Kennedy managed to guide the discussion back to safe ground. Surely, he said, Washington and Moscow could press their respective clients in Laos to observe a neutralist settlement. By this stage, Khrushchev was so wrought up that he blamed the United States for starting Laos's civil war "from Thailand," but he soon calmed down. Yes, of course, he commented, the Soviets and Americans ought to "use their influence so as to bring about agreement among the forces participating in the Laotian struggle."[53]

Day two was a nightmare for Kennedy, dominated by exchanges over the future of Berlin, which Khrushchev wanted to turn into a "free city," thereby terminating U.S. occupation and access rights. Kennedy found that unacceptable, and he responded to Khrushchev's threats by standing fast. The two men traded insults and warnings while their aides looked on in horror. Khrushchev accused Kennedy of "megalomania" and "delusions of grandeur" and roared, "If the U.S. wants to start a war over Germany, then let it be so." The president replied that it was Khrushchev who sought to "force a change" and that if Washington submitted to coercion, the world would lose confidence in the United States. He had not assumed office, he said, to "accept arrangements totally inimical to U.S. interests." Bullying and recklessness were the hallmarks of Vienna—except, as had been the case the previous day, when Kennedy and Khrushchev discussed Laos. Then, Khrushchev became coolheaded, if impatient to move on to weightier matters. He agreed with Kennedy's contention that "Laos is not so important as to get us as involved as we are" and even proclaimed that the Soviet and American foreign ministers "should be locked in a room and told to find a solution." Capitalizing on this point of assent, Kennedy again blamed his predecessor for the Lao crisis. He noted that Eisenhower had not turned over the presidency until January 1961 and that the "commitments [to Laos] had been undertaken before that time." For his part, he wanted to change American policy and was "anxious to get the U.S. military out of Laos." Khrushchev expressed pleasure at hearing this, observing that he could "add little to what had already been said." For a moment, the meeting became almost cordial— and then the two men returned to Berlin, and verbal warfare resumed.[54]

Given the white-knuckle mood in which the summit broke up, it was easy to ignore the communiqué issued to reporters at the end. In it, Kennedy and Khrushchev affirmed their "support of a neutral and independent Laos" and of "international agreements for insuring that neutrality and independence." Kennedy thus did not leave Vienna empty-handed. Determined to make the most of the meeting's single accomplishment, he telephoned Harriman at Geneva. "Do you understand what I want?" he asked. "I want to have a negotiated settlement. I do not want to become militarily involved." Harriman assured the president that he understood.[55]

Salvaging one diplomatic draw out of an otherwise calamitous summit did nothing to ease Kennedy's mortification. Khrushchev had treated him, as he put it, "like a little boy." Vienna was the "worst thing in my life," he confided to *New York Times* correspondent James Reston. "He savaged me." Details of the Kennedy-Khrushchev conversations would not emerge for decades, and American press accounts at the time made it seem as though the president had held his own, but there was no mistaking the fact that the summit, far from reducing cold war tensions, had heightened them. Kennedy felt humiliated. He moreover felt compelled to display what Khrushchev clearly thought he lacked: "guts." As he declared to Reston in a much-cited plaint, "Now we have a problem in making our power credible, and Vietnam is the place."[56]

Vietnam was the place for a variety of reasons. Next door to Laos, it could prevent communist influence in that country from spreading. Diem had shown himself a resolute foe of communism, and his government, unlike Souvanna's, was red-free. Geography favored the guerrilla insurgents in South Vietnam nearly as much as in Laos, but the former nation had a coastline and transportation network that would make supplying and maneuvering American forces simpler. Above all, as Harriman observed in late August 1961, "The Viet-Nam [*sic*] are known to be much tougher soldiers," while the Lao "are mostly happy-go-lucky people that want to be left alone." Four months later, the roving ambassador told interviewers for CBS's *Capitol Cloakroom* that "the Laotian people are not known to be as warlike as the Vietnamese people, who are known to be great fighters." Both the "North and the South Vietnamese have always been able to fight for their independence, and their armies are well trained and well led," Harriman proclaimed. "Whenever they get a chance, the South Vietnamese are putting up a good fight." The RLA, by contrast, took to their heels at a whiff of grapeshot.[57]

Kennedy once declared that Harriman had held more important posts at home and abroad than any American since John Quincy Adams, a remark that indicated the president's high regard for his roving ambassador and suggested why he might accept Harriman's Lao-Vietnamese comparison as valid even though the venerable diplomat had so little experience in Southeast Asia. Other administration officials drew the same distinction. National Security Adviser McGeorge Bundy told Kennedy that South Vietnam stood "on a footing wholly different from Laos.... Laotians have fought very little. South Vietnam [*sic*] troops are not yet U.S. Marines, but they are usable." Rusk likewise advised the president, "Troops in South Vietnam really fight, and that is quite a crucial difference." William Sullivan, destined to become U.S. ambassador to Laos after serving under Harriman, noted that while the Lao were "not fighters," the South Vietnamese were "tigers and real fighters," and that hence "the advantages would be on our side to have a confrontation and showdown in Vietnam and not get sucked into this Laos operation."[58]

The president's course was therefore clear. "If we have to fight for Southeast Asia," he told advisers, "we'll fight in South Vietnam." He would prove to Khrushchev that Washington's acquiescence in a peaceful solution to the Lao conflict did not mean the United States was weak or open to intimidation. Believing, as did Eisenhower, that America must keep the dominoes from falling, Kennedy expanded the U.S. role in South Vietnam while Harriman bargained at Geneva. He did not retreat one inch in his determination to prevent communism from overrunning the Indochinese peninsula. At the same time, he did not trust the Lao to fight the free world's battles. Like his fellow policymakers, and like the journalists who helped set the parameters within which policy could be made, Kennedy reduced the Lao to a set of stereotypes: childlike, lazy, indifferent. "Because of... the Laotians' own gentle nature," Rusk recalled, "we concluded that an American stand against communist aggression in Laos would have been frustrated by the Laotians themselves." This perception, and not any insight into the virtues of nonalignment or desire to ease cold war tensions, led Kennedy to accept a Souvanna-led RLG.[59]

According to William Bundy, Kennedy's assistant secretary of state for international security affairs, the news that delegates at Geneva had arrived at an agreement neutralizing Laos was greeted with solemnity by the White House. "Certainly there was no cheering," Bundy remembered. "It was the widespread impression... that any new government in Laos would end up under communist domination and that all that the U.S. was doing was to put [sic] the best possible face on a clear defeat." While relieved that Americans would not have to go to war in Laos's jungled mountains, narrow valleys, and blast-furnace climate, the New Frontiersmen experienced what Bundy described as "an accompanying sense that the U.S. must show that it would stand firm in other parts of Southeast Asia." South Vietnam was the place Kennedy chose.[60]

# Epilogue

Perhaps the most infamous editorial in American history appeared in 1902, as Washington's efforts to complete its conquest of the Philippines floundered in the face of a determined anticolonial resistance. Reports of atrocities and U.S. casualties had soured the American public on the war, and many prominent figures, some of them former advocates for empire, were demanding withdrawal. The *San Francisco Argus,* a weekly Republican newspaper, found such calls repugnant. "There have [*sic*] been too much hypocrisy about this Philippine business," declared the anonymous author, capitalizing and italicizing his points for emphasis. "Let us be frank: WE DO NOT WANT THE FILIPINOS. WE WANT THE PHILIPPINES. All of our troubles in this annexation matter have been caused by the presence in the Philippine islands of the Filipinos.... The islands are enormously rich, ... *but, unfortunately, they are infested by Filipinos.*" Americans had to take the bit between their teeth. "[E]very man who believes in developing the islands must admit that it cannot be done successfully while the Filipinos are there," the *Argus* proclaimed. "*They are indolent.* They raise only enough food to live on; they don't care to make money; and they occupy land which may be used to much better advantage by Americans. Therefore, the more of them killed the better." The author conceded that his remedy "seems harsh." Nonetheless, he wrote, the Filipinos "must yield before the superior race."[1]

This piece became notorious almost as soon as it was published. Even turn-of-the-century readers were shocked by its crassness, and it has often been cited by critics of U.S. foreign policy as one of the few instances when a mainstream commentator stated American geopolitical objectives point-blank, without sanctimonious cant. Recently, America's invasion of Iraq prompted invocations of the *Argus* editorial from William Loren Katz, Patrick Barr, and other left-wing bloggers who insisted that the spirit of Theodore Roosevelt was on the march again, driving the United States to plunder foreign lands without regard for native peoples.[2]

As is usually the case with historical analogy, these arguments obfuscated more than they revealed. The international and domestic contexts within which Americans fought the Philippine and Iraq wars were too different for parallels to be instructive. Yet one foreign-policy venture did bear a striking resemblance to Washington's plunge into overseas imperialism, at least insofar as Americans regarded the Other they encountered. Many U.S. statesmen and journalists brooding over their nation's challenge in Laos at midcentury would have endorsed the *Argus*'s premise: that is, they did not want the Lao; they wanted Laos. J. Graham Parsons and likeminded Americans coveted the *territory* of Laos, not as a source of profit but as a link in the free-world chain of defense, and saw the indigenous population as an obstacle, possibly an insurmountable one, to the achievement of U.S. aims. Of course, they did not advocate genocide and would have censured anyone who did. Still, in their certainty that host nationals were incapable of joining the march of civilization, they echoed McKinley-era sentiments and confirmed Andrew Rotter's point that the "relative scarcity of race words in the vocabulary" of early cold war policymakers "suggests that these words were unfashionable, not that the reasons for using them originally had disappeared." Sometimes even the words did not change. "*They are indolent,*" hissed the *Argus,* as if to put the matter beyond debate. Parsons would have agreed.[3]

Other Americans viewed the Lao more sympathetically than did Parsons, but none managed to transcend the toxic ensemble of assumptions that shaped U.S. policy toward Laos during the Eisenhower and Kennedy years. Winthrop Brown, Parsons's polar opposite in many respects, implored his superiors on the eve of the battle for Vientiane to "always remember [the] inherent Lao reluctance to fight," even though his own experience with Kong Le ought to have dispelled that notion. Joel Halpern, whose writings contained so many cold doses of common sense, reported to the Rand Corporation in 1959, "I don't see [in Laos] a great drive for achievement, we have got to do it now, we don't have much time." Despite U.S. warnings that the hour was late, the odds were long, and only a supreme effort could prevent Laos from going under, Halpern noted that the Lao "had no radical ideas that they were even thinking about putting into effect." Instead, they were "resigned" to their fate, a "gentle people," lacking "self-discipline," who "don't see themselves as initiating activity." Even the most perspicacious American asserted some version of the complaint put forth by the *Argus* five decades earlier: Washington's difficulties in a foreign land were due to the local inhabitants—not to problems of distance and terrain, and certainly not to flaws at the core of U.S. foreign policy. The United States had failed to bar communism's progress in Laos because the natives could not be de-Laoed.[4]

American stereotypes of the Lao proved remarkably durable. They persisted as the coalition government set up at Geneva in 1962 came apart, igniting a new round of violence; as conflict in Vietnam escalated and Washington launched its air campaign over the Ho Chi Minh Trail; as the heaviest sustained bombing in history flattened every habitable structure in the Plain of Jars and turned other areas of Laos into moonscapes; as the Central Intelligence Agency's secret war drained Hmong villages of fighting men and forced General Vang Pao to staff his units with boys as young as ten; as ground combat and the rain of fire from the sky caused more than a quarter of Laos's population to become refugees; and as the Pathet Lao completed their march to power, closed the nation's borders, abolished the six-hundred-year-old monarchy, and sent tens of thousands of people to gulags to die of malnutrition, maltreatment, exposure, and disease. Even efforts by the communist Lao People's Democratic Republic (LPDR) to exterminate the Hmong with Soviet-supplied biological weapons, a gruesome exercise in ethnic cleansing that lasted into the 1980s, did not lay the snide caricature to rest.[5]

Indeed, it lives on in works of scholarship, including the best study to date of the CIA's covert war. *Shooting at the Moon,* a prizewinning account by Roger Warner, informs readers in its first pages that midcentury Lao "seemed caught in a languid tropical daydream." They "admired Westerners" but "knew they were incapable of doing what the Westerners did, and so they didn't bother trying." Laos, Warner writes, "always lagged behind its neighboring countries in everything it did." Its people were "impossible to motivate," their "greatest handicap" being "a mentality of passive resistance to change." This made them poor instruments of U.S. policy. Lao civilians were "too apathetic to care" when the bulk of American aid trickled into the pockets of unscrupulous officials, and the "sleepy, inefficient Royal Lao Army," although up to the task of handling the Pathet Lao—whom Warner calls "no better soldiers than their royalist brethren"—proved "no match for the Vietnamese fighting machine" bearing down from the east.

Warner chronicles the human costs of internationalization of the Lao civil war, paints a grim picture of postwar life under the LPDR, and concludes his book with cautious optimism and some very revealing language. The collapse of the Soviet Union, easing of international tensions, and consequent emergence in Laos of a more relaxed political atmosphere augured well for the nation's future, Warner observes:

> It was as though this small, obscure, sweetly retarded country had ridden on a cold war roller-coaster ride, starting with the coup of 1960: Fifteen years of American domination followed by fifteen years of Vietnamese and Soviet domination, and then a few more years to calm down and find its own destiny again, which was merely to be its own sweet, goofy self.[6]

Tom Dooley could have written those lines. Two generations after U.S. troops left Southeast Asia, America's "Laos" remained Never-Never Land.

# Notes

## Abbreviations of Archival Collections

CSC      Charles Stevenson Collection, Washington, DC
CYP      Charles Yost Papers, Seeley Mudd Library, Princeton University, Princeton, NJ
DSCF     Department of State Central Files, National Archives II, College Park, MD
EBP      Edgar Buell Papers, Hamilton, IN
EL       Dwight D. Eisenhower Library, Abilene, KS
FAOHC   Library of Congress Homepage, American Memory Series, Frontline Diplomacy: The Foreign Affairs Oral History Collection of the Association for Diplomatic Studies and Training, http://www.loc.gov/homepage/lchp.html
*FRUS*     State Department, *Foreign Relations of the United States*
IVSAC    International Voluntary Services Archival Collection, Mennonite Historical Library, Goshen College, Goshen, IN
JFDP     John Foster Dulles Papers, Seeley Mudd Library, Princeton University, Princeton, NJ
JFKL     John F. Kennedy Library, Boston, MA
JGPP     J. Graham Parsons Papers, Special Collections, Lauinger Library, Georgetown University, Washington, DC
JHP      Joel Halpern Papers, Archives and Manuscripts Department, University Library, University of Massachusetts, Amherst, MA
RG 59    Record Group 59, General Records of the Department of State, National Archives II, College Park, MD
RG 469   Record Group 469, Records of the U.S. Foreign Assistance Agencies, 1948–1961, National Archives II, College Park, MD

TADC   Thomas A. Dooley Collection, Pius XII Library, St. Louis University, St. Louis, MO
TADP   Thomas A. Dooley Papers, Western Historical Manuscript Collection, University of Missouri–St. Louis, St. Louis, MO
WAHP   W. Averell Harriman Papers, Library of Congress, Washington, DC

## Introduction

1. Persons Memorandum for the Record, January 19, 1961, Eisenhower, Dwight D., Post-presidential Papers, 1961–69, Augusta-Walter Reed Series, box 2, Dwight D. Eisenhower Library, Abilene, KS (hereafter EL); Clifford Memorandum on Conference, January 24, 1961, President's Office Files, Special Correspondence, box 29a, John F. Kennedy Library, Boston, MA (hereafter JFKL); Herter Memorandum for the Record, January 19, 1961, Bureau of Far Eastern Affairs, Assistant Secretary for Far Eastern Affairs, Subject, Personal Name, and Country Files, 1960–63, box 5, Record Group 59, General Records of the Department of State, National Archives II, College Park, MD (hereafter RG 59).

2. Clifford Memorandum on Conference, January 24, 1961, President's Office Files, Special Correspondence, box 29a, JFKL (emphasis in the original); McNamara Memorandum to the President, January 24, 1961 (emphasis added); Aide-mémoire, January 19, 1961, ibid.

3. Kennedy cited in Walt W. Rostow, *The Diffusion of Power: An Essay in Recent History* (New York: Macmillan, 1972), 264; Robert S. McNamara with Brian VanDemark, *In Retrospect: The Tragedy and Lessons of Vietnam* (New York: Random House, 1995), 37.

4. For representative works on Washington's early involvement in Southeast Asia see David L. Anderson, *Trapped by Success: The Eisenhower Administration and Vietnam, 1953–1961* (New York: Columbia University Press, 1991); James R. Arnold, *The First Domino: Eisenhower, the Military, and America's Intervention in Vietnam* (New York: William Morrow, 1991); Ronald H. Spector, *Advice and Support: The Early Years of the U.S. Army in Vietnam, 1941–1960* (New York: Free Press, 1985).

5. President of United States to President of Viet-Nam, July 9, 1962, *Foreign Relations of the United States* (hereafter *FRUS*) 1961–63 (Washington, DC: Government Printing Office, 1990), 2:511.

6. Lawrence Freedman, *Kennedy's Wars: Cuba, Berlin, Laos, and Vietnam* (New York: Oxford University Press, 2000), 298. For other works stressing logistical costs and risks see Robert Dallek, *An Unfinished Life: John F. Kennedy, 1917–1963* (Boston: Little, Brown, 2003), 350–52; Anthony O. Edmonds, *The War in Vietnam* (Westport, CT: Greenwood Press, 1998), 15; George Kahin, *Intervention: How the United States Became Involved in Vietnam* (New York: Alfred A. Knopf, 1986), 127–28; Stanley Karnow, *Vietnam: A History* (New York: Viking, 1983), 265; A. J. Langguth, *Our Vietnam: The War, 1954–1975* (New York: Touchstone, 2000), 178–79; Mark Atwood Lawrence, *The Vietnam War: A Concise International History* (New York: Oxford University Press, 2008), 70; John M. Newman, *JFK and Vietnam: Deception, Intrigue, and the Struggle for Power* (New York: Warner Books, 1992), 17–19; William S. Turley, *The Second Indochina War: A Concise Political and Military History* (Lanham, MD: Rowman & Littlefield, 2009), 60.

7. Observer cited in Bernard B. Fall, *Anatomy of a Crisis: The Laotian Crisis of 1960–1961* (New York: Doubleday, 1969), 51.

8. President of the United States to President of Viet-Nam, July 9, 1962, *FRUS* 1961–63, 2:511; Memorandum for the President: Plan for Possible Intervention in Laos, May 30, 1961, National Security Files, Regional Security, box 231, JFKL. For works exploring how this imagined pecking order influenced U.S. policy toward Asia see Andrew J. Rotter, *Comrades at Odds: The United States and India, 1947–1964* (Ithaca, NY: Cornell University Press, 2000); Naoko Shibusawa, *America's Geisha Ally: Reimagining the Japanese Enemy* (Cambridge, MA: Harvard University Press, 2006).

9. Kenneth L. Hill, "President Kennedy and the Neutralization of Laos," *Review of Politics* 31 (July 1969): 354. For other laudatory treatments see James G. Blight, Janet M. Lang, and David A. Welch, *Vietnam If Kennedy Had Lived: Virtual JFK* (Lanham, MD: Rowman & Little-field, 2009), 7–9; Hugh Brogan, *Kennedy* (London: Longman, 1996), 62–64; Freedman, *Kennedy's Wars*, 293–304; Gordon M. Goldstein, *Lessons in Disaster: McGeorge Bundy and the Path to War in Vietnam* (New York: Times Books, 2008), 44–48; David Kaiser, *American Tragedy: Kennedy, Johnson, and the Origins of the Vietnam War* (Cambridge, MA: Harvard University Press, 2000), 36–57; Barbara Leaming, *Jack Kennedy: The Education of a Statesman* (New York: W. W. Norton, 1994), 268–69, 272–81; Robert Mann, *A Grand Delusion: America's Descent into Vietnam* (New York: Basic Books, 2001), 229–31; Michael O'Brien, *John F. Kennedy: A Biography* (New York: St. Martin's Press, 2005), 613–15; O'Brien, *Rethinking Kennedy* (Chicago: Ivan R. Dee, 2009), 177–78; Lewis J. Paper, *The Promise and the Performance: The Leadership of John F. Kennedy* (New York: Crown Books, 1975), 69–72; John Prados, *Vietnam: The History of an Unwinnable War* (Lawrence: University Press of Kansas, 2009), 79; R. B. Smith, *An International History of the Vietnam War: The Kennedy Strategy* (New York: St. Martin's Press, 1985), 60, 65, 70; Edmund F. Wehrle, "'A Good, Bad Deal': John F. Kennedy, W. Averell Harriman, and the Neutralization of Laos, 1961–1962," *Pacific Historical Review* 67 (August 1998): 349–77.

10. Kennedy cited in Benjamin C. Bradlee, *Conversations with Kennedy* (New York: W. W. Norton, 1975), 86; Theodore C. Sorensen, *Kennedy* (Old Saybrook, CT: Konecky & Konecky, 1965), 645–46.

11. Mark Philip Bradley, *Imagining Vietnam and America: The Making of Postcolonial Vietnam, 1919–1950* (Chapel Hill: University of North Carolina Press, 2000), 6.

12. Igor Oganesoff, "Languid Laos," *Wall Street Journal*, September 17, 1959; "Laos: Boxed In," *Newsweek* 59 (March 4, 1962): 45; Jacques Nevard, "Reverses in Laos Laid to 'Myth' of 'Invasion,'" *New York Times*, April 21, 1961; Max Frankel, "View in Washington," *New York Times*, July 23, 1962.

13. Laura A. Belmonte, "Roundtable Review" *Passport* 40 (April 2009): 18; William C. Inboden, *Religion and American Foreign Policy, 1945–1960: The Soul of Containment* (Cambridge: Cambridge University Press, 2008), 25, 5; Rotter, *Comrades at Odds*, 235; Seth Jacobs, *America's Miracle Man in Vietnam: Ngo Dinh Diem, Religion, Race, and U.S. Intervention in Southeast Asia, 1950–1957* (Durham, NC: Duke University Press, 2004), 190. For other works on religion and U.S. cold war foreign relations see Ira Chernus, *Apocalypse Management: Eisenhower and the Discourse of National Insecurity* (Stanford, CA: Stanford University Press, 2008); Mark Edwards, "'God Has Chosen Us': Re-Membering Christian Realism, Rescuing Christendom, and the Contest of Responsibilities during the Cold War," *Diplomatic History* 33 (April 2009): 67–94; Leilah Danielson, "Christianity, Dissent, and the Cold War: A. J. Muste's Challenge to Realism and U.S. Empire," *Diplomatic History* 30 (September 2006): 645–69; David S. Fogelsong, *The American Mission and the "Evil Empire": The Crusade for a "Free Russia" since 1881* (Cambridge: Cambridge University Press, 2007); Diane Kirby, ed. *Religion and the Cold War* (London: Palgrave, 2003).

14. Outline Plan Regarding Buddhist Organizations, January 16, 1957, White House National Security Staff Papers, 1945–61, OCB Central File Series, box 2, EL; Stanley Karnow, "Tale of a Troubled Paradise," *Life* 47 (September 7, 1959): 22; Karnow, *Southeast Asia* (New York: Time-Life Books, 1962), 12.

15. Andrew Rotter, "Gender Relations, Foreign Relations: The United States and South Asia, 1947–1962," *Journal of American History* 81 (September 1994): 521; Kristin Hoganson, *Fighting for American Manhood: How Gender Politics Provoked the Spanish-American and Philippine-American Wars* (New Haven, CT: Yale University Press, 1998); Mary Ann Heiss, "Real Men Don't Wear Pajamas: Anglo-American Cultural Perceptions of Mohammed Mossadeq and the Iranian Oil Nationalization Dispute," in *Empire and Revolution: The United States and the Third World since 1945*, ed. Peter L. Hahn and Mary Ann Heiss (Columbus: Ohio State University Press, 2001),

178–94; Legation in Laos to Department of State, January 28, 1955, *FRUS* 1955–57 (Washington, DC: Government Printing Office, 1990), 21:594; Lippmann cited in Charles A. Stevenson, *The End of Nowhere: American Policy toward Laos since 1954* (Boston: Beacon Press, 1972), 41. Diplomatic historians have found gender a rewarding analytical category. Excellent works include Frank Costigliola, "'Unceasing Pressure for Penetration': Gender, Pathology, and Emotion in George Kennan's Formation of the Cold War," *Journal of American History* 83 (March 1997): 1309–39; Robert D. Dean, *Imperial Brotherhood: Gender and the Making of Cold War Foreign Policy* (Amherst: University of Massachusetts Press, 2001); Petra Goedde, *GIs and Germans: Culture, Gender, and Foreign Relations, 1945–1949* (New Haven, CT: Yale University Press, 2003); Emily Rosenberg, "Revisiting Dollar Diplomacy: Narratives of Money and Manliness," *Diplomatic History* 22 (Spring 1998): 155–76.

16. Dean, *Imperial Brotherhood*, 32; Kennedy cited in William Appleman William, ed., *America in Vietnam: A Documentary History* (New York: W. W. Norton, 1989), 190; Eisenhower cited in Michael Beschloss, *The Crisis Years: Kennedy and Khrushchev, 1960–1963* (New York: Edward Burlingame, 1991), 396; Kennedy cited in Arthur Schlesinger Jr., *Journals, 1952–2000* (New York: Penguin Press, 2007), 152.

17. Shibusawa, *America's Geisha Ally*, 4–5, 57.

18. Foreign Service officials cited in William Prochnau, *Once upon a Distant War* (New York: Vintage, 1995), 102–3; Memorandum of Conversation, January 13, 1958, Bureau of Far Eastern Affairs, Office of Southeast Asian Affairs, Laos Files, 1956–61, box 1, RG 59.

19. Joseph M. Henning, *Outposts of Civilization: Race, Religion, and the Formative Years of American-Japanese Relations* (New York: NYU Press, 2000); Interview: William Sebald, July 22, 1965, John Foster Dulles Oral History Project, Seeley Mudd Library, Princeton University, Princeton, NJ; Matt J. Menger, *Slowly Climbs the Sun* (New York: Twin Circle Publishing, 1973), 221.

20. The best studies of modernization theory's impact on U.S. relations with the developing world are David Ekbladh, *The Great American Mission: Modernization and the Construction of an American World Order* (Princeton, NJ: Princeton University Press, 2010); Nils Gilman, *Mandarins of the Future: Modernization Theory in Cold War America* (Baltimore: Johns Hopkins University Press, 2003); Michael E. Latham, *Modernization as Ideology: American Social Science and "Nation Building" in the Kennedy Era* (Chapel Hill: University of North Carolina Press, 2000); Latham, *The Right Kind of Revolution: Modernization, Development, and U.S. Foreign Policy from the Cold War to the Present* (Ithaca, NY: Cornell University Press, 2011).

21. Race, as Linda Gordon remarks, is "a strong, hot idea," and works exploring its influence on U.S. policy number in the dozens (at least). For noteworthy recent studies see Thomas Borstelmann, *The Cold War and the Color Line: American Race Relations in the Global Arena* (Cambridge, MA: Harvard University Press, 2001); Mary Dudziak, *Cold War Civil Rights: Race and the Image of American Democracy* (Princeton, NJ: Princeton University Press, 2001); Paul A. Kramer, *The Blood of Government: Race, Empire, the United States, and the Philippines* (Chapel Hill: University of North Carolina Press, 2006); Eric T. Love, *Race over Empire: Racism and U.S. Imperialism* (Chapel Hill: University of North Carolina Press, 2004). See also Linda Gordon, *The Great Arizona Orphan Abduction* (Cambridge, MA: Harvard University Press, 1999), 99.

22. Transcript of Conversation between Joel Halpern (hereafter JH) and A. M. Halpern, August 24, 1959, Joel Halpern Papers, Archives and Manuscripts Department, University Library, University of Massachusetts, Amherst (hereafter JHP).

23. Interview: Christian Chapman, 1990, Library of Congress Homepage, American Memory Series, Frontline Diplomacy: The Foreign Affairs Oral History Collection of the Association for Diplomatic Studies and Training, http://www.loc.gov/homepage/lchp.html (hereafter FAOHC); Arthur Edson, "Land of Gentle, Courteous People," *Washington Post*, August 27, 1959; Memorandum for Secretary of Defense, January 23, 1961, National Security Files, Countries, box 130, JFKL; Tucker to CINCPAC, May 16, 1962, President's Office Files, Countries, box 121, JFKL;

CIA Report, September 20, 1960, White House Office, Office of the Staff Secretary, Records, 1952–61, International Series, box 10, RG 59; CIA Report, November 16, 1960, White House Office, Office of the Staff Secretary, Records, 1952–61, International Series, box 11, RG 59; "New U.S. Look at Laos Is Indicated," *New York National Observer,* June 3, 1962; "Laos as Pawn," *Washington Post,* May 2, 1961; "Laos Down the Drain?" *Washington Post,* April 28, 1961; Spinks to Cumming, January 21, 1961, Bureau of Far Eastern Affairs, Office of Southeast Asian Affairs, Laos Files, 1956–61, box 14, RG 59; "President Warns of Our Peril in Laos," *Life* 51 (March 31, 1961): 19.

24. Ang Cheng Guan, "Southeast Asian Perceptions of the Domino Theory," in *Connecting Histories: Decolonization and the Cold War in Southeast Asia, 1945–1962,* ed. Christopher E. Goscha and Christian F. Ostermann (Stanford, CA: Stanford University Press, 2009), 324–25; Ang, *Vietnamese Communists' Relations with China and the Second Indochina Conflict, 1956–1962* (Jefferson, NC: McFarland, 1997), 175–76, 196; MacAlister Brown and Joseph J. Zasloff, *Apprentice Revolutionaries: The Communist Movement in Laos, 1930–1985* (Stanford, CA: Hoover Institution Press, 1986), 64–67, 74; Ilya V. Gaiduk, *Confronting Vietnam: Soviet Policy toward the Indochina Conflict, 1954–1963* (Washington, DC: Woodrow Wilson Center Press, 2003), 166; Paul F. Langer and Joseph J. Zasloff, *North Vietnam and the Pathet Lao: Partners in the Struggle for Laos* (Cambridge, MA: Harvard University Press, 1970), 67–70, 89; Qiang Zhai, *China and the Vietnam Wars, 1950–1975* (Chapel Hill: University of North Carolina Press, 2000), 107.

25. Zhou cited in Gaiduk, *Confronting Vietnam,* 127. See also Ang, *Vietnamese Communists' Relations,* 55, 60–62, 170, 232–33; Chen Jian, *Mao's China and the Cold War* (Chapel Hill: University of North Carolina Press, 2001), 141–42; Qiang, *China and the Vietnam Wars,* 93–105, 111.

26. Khrushchev cited in Gaiduk, *Confronting Vietnam,* 122. See also Aleksandr Fursenko and Timothy Naftali, *Khrushchev's Cold War: The Inside Story of an American Adversary* (New York: W. W. Norton, 2006), 323–34; Lorenz M. Luthi, *The Sino-Soviet Split: Cold War in the Communist World* (Princeton, NJ: Princeton University Press, 2008), 197–98.

27. Khrushchev cited in Fursenko and Naftali, *Khrushchev's Cold War,* 521.

28. Unpublished Parsons Manuscript: "Leo the Lao," J. Graham Parsons Papers, Special Collections, Lauinger Library, Georgetown University, Washington, DC (hereafter JGPP), box 12.

29. Norman Cousins, "Report from Laos," *Saturday Review,* February 18, 1961. For Laos's unprotectedness see Timothy N. Castle, *At War in the Shadow of Vietnam: U.S. Military Aid to the Royal Lao Government, 1955–1975* (New York: Columbia University Press, 1993), 3–4; Arthur J. Dommen, *Conflict in Laos: The Politics of Neutralization* (New York: Praeger, 1971), 58–60; Grant Evans, *A Short History of Laos: The Land In Between* (Crows Nest, NSW: Allan & Unwin, 2002), ix; Fall, *Anatomy of a Crisis,* 208–10; David K. Hall, "The Laos Neutralization Agreement," in *U.S.-Soviet Security Cooperation,* ed. Alexander L. George, Philip J. Farley, and Alexander Dallin (New York: Oxford University Press, 1988), 435.

30. Resident cited in Voran to Cool, June 29, 1959, USOM Laos, Office of the Mission Director, Director's Subject Files, 1955–60, box 2, Record Group 469, Records of the U.S. Foreign Assistance Agencies, 1948–61 (hereafter RG 469).

31. David Halberstam, *The Powers That Be* (New York: Alfred A. Knopf, 1979), 58; William A. Dorman and Mansour Farhang, *The U.S. Press and Iran: Foreign Policy and the Journalism of Deference* (Berkeley and Los Angeles: University of California Press, 1987), 2, 19 (emphasis in the original). See Michelle Mart, *Eye on Israel: How America Came to View Israel as an Ally* (Albany: SUNY Press, 2006); Edward W. Said, *Covering Islam: How the Media and the Experts Determine How We See the Rest of the World* (New York: Vintage Books, 1997); Marda Dunsky, *Pens and Swords: How the American Mainstream Media Report the Israeli-Palestinian Conflict* (New York: Columbia University Press, 2008); Heiss, "Real Men Don't Wear Pajamas"; John Foran, "Discursive Subversions: *Time* Magazine, the CIA Overthrow of Musaddiq, and the Installation of the Shah," in *Cold War Constructions: The Political Culture of United States Imperialism, 1945–1966,* ed. Christian Appy (Amherst: University of Massachusetts Press, 2000), 157–82. Dated but useful works

include Douglass Cater, *The Fourth Branch of Government* (New York: Vintage Books, 1959); Bernard Cohen, *The Press and Foreign Policy* (Berkeley: University of California Press, 1963).

32. "Dreary Outlook in Laos," *Washington News*, January 31, 1962.

## 1. "A Long Country Inhabited by Lotus Eaters"

1. Panh cited in Evans, *Short History of Laos*, 94.

2. The President's News Conference of July 21, 1954, *Public Papers of the Presidents of the United States, Dwight D. Eisenhower, 1954* (Washington, DC: Government Printing Office, 1960), 642.

3. McClintock, "A U.S. Policy for Post-Armistice Indochina," August 12, 1954, Records of the Policy Planning Staff—1954, Lot 65D101, box 86, RG 59.

4. Brown to Rusk, January 20, 1961, Bureau of Far Eastern Affairs, Office of Southeast Asian Affairs, Laos Files, 1956–61, box 14, RG 59; Walter Judd, "Review of American Policy in Asia," Transcript of Conference, June 1, 1956, American Friends of Vietnam Papers, Vietnam Archive, Texas Tech University, Lubbock, Texas, box 4; Chargé at Saigon to Department of State, June 19, 1954, *FRUS* 1952–54 (Washington, DC: Government Printing Office, 1982), 13:1721–22; Chargé at Saigon to Department of State, June 24, 1954, ibid., 13:1734–41.

5. International Cooperation Administration—Evaluation of Laos Program, April 15, 1958, USOM Laos, Office of the Mission Director, Director's Subject Files, 1955–60, box 2, RG 469.

6. The synopsis offered here draws principally from *Laos: War and Revolution*, ed. Nina Adams and Alfred McCoy (New York: Harper & Row, 1970); Arthur Dommen, *The Indochinese Experience of the French and the Americans: Nationalism and Communism in Cambodia, Laos, and Vietnam* (Bloomington: Indiana University Press, 2001); Dommen, *Conflict in Laos;* Evans, *Short History of Laos;* Fall, *Anatomy of a Crisis;* Geoffrey Charles Gunn, *Political Struggles in Laos, 1930–1954* (Bangkok: Duang Kamol, 1988); M. L. Manich, *History of Laos* (Bangkok: Watchrin Publishing, 1994); Andrea Matles Savada, ed., *Laos: A Country Study*, 3rd. ed. (Washington, DC: Library of Congress, Federal Research Division, 1994); Peter Simms and Sanda Simms, *The Kingdoms of Laos: Six Hundred Years of History* (Surrey: Curzon Press, 1999); Martin Stuart-Fox, *A History of Laos* (Cambridge: Cambridge University Press, 1997); Hugh Toye, *Laos: Buffer State or Battleground* (New York: Oxford University Press, 1968).

7. Saveng cited in Simms and Simms, *Kingdoms of Laos*, 145.

8. Stuart-Fox, *History of Laos*, 22; Kenneth Conboy, *Shadow War: The CIA's Secret War in Laos* (Boulder, CO: Paladin Press, 1995), viii.

9. Sisavang cited in Evans, *Short History of Laos*, 82.

10. Sisouk Na Champassak, *Storm over Laos: A Contemporary History* (New York: Frederick A. Praeger, 1961), 11.

11. Convention cited in Fall, *Anatomy of a Crisis*, 43.

12. Phoui cited in Stuart-Fox, *History of Laos*, 85.

13. Phoui cited in Dommen, *Indochinese Experience*, 259.

14. Anthem cited in James Eddy, "The Neutralization of Laos, 1959–1962: A Case Study in the Application of a Theory of Equilibrium" (Ph.D. diss., University of Oklahoma, 1971), 119.

15. Loren Baritz, *Backfire: A History of How American Culture Led Us into Vietnam and Made Us Fight the Way We Did* (New York: Ballantine, 1985), 13.

16. Virginia Thompson, *French Indo-China* (New York: Macmillan, 1937), 323, 333, 263, 43, 375–80; Bradley, *Imagining Vietnam*, 47.

17. Norman Lewis, *A Dragon Apparent: Travels in Cambodia, Laos, and Vietnam* (New York: Hippocrene, 1951), 249, 18, 194, 27, 204, 284, 291, 254, 152.

18. Alan Houghton Brodrick, *Little Vehicle: Cambodia and Laos* (New York: Hutchinson & Co., 1950), 101; Harold Coolidge and Theodore Roosevelt, *Three Kingdoms of Indo-China* (New

York: Thomas Crowell, 1933), 188; Harry Franck, *East of Siam* (New York: Grosset and Dunlap, 1926), 288, 327, 343, 344, 304; Brodrick, *Little Vehicle*, 106, 111, 101.

19.  Bernard Newman, *Report from Indo-China* (London: Robert Hale, 1953), 140–41, 146–47. For similar assessments of the Lao in pre–Geneva Conference English-language monographs see Helen Churchill Candee, *New Journeys in Old Asia* (New York: Frederick A. Stokes, 1927), 33, 78; Roland Dorgeles, *On the Mandarin Road*, trans. Gertrude Emerson (New York: Century Co., 1926), 261–329; Thomas Ennis, *French Policy and Developments in Indochina* (Chicago: University of Chicago Press, 1936), 1, 130; Mona Gardner, *The Menacing Sun* (New York: Harcourt, Brace, 1939), 40–41, 81; E. F. Irwin, *With Christ in Indo-China* (Harrisburg, PA: Christian Publications, 1938), 7–8; Sidney Legendre, *Land of the White Parasol and the Million Elephants* (New York: Dodd, Mead & Co., 1936), 171, 188; Max Relton, *A Man in the East* (London: Michael Joseph Ltd., 1939), 138–39; Josephine Hope Westervelt, *The Green Gods* (New York: Christian Alliance Publishing Co., 1927), 102; Woodrow Wyatt, *Southwards from China* (London: Hodder & Stoughton, 1952), 126.

20.  Maynard Owen Williams, "By Motor Trail across French Indo-China," *National Geographic* 68 (October 1935): 487–534; W. Robert Moore, "Strife-torn Indochina," *National Geographic* 98 (October 1950): 499–510; W. Robert Moore and Maynard Owen Williams, "Portrait of Indochina," *National Geographic* 99 (April 1951): 461–90.

21.  George Long, "Indochina Faces the Dragon," *National Geographic* 102 (September 1952): 279–328.

22.  Peggy Durdin, "Laos: Paradise on the Edge of War," *New York Times*, April 4, 1954; Tillman Durdin, "Role with French Pleases Laotians," *New York Times*, June 19, 1954; Durdin, "French Making Gains in Indo-China Struggle," *New York Times*, June 22, 1954; Joseph and Stewart Alsop, "Loss of Laos Could Be Crucial," *Washington Post*, April 26, 1953; Quentin Pope, "Luang Prabang Gets Ready to Meet Viet Minh," *Chicago Tribune*, March 29, 1954.

23.  Press Release: Statement by the Secretary of State, July 23, 1954, John Foster Dulles Papers, Seeley Mudd Library, Princeton University, Princeton, NJ (hereafter JFDP), box 82; Review of U.S. Policy in the Far East, August 20, 1954, *United States–Vietnam Relations* (Washington, DC: Government Printing Office, 1971), 10:731–41; Smith cited in Editorial Note, *FRUS* 1952–54, 13:1860.

24.  Manila Pact cited in Anderson, *Trapped by Success*, 71; Dulles cited in Lloyd Gardner, *Approaching Vietnam: From World War II through Dien Bien Phu* (New York: W. W. Norton, 1988), 323.

25.  Nhou cited in Len Ackland, "No Place for Neutralism: The Eisenhower Administration and Laos," in Adams and McCoy, *Laos: War and Revolution*, 142.

26.  Geneva Accords cited in Castle, *At War in the Shadow of Vietnam*, 16; Ambassador in Saigon to Secretary of State, July 27, 1954, *FRUS* 1952–54, 13:1882.

27.  Department officials cited in George Christopher Eliades II, "United States Decision-Making in Laos, 1942–1962" (Ph.D. diss., Harvard University, 1999), 172–73; Fall, *Anatomy of a Crisis*, 167; Dommen, *Indochinese Experience*, 324.

28.  Memorandum of Discussion at the 141st Meeting of the National Security Council, April 18, 1953, *FRUS* 1952–54, 13:519; Memorandum of Conversation at the 179th Meeting of the National Security Council, January 8, 1954, ibid., 13:949; Eisenhower cited in Anderson, *Trapped by Success*, 71.

29.  Memorandum from Joint Chiefs of Staff to Secretary of Defense, September 22, 1954, *FRUS* 1952–54, 13:2091; Memorandum of Conversation at the 219th Meeting of the National Security Council, September 24, 1954, ibid., 13:2185.

30.  Yost cited in Eliades, "United States Decision-Making," 155; Memorandum from Joint Chiefs of Staff to Secretary of Defense, January 21, 1955, *FRUS* 1955–57, 21:585–87.

31.  Dulles cited in Martin Goldstein, *American Policy toward Laos* (Rutherford, NJ: Farleigh Dickinson University Press, 1973), 97; white paper cited in Robert McMahon, "Introduction," *Empire and Revolution*, 5; Robertson Testimony, March 18, 1959, *United States Aid Operations in Laos* (Washington, DC: Government Printing Office, 1959), 184; Robertson: Talking Points with

Savang, September 21, 1956, Records of the Office of Southeast Asian Affairs (Laos and Economic), 1950–58, Subject File, box 1, RG 59.

32. Robertson cited in Dommen, *Conflict in Laos,* 269; Anthony Eden, *Full Circle* (Boston: Houghton Mifflin, 1960), 126.

33. Parsons to Secretary, n.d., Bureau of Far Eastern Affairs, Office of Southeast Asian Affairs, Laos Files, 1956–61, box 15, RG 59.

34. Legation in Laos to Department of State, May 3, 1955, *FRUS* 1955–57, 21:641; Legation in Laos to Department of State, January 21, 1955, ibid., 21:588; Legation in Laos to Department of State, May 3, 1955, ibid., 21:641–42; Legation in Laos to Department of State, January 29, 1955, ibid., 21:595–96.

35. Department of State to Embassy in Laos, June 9, 1956, *FRUS* 1955–57, 21:774–75; Dulles to American Embassy, Saigon, January 8, 1955, White House Office, National Security Council Staff (Papers, 1948–61), OCB Central File, box 38, EL; Young to Robertson, September 4, 1956, Records of the Office of Southeast Asian Affairs (Laos and Economic), 1950–58, Subject File, box 1, RG 59.

## 2. "A Soft Buffer"

1. For Taipei Chiefs of Mission Conference: General U.S. Government Attitudes and Actions, March 7, 1958, Bureau of Far Eastern Affairs, Office of Southeast Asian Affairs, Laos Files, 1956–61, box 1, RG 59; Notes on Reappraisal of U.S. Policy toward Laos, November 11, 1957, ibid.

2. Interview: John Dean, January 7, 1970, Charles Stevenson Collection, Washington, DC (hereafter CSC); Dommen, *Conflict in Laos,* 103–4.

3. Memorandum of Conversation, November 27, 1959, Bureau of Far Eastern Affairs, Office of Southeast Asian Affairs, Laos Files, 1956–61, box 11, RG 59; Parsons Assessment of Current Lao Situation, September 15, 1958, White House Office, Office of the Special Assistant for National Security Affairs, Records, 1952–61, OCB Series, Subject Subseries, box 6, EL; Legation in Laos to Department of State, February 14, 1955, *FRUS* 1955–57, 21:604–5; Minister in Laos to Director of Office of Philippine and Southeast Asian Affairs, June 4, 1955, ibid., 21:660; Embassy in Laos to Department of State, November 8, 1956, ibid., 21:836; Blanké to Parsons, June 11, 1956, Department of State Central Files (hereafter DSCF), 751J.00/6-1156; Embassy in Laos to Department of State, August 23, 1956, *FRUS* 1955–57, 21:802.

4. Eisenhower cited in Editorial Note, *FRUS* 1958–60 (Washington, DC: Government Printing Office, 1992), 16:450.

5. Yost to Stevenson, November 6, 1969, CSC; relief worker cited in Oden Meeker, *The Little World of Laos* (New York: Charles Scribner's Sons, 1959), 214.

6. Program Evaluation—Laos, October 12, 1956, JGPP, box 12; Parsons Manuscript: "Not Shangri-la," JGPP, box 13; Eliades, "United States Decision-Making," 174.

7. Yost to Elbrick, November 9, 1955, Charles Yost Papers, Seeley Mudd Library, Princeton University, Princeton, NJ (hereafter CYP), box 5; Dulles cited in Arthur M. Schlesinger, *A Thousand Days: John F. Kennedy in the White House* (Boston: Houghton Mifflin, 1965), 324; Memorandum to Special Adviser, June 3, 1954, *FRUS* 1952–54, 16:1024–26; National Intelligence Estimate, November 23, 1954, *FRUS* 1952–54, 13:2298–99; Minister in Laos to Department of State, December 28, 1954, ibid., 13:2432.

8. Evans, *Short History of Laos,* 100; Progress Report, May 25, 1955, White House Office, Office of the Special Assistant for National Security Affairs, Records, 1952–61, NSC Series, Policy Papers Subseries, box 9, EL.

9. Robertson Testimony, March 18, 1959, *United States Aid Operations in Laos,* 191; Legation in Laos to Department of State, December 3, 1954, *FRUS* 1952–54, 13:2336–37.

10. Legation in Laos to Department of State, March 15, 1955, *FRUS* 1955–57, 21:625–27.

11. Eisenhower to Churchill, March 29, 1955, *The Churchill-Eisenhower Correspondence, 1953–1955,* ed. Peter Boyle (Chapel Hill: University of North Carolina Press, 1990), 204–6; Churchill cited in footnote 1, *FRUS* 1955–57, 21:633.

12. Footnote 4, *FRUS* 1955–57, 21:589; Memorandum of Conversation, February 27, 1955, ibid., 21:615–16; Memorandum of Conversation, February 27, 1955, ibid., 21:610–12.

13. Eliades, "United States Decision-Making," 175–76.

14. Yost to Dulles, December 13, 1954, CYP, box 7.

15. Souvanna cited in Dommen, *Indochinese Experience,* 326.

16. Biographic Report, February 1955, Records of the Office of Southeast Asian Affairs (Laos and Economic), 1950–58, Subject File, box 1, RG 59; Embassy in Vietnam to Department of State, February 26, 1954, *FRUS* 1952–54, 13:1078; Legation in Laos to Department of State, October 8, 1954, ibid., 13:2120; Department of State to Embassy in Laos, May 31, 1955, *FRUS* 1955–57, 21:765–66; Embassy in Laos to Department of State, March 31, 1956, ibid., 21:748.

17. Souvanna cited in Dommen, *Indochinese Experience,* 327.

18. Young to Robertson, September 4, 1956, Records of the Office of Southeast Asian Affairs (Laos and Economic), 1950–58, Subject File, box 1, RG 59; Dulles cited in Goldstein, *American Policy toward Laos,* 124.

19. Embassy in Laos to Department of State, March 31, 1956, *FRUS* 1955–57, 21:748.

20. Parsons to Bonbright, March 27, 1956, JGPP, box 2; "Not Shangri-la," JGPP, box 13; Robertson to Parsons, September 17, 1956, JGPP, box 2.

21. Parsons to Cleveland, September 18, 1956, JGPP, box 2; Briggs to Parsons, December 20, 1956; Parsons to Beech, October 24, 1956, ibid.; "Not Shangri-la," JGPP, box 13.

22. Embassy in Laos to Department of State, August 1, 1956, *FRUS* 1955–57, 21:779–81.

23. "Not Shangri-la," JGPP, box 13; Parsons Manuscript: "Three Tragedies," ibid.; Undated Speech: "Decade of Fulfillment," JGPP, box 11.

24. Robertson to Hoover, June 7, 1956, Bureau of Far Eastern Affairs, Office of Southeast Asian Affairs, Laos Files, 1956–61, box 1, RG 59.

25. Embassy in Laos to Department of State, May 29, 1956, *FRUS* 1955–57, 21:763–65; Blanké to Parsons, July 8, 1956, JGPP, box 2; Embassy in Laos to Department of State, August 6, 1956, *FRUS* 1955–57, 21:783–86; Department of State to Embassy in Laos, August 15, 1956, ibid., 21:791–92.

26. Champassak, *Storm over Laos,* 49. For Souvanna's negotiations with the Chinese and North Vietnamese see Fall, *Anatomy of a Crisis,* 72–74.

27. Department of State to Embassy in Laos, August 29, 1956, *FRUS* 1955–57, 21:803–5; Director of the Office of Southeast Asian Affairs to Assistant Secretary of State for Far Eastern Affairs, September 4, 1956, ibid., 21:805–10; Dispatch from Beijing, August 31, 1956, Bureau of Far Eastern Affairs, Office of Southeast Asian Affairs, Laos Files, 1956–61, box 1, RG 59.

28. Department of State to Embassy in Laos, August 29, 1956, *FRUS* 1955–57, 21:803; Department of State to Embassy in Laos, October 16, 1956, ibid., 21:827.

29. Perry Stieglitz, *In a Little Kingdom* (Armonk, NY: M. E. Sharpe, 1990), 33; Interview: Christian Chapman, 1990, FAOHC; "Not Shangri-la," JGPP, box 13.

30. "Not Shangri-la," JGPP, box 13; Oral History Interview, August 22, 1969, JGPP, box 12; Blanké, "Oh Souvanna," undated, JGPP, box 2.

31. Stieglitz, *In a Little Kingdom,* 33; Souvanna cited in Dommen, *Indochinese Experience,* 330.

32. For analysis of the furies unleashed by the artificially high value of the kip see Stevenson, *End of Nowhere,* 48–58.

33. "Three Tragedies," JGPP, box 13.

34. Robertson to Acting Secretary, September 18, 1956, Records of the Office of Southeast Asian Affairs (Laos and Economic), 1950–58, Subject File, box 1, RG 59; Memorandum of

Conversation, September 24, 1956, ibid.; Department of State to Embassy in Laos, November 8, 1956, *FRUS* 1955–57, 21:836.

35. Embassy in Laos to Department of State, November 20, 1956, *FRUS* 1955–57, 21:840–42.

36. Nhou cited in Embassy in Laos to Department of State, November 21, 1956, *FRUS* 1955–57, 21:843; Acting Director of Office of Southeast Asian Affairs to Deputy Assistant Secretary of State for Far Eastern Affairs, November 26, 1956, ibid., 21:847–48; Marek Thee, *Notes of a Witness: Laos and the Second Indochinese War* (New York: Vintage, 1973), 45; Robertson to Dooley, December 4, 1956, Bureau of Far Eastern Affairs, Office of Southeast Asian Affairs, Laos Files, 1956–61, box 14, RG 59.

37. "Not Shangri-la," JGPP, box 13; "Three Tragedies," ibid.

38. Embassy in Laos to Department of State, December 11, 1956, *FRUS* 1955–57, 21:858; Acting Director of the Office of Southeast Asian Affairs to Deputy Assistant Secretary of State for Far Eastern Affairs, November 26, 1956, ibid., 21:847; Kocher to Parsons, November 27, 1956, Bureau of Far Eastern Affairs, Office of Southeast Asian Affairs, Laos Files, 1956–61, box 1, RG 59.

39. Embassy in Laos to Department of State, December 11, 1956, *FRUS* 1955–57, 21:859; Kocher to Robertson, December 29, 1956, DSCF, 751 J/12-2956, RG 59; Memorandum of Conversation, December 7, 1956, Records of the Office of Southeast Asian Affairs (Laos and Economic), 1950–58, Subject File, box 1, RG 59.

40. For standard treatments of the New Look see Stephen E. Ambrose, *Eisenhower,* vol. 2, *The President* (New York: Simon & Schuster, 1984), 171–73, 224–26; Robert A. Divine, *Eisenhower and the Cold War* (New York: Oxford University Press, 1981), 37–39.

41. Embassy in Laos to Department of State, November 24, 1956, *FRUS* 1955–57, 21:846.

42. Embassy in Laos to Department of State, December 29, 1956, *FRUS* 1955–57, 21:868–69; Department of State to Embassy in Laos, January 3, 1957, ibid., 21:870–71.

43. Wilfred Burchett, *Mekong Upstream: A Visit to Laos and Cambodia* (Berlin: Seven Seas Publishers, 1959), 280–82; Souphanouvong cited in Champassak, *Storm over Laos,* 54; embassy cited in Dommen, *Indochinese Experience,* 333.

44. Department of State to Embassy in Laos, May 25, 1957, *FRUS* 1955–57, 21:916.

45. Assembly deliberations cited in Dommen, *Indochinese Experience,* 334.

46. Parsons cited in Editorial Note, *FRUS* 1955–57, 21:922; Embassy in Laos to Department of State, June 3, 1957, ibid., 21:926; Department of State to Embassy in Laos, May 25, 1957, ibid., 21:920; Katay cited in Sedgwick to Kocher, December 10, 1956, Bureau of Far Eastern Affairs, Office of Southeast Asian Affairs, Laos Files, 1956–61, box 1, RG 59; Embassy in France to Department of State, May 25, 1957, *FRUS* 1955–57, 21:918; Embassy in Laos to Department of State, June 3, 1957, ibid., 21:925.

47. For this musical-chairs episode see Fall, *Anatomy of a Crisis,* 75–78.

48. State cited in Stevenson, *End of Nowhere,* 47.

49. Robertson to Dulles, January 11, 1958, Eisenhower, Dwight D., Records as President, White House Central Files, Confidential File, 1953–61, box 75, EL; footnote 2, *FRUS* 1955–57, 21:1062.

50. Robertson to Dulles, November 18, 1957, Bureau of Far Eastern Affairs, Office of Southeast Asian Affairs, Laos Files, 1956–61, box 1, RG 59; Byrne to Dulles, January 11, 1958, ibid.

51. Embassy in Laos to Department of State, December 28, 1957, *FRUS* 1955–57, 21:1062–63; "Not Shangri-la," JGPP, box 13.

52. Memorandum of Conversation, January 13, 1958, Bureau of Far Eastern Affairs, Office of Southeast Asian Affairs, Laos Files, 1956–61, box 1, RG 59.

53. Memorandum of Conversation, January 14, 1958, Eisenhower, Dwight D., Papers as President, 1953–61, Ann Whitman File, International Series, box 37, EL; Memoranda of Conversations, January 14, 1958, Bureau of Far Eastern Affairs, Office of Southeast Asian Affairs, Laos

Files, 1956–61, box 1, RG 59; Editorial Note, *FRUS* 1958–60, 16:419–21; Dommen, *Indochinese Experience,* 370.

54. Memorandum of Conversation, Department of State, January 13, 1958, *FRUS* 1958–60, 16:417; Memorandum of Conversation, January 14, 1958, Bureau of Far Eastern Affairs, Office of Southeast Asian Affairs, Laos Files, 1956–61, box 1, RG 59.

55. Robertson to Dulles, January 11, 1958, Eisenhower, Dwight D., Records as President, White House Central Files, Confidential File, 1953–61, box 76, EL; Memorandum of Conversation, January 15, 1958, *FRUS* 1958–60, 16:422.

56. Draft Communiqué, January 15, 1958, Eisenhower, Dwight D., Records as President, White House Central Files, Confidential File, 1953–61, box 76, EL; Dulles Toast, January 15, 1958, Bureau of Far Eastern Affairs, Office of Southeast Asian Affairs, Laos Files, 1956–61, box 1, RG 59.

57. International Cooperation Administration: Evaluation of Laos Program, April 15, 1958, USOM Laos, Office of the Mission Director, Director's Subject Files, 1955–60, box 2, RG 469; Director of the Office of Southeast Asian Affairs to Assistant Secretary of State for Far Eastern Affairs, May 5, 1958, *FRUS* 1958–60, 16:438–39. My account of the 1958 elections draws principally from Champassak, *Storm over Laos,* 61–64; Eliades, "United States Decision-Making," 198–207; and Fall, *Anatomy of a Crisis,* 83–89. Statistics are from Eliades.

58. Robertson Position Paper, January 6, 1958, Bureau of Far Eastern Affairs, Office of Southeast Asian Affairs, Laos Files, 1956–61, box 1, RG 59; Chief of the Programs Evaluation Office, Laos, to Commander in Chief, Pacific, February 25, 1958, *FRUS* 1958–60, 16:430.

59. Commander in Chief, Pacific, to Chief, Programs Evaluation Office, Laos, February 13, 1958, *FRUS* 1958–60, 16:428; Editorial Note, ibid., 16:435.

60. Fall, *Anatomy of a Crisis,* 85; pamphlet cited in ibid., 86.

61. Interview: Don Ropa, May 15, 1969, CSC.

62. Parsons Statement, May 7, 1958, *Mutual Security Program in Laos* (Washington, DC: Government Printing Office, 1958), 34; Memorandum of Conversation, January 21, 1958, Bureau of Far Eastern Affairs, Office of Southeast Asian Affairs, Laos Files, 1956–61, box 5, RG 59.

63. Discussion at the 367th Meeting of the National Security Council, May 29, 1958, Eisenhower, Dwight D., Papers as President, 1953–61, Ann Whitman File, NSC Series, box 10, EL.

64. Souvanna cited in Robertson to Dulles, May 17, 1958, Bureau of Far Eastern Affairs, Office of Southeast Asian Affairs, Laos Files, 1956–61, box 5, RG 59.

65. Department of State to Embassy in Laos, May 15, 1958, *FRUS* 1958–60, 16:440; Operations Coordinating Board Report on Southeast Asia, May 28, 1958, White House Office, National Security Council Staff, Papers, 1948–61: Disaster File, box 55, EL; Parsons to Robertson, August 15, 1958, White House Office, Office of the Special Assistant for National Security Affairs, Records, 1952–61, OCB Series, Subject Subseries, box 6, EL.

## 3. "Help the Seemingly Unhelpable"

1. American Women's Club of Vientiane Newsletter, vol. 1, no. 17, August 1958, JHP.

2. United States Operations Mission to Laos, Roster of American Personnel, April 1, 1958, JHP.

3. Donna Alvah, *Unofficial Ambassadors: American Military Families Overseas and the Cold War, 1946–1965* (New York: NYU Press, 2007).

4. Rimer to JH, May 16, 1960, JHP; Barbara Kerewsky (hereafter BK) to "Folks," February 21, 1957, ibid.

5. Villager cited in Field Notes, June 19, 1959, JHP.

6. Representative cited in Stanley Karnow, "The Mess in Laos," *Life* 48 (January 13, 1961): 35.

7. Igor Oganesoff, "Living It Up in Laos," *Wall Street Journal,* April 9, 1958; Frederick Othman, "A State of Chaos in Laos," *Washington World Telegram,* May 15, 1958; Haynes Miller, "A Bulwark Built on Sand," *Reporter* 19 (November 13, 1958): 13.

8. JH to "Mom," October 13, 1957, JHP; JH to "Folks," May 8, 1957; JH to "Folks," May 25, 1957, ibid.

9. Miniclier to Stearns, November 16, 1956, JHP; Brown to Gartin, November 23, 1956, ibid.

10. BK to "Folks," January 26, 1957, JHP; BK to "Folks," January 31, 1957, ibid.

11. JH to "Folks," February 13, 1957, JHP.

12. BK to "Folks," February 15, 1957, JHP; BK to "Folks," May 22, 1957, ibid.

13. JH to "Folks," September 4, 1957, JHP; BK to "Folks," May 22, 1957; BK to "Folks," November 13, 1957, ibid.

14. JH to Arensberg, May 16, 1957, JHP; JH to "Folks," March 6, 1957, ibid.

15. JH to Dampf, October 4, 1957, JHP.

16. Functionary cited in Field Notes, June 27, 1957, JHP.

17. JH to "Dad," March 29, 1957, JHP; JH to "Folks," September 4, 1957; villagers cited in JH to Members of Visiting Evaluation Team, November 2, 1957, ibid.

18. JH to "Folks," September 4, 1957, JHP.

19. JH to "Folks," September 4, 1957, JHP; JH Report: Views of Prince Phetsarath on Various Subjects, n.d., USOM Laos, Office of the Mission Director, Director's Subject Files, 1955–60, box 1, RG 469.

20. JH to Miniclier, September 7, 1957, JHP; JH to "Folks," October 13, 1957, ibid.

21. JH to "Folks," October 4, 1957, JHP; JH to Smither, September 25, 1957; JH to "Folks," October 22, 1957, ibid.

22. William J. Lederer and Eugene Burdick, *The Ugly American* (New York: W. W. Norton, 1958), 205–31, 285. For the *Uncle Tom's Cabin* parallel see Renny Christopher, *The Vietnam War / The American War: Images and Representations in Euro-American and Vietnamese Exile Narratives* (Amherst: University of Massachusetts Press, 1995), 192; James T. Fisher, *Dr. America: The Lives of Thomas A. Dooley* (Amherst: University of Massachusetts Press, 1997), 175.

23. Lederer and Burdick, *Ugly American,* 174–88. For representative critiques see Dean, *Imperial Brotherhood,* 172–79; Christina Klein, *Cold War Orientalism: Asia in the Middlebrow Imagination, 1945–1961* (Berkeley and Los Angeles: University of California Press, 2003), 85–89; Jonathan Nashel, *Edward Lansdale's Cold War* (Amherst: University of Massachusetts Press, 2005), 173–86.

24. JH to "Folks," October 13, 1957, JHP; JH to "Folks," September 5, 1957; Field Notes, October 7, 1957, ibid.

25. JH to "Folks," March 8, 1957, JHP; JH to "Mom," October 13, 1957; JH to "Folks," October 22, 1957; JH to "Folks," October 4, 1957; JH to "Folks," July 10, 1957; Field Notes, August 2, 1957; JH to "Folks," August 15, 1957, ibid.

26. BK to "Folks," January 31, 1957, JHP; BK to "Friends," May 22, 1957, ibid.

27. BK to "Folks," February 21, 1957, JHP; BK to "Folks," May 22, 1957, ibid.

28. BK to "Folks," December 30, 1957, JHP; BK to "Folks," October 15, 1957; BK to "Friends," January 31, 1957; BK to "Friends," May 22, 1957; BK to "Folks," October 29, 1957, ibid.

29. BK to "Folks," March 26, 1957, JHP; BK to "Folks," July 23, 1957, ibid.

30. BK to "Folks," February 27, 1957, JHP; BK to "Folks," March 1, 1957; BK to "Folks," February 15, 1957; BK to "Folks," February 21, 1957; BK to "Folks," December 30, 1957; BK to "Folks," October 5, 1957, ibid.

31. BK to "Friends," May 22, 1957, JHP; BK to Annedorle, March 25, 1957, ibid.

32. Interview: Franklin Huffman, January 2006, FAOHC; Interview: Yale Richmond, June 2003; Interview: Leonard Bacon, 1990; Interview: Gerard Gert, 1988, ibid.

33. JH to "Folks," December 6, 1957, JHP; JH to "Folks," December 29, 1957; JH to Barney, February 12, 1959, ibid.

34. JH to Fall, October 17, 1958, JHP; JH to Dooley, October 12, 1959; JH to Droge, November 6, 1958, ibid.

35. Joel Halpern, "Economic Development and American Aid," Council on Economic and Cultural Affairs, 1958, JHP; Lavergne to JH, February 11, 1960; Burk to JH, February 19, 1959; Miniclier to Halpern, November 18, 1958; Corrigan to JH, February 12, 1959, ibid. See also Joel Halpern, "Economic Development and American Aid in Laos," *Practical Anthropology* 6 (July–August 1959): 151–71.

36. Parsons to JH, December 4, 1958, JHP.

37. JH to Parsons, April 20, 1959, JHP.

38. Souvanna cited in "Exiled Laos Chief Lays War to U.S.," *New York Times,* January 20, 1961.

39. Interview: Elden Erickson, 1992, FAOHC; Interview: Gilbert Sheinbaum, September 5, 1995; Interview: Christian Chapman, 1990, ibid.; Stieglitz, *Little Kingdom,* 33.

40. "Not Shangri-la," JGPP, box 13; Parsons Manuscript: "Foster Dulles Visits Laos," ibid.

41. Parsons to Roberts, February 20, 1957, JGPP, box 2; Parsons to Hollister, February 28, 1957, ibid.; Parsons Manuscript: "By Road to Luang Prabang," JGPP, box 13; "Not Shangri-la," ibid.

42. Parsons "Letter to the Family," February 11, 1966, JGPP, box 2; Parsons Manuscript: "Aid to Laos," JGPP, box 13; Embassy in Laos to Department of State, August 23, 1956, *FRUS* 1955–57, 21:801; Memorandum of Conversation, October 25, 1960, Bureau of Far Eastern Affairs, Office of Southeast Asian Affairs, Laos Files, 1956–61, box 11, RG 59; Parsons Manuscript: "Three Tragedies," JGPP, box 13; "Not Shangri-la," ibid.

43. Parsons to Cameron, February 20, 1957, JGPP, box 2; Parsons to Sandford, December 31, 1956; Parsons Briefing Notes for the Fairless Committee, January 27, 1957, ibid.; Oral History Interview, August 22, 1969, JGPP, box 12; Parsons Manuscript: "The Far Eastern Bureau," ibid.; "Not Shangri-la," JGPP, box 13; Parsons Manuscript: "Grand Tour of Vientiane," ibid.

44. Parsons Manuscript: "The Great Mango Caper," JGPP, box 13.

45. "Aid to Laos," JGPP, box 13.

46. "Welcome to Vientiane" Brochure, November 1956, JGPP, box 2.

47. JH to "Folks," March 25, 1957, JHP; Fall, *Anatomy of a Crisis,* 76.

48. 3349, *Iron Man of Laos: Prince Phetsarath Ratanavongsa* (Ithaca, NY: Department of Asian Studies, Cornell University, 1978), xi; JH, "Trip with the Prince," April 11, 1957, USOM Laos, Office of the Mission Director, Director's Subject Files, 1955–60, box 1, RG 469; "Interview with Tiao Phetsarath," *The Last Century of Lao Royalty: A Documentary History,* ed. Grant Evans (Chiang Mai: Silkworm, 2009), 123.

49. Memorandum of Conversation, May 29, 1957, Records of the Office of Southeast Asian Affairs (Laos and Economic), 1950–58, Subject File, box 1, RG 59.

50. "Interview with Tiao Phetsarath," 124.

51. Terminal Report, June 1, 1958, USOM Laos, Office of the Mission Director, Director's Subject Files, 1955–60, box 2, RG 469; Messegee to Smither, September 11, 1957, USOM Laos, Office of the Deputy Director, Subject Files, 1956–59, box 4, RG 469; USIS Country Plan for Laos, May 12, 1958, USOM Laos, Office of the Mission Director, Director's Subject Files, 1955–60, box 2, RG 469; Evaluation of Laos Program, April 15, 1958, ibid.

52. Oral History Interview, August 22, 1969, JGPP, box 12; "Not Shangri-la," JGPP, box 13. For examples of the "revisionist history" to which Parsons referred see David Halberstam, *The Best and the Brightest* (New York: Ballantine Books, 1969), 88, 189; Schlesinger, *Thousand Days,* 325, 327–28, 415–16.

53. Oganesoff, "Living It Up in Laos."

54. Oganesoff, "Living It Up in Laos," *Reader's Digest* 74 (August 1958): 41–45.

55. "Inaccuracies and Distortions," April 1958, Bureau of Far Eastern Affairs, Office of Southeast Asian Affairs, Laos Files, 1956–61, box 7, RG 59; Parsons to Wallace, July 25, 1958,

Records of the Office of Southeast Asian Affairs, 1950–58 (Laos and Economic), Subject File, box 1, RG 59; Parsons Statement, May 7, 1958, *Mutual Security Program in Laos,* 33–34.

56. Zablocki cited in "Congressman Sees 'Mess' in Foreign Aid to Laos," *Albany Argus,* May 14, 1958; Farbstein and Judd cited in *Mutual Security Program in Laos,* 44, 64; Zablocki cited in Washington AP Report, May 12, 1958, Bureau of Far Eastern Affairs, Office of Southeast Asian Affairs, Laos Files, 1956–61, box 7, RG 59.

57. Miller to Robbins, September 13, 1957, USOM Laos, Office of the Deputy Director, Subject Files, 1956–59, box 3, RG 469; Messegee to Miller, September 24, 1957, ibid.; report cited in *Seventh Report of the Committee on Government Operations: U.S. Aid Operations in Laos* (Washington, DC: Government Printing Office, 1959), 28; Miller Testimony, March 20, 1959, *United States Aid Operations in Laos,* 322.

58. Miller, "Bulwark Built on Sand," 11–16.

59. "Far Eastern Bureau," JGPP, box 12; Parsons, "Letter to the Family," February 11, 1966, JGPP, box 2; Kocher to Parsons, November 14, 1958, Bureau of Far Eastern Affairs, Office of Southeast Asian Affairs, Laos Files, 1956–61, box 7, RG 59; Horton to Smith, April 23, 1959, Bureau of Far Eastern Affairs, Office of Southeast Asian Affairs, Laos Files, 1956–61, box 4, RG 59.

60. "Obituary: Porter Hardy, 91," *New York Times,* April 23, 1995; Miller Testimony, March 20, 1959, *United States Aid Operations in Laos,* 322–23; Robbins Testimony, April 14, 1959, ibid., 558; *Seventh Report,* 3; McNamara Testimony, March 13 and April 16, 1959, *United States Aid Operations in Laos,* 84–140, 379–96, 511–17; Harkins Testimony, April 16, 1959, ibid., 652.

61. Parsons Testimony, March 18, 1959, *United States Aid Operations in Laos,* 191–94; Parsons Statement, March 19, 1959, ibid., 221.

62. *Seventh Report,* 3–4, 50, 2.

63. Robertson Testimony, March 18, 1959, *United States Aid Operations in Laos,* 182–84; Shuff Testimony, March 12, 1959, ibid., 79, 81–82; ibid., 184, 29.

64. Oland Russell, "What's Happened to Aid Sent to Laos?" *Washington News,* September 10, 1959; "Luxuries in Laos," *Wall Street Journal,* April 10, 1958; "Postscript from Laos," *Wall Street Journal,* November 14, 1958; "Laos: Scandal on the Mekong," *Time* 70 (November 4, 1957): 12; Greg MacGregor, "Laotian Capital City of Contrast," *New York Times,* February 10, 1958.

65. Raymond Moley, "The Most Important of Auditors," *Los Angeles Times,* November 25, 1958; Othman, "State of Chaos in Laos"; Robert C. Ruark, "Laos's Needs Are on the Earthy Side," *Washington Daily News,* September 22, 1959.

66. JH to Cleveland, October 15, 1959, JHP; Field Notes, June 13, 1959, ibid.

67. JH to BK, undated, JHP; Field Notes, June 17, 1959; Field Notes, June 13, 1959; JH to A. M. Halpern, June 14, 1959, ibid.

68. JH to A. M. Halpern, June 19, 1959, JHP; Tane cited in Field Notes, August 20, 1959; administrator cited in Field Notes, July 23, 1959; Bong cited in Field Notes, July 18, 1959, ibid.

69. Interpreter cited in Field Notes, June 20, 1959, JHP; Ouane cited in Field Notes, July 27, 1959; Field Notes, July 20, 1958; JH to A. M. Halpern, June 19, 1959; CDNI member cited in Field Notes, July 18, ibid.

70. Maha cited in Field Notes, July 4, 1959, JHP.

71. Student cited in Field Notes, July 8, 1959, JHP.

72. Joel Halpern, "America and Laos: Two Views of Political Strategy and Technical Assistance," Rand Corp., 1959, JHP.

73. Joel Halpern, "America and Laos" (Christiansburg, VA: Dalley Book Service, 1990); author interview with JH, July 6, 2009; Fall, *Anatomy of a Crisis,* 165.

## 4. "Foreigners Who Want to Enslave the Country"

1. My account of the battle of Vientiane draws from contemporary news coverage and from Mark Askew, William Logan, and Colin Long, *Vientiane: Transformations of a Lao Landscape*

(London: Routledge, 2007), 134–37; Mervyn Brown, *War in Shangri-La: A Memoir of Civil War in Laos* (London: Radcliffe Press, 2001), 56–72; Winthrop Brown, "Battle of Vientiane," in *The Foreign Service Reader,* ed. Daniel Oliver Newberry (New York: American Foreign Service Association, 1997), 64–67; Dommen, *Conflict in Laos,* 164–70; Michael Field, *The Prevailing Wind: Witness in Indochina* (London: Methuen, 1965), 102–8; Manich Jumsai, *Battle of Vientiane* (Bangkok: Chalermnit, 1961), 1–33. The thirty-to-one estimate comes from Desmond Meiring, *The Brinkman* (Boston: Houghton Mifflin, 1965), 329.

2. Quinim cited in Jacques Nevard, "Pro-Red Rejected by Laos Assembly," *New York Times,* December 13, 1960; Kong Le cited in Jumsai, *Battle of Vientiane,* 4, 8; CIA Situation Report, December 6, 1960, White House Office, Office of the Staff Secretary: Records, 1952–61, International Series, box 11, EL.

3. Brown to Parsons, December 13, 1960, *FRUS* 1958–60, 16: Microfiche Supplement (hereafter MS) Doc. 673.

4. Brown, *War in Shangri-La,* 65.

5. Kong Le cited in "U.S. Embassy Set Afire in Laos Shelling," *Chicago Tribune,* December 16, 1960; Field, *Prevailing Wind,* 104; Pote cited in Roy Essoyan, "Kong Le and 800 Men Retreat," *Washington Post,* December 20, 1960.

6. Jacques Nevard, "Pro-West Troops Mop Up Vientiane," *New York Times,* December 18, 1960.

7. Champassak, *Storm over Laos,* 168; Souvanna cited in "Exiled Laos Chief Lays War to U.S.," *New York Times,* January 20, 1961.

8. Special State-JCS Meeting on Laos, August 23, 1960, *FRUS* 1958–60, 16:MS Doc. 484.

9. RLG–Pathet Lao accord cited in Stevenson, *End of Nowhere,* 46; Souvanna cited in Field, *Prevailing Wind,* 23. My account of Souvanna's political maneuverings in late 1958 is based on Dommen, *Indochinese Experience,* 349–59, 371–73; Eliades, "United States Decision-Making," 214–18; Field, *Prevailing Wind,* 47–53.

10. Department of State to Embassy in Laos, May 27, 1958, *FRUS* 1958–60, 16:449; Department of State to Embassy in Laos, May 15, 1958, ibid., 16:440; *Lao Presse* cited in Chapman to Herter, June 19, 1958, DSCF, 751J.00/6-1958, RG 59.

11. Toye, *Laos,* 147.

12. CDNI platform cited in Evans, *Short History of Laos,* 111; Champassak, *Storm over Laos,* 63–64.

13. Interview: Robert Amory, March 10, 1969, CSC.

14. Brown, *War in Shangri-La,* 23; Wilfred Burchett, *The Furtive War: The United States in Vietnam and Laos* (New York: International Publishers, 1963), 172.

15. Smith to Herter, August 2, 1958, DSCF, 751J.00/8-258. RG 59; Embassy in Laos to Department of State, July 20, 1958, *FRUS* 1958–60, 16:462; Department of State to Embassy in Laos, August 6, 1958, ibid., 16:472–73.

16. Souvanna cited in "Laos Premier Resigns," *New York Times,* July 23, 1958.

17. Oral History Interview, August 22, 1969, JGPP, box 12; Phoui cited in Ackland, "No Place for Neutralism," 149. My account of Phoui's premiership draws upon Dommen, *Indochinese Experience,* 373–83; Field, *Prevailing Wind,* 54–63; Sisouk, *Storm over Laos,* 61–74.

18. Phoui cited in Mishra, *Contemporary History of Laos,* 43.

19. Dulles cited in Editorial Note, *FRUS* 1958–60, 16:474.

20. Phoui cited in Toye, *Laos,* 120; Nhu cited in Durbrow to Dulles, September 13, 1958, Bureau of East Asian and Pacific Affairs, Office of Laotian and Cambodian Affairs, Subject Files, 1961–75, box 14, RG 59.

21. The best account of this confusing episode is Dommen, *Conflict in Laos,* 114–16, and map on p. 339.

22. Phoui cited in Dommen, *Keystone of Indochina,* 59; Souphanouvong cited in Sisouk, *Storm over Laos,* 68.

23. Stuart-Fox, *History of Laos,* 105; Parsons to Murphy, January 29, 1959, DSCF, 751J.00/1-1959, RG 59.

24. My account of the 1958 RLA integration affair draws on Fall, *Anatomy of a Crisis,* 98–106; Fall, *Street without Joy: The French Debacle in Indochina* (Harrisburg, PA: Stackpole, 1964), 331–34; Sisouk, *Storm over Laos,* 75–84; Anna Louise Strong, *Cash and Violence in Laos and Vietnam* (New York: Mainstream Publishers, 1962), 53–57.

25. Ouane cited in "Laos Holdout Troops Give Up," *Washington Post,* May 19, 1959.

26. Sisouk, *Storm over Laos,* 78; Fall, *Anatomy of a Crisis,* 100.

27. Embassy in Laos to Department of State, June 3, 1959, *FRUS* 1958–60, 16:538–40; OCB Report on Southeast Asia, August 12, 1959, White House Office, National Security Council Staff, Papers, 1948–61, Disaster File, box 55, EL.

28. Director of the Office of Southeast Asian Affairs to Assistant Secretary of State for Far Eastern Affairs, December 29, 1958, *FRUS* 1958–60, 16:491; Interview: John Heintges, 1974, *Senior Officers Oral History Program, U.S. Army Military History Institute,* vol. 3 (Christiansburg, VA: Dalley Book Service, 1992), 495–99.

29. Dulles cited in Editorial Note, *FRUS* 1958–60, 16:499; Embassy in Laos to Department of State, March 25, 1959, ibid., 16:515.

30. Editorial Note, *FRUS* 1958–60, 16:544; Heintges cited in Eliades, "United States Decision-Making," 240.

31. Rod Paschall, "White Star in Laos," in *Pawns of War: Cambodia and Laos,* Arnold Isaacs et al. (Boston: Boston Publishing Co., 1987), 64.

32. Statement by Premier Phoui Sananikone, February 11, 1959, Bureau of Far Eastern Affairs, Office of Southeast Asian Affairs, Laos Files, 1956–61, box 2, RG 59; Heintges to Stevenson, June 17, 1969, CSC.

33. My account of the 1959 communist offensive and Washington's reaction is based on Joseph Lasch, *Dag Hammarskjöld: Custodian of the Brush-Fire Peace* (Garden City, NY: Doubleday, 1961), 140–44; George Lemmer, *The Laos Crisis of 1959* (Christiansburg, VA: Dalley Book Service, 1961), 34–50; Denis Warner, *The Last Confucian: Vietnam, Southeast Asia, and the West* (Baltimore: Penguin, 1964), 254–58; Warner, *Reporting South-East Asia* (Sydney: Angus & Robertson, 1966), 162–65.

34. Phoui cited in "Broader Fighting in Laos Reported," *New York Times,* August 1, 1959.

35. Joseph Alsop, "A New Invasion of Laos," *Washington Post,* September 2, 1959; Alsop, "Sam Neua," *Washington Post,* September 9, 1959; Phoui cited in Goldstein, *American Policy toward Laos,* 153.

36. Herter cited in Thomas Foley, "Herter Says Laos War Upsets U.S.," *Washington Post,* August 25, 1959; Stevenson, *End of Nowhere,* 76.

37. UN report cited in Kathleen Teltch, "U.N. Inquiry Finds No Certain Proof of Laos Invasion," *New York Times,* November 7, 1959.

38. Phoumi cited in Memorandum for the Record, November 6, 1959, *FRUS* 1958–60, 16:651; Ambassador in Laos to Assistant Secretary of State for Far Eastern Affairs, December 15, 1959, ibid., 16:690–95.

39. Interview: Charles Gentry, May 12, 1969, CSC; Interviews: Horace Smith, March 3, 1969, and April 19, 1971, ibid.; Memorandum for Deputy Director: Charges by Ambassador Smith against the Agency and the Recent Chief of Station, March 8, 1960, JGPP, box 4; Embassy in Laos to Department of State, November 30, 1959, *FRUS* 1958–60, 16:681.

40. Department of State to Embassy in Laos, December 19, 1959, *FRUS* 1958–60, 16:701; Embassy in Laos to Department of State, December 21, 1959, ibid., 16:702; Smith to Herter, December 22, 1959, DSCF, 751J.00/12-2259, RG 59; Memorandum of Conversation, December 23, 1959, *FRUS* 1958–60, 16:MS Doc. 328.

41. Embassy in Laos to Department of State, December 24, 1959, *FRUS* 1958–60, 16:714; Embassy in Laos to Department of State, December 25, 1959, ibid., 16:715.

42. For the December 1959 coup see Dommen, *Indochinese Experience,* 381–85; Stevenson, *End of Nowhere,* 84–87.

43. Interview: Charles Gentry, May 12, 1969, CSC; Interview: Horace Smith, March 8, 1969, ibid.; Memorandum: Audience of Western Chiefs of Mission with Savang Vatthana, January 4, 1960, *FRUS* 1958–60, 16:MS Doc. 353.

44. Dillon to Smith, January 7, 1960, *FRUS* 1958–60, 16:MS Doc. 352; Department of State to Embassy in Laos, January 28, 1960, *FRUS* 1958–60, 16:733. My account of the 1960 elections draws on Champassak, *Storm over Laos,* 139–49; Dommen, *Conflict in Laos,* 129–34; Fall, *Anatomy of a Crisis,* 181–83. Statistics are from Dommen and Fall.

45. Sisouk, *Storm over Laos,* 142.

46. Heintges to OSD/ISA, March 12, 1960, *FRUS* 1958–60, 16:MS Doc. 366; Heintges to Felt, March 23, 1960, ibid., 16:MS Doc. 370; Dommen, *Conflict in Laos,* 133–34.

47. Discussion at the 445th Meeting of the National Security Council, May 25, 1960, Eisenhower, Dwight D., Papers as President, 1953–61, Ann Whitman File, NSC Series, box 12, EL; Souphanouvong cited in Burchett, *Furtive War,* 183–84.

48. Smith to Herter, May 24, 1960, *FRUS* 1958–60, 16:MS Doc. 397; Smith to Herter, May 25, 1960, DSCF, 751J.00/5-2460, RG 59; USARMA Vientiane to Herter, May 24, 1960, *FRUS* 1958–60, 16:MS Doc. 399; Sisouk, *Storm over Laos,* 150.

49. American analysts cited in Keyes Beech, "How Uncle Sam Fumbled in Laos," *Saturday Evening Post* 277 (April 22, 1961): 89; Dommen, *Indochinese Experience,* 389–91; Kong Le cited in Dommen, *Conflict in Laos,* 145. My account of the Kong Le coup and its aftershocks draws upon Conboy, *Shadow War,* 31–40; Dommen, *Conflict in Laos,* 142–67; Fall, *Anatomy of a Crisis,* 184–97; Field, *Prevailing Wind,* 66–101.

50. Kong Le cited in Brown to Herter, August 9, 1960, *FRUS* 1958–60:MS Doc. 418; Strong, *Cash and Violence,* 64; Warren Unna, "Laotian Leader Leaves Observers Mystified," *Washington Post,* August 11, 1960.

51. CIA Information Report, August 10, 1960, White House Office, Office of the Staff Secretary, Records, 1952–61, International Series, box 10, EL; CIA Information Report, August 13, 1960, ibid.; Memorandum of Conversation, August 17, 1960, Bureau of Far Eastern Affairs, Office of Southeast Asian Affairs, Laos Files, 1956–61, box 11, RG 59; Department of State to Embassy in Laos, August 17, 1960, *FRUS* 1958–60, 16:806.

52. Brown to Herter, August 10, 1960, *FRUS* 1958–60, 16:MS Doc. 428; Brown to Herter, August 15, 1960, ibid., 16:MS Doc. 451.

53. Interview: Winthrop Brown, February 1, 1968, JFKL.

54. Protesters cited in CIA Report, August 13, 1960, *FRUS* 1958–60, 16:MS Doc. 445.

55. Discussion at the 455th Meeting of the National Security Council, August 12, 1960, *FRUS* 1958–60, 16:788; Discussion at the 456th Meeting of the National Security Council, August 18, 1960, ibid., 16:809–11; JCS cited in Editorial Note, ibid., 16:813; Burke to Gates, August 20, 1960, ibid., 16:MS Doc. 476.

56. Leaflets cited in Field, *Prevailing Wind,* 79.

57. Brown to Herter, August 17, 1960, *FRUS* 1958–60, 16:MS Doc. 459; Department of State to Embassy in Laos, August 17, 1960, ibid., 16:806–8.

58. CIA Report, August 31, 1960, White House, Office of the Staff Secretary, Records, 1952–61, International Series, box 10, EL; Brown to Herter, August 30, 1960, *FRUS* 1958–60, 16:MS Doc. 501.

59. Stieglitz, *Little Kingdom,* 31; Boun Oum cited in Dommen, *Conflict in Laos,* 154.

60. Discussion at the 459th Meeting of the National Security Council, September 15, 1960, *FRUS* 1958–60, 16:846; Joint Chiefs of Staff to Secretary of Defense, September 16, 1960, ibid., 16:846–47; Parsons to Brown, August 26, 1960, Bureau of Far Eastern Affairs, Office of Southeast Asian Affairs, Laos Files, 1956–61, box 11, RG 59; Discussions of Special State-JCS Meeting on Laos, August 23, 1960, *FRUS* 1958–60, 16:MS Doc. 484.

61. Embassy in Laos to Department of State, September 15, 1960, *FRUS* 1958–60, 16:842; Interview: Winthrop Brown, February 1, 1968, JFKL; Department of State to Embassy in Laos,

September 16, 1960, *FRUS* 1958–60, 16:849; Brown to Herter, September 18, 1960, DSCF, 751 J.00/9-1860, RG 59; Department of State to Embassy in Laos, September 18, 1960, *FRUS* 1958–60, 16:852.

62. Joint Chiefs of Staff to Commander in Chief, Pacific, October 3, 1960, *FRUS* 1958–60, 16:876.

63. Embassy in Laos to Department of State, October 5, 1960, 7:00 p.m., *FRUS* 1958–60, 16:877–78; Embassy in Laos to Department of State, October 5, 1960, 11:00 p.m., ibid., 16:879.

64. Abramov cited in Fall, *Anatomy of a Crisis,* 190; "Laos Hails Soviet Envoy," *New York Times,* October 14, 1960.

65. Herter to Embassies, October 8, 1960, White House Office, Office of the Staff Secretary, Records, 1952–61, International Series, box 9, EL; Interview: John Irwin, February 13, 1969, CSC; Interview: Herbert Riley, April 3, 1969, ibid.

66. Oral History Interview, August 22, 1969, JGPP, box 12; Parsons "Letter to the Family," February 11, 1966, JGPP, box 2.

67. Parsons cited in Holt to Herter, October 14, 1960, DSCF, 751 J.00/10-1460, RG 59.

68. Parsons cited in Holt to Herter, October 14, 1960, DSCF, 751 J.00/10-1460, RG 59; Souvanna cited in "Laos: The Alarmed View," *Time* 76 (October 24, 1960): 36; Addis cited in Holt to Herter, October 15, 1960, DSCF, 751 J.00/10-1560, RG 59.

69. Johnson to Herter, October 18, 1960, DSCF, 751 J.00/10-1860, RG 59; Irwin and Riley's off-the-record remarks cited in Brown to Parsons, November 7, 1960, DSCF, 751 J.00/11-860, RG 59.

70. Discussions of State–Joint Chiefs of Staff Meeting, October 28, 1960, *FRUS* 1958–60, 16:MS Doc. 600; Editorial Note, ibid., 16:933; Department of State to Embassy in Laos, October 28, 1960, ibid., 16:934.

71. Brown to Herter, November 1, 1960, DSCF, 751 J.00/11-160, RG 59; Department of State to Embassy in Laos, November 10, 1960, *FRUS* 1958–60, 16:948.

72. CIA Report, November 16, 1960, White House Office, Office of the Staff Secretary, Records, 1952–61, International Series, box 11, EL.

73. Souvanna cited in "Laos Chief Scores U.S. Aid to His Foe," *New York Times,* November 17, 1960; Jacques Nevard, "Laos to Seek Ties with Red Chinese," *New York Times,* November 18, 1960; Brown to Herter, November 21, 1960, DSCF, 751 J.00/11-2160, RG 59.

74. Telephone Conversation, November 21, 1960, *FRUS* 1958–60, 16:973; Department of State to Embassy in Vientiane, November 21, 1960, ibid., 16:974.

75. Dulles cited in Editorial Note, *FRUS* 1958–60, 16:982.

76. Embassy in Laos to Department of State, December 7, 1960, *FRUS* 1958–60, 16:993; Embassy in Laos to Department of State, November 17, 1960, ibid., 16:970; Discussions of State–Joint Chiefs of Staff Meeting, September 30, 1960, ibid., 16:MS Doc. 545; Parsons to Brown, August 26, 1960, ibid., 16:MS Doc. 491; Brown to Herter, December 2, 1960, DSCF, 751 J.00/12-260, RG 59.

77. Souvanna cited in Jacques Nevard, "Military Junta Rules Vientiane as Rebels Near," *New York Times,* December 11, 1960.

78. Savang cited in Mishra, *Contemporary History of Laos,* 67–68; Kong Le cited in Brown to Herter, December 12, 1960, DSCF, 751 J.00/12-1260, RG 59.

79. Kong Le cited in "Pathet Lao Joins Kong Le," *Washington Post,* December 13, 1960; Heintges cited in Goldstein, *American Policy toward Laos,* 210–11; Discussions of State–Joint Chiefs of Staff Meeting, December 9, 1960, *FRUS* 1958–60, 16:MS Doc. 670.

80. Brown to Parsons, December 13, 1960, *FRUS* 1958–60, 16:MS Doc. 673; Parsons to Macomber, January 17, 1961, Bureau of Far Eastern Affairs, Office of Southeast Asian Affairs, Laos Files, 1956–71, box 12, RG 59.

## 5. "Doctor Tom" and "Mister Pop"

1. Edgar Buell (hereafter EB) to Howard and Bonnie Buell (hereafter H-BB), September 1, 1961, Edgar Buell Papers, Hamilton, IN (hereafter EBP). See also EB to H-BB, September 5, 1960; EB to "all," October 19, 1960, ibid.

2. Buell cited in Roger Warner, *Shooting at the Moon: The Story of America's Clandestine War in Laos* (South Royalton, VT: Steerforth Press, 1996), 45, 305; Charles Weldon, *Tragedy in Paradise: A Country Doctor at War in Laos* (Bangkok: Asia Books Co., 1999), 24, 76–79; EB to H-BB, "Sunday either Sept 23 or 30 I think," 1961, EBP.

3. *That Free Men May Live* broadcast (hereafter *TFMML*), January 22, 1957, Thomas A. Dooley Papers, Western Historical Manuscript Collection, University of Missouri–St. Louis, St. Louis, MO (hereafter TADP); *TFMML,* October 6, 1956, ibid.; Thomas A. Dooley, *Deliver Us from Evil* (New York: Farrar, Straus, and Cudahy, 1956), 62; Buell cited in "Edgar Monroe Buell: He Was One Top Pop," *Fort Wayne (IN) News-Sentinel,* January 10, 1981; EB to H-BB, August 28, 1962, EBP.

4. James Monahan, *Before I Sleep: The Last Days of Doctor Tom Dooley* (New York: Farrar, Straus, and Cudahy, 1961), 219; Fisher, *Dr. America,* 6; Speech: "Treatment for Terror," undated, TADP, box 1; Dooley, "The Role of Medico," Address to the Society, November 22, 1959, *John Carroll Quarterly,* Spring 1960—clipping in "Lectures III" Scrapbook, Thomas A. Dooley Collection, Pius XII Library, St. Louis University, St. Louis, MO (hereafter TADC); recording of a speech played in lieu of *TFMML,* June 26, 1960, TADP; Buell cited in Don Schanche, *Mister Pop* (New York: David McKay Co., 1970), 30.

5. Vera Brown, "Our Times," *Detroit Times,* May 20, 1958; Bill Dorr, "The Whole World Is His Hospital," *Chicago Sun-Times,* July 9, 1960; Schanche, *Mister Pop,* 9.

6. Thomas A. Dooley, *The Night They Burned the Mountain* (New York: Farrar, Straus, and Cudahy, 1960), 15.

7. Officer cited in James Fisher, *The Catholic Counterculture in America, 1933–1962* (Chapel Hill: University of North Carolina Press, 1989), 168; Buell cited in Schanche, *Mister Pop,* 20.

8. Nooter to Buell, April 23, 1974, EBP.

9. Dooley cited in Murray Fromson, "Dr. Dooley of St. Louis in Bangkok," *St. Louis Post-Dispatch,* October 26, 1958; "He Found His Mission in the Jungle," *Petersburg (VA) Progress-Index,* February 16, 1958.

10. Buell cited in Don Schanche, "An American Hero, Part II," *Saturday Evening Post* 252 (June 9, 1962): 95.

11. Abe Weiner, "Books in Brief," *San Antonio Explorer,* July 31, 1960; *TFMML,* November 11, 1957, TADP.

12. For Dooley's misspelling of "Laos" see Thomas A. Dooley (hereafter TAD) to Agnes Dooley (hereafter AD), August 28, 1954, TADP, box 2; TAD to AD, September 9, 1954; TAD to AD, January 9, 1955; TAD to Gilmore, August 25, 1955, ibid. For popular response to *Deliver Us from Evil* see Jacobs, *America's Miracle Man,* 158–61.

13. Dooley cited in Marchmont Kovas, "Dooley Tells of Red Torture," *South Bend (IN) Tribune,* April 14, 1956. For the navy's witch hunt see Fisher, *Dr. America,* 81–89.

14. Pell to Cherne, June 29, 1956, Leo Cherne Collection, Howard Gotlieb Archival Research Center, Mugar Library, Boston University, Boston, MA, box 28; Fisher, *Dr. America,* 113, 129.

15. "Plans for Medical Mission to the Kingdom of Laos," n.d., TADP, box 2; Danielle Glassmeyer, "Sentimental Orientalism and American Intervention in Vietnam" (Ph.D. diss., Loyola University, 2001).

16. Thomas A. Dooley, *The Edge of Tomorrow* (New York: Farrar, Straus, and Cudahy, 1958), 7–10.

17. Kenneth Gilmore, "Dr. Dooley Prescribes Movies with His Pills," *Washington Daily News,* July 17, 1956; "Dr. Dooley Will Return to Laos," *San Francisco Examiner,* August 7, 1956; Bish Thompson, "Meet Do-It-Yourself Diplomat Dooley," *Evansville (IN) Press,* July 26, 1956; Dooley cited in Fred Dickenson, "Back to the Rim of Hell," *Los Angeles Sunday Mirror,* June 24, 1956; "Medicine Shown to Fight Communism," June 11, 1956, *Los Angeles Times;* Ruth Wagner, "To Laos," *Washington Post,* August 9, 1956; "Godspeed," *Oregon Statesman,* August 25, 1956.

18. TAD to AD, September 27, 1956, TADP, box 2.

19. TAD to AD, September 29, 1956, TADP, box 2; TAD to AD, September 16, 1956, ibid.; Dooley, *Edge,* 28–29.

20. Blancké to Parsons, October 5, 1956, Bureau of Far Eastern Affairs, Office of Southeast Asian Affairs, Laos Files, 1956–61, box 14, RG 59; de Paul to Parsons, October 26, 1956, USOM Laos, Office of the Mission Director, Director's Subject Files (Central Files), 1955–59, box 17, RG 469; Moore to de Paul, October 16, 1956, ibid.; Parsons to de Paul, October 17, 1956, Bureau of Far Eastern Affairs, Office of Southeast Asian Affairs, Laos Files, 1956–61, box 14, RG 59; Parsons to Young, October 23, 1956, ibid.

21. Memorandum of Conversation, October 17, 1956, Bureau of Far Eastern Affairs, Office of Southeast Asian Affairs, Laos Files, 1956–61, box 14, RG 59; Fisher, *Dr. America,* 182; Diana Shaw, "The Temptation of Tom Dooley," *Los Angeles Times,* December 15, 1991; Parsons to Young, August 23, 1957, Bureau of Far Eastern Affairs, Office of Southeast Asian Affairs, Laos Files, 1956–61, box 14, RG 59.

22. KMOX Press Release, "Laos II" Scrapbook, TADC; "KMOX Series to Be Taped in Red China [sic]," *Variety,* August 1, 1956.

23. Dooley, *Edge,* 39; *TFMML,* November 15, 1959, TADP.

24. *TFMML,* December 15, 1956, TADP.

25. Dooley, *Edge,* 47–49.

26. *TFMML,* April 26, 1957, TADP; *TFMML,* October 30, 1957; *TFMML,* January 12, 1957; *TFMML,* July 3, 1960; *TFMML,* June 29, 1957, ibid.

27. *TFMML,* April 26, 1957, TADP; *TFMML,* May 18, 1957; *TFMML,* January 12, 1957; *TFMML,* September 13, 1959; *TFMML,* June 22, 1957; *TFMML,* January 22, 1957; *TFMML,* October 30, 1957; *TFMML,* November 20, 1960; *TFMML,* January 24, 1960; *TFMML,* November 11, 1957, ibid.

28. *TFMML,* January 5, 1957, TADP; *TFMML,* March 9, 1957, ibid.

29. State Department bureaucrat cited in Fisher, *Dr. America,* 128; Dooley, *Night,* 112, 11, 36, 32, 68, 83, 90; Dooley, *Edge,* 98, 113; Dooley, *Night,* 32, 101, 87; Dooley, *Edge,* 126, 107, 32.

30. Peggy Durdin, "Mission to Laos," *New York Times,* September 7, 1958; "Medical Mission to Asia's Jungles," *New Haven (CT) Journal Courier,* May 19, 1958; "Dr. Dooley's New Book: 'The Edge of Tomorrow,'" *Peoria (IL) Register,* September 21, 1958; Frances Burns, "The Dedicated Tom Dooley," *Boston Globe,* June 15, 1958; Fisher, *Dr. America,* 119; Klein, *Cold War Orientalism,* 90.

31. Fisher, *Catholic Counterculture,* 174; Dooley Address, Reception at Mutual of Omaha Auditorium, Omaha, NE, November 9, 1959, TADP, box 3; Thomas A. Dooley, "The Night They Burned the Mountain," *Reader's Digest* 76 (May 1960): 93; Dooley cited in "Dr. Tom Dooley, Now Serving in Laos," *Brooklyn (NY) Tablet,* April 6, 1957; Dooley, *Edge,* 53; *TFMML,* November 22, 1959, TADP; Teresa Gallagher, *Give Joy to My Youth: A Memoir of Dr. Tom Dooley* (New York: Farrar, Straus, and Giroux, 1965), 8.

32. Dooley cited in Willard Clopton, "U.S. Using Wrong Approach in Asia, Jungle Doctor Says," *Cincinnati Post,* May 26, 1958; Luther Nichols, "U.S. Aid at Village Level," *San Francisco Examiner,* May 29, 1958; "Thomas A. Dooley, M.D.," *Modern Medicine,* February 15, 1960; Dooley Address, January 22, 1958, TADP, box 4.

33. Dooley disc, dictated, October 3, 1960, TADP, box 6; *TFMML,* November 11, 1958, TADP.

34. *TFMML,* November 22, 1957, TADP; *TFMML,* September 19, 1960, ibid.; Dooley disc, dictated October 3, 1960, TADP, box 6; *TFMML,* November 13, 1960, TADP; *TFMML,* October 23, 1960, ibid.

35. Dooley, *Night,* 111; *TFMML,* January 24, 1960, TADP; Dooley, *Night,* 116; TAD to AD, August 23, 1960, TADP, box 4; *TFMML,* November 26, 1960, TADP; Dooley, *Edge,* 140.

36. TAD to Gilmore, January 10, 1957, TADP, box 2; TAD to AD, September 15, 1958; TAD to AD, October 18, 1958; TAD to AD, October 28, 1958; TAD to AD, September 28, 1958, ibid.; TAD to "All," July 2, 1958, TADP, box 7; TAD to "All," October 5, 1958; TAD to "All," October 23, 1958; TAD to "All," October 29, 1958, ibid.; TAD to Copenhaver, February 16, 1960, TADP, box 3.

37. Bill Cunningham, "Tom Dooley Story One of Greatest of Our Times," *Boston Herald,* October 28, 1959; Blair Justice, "Doomed Doctor to Push Medico until the End," *Fort Worth Star-Telegram,* August 28, 1959; Eisenhower to Dooley, September 25, 1959, "Clippings IV" Scrapbook, 1958–61, TADC; Nixon to Dooley, September 24, 1959, "Jaycee" Scrapbook, TADC; Judd to Dooley, August 25, 1959, "Lectures II" Scrapbook, TADC; Parsons to Dooley, August 28, 1959, ibid.; Dooley to Menger, November 4, 1959, box 3, TADP.

38. Ferdinand Kuhn, "A Candle for the Jungle's Dark," *Saturday Review* 72 (June 18, 1960): 21; Paul Coates, "Dr. Dooley Is in a Hurry," *Los Angeles Mirror,* July 11, 1960; Henry Vance, "Selfless Example," *Worcester (MA) Gazette,* July 23, 1960; Helen Gould, "Modern Authors," *Bellows Falls (VT) Times,* July 21, 1960; "Dr. Dooley of Muong Sing," *Honolulu Star-Bulletin,* September 24, 1959; Murphy to Dooley, November 26, 1959, TADP, box 4; Merz to Dooley, December 17, 1959, TADP, box 3; "Most Esteemed Men," *Honolulu Star-Bulletin,* January 23, 1961; Mary Ellen Vaughan, "Dr. Thomas Dooley, Splendid American," *Static,* November 24, 1959.

39. Spellman cited in Gallagher, *Give Joy to My Youth,* 153–54; Senate and House of Representatives, Joint Resolution, January 23, 1961, TADC.

40. Andrew Greeley, *Strangers in the House* (Chicago: Loyola University Press, 1962), 20.

41. Fisher, *Dr. America,* 114, 34–35; Will Brownell, "The Vietnam Lobby: The Americans Who Lobbied for a Free and Independent South Vietnam in the 1940s and 1950s" (Ph.D. diss., Columbia University, 1993), 273, 346–48; Jacobs, *America's Miracle Man,* 142–43, 169–71; TAD to Gilmore, January 10, 1957, TADP, box 2.

42. Buell cited in Schanche, *Mr. Pop,* 21; John Lewallen, "The Reluctant Counterinsurgents: International Voluntary Services in Laos," in *Laos: War and Revolution,* ed. Adams and McCoy, 361.

43. Form Letter: "So You're Coming to Laos," 1960, IVS Archival Collection, Mennonite Historical Library, Goshen College, Goshen, IN (hereafter IVSAC), box 9; Orientation Brochure, 1960, ibid.

44. Role-Playing Instructions, 1960, IVSAC, box 9; "Ideas, Customs, and Peoples: A Fundamental Discussion Prepared for IVS Team Members," 1960, IVSAC, box 1; Noffsinger cited in Schanche, *Mr. Pop,* 19.

45. EB to H-BB, June 23, 1960, EBP; EB to H-BB, "Sat. night"; EB to H-BB, "Tues. evening"; EB to H-BB, July 1, 1960, ibid.

46. EB to H-BB, July 1, 1960, EBP; EB to H-BB, October 3, 1960, ibid.; Russell: Report on Laotian Team, July 1960, IVSAC, box 1.

47. EB to H-BB, July 29, 1960, EBP; co-worker cited in Don Schanche, "An American Hero, Part I," *Saturday Evening Post* 252 (June 2, 1962): 16.

48. EB to H-BB, July 1, 1960, EBP; EB to "all," October 19, 1960; EB to H-BB, October 10, 1960; EB to H-BB, December 4, 1960, ibid.

49. EB to H-BB, July 1, 1960, EBP; EB to "all," August 15, 1960; EB to H-BB, September 1, 1960, ibid.

50. EB to HB, November 14, 1960. The Edon State Bank was in Edon, Ohio, just across the border from the Buell farm in Steuben County, Indiana.

51. Vang Pao is a legendary figure, and it is difficult to separate fact from fantasy in accounts of his early life. Probably the best treatment is Keith Quincy, *Hmong: The History of a People* (Spokane: Eastern Washington University Press, 1995), 174–84.

52. EB to H-BB, October 16, 1960, EBP; EB to Elson and Clara Buell, October 1960, ibid.

53. EB to H-BB, January 15, 1961, EBP.

54. EB to Elson and Clara Buell, January 8, 1961, EBP; Honor Award, March 3, 1961; Noffsinger to EB, March 21, 1961, ibid.

55. EB to H-BB, January 29, 1961, EBP; Buell to "Kids," April 23, 1961.

56. EB to "both," March 12, 1961, EBP; EB to H-BB, June 14, 1961; EB to H-BB, June 25, 1961, ibid.

57. John Prados, *Safe for Democracy: The Secret Wars of the CIA* (Chicago: Ivan R. Dee, 2006), 349. Study of the secret war has become a cottage industry, in which some of the more informative works include Thomas Ahern, *Undercover Armies, 1961–1973: CIA and Surrogate Warfare in Laos* (Washington, DC: Center for the Study of Intelligence, 2006); Thomas Leo Briggs, *Cash on Delivery: CIA Special Operations during the Secret War in Laos* (Rockville, MD: Rosewood Books, 2009); Keith Quincy, *Harvesting Pa Chay's Wheat: The Hmong and America's Secret War in Laos* (Spokane: Eastern Washington University Press, 2000); Warner, *Shooting at the Moon*.

58. EB to H-BB, February 8, 1961; EB to H-BB, June 14, 1961; EB to "both," March 19, 1961; EB to H-BB, January 15, 1961; EB to H-BB, August 24, 1961; EB to H-BB, March 14, 1961; EB to H-BB, March 12, 1961, ibid.

59. Schanche, "An American Hero, Part I," 15–21; Schanche, "An American Hero, Part II," 91–95.

60. "Hoosier Farmer Braves Red Peril to Help Poverty-Stricken Laotians," *Edon (OH) Commercial,* July 25, 1962; EB to H-BB, June 7, 1962, EBP; EB to H-BB, June 25, 1962, ibid.; Edgar Buell cited in e-mail to author from Jeff Buell, June 8, 2010; "Hoosier Farmer Helps Laotians Resist Reds," *Indianapolis Star,* March 25, 1962.

61. Buell cited in Daniel Southerland, "Edgar Buell: The Indiana Farmer Who Finally Left the Hills of Laos," *Christian Science Monitor,* February 7, 1971; John Steinbeck, "Letter from Laos," reprinted in *Mr. Pop,* vii–viii.

## 6. "Retarded Children"

1. Warren Rogers, "Typical Laotian Soldier Is Not Mad at Anyone," *New York Herald Tribune,* May 22, 1962.

2. Menger cited in "Red War in Southeast Asia: An Eyewitness Account," *U.S. News & World Report* 30 (June 11, 1962): 79; Meeker, *Little World of Laos,* 38; "Laos: Test of U.S. Intentions," *Time* 77 (March 17, 1961): 21.

3. Kong Le cited in Burchett, *Furtive War,* 189.

4. For Dooley's relationship with Meeker see TAD to AD, July 28, 1959, TADP, box 3; Meeker, *Little World,* 229–31. For his bond with Menger see Menger to TAD, December 24, 1958, TADP, box 3; Menger to TAD, October 18, 1959, ibid.; Menger to TAD, January 1, 1961, TADP, box 4.

5. Oden Meeker, "Don't Forget Madame's Elephant," *Saturday Evening Post* 269 (January 14, 1956): 30, 64–65, 68.

6. Meeker, *Little World,* 207–8, 242, 39, 89, 46, 37, 14, 78, 102, 33, 206, 194, 45–46, 66, 38, 78, 59, 206, 93, 110, 39.

7. Menger cited in "Red War in Southeast Asia," 80; Matt J. Menger, *In the Valley of the Mekong: An American in Laos* (Paterson, NJ: St. Anthony Guild Press, 1970), 146.

8. Menger to "Indochina Mission Crusaders," "Easter Sunday" 1959, Bureau of Far Eastern Affairs, Office of Southeast Asian Affairs, Laos Files, 1956–61, box 10, RG 59; Bundy to Sheehle, June 20, 1962, White House Central Files, Subject File, box 63, JFKL.

9. Menger, *Slowly*, 82, 140, 43, 80–82, 220–226; Menger, *Valley*, 52.

10. Menger, *Valley*, 12; Menger, *Slowly*, 14; Menger, *Valley*, 61–62; Menger, *Slowly*, 221; Menger, *Valley*, 173; Menger, *Slowly*, 130; Menger, *Valley*, 215; Menger, *Slowly*, 183, 225.

11. Menger cited in "Red War in Southeast Asia," 78–80.

12. Karnow, "Tale of a Troubled Paradise," 22–23.

13. Karnow, "Mess in Laos," 35–39.

14. "Letter from the Publisher," *Time* 77 (March 17, 1961): 3; "Laos: Test Of U.S. Intentions," ibid., 20–25.

15. Harold Jacobson, the American consul at the Hong Kong embassy, obtained a copy of Karnow's manuscript and sent it to his superiors at Foggy Bottom. Jacobson to Department of State [manuscript attached], March 29, 1961, DSCF, 751 J.00/3-2961, RG 59.

16. Robert E. Herzstein, *Henry R. Luce, Time, and the American Crusade in Asia* (Cambridge: Cambridge University Press, 2005), 1. See also T. Christopher Jespersen, *American Images of China, 1931–1949* (Stanford, CA: Stanford University Press, 1996); W. A. Swanberg, *Luce and His Empire* (New York: Charles Scribner's Sons, 1972); Halberstam, *Powers That Be*; Michael Hunt, "East Asia in Henry Luce's 'American Century,'" in *The Ambiguous Legacy: U.S. Foreign Relations in the "American Century*," ed. Michael J. Hogan (Cambridge: Cambridge University Press, 1999), 232–78.

17. John Kobler, *Luce: His Time, Life and Fortune* (New York: Random House, 1968), 2. For journalists' complaints about Luce see Alan Brinkley, *The Publisher: Henry Luce and His American Century* (New York: Alfred A. Knopf, 2010), 293–300, 447–48; Halberstam, *Powers That Be,* 77–85, 459–67; Herzstein, *Henry R. Luce,* 41–46, 220–25; Swanberg, *Luce,* 472.

18. "Battle of Indo-China: Reds in Shangri-La," *Time* 61 (April 27, 1953): 33; "Danger Zones: Black, White, & Red Thais," *Time* 61 (May 4, 1953): 34; "Battle of Indo-China: Monsoon Mystery," *Time* 61 (May 18, 1953): 31; "Cold War: Victor's Progress," *Time* 63 (July 5, 1954): 18; "Foreign News: 48 Hours to Midnight," *Time* 63 (August 2, 1954): 18.

19. "Laos: On the Road to Chaos," *Time* 67 (August 20, 1956): 23; "Laos: The Turnip Watchers," *Time* 68 (March 25, 1957): 33; "Laos: Trouble in the Hills," *Time* 65 (July 25, 1955): 25; "Laos: Nehru on the Rubicon," *Time* 65 (October 3, 1955): 29; "Laos: Conquest by Negotiation," *Time* 69 (January 21, 1957): 27; "Laos: The Umbrella Man," *Time* 70 (June 17, 1957): 33; "Laos: The Long Reign," *Time* 74 (November 9, 1959): 30; "Laos: The Other Party," *Time* 71 (June 2, 1958): 28.

20. "Laos: The Unloaded Pistol," *Time* 74 (September 21, 1959): 33; "Laos: The Alarmed View," 36; "Laos: Desperation's Child," *Time* 75 (June 13, 1960): 31; "Laos: Bell for the Middle Man," *Time* 76 (December 19, 1960): 33; "Laos: Time to Reconcile," *Time* 76 (October 10, 1960): 38; "Laos: Fire & Water," *Time* 76 (August 29, 1960): 25; "Laos: The Price of Peace," *Time* 75 (January 18, 1960): 31.

21. "Laos: No Hard Feelings," *Time* 75 (January 11, 1960): 26; "Laos: Time to Reconcile," 38; "Laos: Spreading the Word," *Time* 76 (September 7, 1960): 6; "Laos: Much for Little," *Time* 76 (October 31, 1960): 21.

22. "Laos: Tale of Two Cities," *Time* 76 (August 22, 1960): 22; "Laos: Fire & Water," 25; "Laos: Threat from the North," 26.

23. "Southeast Asia: Double Trouble," *Time* 76 (November 28, 1960): 26; "Laos: Bell for the Middle Man," 33.

24. "Laos: Battle for Vientiane," 24–26. See also "South Vietnam: Revolt at Dawn," *Time* 76 (November 21, 1960): 30–32.

25. "Laos: Shaky Rule," *Time* 77 (January 2, 1961): 24.

26. "Laos: Unattractive Choice," *Time* 77 (January 27, 1961): 23; "Laos: Collapse," *Time* 77 (May 5, 1961): 22; "Laos: Time Out," *Time* 77 (February 10, 1961): 19; "Laos: Time for Poets," *Time* 77 (February 3, 1961): 26; advisers cited in "Laos: Americans at Work," *Time* 77 (April 7,

1961): 26; "Laos: Toward Nirvana," *Time* 77 (April 28, 1961): 34; "Laos: Attack & Talk," *Time* 78 (June 23, 1961): 20; "Laos: Bogged Down," *Time* 77 (March 24, 1961): 26; "Southeast Asia: Falling Back," *Time* 77 (May 12, 1961): 17.

27. Foran, "Discursive Subversions," 158; Jacques Nevard, "Reverses in Laos Laid to 'Myth' of 'Invasion' by Powerful Foes," *New York Times,* April 21, 1961; Richard Starnes, "A Dreamy Never-Never Land," *Washington News,* March 23, 1961; "Laos: Another Korea?" *Newsweek* 57 (January 9, 1961): 31; Hanson W. Baldwin, "Troubled Laos Now the Vortex of the East-West Struggle," *New York Times,* March 26, 1961; "Backward Land a Pawn in Cold War," *Philadelphia Inquirer,* March 6, 1961; "A Determined Laotian: General Phoumi Nosavan," *New York Times,* June 29, 1961; Oganesoff, "Languid Laos"; Peggy Durdin, "Gentle Laos Is Caught in Cold War," *New York Times,* April 23, 1961; Keyes Beech, "'Our Man in Laos' a Big One," *Philadelphia Inquirer,* September 16, 1959; Beech, "How Uncle Sam Fumbled in Laos," 87; Starnes, "A Dreamy Never-Never Land"; Peter White, "Report on Laos," *National Geographic* 120 (August 1961): 242; "Our Loss in Laos," *Wall Street Journal,* March 15, 1962.

28. Santha Rama Rau, "Land of Leisure," *Holiday* 20 (July 1956): 57–59, 67, 70.

29. David Lancashire, "Laos Important to Free World," *Providence Journal,* November 29, 1959; Warren Unna, "Laos Capital Pursues Happiness," *Washington Post,* April 5, 1961.

30. R. H. Shackford, "Crisis Involves Much More Than Tiny Laos," *Washington News,* March 27, 1961; "Laos: At the Brink," *Newsweek* 57 (April 3, 1961): 21–23; "Little Hope in Laos," *Washington Star,* May 4, 1961.

31. "Laos: The Struggle Shifts," *Christian Science Monitor,* March 28, 1961; "Truce—But Laotian Troops Lose Feet to Own Mines," *New York Herald Tribune,* May 10, 1961; Jacques Nevard, "Reverses in Laos Laid to 'Myth'"; Warren Unna, "Laos Seen as 'Front' in Asia Defense Line," *Washington Post,* April 6, 1961; Igor Oganesoff, "Laos 'Peace' Would Promise Red Victory," *Wall Street Journal,* May 18, 1962.

32. "Laos People Ignore Crisis, Sleep Off Big Celebration," *New York Herald Tribune,* March 25, 1961; John Roderick, "Laos Yearns Only for Peace," *Washington Star,* May 26, 1961; Drew Pearson, "Laotians Laugh as World Worries," *Washington Post,* April 21, 1961.

33. Mark Watson, "Rebels Rely on Discipline in Laos War," *Baltimore Sun,* May 3, 1961.

34. "While Laos Burns," *Newsweek* 57 (April 3, 1961): 22–24; Drew Middleton, "Geneva Talks: Laos Roadblocks," *New York Times,* June 11, 1961; "New Look at Laos," *New York Times,* May 12, 1962; Robert Shaplen, "Letter from Laos," *New Yorker* 74 (October 20, 1962): 211.

35. Durdin, "Gentle Laos Is Caught in the Cold War"; "Laos: What Went Wrong," *Newsweek* 57 (May 15, 1961): 44; "Laos: Another Korea?" *Newsweek* 57 (January 9, 1961): 31; Chester Morrison, "There Goes Asia," *Look* 25 (June 6, 1961): 26; Beech, "How Uncle Sam Fumbled in Laos," 28, 87.

36. "Laos People Ignore Crisis, Sleep Off Big Celebration," *New York Herald Tribune,* March 25, 1961; "Laotians Fighting Reds Show 'Battle Shyness,'" *Washington Star,* March 18, 1961; "Southeast Asia: The Puritan Crusade," *Time* 74 (July 13, 1959): 25; "Laos: Test of U.S. Intentions," 24; "Laos: Toward Nirvana," 34; "Laos: Much for Little," 21; "President Warns of Our Peril in Laos," 21; Shackford, "Crisis Involves Much More Than Tiny Laos"; William L. Ryan, "Laos Fall to Reds to Mean Perilous Days for America," *Denver Post,* May 7, 1961.

37. TFMML, August 28, 1960, TADP; "Laos: The Ugly Record," *Time* 77 (May 26, 1961): 23; Relman Morin, "How We Drifted into the Laos Situation," *Washington Star,* May 14, 1961; "Tom Dooley at Work," *Life* 48 (April 18, 1960): 114; Rogers, "Typical Laotian Soldier"; Durdin, "Gentle Laos Is Caught in the Cold War"; Durdin, "Laos: Paradise on the Edge of War."

38. Cousins, "Report from Laos," 13, 47; Chalmers Roberts, "Laos Is a Story of Change," *Washington Post,* March 26, 1961; "Laos: Test of U.S. Intentions," 21–22.

39. "Laos: Test of U.S. Intentions," 22; "Laos: The Unloaded Pistol," 33; Karnow, "Tale of a Troubled Paradise," 22–23.

40. "Laos: The Nameless Menace," *Time* 71 (May 19, 1958): 26.

41. U. Alexis Johnson, *The Right Hand of Power: The Memoirs of an American Diplomat* (Englewood Cliffs, NJ: Prentice-Hall, 1985), 295.

42. "Our Loss in Laos," *Wall Street Journal,* March 15, 1962.

## 7. "No Place to Fight a War"

1. U. Alexis Johnson, Oral History, April 11, 1967, JFKL.

2. C. V. Clifton, Notes from the Meeting of Congressional Leaders with the President, April 27, 1961, National Security Files, Chester V. Clifton Series, Conferences with the President, JFKL; U. Alexis Johnson, Memorandum on the President's Meeting with Congressional Leaders, April 27, 1961, ibid.; Department of State to Secretary of State, April 27, 1961, *FRUS* 1961–63 (Washington, DC: Government Printing Office, 1994), 24:147.

3. U. Alexis Johnson, Oral History, April 11, 1967, JFKL.

4. Bundy cited in Goldstein, *Lessons in Disaster,* 47.

5. Brinkley and Kennedy cited in Richard Reeves, *President Kennedy: Profile of Power* (New York: Simon & Schuster, 1993), 592–93; Galbraith to Kennedy, May 10, 1961, President's Office Files, Special Correspondence, box 29a, JFKL. For Kennedy as cold warrior see in particular James Giglio, *The Presidency of John F. Kennedy* (Lawrence: University Press of Kansas, 1991); Herbert Parmet, *JFK: The Presidency of John F. Kennedy* (New York: Penguin, 1983); Thomas Paterson, ed., *Kennedy's Quest for Victory: American Foreign Policy, 1961–1963* (New York: Oxford University Press, 1989).

6. Dwight D. Eisenhower, *Waging Peace* (Garden City, NY: Doubleday, 1965), 612; Memorandum of Conference, January 2, 1961, *FRUS* 1961–63, 24:2.

7. Kennedy cited in Schlesinger, *Thousand Days,* 507; John-Thomas Homsany, "John F. Kennedy, the Soviet Union, and the Laos Crisis, 1961–1962" (Ph.D. diss., California State University, Fullerton, 2000), 88; Sorenson, *Kennedy,* 640; Thomas Schoenbaum, *Waging Peace and War: Dean Rusk in the Truman, Kennedy, and Johnson Years* (New York: Simon & Schuster, 1988), 384.

8. Inter-Agency Task Report, January 23, 1961, National Security Files, Countries, box 130, JFKL.

9. Memorandum for Secretary of Defense, January 23, 1961, National Security Files, Countries, box 130, JFKL; Memorandum of Conference, January 25, 1961, *FRUS* 1961–63, 24:43–44.

10. Kaiser, *American Tragedy,* 40; Rostow cited in Interview: Winthrop Brown, February 1, 1968, JFKL.

11. Interview: Winthrop Brown, February 1, 1968, JFKL; Memorandum of Conversation, February 3, 1961, Bureau of Far Eastern Affairs, Office of Southeast Asian Affairs, Laos Files, 1956–61, box 12, RG 59; Interview: Winthrop Brown, January 13, 1969, CSC; Kennedy cited in Schlesinger, *Thousand Days,* 332.

12. Rostow to Kennedy, February 28, 1961, National Security Files, Countries, box 130, JFKL; Rostow to Kennedy, March 7, 1961; Clifton to Kennedy, March 10, 1961; Landon to Rostow, March 7, 1961, ibid.

13. Wallace Carroll, "U.S. Ready to Face All Risks," *New York Times,* March 21, 1961.

14. Memorandum of Conversation, March 12, 1961, National Security Files, Countries, box 130, JFKL; Memorandum of Conference, March 9, 1961, *FRUS* 1961–63, 24:77; Memorandum for Record, March 21, 1961, ibid., 95.

15. The President's Press Conference, March 23, 1961, *Public Papers of the Presidents: John F. Kennedy, 1961* (Washington, DC: Government Printing Office, 1962), 212–20.

16. Reeves, *President Kennedy,* 75; "Text of Kennedy-Macmillan Statement," *Washington Post,* March 27, 1961; SEATO communiqué cited in Telegram from President to Secretary of State, March 27, 1961, *FRUS* 1961–63, 24:106; William Jorden, "Gromyko Sees Kennedy; They Voice Hope on Laos," *New York Times,* March 28, 1961.

17. Kennedy cited in Chalmers Roberts, *First Rough Draft* (New York: Praeger, 1973), 192–93.

18. Parsons to Boulton, September 7, 1960, JGPP, box 3; Kennedy cited in Parsons Interview, June 22, 1969, JGPP, box 12.

19. Kennedy cited in Sorenson, *Kennedy,* 644. See also Roger Hilsman, *To Move a Nation: The Politics of Foreign Policy in the Administration of John F. Kennedy* (Garden City, NY: Doubleday, 1967), 34–35; William Bundy, unpublished book manuscript, JFKL.

20. Department of State to Embassy in United Kingdom, April 15, 1961, *FRUS* 1961–63, 24:132.

21. Lemnitzer cited in Schlesinger, *Thousand Days,* 338.

22. Memorandum: Subject—Laos, n.d., Bureau of Far Eastern Affairs, Office of Southeast Asian Affairs, Laos Files, 1956–61, box 15, RG 59; Message [text not declassified] to Director of Central Intelligence, May 13, 1962, *FRUS* 1961–63, 24:762–63; National Intelligence Estimate, May 14, 1962, President's Office Files, Countries, box 121, JFKL; Record of the 512th National Security Council Meeting, April 20, 1963, *FRUS* 1961–63, 24:980; Notes by General Eisenhower on Luncheon Meeting with President Kennedy, April 22, 1961, Eisenhower, Dwight D., Post-presidential Papers, Augusta-Walter Reed Series, box 2, EL; Eisenhower cited in Beschloss, *Crisis Years,* 397.

23. Henry Fairlie, *The Kennedy Promise* (Garden City, NY: Doubleday, 1973), 185; Bowles cited in Statements on Laos—Foreign Affairs Committee, July 7, 1961, Bureau of Far Eastern Affairs, Office of Southeast Asian Affairs, Laos Files, 1956–61, box 13, RG 59; Memorandum of Conversation, May 15, 1962, *FRUS* 1961–63, 24: 770; Schlesinger, *Thousand Days,* 332; Sorenson, *Kennedy,* 641; Memorandum of Conversation, May 11, 1962, *FRUS* 1961–63, 24:740–41; George Ball, *The Past Has Another Pattern: Memoirs* (New York: W. W. Norton, 1982), 361, 363.

24. Rusk cited in Statements on Laos—Foreign Affairs Committee, July 7, 1961, Bureau of Far Eastern Affairs, Office of Southeast Asian Affairs, Laos Files, 1956–61, box 13, RG 59; Telegram from Secretary of State to Department of State, April 28, 1961, *FRUS* 1961–63, 24:149; Memorandum of Conversation, March 12, 1961, National Security Files, Countries, box 130, JFKL; Memorandum of Conversation, April 29, 1961, National Security Files, Countries, box 130a, JFKL; Memorandum of Conversation, June 29, 1961, ibid.; Dean Rusk, *As I Saw It* (New York: Penguin Books, 1990), 428.

25. Briefing by Brigadier General Craig, September 15, 1961, National Security Files, Regional Security, box 231, JFKL; Lemnitzer cited in Interview: Winthrop Brown, February 1, 1968, JFKL; Boyle cited in Bundy to Kennedy, February 21, 1961, National Security Files, Countries, box 131, JFKL; CHMAAG Laos to CINCPAC, Joint Chiefs of Staff, May 16, 1962, President's Office Files, Countries, box 121, JFKL; Kennedy cited in Bradlee, *Conversations with Kennedy,* 84.

26. Critique of U.S. Policies in Laos and South Vietnam, n.d., National Security Files, Countries, box 130a, JFKL; Contingency Policy for Laos, n.d., Bureau of Far Eastern Affairs, Office of Southeast Asian Affairs, Laos Files, 1956–61, box 12, RG 59; Lessons from Laos, August 7, 1961, Bureau of Far Eastern Affairs, Assistant Secretary for Far Eastern Affairs, Subject, Personal Name, and Country Files, 1960–63, box 5, RG 59.

27. Memorandum of Meeting, April 26, 1961, *FRUS* 1961–63, 24:143.

28. *Combat* cited in Fall, *Anatomy of a Crisis,* 224; Memorandum from Acting Secretary to President, April 26, 1961, *FRUS* 1961–63, 24:141; Rusk to State Department, May 17, 1961, National Security Files, Countries, box 130a, JFKL.

29. Terms cited in Eddy, "Neutralization of Laos," 222.

30. Biographical treatments of Harriman include Rudy Abramson, *Spanning the Century: The Life of W. Averell Harriman* (New York: William Morrow, 1992), 582–91; Walter Isaacson and Evan Thomas, *The Wise Men: Six Friends and the World They Made* (New York: Simon & Schuster, 1986).

31. Kennedy cited in Interview: W. Averell Harriman, May 16, 1969, CSC; Interview: William H. Sullivan, June 28, 1969, ibid.; Delegation to Conference on Laos to Embassy in Thailand, June 16, 1961, *FRUS* 1961–63, 24:248; Wehrle, "'A Good, Bad Deal,'" 351. The most thorough study of Harriman's role in fashioning the Laos accords is Terence Robert Fehner,

"W. Averell Harriman and the Geneva Conference on Laos, 1961–1962" (Ph.D. diss., George-town University, 1984).

32. Chester Cooper, *The Lost Crusade: America in Vietnam* (New York: Fawcett, 1972), 234.

33. Bhumibol cited in Dommen, *Indochinese Experience,* 450; Memorandum of Conversation, July 22, 1962, *FRUS* 1961–63, 24:868; Harriman-Sparkman Telecon, May 12, 1962, W. Averell Harriman Papers, Library of Congress, Washington, DC (hereafter WAHP), box 581; Memorandum of Meeting, July 27, 1962, *FRUS* 1961–63, 24:873; Record of the 511th National Security Council Meeting, April 10, 1963, ibid., 24:964; Interview: W. Averell Harriman, May 14, 1969, CSC; Telegram from Delegation to Conference on Laos to Department of State, June 21, 1961, *FRUS* 1961–63, 24:250.

34. Hilsman, *To Move a Nation,* 138–39; Delegation in Laos to Department of State, September 26, 1961, *FRUS* 1961–63, 24:432.

35. Memorandum for the Record, November 2, 1961, *FRUS* 1961–63, 24:494; Delegation to Conference on Laos to Department of State, November 21, 1961, ibid., 24:523; Harriman to State Department, November 6, 1961, WAHP, box 529.

36. For the "massacre" see Schlesinger, *Thousand Days,* 442–47.

37. Interview: W. Averell Harriman, May 13, 1961, CSC; Phoumi cited in Brown to Rusk, March 6, 1962, National Security Files, Countries, box 131, JFKL.

38. Dommen, *Conflict in Laos,* 216; Memorandum of Conversation, March 24, 1962, WAHP, box 529.

39. Memorandum of Conversation, March 25, 1962, WAHP, box 529; Harriman cited in Abramson, *Spanning the Century,* 590; interpreter cited in Brown, *War in Shangri-la,* 119–20.

40. Sisouk cited in Harriman to Rusk, March 27, 1962, WAHP, box 529; Harriman cited in Donald Nuechterlein, *Thailand and the Struggle for Southeast Asia* (Ithaca, NY: Cornell University Press, 1965), 234.

41. Memorandum for Record, April 2, 1961, *FRUS* 1961–63, 24:678; Cooper, *Lost Crusade,* 233.

42. Boyle cited in footnote 2, *FRUS* 1961–63, 24:719. The best account of this episode is Conboy, *Shadow War,* 67–74.

43. White House Announcement, May 15, 1962, WAHP, box 529.

44. Interview: Paul Gardner, 1991, FAOHC; Transcript of Background Press and Radio Briefing, March 30, 1962, WAHP, box 789; Harriman to Rusk, July 21, 1962, WAHP, box 531; Cooper cited in Eliades, "United States Decision-Making," 397.

45. Harriman to Rusk, September 13, 1961, WAHP, box 534; "Pushkin-Harriman Understanding Re: Laos," April 14, 1962, ibid.

46. Treaty terms cited in Jane Hamilton-Merritt, *Tragic Mountains: The Hmong, the Americans, and the Secret Wars for Laos* (Bloomington: Indiana University Press, 1993), 119.

47. Harriman to Kirk, October 12, 1962, WAHP, box 565; Wehrle, "'Good, Bad Deal,'" 351.

48. Kennedy cited in Schlesinger, *Thousand Days,* 329.

49. Kennedy and de Gaulle cited in Sorenson, *Kennedy,* 560, 562.

50. Memorandum of Conversation, May 31, 1961, National Security Files, Trips and Conferences, box 233, JFKL.

51. "Communiqué on Paris Talk," *New York Times,* June 3, 1961; C. L. Sulzberger, "Mr. Kennedy Succeeds in Paris," *New York Times,* June 3, 1961.

52. Excellent treatments of the Vienna summit include Beschloss, *Crisis Years,* 182–236; Dallek, *Unfinished Life,* 401–14; Fursenko and Naftali, *Khrushchev's Cold War,* 360–65; Reeves, *President Kennedy,* 156–74; Schlesinger, *Thousand Days,* 358–74; William Taubman, *Khrushchev: The Man and His Era* (New York: W. W. Norton, 2003), 493–500.

53. Memorandum of Conversation, June 3, 1961, National Security Files, Trips and Conferences, box 234, JFKL.

54. Memoranda of Conversations, June 4, 1961, National Security Files, Trips and Conferences, box 234, JFKL.

55. "Communiqué on Talks at Vienna," *Washington Post,* June 5, 1961; Kennedy cited in Isaacson and Thomas, *Wise Men,* 616.

56. Kennedy cited in Reeves, *President Kennedy,* 166, 172; Karnow, *Vietnam,* 265; Langguth, *Our Vietnam,* 136.

57. Transcript of Background Press and Radio News Briefing, August 24, 1961, WAHP, box 788; W. Averell Harriman Interviewed on *Capitol Cloakroom,* December 21, 1961, ibid.

58. Kennedy cited in Sorenson, *Kennedy,* 289; Bundy cited in Kai Bird, *The Color of Truth: McGeorge Bundy and William Bundy, Brothers in Arms* (New York: Touchstone, 1998), 222; Memorandum of Conversation, May 15, 1962, *FRUS* 1961–63, 24:773; Sullivan cited in Castle, *Shadow of Vietnam,* 41.

59. Kennedy cited in Gregory Alan Olson, *Mansfield and Vietnam: A Study in Rhetorical Adaptation* (East Lansing: Michigan State University Press, 1995), 94; Rusk, *As I Saw It,* 428–29.

60. Bundy unpublished manuscript, JFKL.

## Epilogue

1. "A San Francisco Weekly Defends the Army," in *To Serve the Devil,* vol. 2, *Colonials and Sojourners,* ed. Paul Landau, Saul Jacobs, and Eve Pell (New York: Vintage, 1971), 335–37.

2. William Loren Katz, "We Are Repeating the Mistakes We Made in the Philippines 100 Years Ago," History News Network, May 3, 2004, http://hnn.us/articles/4915.html; Patrick Barr, "Terrorists R U.S.," Counterpunch, May 5, 2004, http://www.counterpunch.org/barr05052004.html.

3. Rotter, *Comrades at Odds,* 160.

4. Embassy in Laos to Department of State, October 5, 1960, *FRUS* 1958–60, 16:878; Transcript of Conversation between JH and A. M. Halpern, August 24, 1959, JHP.

5. For the U.S. air war over Laos see Fred Branfman, *Voices from the Plain of Jars* (New York: Harper & Row, 1972). For policies adopted by the LPDR in the aftermath of the Second Indochina War see Christopher Kremmer, *Bamboo Palace* (Sydney: Flamingo, 2003), 124–30, 152–57, 195–211, 217–30. For the campaign to wipe out the Hmong see Hamilton-Merritt, *Tragic Mountains,* 355–410.

6. Warner, *Shooting at the Moon,* 3, 6, 378, 376, 7, 29, 38, 58, 379.

# Index

Note: Page numbers in *italics* indicate illustrations.

Abramov, Aleksandr, 163, 168
Addis, John, 132, 165
Agency for International Development, 175
aid. *See* foreign aid
Albert, Carl, 236
Algeria, 267
Alsop, Joseph, 42, 148–49
Alsop, Stewart, 42
Alvah, Donna, 84
American Women's Club of Vientiane, 82–84
Amory, Robert, 139
Anderson, Daniel, 157
Annam, 26, 27. *See also* Vietnam
Arends, Leslie, 236
Auer, Bernhard, 218
Auriol, Vincent, 33
Australia, 43, 135, 152, 160

Babcock, James, 77
Bacon, Leonard, 98
Ball, George, 251
Bandung Conference of Nonaligned
    Nations, 57, 62

Baritz, Loren, 37
Barr, Patrick, 272
Bay of Pigs invasion, 249, 250, 266, 267
Beech, Keyes, 230–31
Berlin Airlift, 77
Berlin Wall crisis, 1, 253, 266–68
Bhumibol Adulyadej, King of Thailand, 256
Bird, Willis, 117, 120
Blanké, Wendell, 62, 64
Bong Souvannavong, 72, 78, 124
*bo pen nyang* ("it doesn't matter"), 94–97;
    Dooley on, 184, 190–91; Long on, 41;
    Meeker on, 213–14
Boun Oum, Prince, 30, 160–61, 169, 226;
    Brown on, 243; Eisenhower's support of,
    241; Kennedy's support of, 242, 254;
    personality of, 219; photograph of, *262;*
    and Phoumi Nosavan, 257, 260, 261;
    retirement of, 262–63
Bowles, Chester, 9, 236, 251, 254
Bowman, Dick, 197, 199
Boyle, Andrew, 250, 252, 260
Bradley, Mark, 8

Bridges, Styles, 236, 237
Briggs, Ellis, 60
Brinkley, David, 239
Brodrick, Alan, 40
Brown, Mervyn, 132, 139
Brown, Rothwell, 83, 146
Brown, Vera, 173
Brown, Winthrop, 14, 272; and Kennedy,
242–43; and Kong Le, 157–59; on Lao
civil war, 132, 134, 168–70; and Phoumi
Nosavan, 161–63, 166–67; on Savang,
220; on SEATO intervention, 236; and
Souvanna, 165–67
Buddhism, 23, 24; alleged national
characteristics of, 10, 23, 37–40, 95,
113–15; Dooley's view of, 172, 184;
establishment in Laos of, 25; Karnow's
view of, 10, 219; Meeker's view of,
213, 214; Menger's view of, 215;
supposed pacifism of, 42, 96, 134, 210,
219, 230–31
Buell, Edgar Monroe "Pop," 12, 171–77,
194–208; and Dooley, 171–77, 204, 206,
207, 210–11
Bundy, McGeorge, 215, 236, 239, 269, 270
Burchett, Wilfred, 71, 155
Burdick, Eugene, 84–85, 93–94, 188, 204, 206
Burk, Monroe, 101
Burke, Arleigh, 159, 168, 235, 236, 237
Burma, 26, 28, 45, 267
Burns, Frances, 186
Byrne, Patricia, 50–52, 74

Cambodia, 21, 23–24, 35, 43; cultural
stereotypes of, 23, 37–39, 98; Laos
policies of, 17; neutrality of, 267; and
SEATO, 44
CARE (Cooperative for American Relief to
Everywhere), 211
Castro, Fidel, 1, 249, 250, 253, 266, 267
CDNI. See Committee for Defense of
National Interests
Central Intelligence Agency (CIA), 4, 167;
and Brown, 243; and Buell, 199–200; and
CDNI, 137–43, 151, 152; gerrymandering
by, 135, 153–54; and Kong Le, 159; and
Phoui, 149–50; and Phoumi, 166–70,
258; on Royal Lao Army, 55; secret
war in Laos of, 201–2; in Vientiane,
52–53, 83

Cham Nien, 145
Chao Anou, Prince, 26–27, 35–36
Chapman, Christian, 14, 64
Cherne, Leo, 177–79
Chiang Kai-shek, 33, 50, 121, 222
China, 215, 221; Civil War of, 22, 33;
emigrants to Laos from, 95, 97–98; and
French Indochina, 28, 39–40; Great
Leap Forward in, 16; Kennedy's views of,
238, 240; Laos policies of, 2, 16–17; and
Souvanna, 61–63, 71, 73; and Taiwan,
45–46, 142, 267; U.S. recognition of, 222;
and Viet Minh, 33, 35
Chiperfield, Robert, 236
Christian Science Monitor, 19–20, 208, 228
Churchill, Winston, 56, 225
Cillis, Vincent, 112
Clifford, Clark, 2–3
Clifton, Chester, 244–45
cold war, 232; Buell on, 197, 199; Churchill
on, 56; Dooley on, 172, 174, 186, 189;
Dulles on, 9–10, 18, 25, 50, 59, 61, 103;
Halpern on, 92; Harriman on, 255;
Karnow on, 217–18; Khrushchev on, 264;
Laotian view of, 60, 104–5; Meeker on,
213, 214; Menger on, 214–15; Parsons on,
61, 68, 103, 110–13; Souvanna on, 59–61.
See also domino theory; neutralism
colonialism, 21, 27–35, 85, 110. See also
neocolonialism
Committee for Defense of National Interests
(CDNI), 137–44, 150–52, 190
Commodity Import Program (CIP), 65–66,
114
community development projects, 66, 78–79,
88–95, 90, 100–102, 106
Congo, Democratic Republic of, 1, 226, 267
Coolidge, Harold, 39
Cooper, Chester, 260, 261
Corcoran, Thomas, 52
Corrigan, Frank, 101
corruption: electoral, 52, 78–79, 135, 153–54;
with import licenses, 65–66, 86, 114, 139;
and kip exchange rates, 65, 114, 117; with
U.S. foreign aid, 65–66, 86, 91, 92, 99–102,
110, 114–27
Cousins, Norman, 18
Craig, William, 252
Cronkite, Walter, 208
Cuba, 1, 249, 250, 253, 266, 267

cultural stereotypes of Lao, 6–19, 36–43,
84–86, 94–98, 211–17; by Brown, 243–44;
by Buell, 196–97; by Byrne, 50–52; versus
Cambodians, 23, 37–39, 98; by Dooley,
172–73, 176, 178–80, 184–86, 190–91; by
Franck, 39–40; by French, 28–29, 34; by
Halpern, 94–95; by Karnow, 10, 218–20;
by Kerewsky, 96–97; by McClintock,
23–24, 37; by Meeker, 212–14; by Menger,
13, 211, 215–17; by Newman, 40; by
Parsons, 53, 103–5, 112–14, 175, 241;
paternalistic, 7–8, 12–14, 178, 187, 206;
by Rogers, 209–10; by Schanche, 205; by
Thompson, 37–38; versus Vietnamese, 9, 13,
37–41, 97–98, 184–85, 225–26, 230, 237,
269. *See also* race; work ethic
Cunningham, Bill, 191
Czechoslovakia, 11, 51, 80, 234; Dulles on,
74; Parsons on, 61; Robertson on, 56;
Souvanna on, 75

dam and irrigation projects, 78, 89, *90*
Dean, Robert, 11
Declaration on the Neutrality of Laos
(1962), 262–63
de Gaulle, Charles, 30, 147, 264–66
*Deliver Us from Evil* (Dooley), 174, 177, 178,
180, 193
de Paul, Carter, 119, 120, 180, 181
Diem, Ngo Dinh, 10, 23–24, 46, 50, 142;
assassination of, 3; attempted coup against,
225; and Dooley, 180, 184–85, 189, 190;
Harriman on, 261–62; and Katay, 72; and
Kennedy, 5, 6, 269–70; and Laos Accords,
263; McClintock on, 23; Parsons on, 60;
press coverage of, 230; on SEATO, 44;
U.S. visit of, 111
Dien Bien Phu, battle of, 3, 21, 34, 52, 69
Dillon, Douglas, 157, 159
Dirksen, Everett, 236, 237
Disney films, 12, 179–80, 185, 193
domino theory, 6; Burke on, 237; Byrne on,
51; Dulles on, 43; Eisenhower on, 2, 4, 22,
45, 241; Kennedy on, 239, 246–47, 265,
269–70. *See also* cold war
Dommen, Arthur, 53, 153–54, 259
Dong, Pham Van, 142
Dooley, Thomas Anthony, III, 12, 171–93;
and Buell, 171–77, 204, 206, 207, 210–11;
cultural stereotypes of, 172–73, 176,

178–80, 184–86, 190–91; and Diem, 180,
184–85, 189, 190; and Eisenhower, 191,
192; legacy of, 192–93; and Meeker, 212;
and Menger, 212; Operation Laos of,
178–81, 185, 188, 191; and Parsons, 180–81,
188–90; personality of, 172–73; photograph
of, *187;* radio show of, 172, 181–86, 231
Dooley, Thomas Anthony, III, works of:
*Deliver Us from Evil,* 174, 177, 178, 180,
193; *Edge of Tomorrow,* 184, 186, 193; *Night
They Burned the Mountain,* 186, 190, 193
Dorman, William, 19–20
Dorr, Bill, 173
Douglas-Home, Alexander Frederick, 250
Drew, Alice, 82
Duke, Angier Biddle, 178
Dulles, Allen, 76, 168; on elections of 1958,
80; on French military training, 146–47;
on Phoui Sananikone, 141–42
Dulles, John Foster, 13, 241; on cold war,
9–10, 18, 25, 50, 59, 61, 103; on Indochina,
43, 47, 49; on Kong Le, 159; Laos trip of,
57; on RLA, 81; and Savang, 57, 66–67;
on SEATO, 44; and Souvanna, 62, 71–77,
81, 137; successor of, 149; on withholding
Laos aid, 63–64, 68–69
Dunsky, Marda, 19
Durbrow, Elbridge, 142
Durdin, Peggy, 42, 186, 230

Eden, Anthony, 47
*Edge of Tomorrow* (Dooley), 184, 186, 193
education, 24, 92, 97; during French rule, 29;
of Hmong, 205, 208; and Savang, 219
Eisenhower, Dwight: on British cold war
policies, 56; decision-making style of, 235;
domino theory of, 2, 4, 22, 25, 45, 241;
and Dooley, 191, 192; on Geneva Accords,
22, 44–45, 69; and Kennedy, 1–4, 12, 235,
239–41, 246, 249–53, 264–69, 272; on
1958 Laos elections, 54; on Laos policies,
240–41; "New Look" foreign policy of,
69–70; on Pathet Lao, 2–3; on RLA, 12,
251; and Souvanna, 69–70, 75–76, 239;
Truman versus, 69; on Vietnam, 3
elections in Laos: of 1955, 57–58; of 1958, 52,
54, 77–81, 99, 135; of 1960, 152–54, 190

Fairlie, Henry, 251
Falaize, Pierre-Louis, 165

Fall, Bernard, 79, 127
Fa Ngum, King of Laos, 25–26, 35–36
Farbstein, Leonard, 116
Farhang, Mansour, 19–20
Felt, Harry, 162, 167
Field, Michael, 133
films, propaganda, 58, 77, 179–80, 185, 193
Finland, 75
Fisher, James, 172, 193
Foran, John, 19, 226–27
foreign aid (U.S.), 71, 175, 211; for
    community development, 66, 78–79,
    88–95, *90,* 100–102, 106; misuse of, 86,
    91–93, 99–102, 110, 114–27, 188–89,
    218; for Royal Lao Army, 46–47, 75, 86,
    149, 217, 258; withholding of, 63–64,
    68–69, 76
France, 254; Communist Party in, 80; Indochina
    as colony of, 21, 27–35, 85, 110; Laotian
    rebellions against, 28–29, 32; and Munich
    Conference, 234; and SEATO, 2, 43–44,
    135, 237, 238, 248; Vichy regime of,
    29–30
Franck, Harry, 39–40
Franco-Laotian Convention, 33
Franco-Viet Minh War, 22, 23, 40, 57; and
    Kong Le, 156, 170; and Phoumi, 138; U.S.
    assistance in, 44–45
Frankel, Max, 9
Fulbright, J. William, 236

Galbraith, John Kenneth, 240
Gandhi, Indira, 215
Gardner, Richard, 152
Gassouin, Jean, 152
Gates, Thomas, 135, 159
Gaulle, Charles de, 30, 147, 264–66
gender issues, 10–12, 223, 232–33, 251
Geneva Accords on Indochina (1954), 16,
    21–22, 34–35; and Eisenhower, 22, 44–45,
    69, 146; implementation of, 55–57, 81;
    and Kennedy, 249; *Time*'s coverage of, 223;
    U.S. policies after, 43–49
Geneva Conference on Laos (1961–62), 6–9,
    15, 175, 234, 254–63, 265, 270
Gert, Gerard, 98
Giap, Vo Nguyen, 33, 40, 42, 221, 223
Glassmeyer, Danielle, 178
Government Operations Committee (U.S.),
    119, 164, 189
Greater East Asia Co-Prosperity Sphere, 29–30

Greece, 252
Greeley, Andrew, 193
Gromyko, Andrei, 248, 250

Halberstam, David, 19
Halleck, Charles, 236
Halpern, Joel, 14, 86–95, *90,* 272–73;
    academic career of, 98–102, 122–23, 127;
    and Parsons, 101–2, 109; Rand report by,
    123–28
Hammarskjöld, Dag, 148, 149
Hardy, Porter, 119–21, 124, 164, 189
Harkins, Daniel, 119
Harriman, W. Averell, 9, 14, 17, 172, 255–63,
    268, 269
Harting, Harry, 117, 120
Hazey, Jack, 258
health care, 29, 92, 96, 214, 250
Heath, Donald, 45
Hecksher, Henry, 83, 137, 150
Heintges, John, 146–48, 169; and CDNI,
    150, 151, 153
Heiss, Mary Ann, 11, 19
Henry, Joseph, 13
Herter, Christian, 2, 140, 149, 153;
    and Eisenhower, 241; on Phoumi,
    161–64, 166–67
Herzstein, Robert, 222
Hickenlooper, Bourke, 236–38
Hill, Kenneth, 7
Hilsman, Roger, 257
Hitler, Adolf, 29, 133, 177, 234
Hmong, 89, 196–201, 203–8; ethnic cleansing
    of, 273
Ho Chi Minh, 8, 15, 23; and Souphanouvong,
    31, 32; and Souvanna, 62, 63, 73
Ho Chi Minh Trail, 15, 142, 263, 273
Hoganson, Kristin, 11
Holt, John, 132, 145–46
Horton, Philip, 119
Huffman, Franklin, 97
Humphrey, Hubert, 236
Hungary, 10, 75
Huntley, Chet, 207
Hyland, Robert, 182

ICC. *See* International Control Commission
imperialism. *See* colonialism
import licenses, 65–66, 86, 114, 139
Inboden, William, 9–10
Independent Party (Laos), 58, 78, 137

India, 10, 45, 95, 215, 265; emigrants to Laos from, 97–98
Indochinese Union, 27–29
Indonesia, 6, 45, 50
Inpeng Suryadhay, 137, 141
International Control Commission (ICC), 21, 67, 68; and elections of 1955, 55–56; and elections of 1958, 81; and Kennedy, 245, 250, 263; and Laos-Vietnamese conflicts, 142
International Cooperation Administration (ICA), 25, 77, 87, 113, 119
International Rescue Committee (IRC), 177, 178
International Voluntary Services (IVS), 97, 172, 174, 194, 195
Iran, 11, 19, 267
Iraq, 272
Irwin, John, 163–66

Jackson, Andrew, 6
Japan, 265; modernization of, 13; and World War II, 12, 13, 29–31, 233
Jefferson, Joseph, 82
Jespersen, T. Christopher, 222
*Jeunes. See* "Young Ones"
Johnson, Lyndon, 3, 236
Johnson, U. Alexis, 233, 235, 238–39
Jonas, Gilbert, 178, 179
Jones, Howard, 80
Judd, Walter, 24, 116

Kamphan Panya, 137, 138, 141, 190
Karnow, Stanley, 10, 85–86, 211, 217–22, 233
Katay Don Sasorith, 46, 48, 220, 223; Dulles's meeting with, 57; in elections of 1955, 58–59; in elections of 1958, 78, 137; on neutralism, 72; Pathet Lao negotiations with, 55–57; and Phoui Sananikone, 141; in Souvanna's coalition, 72
Katz, William Loren, 272
Kennedy, John F., 7, 226, 233–70; and Buell, 172, 202; and Cuba, 249, 250, 266, 267; decision-making style of, 235, 243; on domino theory, 239, 246–47, 265, 269–70; and Dooley, 192; and Eisenhower, 1–4, 12, 235, 239–41, 246, 249–53, 264–69, 272; on foreign aid, 241; and de Gaulle, 264–66; and ICC, 245, 250, 263; and Khrushchev, 264, 266–68; Laos Task Force of, 242, 244, 250, 253; and Menger, 215; photograph

of, *247;* and South Vietnam, 5, 6, 9, 239, 268–70
Kerewsky, Barbara, 87–88, 95–97, 101–2, 109, 115
Kessinger, Saxon White, 59
Khmer Resistance Government, 35
Khmu (ethnic group), 89, 196
Khrushchev, Nikita, 1, 269; and Kennedy, 264, 266–68; Laos policies of, 16–17, 250, 267–68
kip, 65, 114, 117; devaluation of, 66, 76, 139
Kipling, Rudyard, 15, 211
Kobler, John, 222
Kocher, Eric, 68, 77, 118–19
Kong Le, 5, 15, 155–67, 212, 225; and battle of Vientiane, 15, 129–36, 169–70; Brown on, 243; Buell on, 197; coup by, 15, 156–57, 221; Dooley on, 189; Harriman on, 256; Karnow on, 219, 221; personality of, 11, 157; and Phoumi, 159–63, 167–70; and Souphanouvong, 240
Korean War, 16, 46, 222, 233; Dulles on, 49; Eisenhower on, 69; Khrushchev on, 267; Rusk on, 252
Kou Abhay, 152
Kouprasith Abhay, 130–31, 168–69
Kuhn, Ferdinand, 191

Lair, William, 200, 201
Lancashire, David, 228
Landon, Kenneth, 245
Lan Xang kingdom, 25–27
Lao Issara (Free Lao) government, 31–33
Lao People's Democratic Republic (LPDR), 273
Lavergne, Daly, 101
Lederer, William J., 84–85, 93–94, 188, 204, 206
LeMay, Curtis, 161
Lemnitzer, Lyman, 159, 236, 242, 250, 252
Lewallen, John, 194
Lewis, Norman, 38–39
*Life* magazine, 211, 218, 231–33
Lincoln, Anthony, 152
Lippmann, Walter, 11
"Little America," 18–19, 99–102, 123, 138; Halpern on, 87–88, 123, 124, 126–27; Kerewsky on, 88; Miller on, 116–17; Parsons on, 107–9, 112–14. *See also* U.S. Operations Mission
Long, George, 41

Long Chieng, 201–2, 206
Luang Prabang kingdom, 27–29
Luce, Henry, 19, 222–27, 231

MAAG. *See* Military Assistance Advisory Group
MacGregor, Greg, 122
Macmillan, Harold, 246, 247
magical beliefs of Lao, 104, 130, 228
Magsaysay, Ramón, 50, 139
Malaya, 50, 230
Mansfield, Mike, 65, 236, 238
Mao Zedong, 215, 221; and Chiang Kai-shek, 33; Laos policies of, 16–17; and Souvanna, 61–63, 71, 73; writings of, 93
Mart, Michelle, 19
McCarthy, Joseph, 172, 255
McClintock, Robert, 22–24, 37, 42
McConaughy, Walter, 258
McKinley, William, 272
McNamara, Edward, 117, 119–21
McNamara, Robert, 2–3, 236, 238, 251
Medical International Cooperation (MEDICO), 174, 191–93
Meeker, Oden, 211–14, 233
Mendès-France, Pierre, 223
Menger, Matt, 191; on Catholic converts, 215–16; on cold war, 214–15; and Dooley, 212; on Lao character traits, 13, 211, 215–17
Meo. *See* Hmong
Merchant, Livingston, 166
Messegee, Gordon, 112–13
Military Assistance Advisory Group (MAAG), 44, 45, 149, 249–50, 252
Miller, Hank, 113
Miller, Haynes, 116–20
Minges, Robert, 89, 91
Miniclier, Louis, 87, 92, 101
Moley, Raymond, 122
Morgan, Thomas, 236
Morrison, Chester, 230
Mua Chung, 198
Muong Sing, 28–29
Mutual Security Act, 46
Myanmar, 26, 28, 45, 267

Nasser, Gamal Abdel, 66
*National Geographic,* 40–41, 227
nationalism, Lao, 30–36, 65, 103–4, 135–36, 155–58
Nationalist Party, 78–80, 137

National Progressive Party, 58
NATO (North Atlantic Treaty Organization), 43, 264, 267
Navarre, Henri-Eugène, 34
neocolonialism, 81, 105, 136; and race, 8, 126, 272
Neo Lao Hak Xat (NLHX), 54, 59, 76; censorship of, 145; Dooley on, 189–90; in elections of 1958, 78–81, 118, 136, 141; in elections of 1960, 153; at Geneva Conference, 254–55; legalization of, 70, 72
neutralism, 16–20, 224, 262–63, 270; de Gaulle on, 265–66; Dulles on, 59, 61; Katay on, 72; Kennedy on, 241, 246–47; of Kong Le, 158, 169; Parsons on, 103, 110–13; of Phoui, 141, 142; of Sihanouk, 24; of Souvanna, 61–65, 105, 137, 166, 185, 219. *See also* cold war
Nevard, Jacques, 134
"New Frontier," 12, 251, 256, 270
"New Look" foreign policy, 69–70
Newman, Bernard, 40
*Newsweek* magazine, 9, 19–20, 228, 230
*New York Times,* 9, 42, 230; on battle of Vientiane, 129; on Dooley, 186; on Kennedy's diplomacy, 266, 268; on misuse of U.S. aid, 122
Ngon Sananikone, 79
Nhou Abhay, 44, 67
Nhu, Ngo Dinh, 142
*Night They Burned the Mountain* (Dooley), 186, 190, 193
Nixon, Richard, 76, 191, 215
NLHX. *See* Neo Lao Hak Xat
Noffsinger, John, 195, 200
nonaligned nations. *See* neutralism
North Atlantic Treaty Organization (NATO), 43, 264, 267
nuclear weapons, 30, 69, 236–39, 250, 254, 264

Oblates of Mary Immaculate (OMI), 211, 216
Office of Naval Intelligence (ONI), 174, 177
Oganesoff, Igor, 114–17
Operation Booster Shot, 78–79. *See also* community development projects
Operation Cleanup, 153
Operation Laos, 178–81, 185, 188, 191
Operation Passage to Freedom, 174, 177
Operations Coordinating Board, 10, 81, 146

opium, 28, 131, 201, 205, 207
Orientalism, 7–8, 40, 114, 178, 219–20
Othman, Frederick, 122
Ouane Rathikoun, 144, 157, 160

Pakistan, 10, 248, 267; and SEATO, 43, 135
Palmer, Gardner, 76
Panh Ngaosyvathn, 21–22
Parsons, J. Graham, 9, 14, 17, 102–20, 272;
    as ambassador to Laos, 47–48, 60–70, 74,
    175; as ambassador to Sweden, 248–49;
    Chapman on, 64; on cold war, 61, 68,
    103, 110–13; and Dooley, 180–81,
    188–90; on elections of 1958, 78–81;
    and Halpern, 101–2, 109; and Kennedy,
    242; and Kong Le, 161, 169; on Lao
    character traits, 53, 103–5, 112–14, 175,
    241; and Lao nationalism, 65, 103–4;
    on "Little America," 107–9, 112–14; and
    Miller, 118, 119; on Pathet Lao, 164; perso-
    nality of, 103, 107–9; and Phetsarath,
    109–12; and Phoui Sananikone, 141, 143;
    and Phoumi Nosavan, 151, 168; And
    Robertson, 81, 113; and Souvanna, 61–70,
    74, 102–3, 110–11, 163–66
paternalism, 7–8, 12–14, 178, 187, 206.
    *See also* cultural stereotypes
Pathet Lao, 2–3, 33–35, 57–61, 254, 273;
    effectiveness of, 194, 210, 229; in 1958
    elections, 54; in 1960 elections, 153–54;
    Katay's negotiations with, 55–57; and
    Kennedy, 4, 245, 246, 248; and Kong Le,
    135, 169; Lippmann on, 11; Parsons's
    view of, 164; popularity of, 124–26; RLA
    integration with, 62, 68, 71, 72, 111, 136,
    144; Robertson's view of, 67; and Savang
    Vatthana, 136; Souvanna's coalition with,
    61–62, 67–68, 70–74; Viet Minh support
    for, 15–16, 33–34, 219
Pavie, August, 27
Paxa Sangkhom ("People's Society") Party,
    154
Peabody, Gerald, 117, 120, 121
Peace Corps, 192, 193
Pearson, Drew, 229
Pell, Claiborne, 178
PEO. *See* Programs Evaluation Office
Pfizer Corporation, 172, 179
Pha That Luang ("Great Sacred Stupa"), 26
Phaya Khammao, 32

Phetsarath, Prince, 30–33, 223; and Parsons,
    109–12; personality of, 31; and Souvanna,
    110; on U.S. foreign aid, 92
Philippines, 11, 50, 139; and SEATO, 43–44,
    135, 248; U.S. annexation of, 271–72
Phoui Sananikone, 15–16, 72; Dooley on,
    189–90; and Geneva Accords, 34–35;
    Independent Party of, 58, 78, 137; and Katay,
    58; and Phoumi, 141, 150–51, 166, 224; as
    prime minister, 140–43, 147–51; resignation
    of, 152; and Souvanna, 141, 166–67
Phoui Vongvichit, 72
Phoumi Nosavan, 5; and battle of Vientiane,
    129–36, 168–70; and Boun Oum, 257, 260,
    261; Brown on, 243; career of, 138; Dooley
    on, 190; and Harriman, 256–63; and
    Kennedy, 7, 238, 242, 244–45, 249–52; and
    Kong Le, 159–63, 167–70; as military leader,
    15, 219; Paxa Sangkhom Party of, 154;
    personality of, 11, 150, 168; photograph
    of, *262;* and Phoui, 141, 150–51, 166,
    224; and Savang, 152, 155, 168–69; and
    Souphanouvong, 138, 169, 240, 257, 261;
    and Souvanna, 139–40, 160, 162–67, 257,
    261; *Time* magazine on, 224–26; U.S.
    support of, 151, 159–70, 224–25, 240
Plain of Jars incident (1959), 144–46, 200,
    202, 219, 221
Poland, 75, 267
Pote Sarasin, 133
Prados, John, 201–2
Programs Evaluation Office (PEO), 43, 48,
    158, 226; and Buell, 198; establishment
    of, 44–45, 47, 52; gerrymandering by,
    135, 153; Joint Chiefs of Staff on, 46;
    Kennedy's upgrading of, 239, 242, 249;
    and Phoui, 149–50; and Phoumi, 152, 166;
    staffing of, 55, 83, 147; and U.S. military
    buildup, 146–47
Progressive Party, 78–81
propaganda films, 58, 77, 179–80, 185, 193
Pushkin, Georgi, 254, 256, 261–63

Quinim Pholsena, 129, 154, 168, 169, 221

race, 13–14, 211–12; Japanese views of, 29;
    and neocolonialism, 8, 126, 272. *See also*
    cultural stereotypes
Rally of the Lao People (RLP) coalition,
    137–38, 143

Rama Rau, Santha, 227, 233
Rand Corporation, 123–28
Rayburn, Sam, 236
*Reader's Digest,* 95, 115–16
Reeves, Richard, 247
Reston, James, 268
Richmond, Yale, 97
Riley, Herbert, 163–66
Rimer, J. T., 85
RLA. *See* Royal Lao Army
RLP. *See* Rally of the Lao People coalition
Robbins, Carl, 117–20
Roberts, Chalmers, 248
Roberts, George, 259
Robertson, Walter, 47, 56, 121; and Parsons,
    81, 113; and Savang, 66; and Souvanna, 62,
    67, 73–77
Roderick, John, 229
Rogers, Warren, 209–10
Roosevelt, Theodore, 272
Rostow, Walt, 3, 243, 245
Rotter, Andrew, 10, 17, 272
Royal Lao Army (RLA), 15, *36;* Dulles on, 81;
    effectiveness of, 69–70, 99, 118, 145–46,
    194, 197, 231, 250–51; Eisenhower on, 12,
    251; Harriman on, 256; and Kennedy, 238,
    243, 248–53; Pathet Lao integration with,
    62, 68, 71, 72, 111, 136, 144; revolt within,
    167; Rusk on, 251–52, 270; U.S. advisors
    for, 44–47, 147; U.S. financing of, 46–47,
    75, 86, 149, 217, 258; U.S. view of, 53, 55,
    56, 86, 209–10, 220–21, 226–30, 243–45;
    against Viet Minh, 34, 40
Ruark, Robert, 122
Rusk, Dean, 9, 18–19, 238, 245; on Geneva
    Conference, 254–55; on RLA, 251–52,
    270; and SEATO, 247–48; on Vietnamese
    soldiers, 269
Russell, Richard, 236, 237

Said, Edward, 19
Saltonstall, Leverett, 236
Santiphab ("Peace through Neutrality") Party,
    78–81, 118, 136, 141
Saraburi, Battle of, 27
Sarit Thanarat, 5, 130; as autocrat, 138,
    154; blockade of Vientiane by, 130, 159,
    166; and Harriman, 258–59; and Laos
    Accords, 263
*Saturday Evening Post,* 202–3, 208, 212–13,
    231

Savang Vatthana, Crown Prince, 33–34, 58;
    and Dulles, 57, 66–67; during World
    War II, 30
Savang Vatthana, King of Laos, 214, 220,
    223–24; Brown on, 243; Harriman on,
    256; Karnow on, 218–19; and Pathet Lao,
    136; and Phoui, 150; and Phoumi, 152,
    155, 168–69
Saveng Phinith, 27
Schanche, Don, 173, 202–7
Schechter, Jerrold, 221
Schlesinger, Arthur, Jr., 244, 251
SEATO. *See* Southeast Asia Treaty Organization
Sebald, William, 13
Shackford, R. H., 228
Shaplen, Robert, 230
Shibusawa, Naoko, 12
Shuff, Charles, 121
Siam, 26–27, 35. *See also* Thailand
Sihanouk, Norodom, King of Cambodia, 17,
    24, 44
Sisavang Vong, King of Laos, 29–34, 110
Sisouk Na Champassak, 31, 62, 134; and
    CDNI, 137, 138, 141, 153; on Harriman,
    259; and Plain of Jars incident, 144–46
Smith, Horace, 14; and CDNI, 150–52; on
    Heintges, 146, 147; and Souvanna, 140
Smither, Robert, 92–93, 113
Somsanith, Tiao, 155, 157, 158
Sorensen, Theodore, 7, 241, 249, 251
Sounthone Pathammavong, 168, 225
Souphanouvong, Prince, 15, 30–32, 57–59,
    223, *265;* arrest of, 145, 148, 153; Dooley
    on, 179, 189; in elections of 1958, 78, 80;
    Harriman on, 256; Karnow on, 221; "long
    march" of, 136, 155; North Vietnamese
    support of, 15–16, 33, 246; pardon of, 162;
    Parsons on, 111–12; and Pathet Lao, 55–57,
    144, 246; personality of, 31; photograph of,
    *262;* and Phoui Sananikone, 35, 143; and
    Phoumi Nosavan, 138, 169, 240, 257, 261;
    popularity of, 76, 125–27; prison escape
    by, 135–36, 154–55; refusal of U.S. aid by,
    91–92; Robertson on, 67; and Souvanna,
    58–59, 62, 63, 67–74, 167, 169, 261; and
    Viet Minh, 31–33, 35, 221
Southeast Asia Treaty Organization (SEATO),
    2, 43–47; Dulles on, 44, 57; Laos policies
    of, 135, 150, 236–38, 250; Rusk on, 247–48
Souvanna Phouma, Prince, 4–7, 30–33, 58–64,
    220, 225; as ambassador to France, 141; and

battle of Vientiane, 134–35, 219; Brown on, 243; character of, 11–13, 31, 59, 74; on cold war, 59–61; on Czechoslovakia, 75; de Gaulle on, 265; and Dooley, 181, 185, 189; and Dulles, 62, 71–77, 81, 137; and Eisenhower, 69–70, 75–76, 239; exile of, 134, 168; at Geneva Conference, 254–55, 265; Harriman on, 256, 259; and Ho Chi Minh, 62, 63, 73; and Kennedy, 270; and Mao Zedong, 61–62, 71, 73; neutralism of, 61–65, 105, 137, 166, 185, 219; and Parsons, 61–70, 74, 102–3, 110–11, 163–66; and Pathet Lao coalition, 61–62, 67–68, 70–74, 110–11; and Phetsarath, 110; photograph of, *262;* and Phoui Sananikone, 141, 166–67; and Phoumi Nosavan, 139–40, 160, 162–66, 257, 261; resignation of, 71–72, 140; song parody on, 64; and Souphanouvong, 58–59, 62, 63, 67–74, 167, 169, 261; Soviet aid for, 163; U.S. visit of, 73–77

Souvanna Phouma, Princess, 68

Sparkman, John, 256

Spellman, Francis, 192

*Sputnik* launch, 93

Stalin, Joseph, 230

Steeves, John, 253

Steinbeck, John, 208

Stevenson, Robert Louis, 88

Stieglitz, Perry, 65, 103, 161

Stuart-Fox, Martin, 27, 143

Stump, Felix, 78

Suez Crisis (1956), 66

Sullivan, William, 256, 269

Swanberg, W. A., 222

Taipei conference (1958), 50–54

Taiwan, 49; Chinese attacks on, 45–46; Khrushchev on, 267; Lao recognition of, 142

Tane Chounlamountri, 124

Thailand, 65; blockade of Vientiane by, 130, 159, 166; as Boun Oum supporter, 245; early history of, 26–27, 35; government of, 138, 150, 154; and SEATO, 43–44, 248; U.S. military personnel in, 45; as U.S. ally, 5, 118–19

Thao Leuam, 141

*That Free Men May Live* (radio show), 172, 181–86, 231

Thee, Marek, 67

Thompson, Bish, 179

Thompson, Virginia, 37–38, 42

*Time* magazine, 19–20, 211, 231–33; Karnow's articles in, 218–22; Luce's control of, 222–27; on misuse of U.S. aid, 86, 121–22

Truman, Harry S., 12, 69

Tucker, Reuben, 252–53, 256

*Ugly American* (Lederer & Burdick), 84–85, 93–94, 188, 204, 206

UNESCO, 95

Union of Soviet Socialist Republics (USSR): collapse of, 274; at Geneva Conference, 254, 256; Laos policies of, 2, 16–17, 73, 240, 245–50, 261–62, 267–68; *Sputnik* launch of, 93

United Kingdom: and Burma, 28; China policies of, 22; and Geneva Accords, 22; as Laos mediator, 245, 246, 261; and Munich Conference, 234; and NATO, 264; and SEATO, 2, 43–44, 135, 237, 238, 247

Universal Construction Company, 117, 119, 120

U.S. Information Service (USIS), 84–85; country plan of, 113; propaganda films of, 58, 77; in Vientiane, 52, 85

U.S. Operations Mission (USOM), 52, 64; accommodations of, 54, 87–88, 99–100, 107, 123; and Buell, 200; community development projects of, 88–95, *90,* 100–102, 106; corruption charges against, 116–19; and Dooley, 180, 188; and elections of 1958, 77; and Parsons, 112; refugee relief by, 201; women's club at, 82–84. *See also* "Little America"

Vang Pao, 198–202, 273

Vienna conference (1961), 264, 266–68

Vientiane, 26–27; American Women's Club of, 82–84; battle of, 15, 129–36, 168–70, 219, 225, 241; CIA in, 52–53, 83; under French rule, 27–28, 32–34; Kong Le's coup in, 15, 156–57, 221; Thai blockade of, 130, 159, 166

Viet Minh, 21–22; and China, 33, 35; France's war with, 22, 23, 40, 44–45, 57, 138, 156, 170; and Khmer Resistance Government, 35; Lao advisors of, 214; Laos incursion by, 33–34, 38, 40, 42, 223; and Pathet Lao, 15–16, 33–34, 219; and Souphanouvong, 31–33, 35, 221

Vietnam, 3, 104; cultural stereotypes of, 9, 13, 37–41, 97–98, 184–85, 225–26, 230, 237, 269; early history of, 26, 27; emigrants to Laos from, 42, 97–98; as French colony, 21, 28, 29, 33; partitioning of, 35

Vietnam, North: as Souphanouvong's allies, 15–16, 246; and Souvanna, 62, 63, 73; troops in Laos from, 142–43, 263. *See also* Ho Chi Minh

Vietnam, South, 23, 60, 118–19; and Boun Oum, 245; and Kennedy, 5, 6, 9, 239, 268–70. *See also* Diem, Ngo Dinh

Vinson, Carl, 236

Volunteers in Service to America, 193

Wallace, De Witt, 116

*Wall Street Journal,* 9, 227, 234; on misuse of U.S. aid, 86, 114–17, 121

Warner, Roger, 273–74

*Washington Post,* 42, 228, 229, 232; on Kennedy's Laos policies, 248; on misuse of U.S. aid, 86; on Pathet Lao rebellion, 148–49

Watson, Mark, 229–30

Wilson, Charles, 46

work ethic, 89, 97–98, 194–95, 227–28; Dooley on, 190–91; Durdin on, 42; Franck on, 39–40; Halpern on, 95; Karnow on, 218; Kerewsky on, 96–97; Meeker on, 214; Oganesoff on, 115; Parsons on, 105; Thompson on, 38. *See also* cultural stereotypes

Yost, Charles, 11, 46–48, 54–60, 105

Young, Kenneth, 59, 61, 62, 181, 255

"Young Ones" *(les Jeunes),* 138–40, 143, 151–52

Zablocki, Clement, 116, 119

Zhou Enlai, 16, 61–63